Protecting Rights Without a Bill of Rights
Institutional Performance and Reform in Australia

Edited by

TOM CAMPBELL
Professorial Fellow, Centre for Applied Philosophy and Public Ethics, Charles Sturt University, Australia

JEFFREY GOLDSWORTHY
Professor of Law, Monash University, Australia

ADRIENNE STONE
Fellow, Law Program, Research School of Social Sciences, Australian National University, Australia

Routledge
Taylor & Francis Group
LONDON AND NEW YORK

First published 2006 by Ashgate Publishing

Reissued 2018 by Routledge
2 Park Square, Milton Park, Abingdon, Oxon OX14 4RN
711 Third Avenue, New York, NY 10017, USA

Routledge is an imprint of the Taylor & Francis Group, an informa business

First issued in paperback 2018

A Library of Congress record exists under LC control number: 2006000087

Notice:
Product or corporate names may be trademarks or registered trademarks, and are used
only for identification and explanation without intent to infringe.

Publisher's Note
The publisher has gone to great lengths to ensure the quality of this reprint but points
out that some imperfections in the original copies may be apparent.

Disclaimer
The publisher has made every effort to trace copyright holders and welcomes
correspondence from those they have been unable to contact.

ISBN 13: 978-0-815-39120-3 (hbk)
ISBN 13: 978-1-138-62023-0 (pbk)
ISBN 13: 978-1-351-15124-5 (ebk)

Contents

List of Contributors

Tom Campbell is a Professorial Fellow in the Centre for Applied Philosophy and Public Ethics, Charles Sturt University, and a former Dean of the Faculty of Law, Australian National University. He is the author of *The Left and Rights* (Routledge, 1983), *Justice* (2nd edn, Macmillan, 2001) and *The Legal Theory of Ethical Positivism* (Dartmouth, 1996). He is also co-editor of numerous books, most recently *Protecting Human Rights, Instruments and Institutions* (OUP, 2003), with Adrienne Stone and Jeff Goldsworthy, and *Sceptical Essays on Human Rights* (OUP, 2001), with Keith Ewing and Adam Tomkins.

Hilary Charlesworth is an ARC Federation Fellow in the Regulatory Institutions Network in the Research School of Social Sciences at the Australian National University, where she is also Professor of International Law in the Faculty of Law. She was chair of the ACT Bill of Rights Consultative Committee in 2002–3. Her scholarly interests include international law, human rights law and feminist legal theory. Among her many publications are *Writing in Rights: Australia and the Protection of Human Rights* (UNSW Press, 2002), and *International Law and World Order: a Problem-oriented Coursebook* (3rd edn, West Pub, 1997), with Burns Weston and Richard Falk.

Robin Creyke is Alumni Professor of Administrative Law in the Faculty of Law, Australian National University. She specializes in administrative law, constitutional law and administrative tribunals. She has co-edited many books of essays on Australian administrative law, most recently *The Brennan Legacy: Blowing the Winds of Legal Orthodoxy* (Federation Press, 2002), with Patrick Keyzer. She is also the author of numerous book chapters and journal articles in that field.

Megan Davis is a member of the Jumbunna Indigenous House of Learning in the Faculty of Law, University of Technology Sydney, and Director of the Bill of Rights Project in the Gilbert and Tobin Centre of Public Law, University of New South Wales. Her research interests include aboriginal women's issues, customary Aboriginal law, the rights of indigenous peoples, especially to intellectual property, and the right to democratic governance in international law. She is the author of book chapters and journal articles in these areas.

Simon Evans is Director of the Centre for Comparative Constitutional Studies in the Faculty of Law, Melbourne University. He researches and teaches in constitutional law and theory. He is particularly interested in non-judicial mechanisms for protecting human rights, accountability of the executive government and constitutional protection of property rights. He is the author of numerous articles and book chapters on these and other topics.

Brian Galligan is a Professor of Political Science at the University of Melbourne. He researches and teaches mainly in Australian constitutional politics and political economy. His most recent books are *Australian Citizenship* (MUP, 2004) with Winsome Roberts, *Australians and Globalisation* (CUP, 2001), with Winsome Roberts and Gabriella Trifiletti, *Citizens Without Rights: Aborigines and Australian Citizenship* (CUP, 1997), with John Chesterman, and *A Federal Republic* (CUP, 1995). He is also the author of *The Politics of the High Court* (University of Queensland Press, 1987), and is currently editing the *Oxford Companion to Australian Politics*.

Jeffrey Goldsworthy is Professor of Law at Monash University. He specializes in constitutional law, history and theory, and legal philosophy. He is author of *The Sovereignty of Parliament, History and Philosophy* (OUP, 1999), and co-editor of *Protecting Human Rights, Instruments and Institutions* (OUP, 2003), with Tom Campbell and Adrienne Stone, and of *Legal Interpretation in Democratic States* (Ashgate, 2002) and *Judicial Power, Democracy and Legal Positivism* (Ashgate, 2000), both with Tom Campbell.

Bryan Horrigan is a Professor in the Division of Law at Macquarie University. His research and teaching cover a broad range of topics in the areas of governmental and business law. His human rights work covers native title, corporations and human rights, and parliamentary scrutiny of legislation for human rights implications. He is the author of *Adventures in Law and Justice: Exploring Big Legal Questions in Everyday Life* (UNSW Press, 2003), and editor of several books including *Government Law and Policy: Commercial Aspects* (Federation Press, 1998).

Helen Irving is an Associate Professor of Law at the University of Sydney. Her interests include constitutional history, jurisprudence and law, federalism, and intergovernmental relations. She is the author of *Five Things to Know about the Australian Constitution* (Cambridge University Press, 2004), *To Constitute a Nation: A Cultural History of Australia's Constitution* (rev. ed., CUP, 1999), and editor of *The Centenary Companion to Australian Federation* (CUP, 1999) and several other collections.

Christopher Manfredi is a Professor in the Department of Political Science, McGill University, Canada. He specializes in comparative constitutionalism and judicial politics, American public law and Canadian politics. He is the author of *Feminist Activism in the Supreme Court of Canada* (UBC Press, Vancouver, 2004), *Judicial Power and the Charter: Canada and the Paradox of Liberal Constitutionalism* (2nd edn, OUP, Toronto, 2001), *The Supreme Court and Juvenile Justice* (Kansas UP, Lawrence, Kansas, 1997), and numerous book chapters and journal articles.

F.L. (Ted) Morton was a Professor of Political Science at the University of Calgary, until he became a Member of the Albertan Legislative Assembly in 2004. He specializes in constitutional politics and rights protection, and has published extensively on Canadian politics since the adoption of the Charter of Rights and Freedoms in 1982. He is the author of *The Charter Revolution and the Court Party* (Broadview Press, 2000) with Rainer Knopff, *Charter Politics* (Nelson Canada, 1992) with Rainer Knopff, and *Morgentaler v. Borowski: Abortion, The Charter and The Courts* (McClelland and Stewart, 1992).

Robert Nagel is Ira C. Rothgerber Jr. Professor of Constitutional Law, University of Colorado School of Law. He is the author of *The Implosion of American Federalism* (OUP, New York, 2001), *Constitutional Cultures: the Mentality and Consequences of Judicial Review* (University of California Press, Berkeley, 1989), and *Judicial Power and American Character: Censoring Ourselves in an Anxious Age* (OUP, New York, 1994).

Adrienne Stone is a Fellow in the Law Program at the Research School of Social Sciences, Australian National University. She is interested in Australian and comparative constitutional law and theory, particularly in relation to freedom of speech. She is co-editor of *Protecting Human Rights, Instruments and Institutions* (OUP, Oxford, 2003), with Tom Campbell and Jeff Goldsworthy, and the author of many journal articles and book chapters.

John Uhr is Reader in Politics, Asia Pacific School of Economics and Government, Australian National University. His current research interests concern efforts to improve democratic governance, including strategies for greater public participation and accountability, parliamentary reform and ethics in government. He is the author of *Terms of Trust: Arguments Over Ethics in Australian Government* (UNSW Press, Sydney, 2005) and *Deliberative Democracy in Australia* (CUP, Cambridge, 1998), and editor of *The Australian Republic: The Case for Yes* (Federation Press, 1999), among many other books.

Jeremy Webber holds the Canada Research Chair in Law and Society, Faculty of Law, University of Victoria; Director, Consortium on Democratic Constitutionalism; Visiting Professor of Law, University of New South Wales. He is internationally known as a law and society scholar working in the areas of cultural diversity, constitutional theory and indigenous rights. He is the author of *Reimagining Canada: Language, Culture, Community and the Canadian Constitution* (McGill-Queen's UP, 1994).

George Winterton is Professor of Constitutional Law at the University of Sydney. His interests include constitutional law, comparative constitutional law and legal history. He is the author of *Parliament, the Executive and the Governor-General: A Constitutional Analysis* (Melbourne UP, 1983), *Monarchy to Republic; Australian*

Republican Government (OUP, 1994), the co-author of *Australian Federal Constitutional Law* (LBC, Sydney, 1999), with H.P. Lee, Arthur Glass and James Thomson, and the co-editor of many books including *Australian Constitutional Landmarks* (CUP, Cambridge, 2003), with H.P. Lee.

Introduction

Jeffrey Goldsworthy

Australian Exceptionalism

Australia is now the only major Anglophone country that has not adopted a bill of rights. Since 1982, Canada, New Zealand and the United Kingdom have all adopted either constitutional or statutory bills of rights. But to protect rights, Australia continues to rely mainly on the common law, a vigorous parliamentary democracy, statutes dealing with specific issues such as racial and sexual discrimination and a generally tolerant culture.

Australia's federal Constitution has been described as 'a prosaic document expressed in lawyer's language'.[1] It does not include grand declarations of national values or aspirations. It includes a number of provisions designed to suppress regional favouritism, but no bill of rights. Despite borrowing heavily from the United States in designing the federal system, the framers included only a few scattered provisions that arguably protect individual rights. The Commonwealth, but not the states, is prohibited from compulsorily acquiring property without just compensation, removing trial by jury for prosecutions on indictment, or violating freedom of religion.[2] The states are not permitted to discriminate against the residents of other states.[3] It should also be mentioned that for many years, the High Court interpreted s. 92 of the Constitution, which guarantees freedom of interstate trade and commerce, as if it protected individual rights to engage in such trade and commerce free of unreasonable legal burdens. But that 'laissez faire' interpretation was abandoned in 1986.[4]

With respect to rights, the framers were influenced more by the British than the American constitutional tradition. Australian federation resulted not from armed rebellion against perceived tyranny, but from calm, pragmatic reform by colonial politicians encouraged and assisted by the imperial government. Utilitarianism had

---

1   Sir A. Mason, 'The Australian Constitution in Retrospect and Prospect' in R. French, G. Lindell and C. Saunders (eds) *Reflections on the Australian Constitution* (The Federation Press, Sydney 2003) 8.

2   The Constitution of the Commonwealth of Australia, ss.51(31), 80, and 116 respectively.

3   Ibid. s. 117.

4   See *Cole* v *Whitfield* (1988) 165 CLR 360.

replaced natural rights as the main currency of British political thought, and Australia has been described as a paradigmatically utilitarian society.[5] In general, the framers deemed it both unnecessary and unwise to fetter their parliaments. Given the progress of liberal ideas under British institutions, democratically elected parliaments seemed to them the best possible guardians of liberty. The harsh Australian environment was still being settled by Europeans, who wanted strong government to underwrite enterprise, provide necessary infrastructure and enact social regulation. The framers feared that judicial interpretations of abstract rights could have unpredictable and undesirable consequences. For one thing, they did not want to be prevented from discriminating against people of other races in order to protect the racial and cultural homogeneity of their communities.[6]

It was necessary to arm an independent federal judiciary with power to enforce the terms of the federal compact. But, with a few minor exceptions, the traditional British doctrine of parliamentary sovereignty was disturbed only to that extent. Provided they were acting within their respective spheres of responsibility and not violating either paramount Imperial laws or constitutional limits, Australian parliaments were deemed to exercise powers as plenary and ample – as sovereign – as that of the United Kingdom Parliament itself.[7]

Over the years, many prominent Australians have expressed faith in the country's reliance on parliamentary democracy and the common law to protect rights adequately, and denied that there was any pressing need to adopt a bill of rights. Statements along these lines by Sir Owen Dixon, reputedly Australia's greatest judge, and Sir Robert Menzies, its longest serving Prime Minister, are quoted in the first chapter of this book.[8] Menzies was a conservative politician who led the Liberal Party. But at least until the 1970s, his counterparts on the left of the political spectrum agreed with him. The traditional attitude of the Australian Labor Party towards rights was forcefully expressed by Gough Whitlam, a future party leader and Prime Minister, in 1955:

> British history shows that Parliament has been our great liberating force. Parliament has conferred political freedom on those represented in it, first of all the barons and squires and then the merchants and now all adults. There is no freedom without equality. To redistribute and equalize liberty has been one of the principal functions of Parliament. Parliament alone can give equality of opportunity and thereby increase liberty for all. If we are to have economic equality of opportunity, which is the next stage in the advance of liberty, we must have effective parliamentary government and, accordingly, dispense with

---

5   For example, H. Collins (1985, Winter), 'Political Ideology in Australia: The Distinctiveness of a Benthamite Society', *Daedalus*: 147.

6   J. Goldsworthy (1992), 'The Constitutional Protection of Rights in Australia', in G. Craven, ed., *Australian Federation, Towards the Second Century* (Melbourne University Press, Melbourne), pp. 151, 152–54.

7   See Quick and Garran, pp. 509–510; *D'Emden* v *Pedder* (1904) 1 CLR 91, 110 per Griffith CJ; *Nelungaloo* v *Cth* (1948) 75 CLR 495, pp. 503–4 per Williams J.

8   See Chapter 1 below, p. 17.

fetters on parliament rather than contrive them. For every person whose liberty has been prejudiced by government action, there are many whose liberty has been enhanced. The virtue of Parliament is that it provides publicity and works in the open. When Parliament is sitting, there are a great number of opportunities for calling its Government to account. The forum which Parliament provides is the best guardian of our liberties. As long as we have members on both sides of our Parliament who are able and willing to express many and varied points of view, we have some liberty and can aspire to greater liberty. The price of liberty is eternal vigilance. Parliament has hitherto proved the best instrument for exercising that vigilance.[9]

The High Court ... is less representative of the Australian people than are their elected representatives. Judges are irresponsible in that they hold office for life, which is sometimes a very long life. Some have used that asset for a political purpose ... We are constrained by our present Federal Constitution to leave the final disposition of many matters in the hands of lawyers. We are forbidden to do not so much what the Constitution forbids us to do but what the judges forbid us to do. If counsel has to advise whether a certain action is constitutional, he is less concerned with the Constitution than with the composition of the court. We thus run the risk that we shall be granted only such liberties as commend themselves to lawyers. Australians have developed a habit of asking the High Court to invalidate Acts of Parliament whenever they conceive their liberties have been infringed by those Acts. Advocacy has been so successful in recent years that the Court itself has developed an attitude of almost supercilious suspicion towards Acts of Parliament and actions of the administration. People who have successfully approached the Court in these matters are loud in their praise for the safeguard the Court affords. There are, however, hundreds and thousands of persons who have not a sufficient interest to be heard by the Court but who would have received benefits and enhanced liberties from the legislation in question. The Court, in other words, gives liberty to those who can establish a sufficient interest or a right of action and to them alone.[10]

The policies of the Labor Party changed when it was in government in the early 1970s and 1980s, when two unsuccessful attempts were made to adopt a bill of rights. But Australians remain wary of constitutionally entrenched rights. In 1988, a modest proposal to amend the Constitution by extending to the states the existing guarantees of religious freedom, jury trial and just terms for the expropriation of property, suffered the worst defeat of any amendment ever proposed, being approved by less than 31 per cent of the electorate. Since then, there has been no significant political impetus towards strengthening the protection of rights in the Constitution. As Professor Winterton states in Chapter 13, 'the prospects of securing referendum approval for the introduction of [an entrenched] bill of rights are minimal in view of the inevitable controversy it would generate'.[11]

On the other hand, with the tide of international opinion continuing to run strongly in favour of increased judicial participation in human rights protection, and

---

9   Whitlam, E.G. (1955) in The Australian Institute of Political Science, *Liberty in Australia* (Sydney: Angus and Robertson), pp. 177–78.

10   Ibid. 174.

11   Chapter 13 below, p. 306.

Australians occasionally seeking redress from the United Nations Human Rights Committee, it is inevitable that demands for major statutory if not constitutional reform will grow over the coming years. It is apparent that Australian judges are increasingly amenable to the prospect of protecting rights, and among younger generations of lawyers, older ideas of legislative supremacy often seem almost incomprehensible. They are right not to be complacent about Australia's human rights performance. In Chapter 14, Tom Campbell lists many recent failings:

> ... the continuing relative deprivations of indigenous people and the lack of substantial recognition of their interests as the original inhabitants, oppressive laws against voluntary euthanasia, inadequate services for disabled people (particularly those suffering from mental illness), failure to protect children at risk, harsh treatment of asylum seekers, acquiescence in child poverty and gross economic inequality, readiness to introduce potentially oppressive anti-terrorist legislation, the use of mandatory sentencing for juvenile offenders (in Western Australia and the Northern Territory), and the Commonwealth Government's repeated and forceful rejection of quite reasonable criticism of these policies by the UN Committee on Human Rights.[12]

Australia's exceptionalism should ensure that comparisons between its experience and those of other countries are of increasing interest, both locally and internationally. Locally, the debate between proponents and opponents of a bill of rights already turns partly on such comparisons. Internationally, continuing controversies over the role of judges in protecting rights, alleged judicial activism, and its impact on democracy, means that Australia's experience should be keenly studied. If it is true that western liberal democracies have embarked on an experiment, in which much greater reliance is placed on judicial enforcement of constitutional rights, then Australia might serve as a 'control'.

The object of this book is to provide useful background for evaluating how well Australian institutions – governments, legislatures, courts, and tribunals – have been protecting human rights in the absence of a bill of rights, and for assessing proposals for practical reform aimed at enhancing such protection. These proposals are not limited to the traditional model of a judicially enforceable bill of rights: indeed, emphasis is placed on other possible reforms. An essential aim of the book is to take the debate over rights protection beyond the usual, familiar arguments between supporters and opponents of a constitutionally entrenched bill of rights, although the reconciliation of human rights protection and democracy remains a major theme. The Canadian, New Zealand and British models now present us with a more varied set of options than the either/or choice of American-style judicial supremacy. They appear to offer ways of shifting more power to courts, while retaining ultimate legislative supremacy. And our imaginations should not be limited to these models. We should be open to other possible ways of enhancing the protection of human rights without sacrificing what Jeremy Waldron has called the right of rights: the

---

12 Chapter 14 below, p. 324.

right of all citizens, and not just a highly educated, lawyerly elite, to participate on an equal basis in determining how their community will be governed.

It is often assumed that a legislature whose power is not subject to judicially enforceable limits has 'arbitrary' power that is uncontrolled by law.[13] But laws governing the composition of legislatures, and the procedure and form by which they must legislate, in themselves exert a powerful kind of legal control.[14] Historically, the requirement that legislation desired by a monarch could not be enacted without the assent of community representatives was a major advance for the protection of rights, even though this did not involve the imposition of substantive limits on the power to legislate. The same goes for the other constitutional reforms that gave birth to modern democracy: the development of bicameralism, electoral reform, the extension of the franchise and so on. These methods of controlling legislative power exemplify what Kenneth Culp Davis called 'structuring', as opposed to 'confining' and 'checking', the exercise of power.[15] They involve controlling by law the exercise of what would otherwise be arbitrary power, and all contribute to the protection of rights.

It follows that the protection of rights might possibly be improved by reforming the laws that govern the electoral process, the composition of the legislature, and the procedure and form by which legislation is proposed and scrutinized. It is often argued that such reforms would be preferable to an American-style bill of rights on democratic grounds. Why not improve the system of representative democracy rather than further diminish it? Less obviously, it can also be argued that such reforms would be preferable on rule of law grounds. They could make more effective review or veto of legislation part of the legislative process itself, taking place before legislation is enacted and relied on as law by the community. A bill of rights typically inserts a power of legislative review and veto into subsequent judicial processes, where its exercise on grounds of political morality can have unpredictable, retrospective effects on legislation that has already been enacted, and may have been relied on as law. It is curious that in common law countries we do not worry much about the impact of retrospective judicial law-making on the rule of law and rights associated with it.

Structure of the Book

In Part I, five essays contribute to an evaluation of the performance of Australian institutions in the protection of rights. In Part II, three essays discuss particular human

---

13 For extended discussion, see J. Goldsworthy (2001), 'Legislative Supremacy and the Rule of Law', in T. Campbell, K.D. Ewing and A. Tomkins (eds), *Sceptical Essays on Human Rights* (Oxford: OUP), p. 61.

14 See A.L. Goodhart (1958), 'The Rule of Law and Absolute Sovereignty' 106 *University of Pennsylvania Law Review*: 943, 950–52.

15 K.C. Davis (1969), *Discretionary Justice, A Preliminary Inquiry* (Baton Rouge: Louisiana State University Press), chs. 3–5.

rights issues of particular salience in Australia: citizenship, the rights of indigenous people and property rights. In Part III, two essays examine major alternative models for the protection of rights – those of the United States and of Canada. These essays are included because, as previously explained, comparisons between the Australian experience and those of other countries bear directly on debates over rights protection both locally and internationally. Their systems are distinct, and constitute two of the major models of rights protection that Australians must consider. In the final Part IV of the book, four essays discuss a variety of concrete, practical reforms that might be made in Australia to enhance the protection of rights without undermining its democratic system of government.

In the first chapter, Brian Galligan and Ted Morton discuss the extent to which there has recently been a 'rights revolution' in Australia. They criticise Charles Epp's well known theory of the nature and causes of recent 'rights revolutions' in the United States and Canada. That theory, they object, is ethnocentric in taking the United States as the norm that is used to evaluate developments elsewhere. This over-emphasizes the protection of rights through advocacy litigation in courts, and under-emphasizes their protection through normal politics and the enactment of legislation. Galligan and Morton acknowledge that in Australia, there has been only a weak rights revolution in the judicial arena, both because the absence of a bill of rights limits the scope for judicial activism, and because what Epp calls the 'support structure for legal mobilization' (well-funded advocacy groups that use litigation to advance rights) is relatively weak. Nevertheless, they suggest that Australia has undergone a 'fully blown' rights revolution in the political arena, which might be as effective in terms of the overall protection of rights as the judicial revolutions in otherwise comparable countries.[16] However, they point out that the protection of rights provided by courts differs from that usually offered by parliaments:

> We would expect the legislative process to favour rights that are of primary concern to the people and mass-based parties, such as voting rights, certain social and economic rights such as welfare entitlements and working conditions and wages, health care provision and education. In contrast, judicial decision making would likely benefit special groups with the knowledge and resources to work the court system to their advantage.[17]

In Chapter 2, John Uhr's discussion of the role of parliaments in protecting rights explores the metaphor of 'dialogue' between the branches of government, which has attracted considerable attention in Canada. But Uhr is interested in dialogue between parliaments on the one hand, and executive governments, rather than courts, on the other. He distinguishes between two models of rights-protection: an earlier model of civil liberty, which emphasizes popular self-government and the need for a separation of powers to ensure that government remains subordinate to the people's will, and the more recent model of civil liberties, which is concerned

---

16 Galligan and Morton acknowledge that a more extensive study would be required to vindicate the latter claim.

17 Chapter 1 below, p. 21.

with protecting individual rights. He is concerned with the former. He argues that in a system of responsible government, in which the lower house is dominated by the executive government, the existence of a strong upper house with real power to hold the executive government to account is a vital component of the separation of powers. The Australian Senate, which is much more powerful than that of Canada, is an example. Uhr describes the development and performance of the Regulations and Ordinances Committee within the Australian Senate, which played a crucial role in preventing rule by 'executive decree'. He identifies a variety of factors that have facilitated the Committee's effectiveness, factors that might also be crucial in other contexts.

In Chapter 3, Bryan Horrigan describes the work within Australian parliaments of bipartisan committees charged with pre-enactment scrutiny of legislation according to human rights standards and other principles for good legislation. He regards their work as imperfectly understood and undervalued, and as having a potential that is yet to be fully realised, both in terms of improvements in the quality of legislation and in the promotion of a 'culture of rights' within parliaments, governments and bureaucracies. He identifies the similarities and differences between committees operating in different Australian jurisdictions, as well as the UK Joint Committee on Human Rights. Because these committees lack authority to enforce their recommendations, their influence depends on retaining the respect of all major political parties. It follows that they must pursue a strictly non-partisan approach and attempt to separate criticisms of legislation on human rights grounds from attacks on the political policies underlying it. This is a distinction that can be difficult to maintain, although Horrigan distinguishes 'legal policy' from 'public policy'.[18] Statutory committees attempt to offer constructive advice rather than just criticism, such as by suggesting alternative ways of achieving desired policies that have a lesser impact on rights. Horrigan makes a number of recommendations to enhance their effectiveness, including (a) the enactment of a bill of rights, either constitutional or statutory, to provide greater clarity and focus for scrutiny, (b) improved tools and resources, (c) more generous time-frames within which scrutiny can take place, (c) more frequent use of exposure drafts, together with opportunities for public consultation, and (d) a higher public and media profile.

In Chapter 4, Robin Creyke describes part of the 'rights revolution' that has been achieved through legislation in Australia since the 1970s. This is the massive expansion of administrative law, brought about partly by judicial, but mainly by legislative, innovations. The latter were a response to deficiencies in pre-existing avenues for judicial review of administrative action available at common law. In the 1970s, the Commonwealth Parliament enacted a comprehensive package of legislation that has collectively been called the 'new administrative law'. This included legislation simplifying the procedures for judicial review of legality of administrative actions, establishing a new system of merits review by non-judicial tribunals, creating the office of ombudsman, and conferring new rights to reasons for

---

18 Chapter 3 below, p. 82.

decisions and access to government information. In addition, Parliament established the Human Rights and Equal Opportunity Commission, which investigates complaints of racial, sexual and disability discrimination made against private citizens as well as government officials. Many of these reforms have now been copied at the state level and overseas. Creyke describes the richness and complexity of these diverse avenues for protecting rights against government, and the many advantages they have compared with litigation before courts, such as informality, inexpensiveness and specialized expertise. They arguably constitute 'the best established and most sophisticated system of administrative law in any common law jurisdiction'.[19]

In Chapter 5, Adrienne Stone discusses rights in the Australian Constitution, including both express rights and those that the High Court has found to be implied. She agrees with critics that these rights are comparatively weak. The express rights have been narrowly interpreted by the High Court, and the framers of the Constitution may have envisaged them as part of the federal distribution of legislative powers rather than as guarantees of rights. The weakness of implied rights, such as to freedom of political communication, is due to the interpretive theories on which they are based being highly controversial and therefore vulnerable to challenge. Stone does not, however, conclude that an express bill of rights is therefore desirable. This might make Australian constitutional law even more complex and uncertain.

Part II of the book is devoted to brief discussions of some concrete rights issues that have been of particular salience in Australia. Chapter 6, by Helen Irving, discusses the relationship between rights and citizenship. She shows that there is no necessary connection between citizenship and any particular right, not even the right to vote or the right to a passport, both of which can be legitimately denied on various grounds. She also rejects putative ideals of 'good' (that is, active) citizens, whose rights depend on their fulfilling civic duties, once again on the ground that these ideals fail to account for necessary or desirable exceptions. The only rights that are immune from erosion, she concludes, are universal human rights that attach to everyone, rather than just citizens. But she concludes with the provocative suggestion that when rights are exhaustively defined by the state, opportunities to challenge and expand concepts of rights are narrowed or even closed. 'The state should not cover the field of what is intended by the language of citizenship and rights. Fortunately ... it has not attempted to do so in Australia.'[20]

In Chapter 7, Megan Davis uses the experience of indigenous Australians to challenge the claim that no bill of rights is needed in Australia because the democratic system adequately protects rights. She argues that indigenous Australians cannot rely on parliaments to protect their rights because they constitute a very small (2 per cent) proportion of the population and have historically been excluded from Australia's public institutions. As a result, their rights are subject to 'the ideological fashions and the governing political party of the day'.[21] Australia is the only common law country that lacks both a treaty with its indigenous peoples and a bill of rights.

---

19 Chapter 4 below, p. 127.
20 Chapter 6 below, p. 173.
21 Chapter 7 below, p. 177.

Yet a bill of rights is not necessarily the solution either, if it protects only 'universal' human rights that are possessed by all members of the community. Rather, indigenous peoples need recognition as a distinct cultural minority, with special communal rights such as the operation of their own laws within their communities. When their cultural traditions clash with universal human rights, an appropriate balance must be achieved through consultation between them and the broader community.

In Chapter 8, Simon Evans discusses one of the few provisions in the Australian Constitution that has come to be regarded as protecting an important right, namely s. 51(xxxi), which grants power to the Commonwealth Parliament to make laws with respect to the compulsory acquisition of property but only on just terms. Evans agrees with Stone that the framers seem to have envisaged this provision as a grant of power, rather than a guarantee of a right, but argues that it would not be desirable now to return to that more limited objective. He explains how, as a result of it being construed as a constitutional guarantee, judicial interpretation has become complex and confused, and 'in some areas is close to incoherent'.[22] He believes that this is the inevitable result of our understanding of such guarantees depending on deeply contested and competing moral values – in this case, the need for stability in entitlements, as against the need for modifications in response to changed circumstances. Judges of the High Court have proposed at least six different limiting principles to constrain the scope of the guarantee, principles that are based on different understandings of, and assessments of the appropriate balance between, the competing, underlying moral values. The Court's judgments have been characterized by sharp division because the judges have adopted conflicting substantive value commitments, although only occasionally have these been explicitly articulated. Evans considers three alternative ways of reducing these interpretive disagreements, which cannot be eliminated. He concludes that the Court should more clearly articulate the moral values that are at stake and formulate a standard of judicial review that is more deferential to legislative judgment while insisting on a 'minimal impairment' test.[23] But if legislatures are to be worthy of such deference, Evans recommends that they should improve the processes that ensure that they pay due regard to the competing moral values at stake. Here, Evans's paper connects with other papers that discuss legislation scrutiny committees and how they might be made more effective. Thus, changes in both judicial and legislative approaches to property rights issues are required to improve the quality of decision-making, changes that harness the different strengths of both institutions.

Part III of the book contains two chapters that provide international perspectives, one from the United States and the other from Canada. In Chapter 9, Robert Nagel acknowledges that the judicial enforcement of constitutional rights in the United States 'has sometimes been a useful, even an admirable, practice', and 'has on important occasions vindicated high ideals'.[24] But he plainly believes that its benefits

---

22 Chapter 8 below, p. 197.
23 Chapter 8 below, p. 213.
24 Chapter 9 below, p. 236.

are outweighed by its less desirable consequences. The latter are attributable to the practice becoming routine and all-pervasive, dealing with ever more minute details of social life, rather than being reserved for exceptional cases involving matters of high principle. An example is the way that free-speech jurisprudence now controls mundane matters such as billboards, door-to-door solicitation, school dress codes and automobile licence plates. On the other hand, seemingly insignificant decisions are subsequently taken to establish broad principles that are then used to institute sweeping social change. As the scope of judicial review has inexorably expanded, political culture at the local level has been weakened and demoralized, with policy making becoming provisional and subordinate to judicial doctrine. Lay-people are discouraged from questioning 'revolutionary change imposed by distant and alien figures', partly because of their use of inaccessible, technical legal jargon and partly because of judicial accusations of base motives. There has been 'a tendency to distort and belittle the public's understanding of its own objectives and traditions', eroding its self-confidence and self-respect.[25] It has also exacerbated cultural and political conflict, by removing opportunities normally available in the political sphere for compromise. Nagel offers some concluding speculations on whether Australia could avoid these consequences if it adopted the American model.

The United States exemplifies what is called 'strong' judicial review, in which judicial interpretations of constitutional rights necessarily prevail over political decision making. By contrast, so-called 'weak' forms of judicial review either do not lead directly to judicial invalidation of legislation (the British model), or allow for legislative override of judicial invalidations (the Canadian model). In Chapter 10, Christopher Manfredi discusses the Canadian model, which is often defended as promoting a healthy form of dialogue between the political and judicial branches of government, rather than judicial supremacy, thereby enhancing rather than diminishing Canadian democracy. Manfredi rejects the dialogue metaphor, which rests mainly on the possibility of legislatures making use of sections 1 and 33 of the Canadian Charter of Rights. As for section 1, Manfredi objects that it provides the legislature with only a very limited range of potential responses to judicial decisions. Supposed examples of legislative modifications of judicial rulings under section 1 are, in fact, really examples of legislative capitulation. As for section 33 (the famous 'override clause'), the early history of its use has made its invocation politically unfeasible, which leaves the advantage in debates about rights 'squarely in the hands of the Supreme Court.'[26] Instead of 'dialogue', Manfredi prefers to characterize the interaction of legislatures and the Supreme Court in terms of a strategic model – which he calls the 'separation of powers game' – in which both sides seek to advance their policy preferences, subject to institutional constraints, in ways that can be modelled in game-theoretic terms. In the course of this game, the practical inability of legislatures to invoke the override clause has greatly strengthened the power of the Court. Indeed, 'where the judicial will exists to trump legislative policy

---

25 Ibid. p.232.
26 Chapter 10 below, p. 252.

preferences, the judicial capacity to do so is incontestable'.[27] This sounds much like American-style judicial supremacy.

Part IV of the book consists of four essays discussing alternative ways in which the Australian legal system could be or has been reformed so as to enhance the protection of rights.

Chapter 11, by Jeremy Webber, offers a powerful defence of statutory, as opposed to constitutional, bills of rights. He regrets the fact that both supporters and critics of statutory bills of rights rely on arguments that are much more pertinent to constitutionally entrenched bills, thereby ignoring crucial differences between the two methods of rights protection. After summarizing the ways in which statutory bills can offer substantial protection of rights, not only from executive but also from thoughtless legislative intrusions, he offers a justification that is consistent with democratic values and avoids many of the usual objections to bills of rights. Statutory bills, unlike constitutionally entrenched ones, remain at all times under the control of legislatures, which can at any time choose to override, amend or repeal them. Yet they can still play a vital role, because of the courts' distinctive institutional role of focusing on individual cases, as distinct from the legislature's role in assessing general normative principles and balancing broad social concerns. By focusing on individual cases, courts may reveal particular circumstances of normative significance that the legislature overlooked and which justify a restrictive interpretation of the law in order to prevent a violation of rights that the legislature did not intend. If the legislature disagrees with the court's decision, it can clarify the law accordingly, but at least it will have had the opportunity to take into account the individual circumstances that judicial inquiry has revealed. As Webber concludes, 'statutory bills provide one means of fostering the process of attention and revision. They do so by combining adjudication's intense focus on the particular case with, at the end of the day, legislative determination of the general normative order of society'.[28]

In Chapter 12, Hilary Charlesworth discusses the recent adoption of a statutory bill of rights in the Australian Capital Territory ('the ACT'). It is the first bill of rights to be adopted anywhere in Australia and its effects will be closely studied in other Australian jurisdictions. The ACT, which includes the national capital Canberra, is one of two mainland Territories. Like other Territories, it can be controlled directly by the federal Parliament under s. 122 of the Constitution, but it was granted self-government by federal legislation enacted in 1988. Acting on the recommendations of a Consultative Committee, which Charlesworth chaired, the ACT legislature has adopted a statute that is intended to create a 'dialogue' about rights involving the government, legislature, courts and people of the Territory. She describes the main features of the statute, and in particular, the way in which it differs from its counterparts in the United Kingdom and New Zealand, by including potentially inconsistent directives: one (s.30) requiring interpretation of legislation consistent

---

27 Ibid. p. 257.
28 Chapter 11 below, p.284 .

as far as possible with human rights, and the other (s.32) requiring interpretation that would best achieve the purpose of the legislation in question. It is not yet clear what effect this will have. Charlesworth also discusses the impact of the bill of rights to date, although it is still in its infancy, and concludes that so far it has affected government and legislative policy more than judicial reasoning.

George Winterton, in Chapter 13, proposes a very different way of achieving more effective rights protection without imposing judicial supremacy over elected legislatures. This is to establish an Australian Rights Council, modelled on France's *Conseil Constitutionnel*, to provide pre-enactment, abstract, quasi-judicial scrutiny of proposed legislation to assess its consistency with human rights. There are various ways of doing this, but Winterton favours a single, national Rights Council, able to scrutinize both state and Commonwealth legislation, consisting of five former judges or other experts in constitutional or human rights law, two elected by two-thirds majorities in both Houses of the Commonwealth Parliament, and three elected by special majorities of state governments or parliaments. The Council would conduct a quasi-judicial hearing into proposed legislation, in which legal counsel and others could make submissions, with generous rules governing standing to seek review. It could suggest amendments to the parliament concerned, but not require that they be made: ultimate authority would remain with the elected legislators, subject to a special majority requirement. This method of scrutiny would suffer from the disadvantage of abstract forms of review: the lack of focus on the concrete facts of an individual case, which is the advantage of adjudication that Webber emphasizes. But Winterton argues that his proposal has compensating benefits. It is plainly a proposal worthy of further consideration.

Tom Campbell in Chapter 14 is not as convinced as Jeremy Webber of the merits of statutory bills of rights, because they often lead to activist judges 'overstep[ping] their interpretive powers to intervene in ways to which it is difficult for legislatures to respond'.[29] Campbell advocates the enactment of a 'democratic bill of rights', which he defines as one that is directly endorsed by the electorate in a referendum, and aims to improve the human rights performance of elected legislatures rather than confer additional powers on courts. It would establish a joint Parliamentary Committee on Human Rights with constitutional powers to scrutinize draft legislation, hold inquiries and also design a comprehensive set of human rights legislation to be given a higher status than ordinary legislation. Courts would be required to give human rights legislation priority. The Committee would be empowered to delay the passage of legislation, to hold public hearings, to question government ministers and public servants and obtain government information, to require that human rights issues be debated in Parliament, and to require that legislation be brought forward to deal with human rights deficits. It would have many advantages compared with courts, including: (a) being able to deal with social and economic as well as civil and political rights; (b) not having to adopt a technical, legal approach to issues, which would enable it to take into account philosophical, political and economic, as well as

---

29 Chapter 14 below, p.331.

legal, literature; and (c) being able to focus on human rights violations by corporate as well as government actors.

The essays in this book were originally presented as papers at a workshop on 'Protecting Human Rights in Australia: Past, Present And Future', held in Melbourne in December 2003.

I conclude by thanking my co-editors, Tom Campbell and Adrienne Stone, for helping me organize both the workshop and the publication of this book. The three of us have been collaborators in a research project, funded by the Australian Research Council, on the subject of the protection of human rights in Australia. A book that emerged from an earlier stage in that project is *Protecting Human Rights, Instruments and Institutions* (Oxford: OUP, 2003).

We thank the Australian Research Council for its generous support. We also thank Michael McIver for his invaluable assistance in style checking and correcting all chapters for publication, Tamara Shanley for compiling the index, and the team at Ashgate, both for their patience in awaiting the manuscript for this book, and for their expert assistance in preparing it for publication.

PART I
Institutional Performance

Chapter 1

Australian Exceptionalism: Rights Protection Without a Bill of Rights

Brian Galligan and F.L. (Ted) Morton[1]

The purpose of this chapter is to open up the theoretical and comparative space for considering Australia's exceptionalism in being the last English-speaking democracy without a judicially enforceable bill or charter of rights. We point out that Australia has experienced a significant judicial development of civil rights and liberties in the absence of a written bill of rights, and that this development is consistent with Charles Epp's paradigm for explaining 'rights revolutions' in the United States and Canada (Epp, 1998). The key element in Epp's theory – a 'support structure for legal mobilization' (SSLM) – exists in Australia, albeit in a relatively weak and under-developed form. We suggest that the Mason Court era of the early 1990s is analogous to what Epp describes as the partial rights revolution that occurred pre-1998 in the United Kingdom in the absence of a bill of rights. We then use the Australian rights experience to critique Epp's model. Australia has a relatively well-developed legislative and administrative rights regime quite apart from any judicial involvement. This pattern suggests that Epp's explanation is flawed because it does not account for rights protection that takes place outside the courts and advocacy group litigation. His model is ethnocentric in taking US experience as the norm and evaluating that of other countries in terms of replicating the American pattern of advocacy group litigation and judicial activism. Epp's paradigm also suffers from being apolitical. It assumes that 'rights' are a public good, irrespective of whether they are self-serving claims by particular groups that advance their policy objectives. Nor does he recognize that in many cases, rights claims conflict with each other (Sniderman et al., 1996).

We suggest that the primary effect of adopting a bill of rights is institutional, shifting primary responsibility for making decisions about rights claims from legislatures to courts. The secondary effect of adopting a bill of rights is to privilege different types of political resources and, since these resources are not evenly distributed, to privilege different societal interests. Legislative decision making is more susceptible to being influenced by interests with large or mass memberships that can influence electoral outcomes with votes and financial contributions. Judicial

1 Acknowledgment is made of the University of Melbourne's support through a Visiting Collaborative Fellowship for Ted Morton.

decision making is more susceptible to influence by interests with large numbers of lawyers or whose policy objectives and social values are shared by elite groups. Which forums and which societal interests are more supportive of 'rights' varies over time, and depends upon which rights and whose rights are in play.

This chapter is exploratory in opening up the topic, and reports on an initial investigation of the SSLM in Australia. It summarizes the limited scope for judicial innovation in human rights protection allowed by the *Australian Constitution*, which does not include a bill of rights, and examines the High Court's foray into implied constitutional rights and its more substantial transformation of native title law in the 1990s. These two elements – limited scope for judicial activism and relatively weak SSLM – explain Australia's limited rights revolution by judicial means. However, this is only part of the Australian story whose rights revolution has occurred mainly through parliamentary and political means. While the case for this is outlined and some illustrations given, its substantiation requires more extensive research and comparative analysis along lines suggested in the chapter.

Australian Exceptionalism in Human Rights Protection

Australia is the only English-speaking democracy not to have a judicially enforceable bill of rights, either constitutional or statutory. Such exceptionalism is lamented by bill of rights advocates and used as evidence of grave deficiency in rights protection in Australia. In a recent book advocating 'writing in rights' in the *Constitution*, Hilary Charlesworth characterized Australia's century of nationhood celebrated in 2001 as 'a century of reluctance about rights' (Charlesworth, 2002, p. 35). According to Charlesworth, the most urgent constitutional task for the nation is 'to devise an Australian system to protect rights: We are now the only common law country in the world without such a system' (Ibid., p. 76). Without a bill of rights, George Williams argues that rights protection in Australian is deficient: 'There is need for greater protection entrenched in a statutory or constitutional Bill of Rights' (Williams, 1999, p. 24). While acknowledging that there are arguments for and against adopting a bill of rights, Williams concludes that 'the importance of protecting fundamental rights against the exercise of arbitrary government power makes the case for a Bill of Rights compelling' (Ibid., p. 258; see also Williams, 2004).

Our purpose in this chapter is to explore two interrelated aspects of Australian exceptionalism. One is the extent to which Australian human rights protection has developed through judicial means usually associated with a bill of rights regime. As we show using the framework of Charles Epp, this has been significant but limited and does not amount to a full-blown rights revolution. That is hardly surprising since one would not expect a judicially based rights revolution to be possible without a bill of rights for judges to interpret. What is probably more surprising is the extent to which judges have developed implied constitutional rights and incorporated international human rights norms into Australian constitutional jurisprudence. This in turn is explicable by the existence of Australia's weak but functioning SSLM,

Epp's necessary condition for a rights revolution. In evaluating Australia's record on rights protection, we need to take account of this partial rights revolution by judicial means. More importantly, however, we need to recognize that this is only part of the Australian story on human rights protection.

The other purpose of the chapter is to suggest that Australia has in fact had a fully blown rights revolution mainly through political means. The great rights victories attributed to judges and constitutional courts in other countries have been achieved in Australia mainly through legislative and administrative decision making. While this has been supplemented in significant ways by judicial decision making, Australia's rights revolution has been predominantly political and democratic. If correct, this finding challenges the case of the bill of rights advocates, mainly lawyers, who have been looking in the wrong direction for evidence of Australian rights protection. The Australian experience also shows up a flaw in Epp's paradigm: his assumption that rights are only protected through judicial decisions is ethnocentric and based upon the highly judicialized American model. Australia provides comparative evidence that a political model of rights protection is possible and effective. This finding vindicates the theoretical argument of Jeremy Waldron (1993) that human rights protection can be achieved without excessive reliance upon a bill of rights or judicial activism. Moreover, such a model of rights protection helps ensure political vigour and democratic legitimacy.

Epp's Thesis and Australia

Epp defines 'rights revolution' as 'a sustained, developmental process that produced or expanded the new civil rights and liberties'. The 'new rights', according to Epp, encompassed 'among other rights, freedom of speech and the press; free exercise of religion and prohibitions on official establishment of religion; prohibitions against invidious discrimination on the basis of race, sex, and a few other more or less immutable characteristics; the right of privacy; and the right to due process in law enforcement and administrative procedure'. The rights Epp focuses upon are women's rights and the rights of criminal defendants and prisoners (Epp, 1998, p. 7).

The rights revolution that Epp has in mind is based upon generalizing from American practice and scholarship that attributes advances in rights protection mainly to courts and judges. Gerry Rosenberg's (1991) contrary view, that discounts the role of the Supreme Court in United States landmark rights cases in favour of political and social causes, is ignored. According to Epp, the process of rights revolution has had three components: 'judicial attention to the new rights, judicial support for the new rights, and implementation of the new rights'. But judicial attention to and support for new rights plus their court-based implementation are not enough, according to Epp. Even in combination with the other two explanatory components that others have relied upon – a constitutional bill of rights and a sympathetic popular culture – the explanation of rights revolutions is incomplete. Hence, Epp broadens the top-down judicial fiat model of rights advancement predominant among judges and lawyers by adding a bottom-up political component of group mobilization that he calls a 'support structure for legal mobilization'.

This additional factor is crucial, Epp claims, based upon his empirical investigation of the United States and comparative practice of Canada, Britain and India. This SSLM requires dedicated material resources and organizational structures that provide expert legal advice, develop and coordinate legal research, plan and sustain the launching of strategic cases, and provide publicity and communication networks to spread ideas. Such support structures form independently of judicial politics and provide the stimulus and support for the processes of the rights revolution. To sum up, Epp's thesis is that without a sufficient SSLM, the other components of constitutional provisions, judicial politics and popular culture are insufficient. In his words: 'If the *support-structure* explanation is correct, we should find that rights revolutions have occurred only where and when and on those issues for which material supports for rights litigation – rights-advocacy organizations, supportive lawyers, and non-membership sources of financing – have developed' (Epp, 1998, p. 23, emphasis in original).

We use Epp's framework to examine Australia's experience with court-based rights protection. This includes the three usual explanatory components invoked by constitutional scholars – a bill of rights, sympathetic judges and a supportive popular culture – plus Epp's fourth essential SSLM requirement. Our review finds a moderate but fluctuating degree of judicial support for rights, some evidence of a supportive popular culture and a thin but vocal SSLM. The absence of a bill of rights is no doubt crucial in explaining the latter's weakness: why mobilize to litigate rights if there are no justiciable rights? Nevertheless, the High Court has recognized certain 'implied rights' in the *Constitution* while deciding test cases brought by rights advocacy groups and dedicated human rights activists.

Such judicial developments in Australian rights protection have been significant but limited. There has not been a court-based rights revolution, or sufficient support for adopting a bill of rights despite periodic agitation and several attempts to implement a statutory bill of rights in the 1970s and 1980s. The absence of both is assumed by critics to be evidence of Australian apathy towards rights protection. If Australia has experienced a rights revolution by mainly political means, however, the relative weakness of support for a bill of rights and the limited scope of judicial developments in rights protection without a bill of rights are to be expected. Once we allow that a rights revolution can be achieved by political as well as judicial means, Australian exceptionalism becomes theoretically more significant. It can assist us in correcting Epp's thesis. Whereas Epp broadened the court-based judicial model of rights protection by adding the political component of group mobilization, we show that this is only one way, or one partial way, of securing a rights revolution. The other way that has been significant in the countries that Epp examines, including the United States but especially Britain, India and Canada, and remains predominant in Australia, is legislative protection through the political process. Indeed, the legislative/political protection of human rights has often been more significant, and in most countries is an ongoing part of a combination of legislative and judicial processes. Without a bill of rights, Australia is at the legislative end of the spectrum, but the judicial component of rights protection has been significant.

In addition, the Australian case allows us to test the institutional hypothesis that institutions matter in determining, to an important extent, the sorts of rights that get attention and action. We would expect the legislative process to favour rights that are of primary concern to the people and mass-based parties, such as voting rights, certain social and economic rights such as welfare entitlements and working conditions and wages, health care provision and education. In contrast, judicial decision making would likely benefit special groups with the knowledge and resources to work the court system to their advantage.

Rights Protection by the Courts and Judiciary

Despite having no bill of rights, Australia has had a range of judicial developments in rights protection during the last couple of decades. The Australian experience shows that sympathetic judges can advance rights protection in innovative ways, but it also shows the limitations of such advances without a bill of rights.

The *Australian Constitution* is not entirely bereft of rights protection clauses. There are three express rights guarantees: s. 80 that guarantees jury trial for indictable offences under Commonwealth law; s. 116 that guarantees freedom of religion; and s.117 that prohibits discrimination against those from another State. In addition there is the requirement of 'just terms' in the Commonwealth's acquisition power under s. 51(xxxi). The three explicit guarantees have provided limited rights protection, although the just terms provision has been quite robust. Least significant of all has been the jury trial provision that was gutted early on when the Court held that the Commonwealth government could decide to have offences tried summarily rather than on indictment.

The most significant guarantee is that of freedom of religion, which was closely copied from the *United States Constitution*. It was added to the *Australian Constitution* after the invocation 'humbly relying on the blessing of Almighty God' was added to the preamble. This invocation was adopted because of a groundswell of support from God-fearing people, but this in turn sparked concern among non-conformists that was addressed by also adopting the guarantee of religious freedom. The wording of the section is clear and comprehensive:

> The Commonwealth shall not make any law for establishing any religion, or for imposing any religious observance, or for prohibiting the free exercise of any religion, and no religious test shall be required as a qualification for any office or public trust under the Commonwealth.

The High Court has interpreted it literally and narrowly, rejecting the proposal of the Defence of Government Schools (DOGS) lobby to read in the American doctrine of strict separation of church and state so as to deny government provision of state-aid to Catholic schools. Justice Lionel Murphy, a leading rights activist as a judge and previously as Attorney-General in the Whitlam Labor government, was the only dissenting judge to support the DOGS claim.[2]

The s. 117 prohibition of discrimination based on State residence fared better with a differently constituted Court in *Street* v *Queensland Bar Association*.[3] The decision barred professional associations from restricting out-of-State practitioners, in this case a prominent Sydney barrister, from becoming a member of the Queensland bar. Section 117, however, was narrowly drafted by the constitutional founders to prevent only discrimination against residents of other States. The original proposal for a broader American style Fourteenth Amendment banning State discrimination against citizens per se was rejected. Overall, these specific guarantees have provided limited scope for rights protection and have not been broadly embellished by judicial review. This result has been more or less as the Australian founders intended and anticipated: they preferred to leave rights protection mainly to parliamentary democratic processes and designed the *Constitution* accordingly.

Until the foray into implied rights by the Mason Court in the early 1990s, the most significant rights implication that the High Court drew from the *Constitution* was that of an individual right to freedom of interstate trade. Despite the misgivings of some, the founders incorporated the popular commercial slogan of 'absolute freedom' of interstate trade in s. 92 of the *Constitution*. This became one of the most litigated sections – not least because it conflicted with the Commonwealth's designated power over interstate trade and commerce – and was variously interpreted by changing coalitions of High Court judges. That s. 92 protected the right of individual traders to engage in interstate trade was suggested by Dixon J during the 1930s and adopted by the Privy Council in confirming the High Court's landmark decision declaring bank nationalization by the Chifley Labor government unconstitutional in 1949. The individual right theory of s. 92 was dominant for the Dixon and Barwick Courts, and was finally discarded by the Mason Court in 1988. In *Cole* v *Whitfield*,[4] the Court returned to a restricted reading that allowed government regulation of interstate trade and only prevented discriminatory burdens of a protectionist kind. Significantly, it was the rights activist Murphy who proposed an even more restrictive interpretation of s. 92 as preventing only fiscal burdens that resembled customs duties.

If the *Australian Constitution* was an unpromising instrument for rights protection, the Australian judiciary was generally unsympathetic to expansive rights claims. Judges were typically appointed from the elite ranks of leading barristers from the Sydney, Melbourne and, to a lesser extent, Brisbane bars and the Supreme Courts of those States. Notable exceptions were the leading founders, Griffith CJ, Barton, O'Connor, Isaacs and Higgins JJ, appointed to the High Court in the first series of appointments in 1903 and 1905, and the controversial appointments of Labor politicians Evatt and McTiernan JJ in 1930 and Murphy J in 1975. Until Murphy J, however, rights enhancement was not on the Court's agenda, which was predominantly focused on

---

2　　*A-G (Vic); Ex rel Black* v *Commonwealth* (1981) 146 CLR 559 ('DOGS case').

3　　(1989) 168 CLR 461.

4　　(1988) 165 CLR 360.

the federal division of powers and the limits of Commonwealth jurisdiction. After the passing of the early founders, the public rhetoric of the Court, as expressed by its leading exponent Sir Owen Dixon, was 'strict and complete legalism'. If this was not always adhered to in practice, as was evident in Dixon CJ's individual rights interpretation of s. 92 and the Court's overturning of a raft of Labor government legislative initiatives for greater regulation, centralization and socialization, the Court favoured old-style liberal economic and property rights. Not until Murphy J's appointment in 1975 was there much attention to the 'new rights' with which Epp is concerned, and not until the late 1980s was there a majority of sympathetic judges on the Court. The Court's complexion changed through judicial appointments by the Hawke Labor government: Mason CJ replaced the more conservative Gibbs CJ as Chief Justice in 1987; while Toohey J and Gaudron J (the first woman ever on the High Court) were appointed at the same time to replace Gibbs CJ who retired and Murphy J who had died. Along with Brennan and Deane JJ, who had been appointed earlier by the Fraser Liberal Coalition government in 1981 and 1982, there was now a majority of High Court judges with varying degrees of sympathy for new rights protection. Labor made a further appointment, that of McHugh J, who replaced Wilson J in 1989.

The implied rights foray of the Court in the early 1990s was a product of sympathetic judges being presented with test cases and novel rights arguments by a growing band of advocacy groups and legal counsel dedicated to rights enhancement. The most notable advance was in finding that a right to freedom of political speech was implied by sections of the *Constitution* implementing representative and responsible government. The requirement that the two Houses of Parliament be composed of senators and members 'directly chosen by the people', specified in ss. 7 and 24, provided the main constitutional basis for such an implication. This was established in a pair of cases in 1992, *Nationwide News* v *Wills*[5] and *Australian Capital Television* v *Commonwealth*.[6] Legislation banning the criticism of Commonwealth industrial relations commissioners was struck down in the former case, and Commonwealth restrictions on radio and television advertising during election campaigns that purported to also bind the States and Territories in the latter case.

These cases sparked an exciting period of judicial review when counsel made more ambitious claims to expand implied constitutional rights and a minority of judges responded sympathetically. One avenue was to incorporate criminal procedure rights into judicial power. For some time the High Court has made strong assertions about the separation of judicial power in the *Constitution*, the overarching role of the High Court as the authoritative interpreter of the *Constitution*, and the exclusive right of courts to exercise judicial power. In a minority position in *Dietrich* v *The Queen*,[7] Deane and Gaudron JJ sought to extend this by holding that certain features of the criminal law procedure are constitutionally entrenched, being inherent in

---

5   (1992) 177 CLR 1.
6   (1992) 177 CLR 106.
7   (1992) 177 CLR 292.

the notion of judicial power. In a controversial public address, Toohey J argued in favour of basic common law principles being implied by the *Constitution*.[8] In *Leeth v Commonwealth*,[9] his Honour and Deane J claimed there was an implied right of equality between citizens derived from the agreement of the people to unite into a federal policy, as evidenced in the preamble declaration. These more ambitious claims never attracted more than a minority of judges.

The implied rights adventure was played out mainly in clarifying the implied right to freedom of communication. In *Theophanous* v *Herald and Weekly Times*[10] and *Stephens* v *WA Newspapers*,[11] the Court was divided over whether the implied right to political communication provided a constitutional defence supplanting the established law of defamation. Australian defamation law was notoriously restrictive on criticism of public figures and the newspapers were keen to have it replaced by a more liberal constitutional regime. Theophanous was a federal politician and Stephens a Western Australian politician, and both sued newspapers for publishing criticisms of their political activities. In a subsequent case, *Lange* v *ABC*,[12] the Court forged a new unanimity in affirming a modified freedom of political communication, not as an individual right but a restriction on the legislative power of government. While this distinction is of arguable validity, the Court ruled that individual redress should be based on development of the common law defence of qualified privilege rather than any constitutional implication. In other words, the constitutional implication of freedom of political speech turned out not to advance individual rights protection, except as a limitation on government powers. There was no judicial consensus for going beyond this modest bridgehead; indeed in the *Lange* case the Court regrouped by retreating somewhat from its earlier diffuse advance.

Nevertheless, the break-out on freedom of speech was sufficient catalyst for further implied rights claims. In *Kruger* v *Commonwealth*,[13] lawyers for the 'Stolen Generation', Aboriginal people who as children in the Northern Territory had been forcibly removed from their mothers and put in government custody, claimed their implied constitutional right to freedom of movement had been infringed by involuntary detention. The Court did not accept this or other claims that freedom of religion had been breached by the policy. In dissent, Gaudron and Toohey JJ affirmed an implied right to freedom of movement that had been infringed. Gaudron, Toohey and McHugh JJ all thought there was an implied right to freedom of movement incidental to the implied freedom of political communication, although McHugh J was stricter in limiting this to movement associated with political communication. In *Levy* v *Victoria*,[14] the Court rejected claims that a Victorian regulation banning

---

8   Justice John Toohey AC, 'A Government of Laws, and Not of Men?' (1993) 4 *Public Law Review*: 158.

9   (1992) 174 CLR 455.

10   (1994) 182 CLR 104.

11   (1994) 182 CLR 211.

12   (1997) 189 CLR 520 ('*Lange*').

13   (1997) 190 CLR 1 ('*Kruger*').

14   (1997) 189 CLR 579 ('*Levy*').

protestors from duck-hunting areas at the beginning of the shooting season breached the protestors' implied right to freedom of political speech. The High Court's rejection of these more ambitious claims spelt the end of its foray into implied constitutional rights.

Native Title

More significant than implied rights was a second novel front that the Court opened up with decisions on racial discrimination and native title in *Mabo* v *Queensland [No 1]*[15] and *Mabo* v *Queensland [No 2]*,[16] and in the subsequent *Wik Peoples* v *Queensland*[17] decision. The *Mabo* cases were ambitious test cases brought by dedicated human rights lawyers from Melbourne, Ron Casten and Bryan Keon-Cohen, to recognize the traditional title to land of indigenous people and overturn two hundred years of common law doctrine of *terra nullius* that had denied any such title. In *Mabo [No 1]*, the High Court ruled that Queensland's pre-emptive attempt to extinguish any residual native title by legislation was invalid on the ground of inconsistency with the Commonwealth's *Racial Discrimination Act 1975* (Cth) ('*Racial Discrimination Act*'). In the earlier case of *Koowarta* v *Bjelke-Petersen*,[18] the High Court had upheld the validity of the *Racial Discrimination Act* as a legitimate exercise of the Commonwealth's s. 51 (xxvi) external affairs power in implementing the *International Convention on the Elimination of All Forms of Racial Discrimination*[19] to which Australia had become a party. In *Mabo [No 2]*, the Court overturned *terra nullius* and upheld the native title claims of the Meriam people to the Murray Islands in Torres Strait. Justice Brennan wrote the leading opinion and relied upon international human rights norms in overturning common law doctrine that was discriminatory. In *Wik*, the Court extended the principle of native title to pastoral leases in Queensland, and by implication to pastoral leases that cover much of northern and western Australia. This was a more contentious decision, with Brennan dissenting as Chief Justice.

Wik sparked unprecedented criticism of the Court from the States, mainly Queensland and Western Australia that were most affected, the pastoral and mining industries, and the Liberal and National parties in federal opposition. Deputy Prime Minister and National party leader, Tim Fischer, accused the Court of delaying publication of its *Wik* judgment and threatened when in government to appoint a capital 'C' conservative judge. Chief Justice Brennan's letter of complaint to Fisher was published in the press and Fisher apologized. Nevertheless, the resolve of the Liberal-National party coalition to use judicial appointments to change the direction

---

15 (1988) 166 CLR 186 ('*Mabo [No 1]*').

16 (1992) 175 CLR 1 ('*Mabo [No 2]*').

17 (1996) 187 CLR 1 ('*Wik*').

18 (1982) 153 CLR 168.

19 Opened for signature 7 March 1966, 660 UNTS 195 (entered into force 4 January 1969).

of the Court was clear, and it was in a position to do so after winning office in 1996. In theory the Howard-Fisher government might have overturned *Wik* by passing legislation that in effect amended the *Racial Discrimination Act*, but in practice that was not politically feasible. It retained the native title legislation passed by the Keating Labor government to provide orderly procedures for dealing with native title claims.

Given the political circumstances of a major backlash from its native title decisions and the change of federal government, it was not surprising that the Court effectively closed down its foray into implied constitutional rights in the series of 1997 decisions – *Lange*, *Kruger* and *Levy* referred to earlier. There were obvious technical difficulties in maintaining a plausible constitutional jurisprudence without a bill of rights. As well, the composition of the Court was changing even before Labor lost federal office. Chief Justice Mason retired in 1995 and was replaced by Gummow J, a Sydney barrister, with Brennan being appointed Chief Justice. The leading proponent of implied rights, William Deane, was appointed Governor-General later in 1995. Although he was replaced by Kirby J, a prominent champion of human rights, the Court became more subdued. After the change of government in 1996, the Howard Liberal Coalition government was able to make three appointments in 1997–98: Callinan and Hayne JJ and Murray Gleeson as Chief Justice. The additional appointment of Dyson Heydon J, a champion of Dixonian legalism, in 2002 to replace Gaudron J has consolidated a traditional and rather more conservative Court, with Kirby J the notable exception as a champion of rights protection by judicial means and the leading dissenter on the Court.

Overall, the contribution of the judiciary to furthering new rights protection has been significant, but mainly through other means than implied constitutional rights. In transforming the common law to allow native title, the Court confirmed a limited and residual right that is subject to legislative override by parliaments. That leaves the matter in the political realm of federal politics, with the Commonwealth able to preserve native title as it has done and the States constrained by the Commonwealth's anti-discrimination law. Constitutionally, the Court's contribution has been through its traditional federal adjudication in giving broad and plenary scope to Commonwealth powers. Again, that leaves the running on rights protection mainly to the legislatures with the Commonwealth able to trump the States in any of the vast array of matters that come within its expansive powers. Through generous interpretation of the external affairs power, the Court has opened up for the Commonwealth a potential super highway for introducing international human rights norms, including a statutory bill of rights, into domestic law. Such legislation takes precedence over that of the States, as established in the challenge to the *Racial Discrimination Act*. Thus, the effect is to leave human rights protection mainly to parliaments and the political process.

Parliamentary Rights Protection

Australian exceptionalism in not having a bill of rights is relatively recent. Until the 1970s Australia was typical of British Commonwealth nations like Canada and New Zealand that followed Britain in relying upon parliamentary responsible government and the common law for human rights protection. Sir Owen Dixon, a leading High Court judge from 1929 to 1952 and Chief Justice until 1964, championed the Australian model that placed no fetters upon legislative power except insofar as that was entailed in distributing legislative power between the federal and State parliaments. Justice Dixon explained to the American Bar Association in 1944 that the Australian founders departed from the *United States Constitution*, otherwise considered an 'incomparable model' of federal constitutionalism, in retaining responsible parliamentary government and rejecting a bill of rights. This was due to 'our steadfast faith in responsible government and in plenary legislative powers distributed, but not controlled'. Justice Dixon recognized the different sensitivities of his American audience but made no apologies for Australia's democratic tradition (Dixon, 1965, pp. 101–2):

> In our steadfast faith in responsible government and in plenary legislative powers distributed, but not controlled, you as Americans may perceive nothing better than a wilful refusal to see the light and an obstinate adherence to heresies; but we remain impenitent.

In a public lecture at the University of Virginia in 1967, Sir Robert Menzies, who as a young man had read law in Dixon's chambers and went on to become Australia's longest serving prime minister, reiterated the Australian orthodoxy. The Australian democratic model of rights protection entailed the executive being answerable to parliament on a day-to-day basis, and parliament being directly elected by the people, Menzies said. This was no recipe for majoritarian tyranny as his audience may have supposed, or arbitrary government power as latter-day Australian constitutionalists like Williams presume. According to Menzies, democratic responsible government was regarded by Australians as 'the ultimate guarantee of justice and individual rights'. That and the common law obviated the need for any formal definition of rights and produced outstanding outcomes, according to Menzies: 'I would say, without hesitation, that the rights of individuals in Australia are as adequately protected as they are in any other country in the world' (Menzies, 1967, p. 54).

Much has changed in the public rhetoric and practice of Australian law and politics since Dixon J and Menzies. Most today would recognize that executive control over the lower House of Parliament through disciplined party politics undermines parliamentary accountability of government, although the Australian Senate has developed an enhanced scrutiny role that partly compensates. There is also a more sober appreciation of the blemishes in Australia's record of rights protection, especially in the historic denial of rights to Aboriginal people (Chesterman and Galligan, 1997) and discrimination against non-whites in immigration policy. With these qualifications, however, Australia's democratic political system of rights protection championed by Dixon J and Menzies remains in place, although under increasing attack from bill of rights advocates.

Before bills of rights became instruments of rights protection in the mid twentieth century, institutional checks and balances were the main institutional constraints on government power. That was the case in the United States and was copied in the *Australian Constitution* (Galligan, 1995). According to the basic principle of federalism, powers for the two spheres of government were divided and, *pace* Dixon J, thereby limited. The powers and structures of national or Commonwealth government were also specified, albeit broadly, and as a consequence subject to judicial review by a High Court whose own judicial power was constitutionally entrenched. Perhaps more significantly, the multiple spheres and branches, as well as the bicameral structure of the Commonwealth Parliament, ensured that power was dispersed among a number of quasi-independent institutions that would diffuse political will and multiply opportunities for political ambition and democratic input. Within this complex system of government, the Commonwealth and State parliaments were left with prime responsibility for rights protection.

To say the least, the tyranny of a majority was made virtually impossible by such a federal constitutional system of parliamentary democracy. John Uhr's chapter shows how the Commonwealth Parliament, and particularly the Senate which the government of the day usually does not control, has incorporated rights considerations and protection into its operation. More could no doubt be done, but the achievement is significant. The review role of the Senate, however, is only one part of system of parliamentary rights protection. Governments and parliaments reflect popular opinion on human rights; they can orchestrate and respond to political mobilization of broad social movements and special interest groups, as well as adopt international and comparative models of improved rights protection. The Commonwealth and State governments and Parliaments have engaged in variations of these options. Aboriginal land rights, for example, was pioneered in South Australia before adoption by the Commonwealth for the Northern Territory. This was prior to the High Court's revolution of common law title in *Mabo [No 2]*. Before federation South Australia and Western Australia granted female suffrage that was copied by the new Commonwealth Parliament in 1902. Under the *Australian Constitution*, criminal law remains primarily a State responsibility and there has been ongoing, if uneven, development in attention to criminal justice rights.

The Commonwealth became more active in rights protection in the latter decades of the twentieth century, implanting through statute a range of new rights that had become the subject of international agreements to which Australia was party (Galligan, Trifiletti and Roberts, 2001, p. 152). These included the *Racial Discrimination Act,* the *Sex Discrimination Act 1984* (Cth), the *Disability Discrimination Act 1992* (Cth) and the *Human Rights and Equal Opportunity Commission Act 1986* (Cth). The Human Rights and Equal Opportunity Commission (HREOC), a statutory body with a brief for monitoring and limited investigation and advocacy functions, is typical of a range of non-judicial bodies with some responsibility for rights enhancement. It also has administrative responsibilities under the *Native Title Act 1993* (Cth) and the *Workplace Relations Act 1996* (Cth).

Towards a Comparative Outcome Method

The hard test of how effective parliamentary protection of rights has been in comparison to judicial protection should be in terms of effective outcomes. This undercuts the often simplistic and essentialist assumptions of those who presuppose rights are limited to what are legally or constitutionally based and focus on processes of judicial review. Such a method allows us to do justice to countries like Australia that have predominantly a parliamentary systems of rights protection with the judiciary playing a significant but subordinate part, as outlined earlier. Because the study of parliamentary and political protection of rights has been relatively neglected in recent decades in favour of judicial protection, this would be a countervailing study that would give a more balanced account. What is suggested here is merely an outline of a methodology and work plan, as there is a good deal of Australian and comparative research to be done.

From a survey of actual advances in, and the literature on, rights protection we should be able to come up with a list of important rights. We can then examine whether and to what extent, and through what institutional means – parliamentary, judicial, or some combination of these and other process, such as the impact of international laws or norms – they have been achieved both in Australia and in otherwise comparable countries that have bills or charters of rights. Epp's comparative study of the judicial process of rights protection in the United States, Britain, Canada and India focusing on 'new rights', mainly women's rights and criminal law rights, is selective and only partial, as rights advances in these areas probably owe a good deal to parliamentary and political processes as well as judicial ones. Obviously, focusing only on the judicial advances would give a very incomplete Australian story. The method we are suggesting is the obvious one of beginning with outcomes in notable human rights areas and working back to see how they have been achieved.

The second part of the approach is comparative: taking a series of comparable countries and examining how well and by what institutional, or combination of institutional means, they have achieved advances in human rights in key areas. A preliminary list of major human rights would include the following (listed in no particular order):

- voting rights
- non-discrimination
- freedom of speech, including political advertising and pornography
- free exercise of religion, including state aid for education
- criminal law rights, including to counsel and the exclusion of evidence
- abortion rights
- gay rights
- social welfare.

A broader prism could be the achievement of equality among citizens, that would include social and economic entitlements as well as substantive and procedural embellishments of due process. Another current avenue for exploration might be procedures for dealing with national security and terrorism, and the treatment of refugees and asylum seekers. Even if we stick with the 'new rights' that Epp singles out – mainly women's rights and criminal law rights – Australia's record probably stands up in comparison with those of Epp's comparator countries.

The Australian case allows us to examine a 'rights revolution' achieved mainly through parliamentary and political means, with a complementary judicial contribution. We expect it to show that Australia compares well with other countries, being concerned with broad political rights such as voting and substantive equality matters such as wage levels and employment practices that have widespread appeal. Whether it is a laggard in more selective individual and group rights, to do with personal privacy and alternative lifestyles, will depend on the strength of the support structure for political mobilization. Investigation of these issues is beyond the scope of this chapter and requires further empirical research. In the final section of the chapter, we make a preliminary review of the SSLM underpinning the limited judicial advances in rights protection that have occurred.

Support Structure for Legal Mobilization in Australia

There are a large number of rights-protection organizations in Australia – within government, in the NGO world and in academia. Most do not use 'test case' litigation as a strategy for advancing their rights goals. This is due in part to lack of resources, and in part to the courts' unreceptive stance toward interveners and amicus curiae participation by advocacy groups of any kind. The legal community's support for rights advocacy organizations is mixed. Australian lawyers appear to be evenly divided on whether parliaments or courts should have the final say on rights issues. A growing number of lawyers volunteer time for public interest litigation, and recent growth in larger law firms has created more opportunities for *pro bono* litigation. In the law schools there is stronger support evidenced in the recent creation of several human rights research institutes, the leading public role of law professors in the bill of rights' debate, and the increasing number of human rights courses being offered to students.

The weak-link in Australia's SSLM, however, is funding with few of the non-government rights-advocacy organizations receiving public or private foundation funding. There is no dedicated test case funding program as in Canada. Legal aid programs exist in all States, but budget constraints and strict government guidelines discourage, if not preclude, funding potentially policy-salient cases beyond the first appeal. To the extent that Australia has a SSLM, it is much weaker than those currently found in the US or Canada, but perhaps on a par with what Epp reports for the UK prior to 1998 before the incorporation of the *European Convention for the Protection of Human Rights and Fundamental Freedoms*[20] into British domestic law.

Although Epp did not include Australia in his comparative study, we can use his framework for assessing its SSLM. As explained earlier, Epp makes the SSLM a necessary condition for a successful rights revolution because this provides the resources to enable sustained and strategic appellate litigation. Funding is one of the three central elements of SSLM, the others being the existence of rights advocacy groups and significant support among lawyers. The Australian case shows there are many rights advocacy groups and that these have support from some lawyers. Australian lawyers, however, are divided in their support for traditional parliamentary protection versus judicial protection of rights (Galligan and McAllister, 1997). The main weakness of Australian SSLM is the lack of non-membership funding, either from private foundations or governments.

Rights advocacy organizations

There are a large number of organizations in Australia that define their mission, in whole or in part, as the protection and promotion of rights. These groups are found within government agencies and among NGOs. As early as 1981, the Human Rights Bureau identified 18 organizations within the Commonwealth government with responsibilities in the human rights field (Commonwealth, Human Rights Bureau, 1981). Today, at the federal and State level, there are scores of public institutions that monitor government legislation and administration for compliance with rights norms. These include ombudsmen; parliamentary committees that scrutinize proposed legislation; government agencies and commissions that promote and conciliate on human rights issues; welfare agencies; administrative tribunals; judicial enforcement of human rights norms that are found in international and common law (Sampford, 1997). The 1981 study identified 34 NGOs that worked to protect and promote human rights, including six international organizations, four women's organizations, three religious organizations, three organizations for the disabled, three youth and children organizations, one general welfare organization, two legal organizations, two refugee organizations, two employer-employee relations organizations, two gay rights organizations and six miscellaneous organizations. By 1992, Cohen identified 462 organizations that indicated a primary concern with the protection of 'civil liberties' (Cohen, 1992). Most of these date from the 1980s or more recently and their policy objectives cover a broad, and often conflicting, range of rights issues. We briefly review some of the major ones.

There is a civil liberties council (CLC) in each State. While the level of organizational activity varies from State to State, and from year to year within each State, most report having several hundred active, dues-paying members. All maintain websites; all publish annual or bi-annual newsletters; and most have

---

20 Opened for signature 4 November 1950, 213 UNTS 222 (entered into force 3 September 1953).

a list-serve capacity to send out policy alerts and copies of news releases to their membership. Interviews and anecdotal evidence suggests that State CLCs regularly inject rights concerns into public policy debates at the State level on issues ranging from asylum seekers, anti-terrorism laws, peaceful assembly legislation, involuntary taking of DNA samples from suspects, and police access to telephone records. Most also participate in national policy development but to a lesser extent. This is the responsibility of their national umbrella organizations, the Australian Council for Civil Liberties.

One of the most active rights advocacy organizations is the Public Interest Advocacy Centre (PIAC) based in Sydney. PIAC was founded in 1982 by activist lawyer Terry Purcell. Purcell envisioned a role for PIAC that fits Epp's model of a modern rights advocacy organization: a policy-oriented litigator that can bring test cases and is funded from non-membership sources. Since 1982, its salaried staff has grown from four to eighteen, and its budget for 2002 was approximately one million dollars. Almost all of this funding comes from governments and law society trust funds. Over the years, PIAC has succeeded in building a significant stable of lawyers willing to do *pro bono* work, including 40 barristers, 10 barristers' chambers and 50 law firms. Law firms, especially large metropolitan ones, are an important source of PIAC support, providing *pro bono* lawyers and contributions, as well as hosting luncheons, guest speakers and funding PIAC's Indigenous Lawyer program.

In its twenty years of operation, PIAC has been involved in rights litigation both as a party to test cases and as an intervener. PIAC usually tries to go to court as part of a coalition, and tries to bring to the judges a perspective or information not available from litigants. Recently, it has experienced some of the High Court's unwillingness to allow third-party participants in its proceedings. In its earlier years PIAC focused primarily on race and sex discrimination issues. More recently PIAC has expanded its focus to include discrimination against the disabled. PIAC has also been involved in many cases raising access to justice issues such as standing, assignment of costs and participation of interveners. In recent years, PIAC has shifted its focus away from civil and political rights toward social and economic rights, especially for Aboriginal people. With this shift in focus has come a shift in tactics away from straight litigation to an integrated approach to public interest advocacy that combines litigation, policy development and education and training.

Another major rights advocacy organization is the Human Rights and Equal Opportunity Commission (HREOC). HREOC differs from PIAC in that it is an independent statutory organization that reports to the Commonwealth government through the Attorney-General. It thus enjoys relatively stable public funding and need not seek financial support in the private sector. HREOC's broad mandate includes hearing and resolving discrimination complaints arising under a variety of federal anti-discrimination statutes, including the *Racial Discrimination Act*, the *Sex Discrimination Act 1984* (Cth) and the *Disability Discrimination Act 1992* (Cth), as well as its own *Human Rights and Equal Opportunity Commission Act 1986* (Cth). It also has administrative responsibilities under the *Native Title Act 1993* (Cth) and the *Workplace Relations Act 1996* (Cth). It has oversight of human rights compliance with international human rights instruments that Australia has joined, including the *International Covenant on Civil and Political Rights*,[21] the *Discrimination (Employment and Occupation) Convention 1958*,[22] the *Convention on the Rights of the Child*,[23] the *Declaration on the Rights of the Child*,[24] the *Declaration on the Rights of Disabled Persons*,[25] the *Declaration on the Rights of Mentally Retarded Persons*,[26] the *Declaration on the Elimination of All Forms of Intolerance and of Discrimination Based on Religion or Belief.*[27] As well, HREOC has a public education mandate to work with the media, develop appropriate curriculum for educators, liaise with unions and employers to reduce discrimination in employment, work with community groups and host awards and conferences. Policy research and development are also significant with HREOC getting involved in issues such as paid maternity leave, detention of children of asylum seekers, prejudice against Australians of Islamic belief or Arab origin, and a wide variety of Aboriginal issues. HREOC can also initiate investigations of suspected public and private sector discrimination or rights violations. It may seek to facilitate a voluntary resolution among the parties involved. If this fails, HREOC may submit a report to Parliament describing the problem and recommending government action to solve it.

HREOC is frequently in the courts as either an amicus curiae or intervener. HREOC enjoys statutory authority to participate in cases arising under human rights statutes and treaties, so has not experienced the same barriers to the courtroom as PIAC and other rights advocacy groups. However, it is barred by statute from initiating test cases on its own. HREOC has a separate legal section that originally adjudicated discrimination complaints that could not be resolved through conciliation. After HREOC had this jurisdiction removed in 1995 by the High Court ruling in *Brandy* v *HREOC*,[28] the six to seven lawyers in the Commission have focused most of their resources on intervention and amicus curiae briefs in rights cases. HREOC occasionally also benefits from *pro bono* representation by high profile private sector lawyers (such as Bret Walker in *Members of the Yorta Yorta Aboriginal Community* v *Victoria*[29]).

HREOC's primary objective in intervener/amicus curiae participation in discrimination cases is policy reform rather than dispute resolution. Continuity in personnel and specialization gives HREOC the advantages of a 'repeat player' in rights litigation. In recent years HREOC has intervened in court cases involving family

---

21 Opened for signature 19 December 1966, 999 UNTS 171 (entered into force 23 March 1976).

22 Opened for signature 25 June 1958, 362 UNTS 31 (entered into force 15 June 1960).

23 Opened for signature 20 November 1989, 1577 UNTS 3 (entered into force 2 September 1990).

24 GA Res 1386, 14 UN GAOR (841st plen. mtg), UN Doc A/4354 (1959).

25 GA Res 3447, 30 UN GAOR (2433rd plen. mtg), UN Doc A/10034 (1975).

26 GA Res 2856 (XXVI), 26 UN GAOR (2027th plen. mtg), UN Doc A/8429 (1971).

27 GA Res 36/55, 36 UN GAOR (73rd plen. mtg), UN Doc A/RES/36/55 (1981).

28 (1995) 183 CLR 245.

29 (2002) 214 CLR 422 (*'Yorta Yorta* case').

law, child abduction, refugees and asylum seekers, sex and marital discrimination, and native title. Some of the more high profile cases in which HREOC participated include *Ruddock* v *Vadarlis*[30] in the Federal Court, and *Re McBain; Ex parte Australian Catholic Bishops Conference*[31] and the *Yorta Yorta* Aboriginal land rights case in the High Court. The Commission's political independence is demonstrated by the fact it intervened on the opposing side to the Commonwealth Attorney-General in the *Lesbian IVF* case.

Another rights advocacy organization that has gained some prominence in New South Wales in recent years is the Australian Lawyers for Human Rights (ALHR). Established in 1993 and incorporated in 1998, it works in conjunction with groups like PIAC and the various State CLCs. ALHR has sent representatives to several international rights conferences; publicly advocated the adoption of bills of rights for both the Commonwealth and New South Wales; and comments in the media on rights issues and incidents. However, its annual budgets are modest – less than $10,000 – and heavily depend on members' dues and contributions. While some of its members have done *pro bono* litigation on rights issues, the ALHR has not.

Other law-related groups step forward on a more ad hoc and sporadic basis to voice various rights concerns. In Melbourne, the Public Interest Law Clearing House (PILCH) coordinates a network of volunteer lawyers who do public interest litigation, often with a rights dimension. PILCH's lack of a stable source of non-membership funding has made its activities somewhat sporadic. The International Commission of Jurists (Australian Branch) unsuccessfully sought leave to appear as amicus curiae in the *Kruger* case involving the removal of aboriginal children. The Law Council of Australia made a submission to the Senate Law and Constitutional Affairs Committee raising civil liberties concerns about the Commonwealth's proposed new anti-terrorism laws. Most of these groups, however, do not rely on litigation to advance their rights agendas, preferring to use a range of conventional means of public advocacy and political representation including submissions and testimony to parliamentary committees, lobbying elected politicians and non-elected senior bureaucrats, issuing press releases, writing guest opinion columns for newspapers, and giving media interviews.

Indeed, high-profile cases involving rights advocacy groups – Aboriginal land rights cases, *Mabo*, *Wik* and *Yorta Yorta*, the *Tampa* case, the *Lesbian IVF* case, and the earlier DOGS challenge to public funding of Catholic schools – are clearly exceptions to the rule. Evidence of the more common form of advocacy group participation in appellate litigation as amicus curiae or intervener is also sparse. While the number of instances of NGO amicus curiae/intervener appearances in the High Court increased substantially from 11 in the 1980s to 36 in the 1990s, it is far below Canada's figure

---

30 *Vadarlis* v *Minister for Immigration and Multicultural Affairs*; *Victorian Council for Civil Liberties Inc* v *Minister for Immigration and Multicultural Affairs* (2001) 110 FCR 491 (FCA); *Ruddock* v *Vadarlis*; *Ruddock* v *Victorian Council for Civil Liberties Inc* (2001) 110 FCR 452 (FCFCA) ('*Tampa case*').

31 (2002) 209 CLR 372 ('*Lesbian IVF* case').

of 431 during the 1990s (Williams, 2000). A final and telling piece of evidence is the complete absence of any reference to 'advocacy groups', 'interest groups', 'pressure groups', 'public interest advocacy groups', 'rights advocacy groups', 'test case' or 'systematic litigation' in the comprehensive *Oxford Companion to the High Court of Australia* (Blackshield, Coper and Williams, 2001).

Advocacy groups' choice not to use strategic litigation to advance rights claims is due in part to lack of resources, but also to the courts' unreceptive stance toward interveners and amicus curiae participation by rights advocacy groups. Canadian experience shows that amicus curiae appearances and intervention are the preferred method of advocacy group participation in appellate litigation because they are much less expensive than direct sponsorship of test cases (Brodie, 2002). In Australia, however, Williams has demonstrated that the High Court has virtually closed the door to third-party participation in its deliberations (Williams, 2000). While the number of NGO amicus curiae/intervener appearances in the High Court has increased, as pointed out above, the Court has turned down many applications and refused to set out any clear guidelines as to its criteria. For example, two of Australia's best established rights advocacy groups, the International Commission of Jurists (Australian Branch) and PIAC, have recently had their petitions to intervene rejected by the High Court, without any reasons being given. Perhaps not surprisingly, these groups are staunch advocates of a bill of rights.

Lawyers' Support

The legal community's preferences on institutions for rights protection and support for rights advocacy organizations are mixed. A 1991 public opinion survey found that for a large sample of Australian lawyers (n=477), opinion was divided 45 per cent to 55 per cent on whether parliaments or courts should have the final say on rights issues. In contrast, citizens were more strongly in favour of courts (59 per cent) rather than parliament (41 per cent) having the final say on rights protection, whereas politicians preferred parliament over the courts (76 per cent v 24 per cent) (Galligan and McAllister, 1997). Lawyers' views are probably changing as rights discourse and advocacy become more prominent.

A growing number of lawyers volunteer time for public interest litigation, and recent growth in larger law firms creates more opportunities for such pro bono litigation. Large law firms can afford to 'loan' lawyers to do pro bono public interest work in a way that small firms and sole practitioners cannot. This pattern is evident in the workings of two of the most active rights advocacy groups discussed above, PILCH and PIAC. Both rely on a network of volunteer lawyers drawn largely, but not exclusively, from larger law firms. Lawyers are also disproportionately represented in the memberships of the various State CLCs, but many of these appear to come from smaller law firms and sole practitioners.

In the law schools there is stronger support for rights advocacy and increased judicialization of rights protection evidenced by the recent creation of several human rights/public law research institutes, the leading public role of law professors in the bill of rights debate, and the increasing number of human rights courses being offered to students. The last decade has witnessed the creation of three new human rights/public law institutes in leading law schools. The Castan Centre for Human Rights Law at Monash University, named after the lead counsel in the celebrated *Mabo* case, the late Ron Castan, was launched in October 2000 to bring together national and international human rights scholars, practitioners and advocates in order to promote and protect human rights through teaching, scholarly publications, public education, applied research, collaboration and advice work, consultancies and advocacy. It was headed until recently by David Kinley, a well-known human rights scholar and advocate (see Kinley, 1998). The Gilbert and Tobin Centre of Public Law at the University of New South Wales has a similar brief, with special attention to the bill or rights debate, indigenous law and international human rights law. This reflects in part the interests of the Centre's founding director, George Williams, a prominent advocate of a bill of rights (Williams, 2004). The largest and best-funded centre is the Centre for International and Public Law (CIPL) at the Australian National University in Canberra. While its mandate is much broader than human rights, its most recent Director, Hilary Charlesworth, is best known as a human rights scholar and advocate whose recent book *Writing in Rights* (2002) is an impassioned plea for adding a bill of rights to Australia's constitution.

Legal academics are generally supportive of the need for a bill of rights and human rights concerns more generally, although there are still sharp divisions. Critics of the bill of rights movement have identified legal academics as some of the strongest supporters. According to political scientist David Tucker, 'British-Australian legal culture is under threat by theories emanating from US universities' and 'the uncritical manner in which the legal intellectuals in Australia are being influenced by US theories'. As Tucker sees it: 'Despite Australia's own longstanding parliamentary traditions, many Australian intellectuals are now encouraging its judges to emulate the Warren activists, trying to recast Australia in the image of the United States two or three decades ago' (Tucker, 1997, pp. 121–2).

In sum, while the legal profession is fairly evenly divided on the desirability of a bill of rights for Australia, university law professors are increasingly supportive. The most vocal and articulate advocates for a bill of rights are almost all academic lawyers. The pattern of support and opposition amongst lawyers is not unique to Australia, but probably similar to what existed in Canada prior to the adoption of the *Canadian Charter of Rights and Freedoms* [32] in 1982 and in the UK prior to adoption of its *Human Rights Act 1998* (UK) c 42.

Adequate Funding

The weak-link in Australia's SSLM is funding. Stephen Cohen, author of the 1992 study *Australian Civil Liberties Organizations*, observed that most groups were 'institutionally weak', in part because they were 'really badly funded'. He estimated

---

32 Schedule B of *Canada Act 1982* (UK) c. 11.

that most depended on donations and perhaps 90 per cent had budgets of less than $500 per year (Cohen, 1992). Even the better known ALHR's annual budgets were less than $10,000, and depended heavily on members' dues and contributions. Few rights-advocacy organizations receive significant and or sustained public or private foundation funding. The only two exceptions are PIAC and HREOC discussed above. There is no dedicated test case funding program as in Canada. Legal aid programs exist in all States, but most have an informal policy of limiting funding to one appeal, thus precluding test cases.

In sum, the SSLM that we find in Australia is much weaker than in the US or Canada, but perhaps on par with what Epp found in the UK prior to 1998. In the same manner in which the British SSLM supported a partial 'rights revolution' in the UK prior to 1998, so the current Australian SSLM probably contributed to the brief period of rights activism associated with the Mason Court in the early 1990s. For instance, without rights activists like Ron Castan, cases like *Mabo* would not have come before the High Court. Nor would the High Court have been encouraged to take novel and precedent-setting stands on rights issues, or been defended for having taken them.

Rights Protection by Other Means

The story of rights protection by judicial means in Australia that has been sketched in this chapter is a comparatively thin one, in terms of both High Court achievements and SSLM. As the only English-speaking democracy not to have a judicially enforceable bill of rights, either constitutional or statutory, Australia is exceptional. That exceptionalism is lamented by bill of rights advocates and used as evidence of grave deficiency in rights protection that can be best remedied by adopting an Australian bill of rights.

Australia is exceptional in continuing to rely primarily upon parliamentary and political means for rights protection, with a complementary judicial contribution. However, it is probably just as successful in achieving a rights revolution as comparable bill of rights countries. This needs to be shown by careful comparative analysis of rights developments and outcomes in Australia and comparable countries, and will be the subject of a larger research project. But to look simply at judicial achievements and gaps in legal protection of rights as most bill of rights advocates do is to take account of only part of the picture.

We hypothesize that Australia has experienced a 'rights revolution' in Epp's terms broadly comparable to that of other countries, but mainly through parliamentary and political means. If so, we might expect to find that Australia has been more concerned with broad political rights such as voting and substantive equality matters such as wage levels and employment practices that have widespread appeal. Whether it is a laggard in more selective individual and group rights, to do with personal privacy and alternative lifestyles, will depend on the strength of the support structure for political mobilization. Investigation of these issues is beyond the scope of this chapter and requires further empirical research. If Australia has indeed experienced a rights revolution by mainly political means, the relative weakness of support for a bill of rights and the limited scope of judicial developments in rights protection without a bill of rights are to be expected. Moreover, Australian exceptionalism becomes comparatively and theoretically more significant.

References

Blackshield, T., Coper, M, and Williams, G. (eds) (2001), *The Oxford Companion to the Australian High Court* (Melbourne: Oxford University Press).

Brodie, I. (2002), *Friends of the Court: The Privileging of Interest Group Litigants in Canada* (New York: State University of New York Press).

Charlesworth, H. (2002), *Writing in Rights: Australia and the Protection of Human Rights* (Sydney: University of New South Wales Press).

Chesterman, J. and Galligan, B. (1997), *Citizens without Rights: Aborigines and Australian Citizenship* (Cambridge: Cambridge University Press).

Cohen, S. (1992), *Australian Civil Liberties Organizations* (Sydney: International Business Communication Pty Ltd).

Commonwealth, Human Rights Bureau (1981), *National Human Rights Organizations in Australia* (Canberra: Commonwealth of Australia).

Dixon, Sir O. (1965), 'Speech to the American Bar Association [1944]', in Judge Woinarski (ed.), *Jesting Pilate and Other Papers and Addresses* (Melbourne: Melbourne Law Book Co.), p. 101.

Epp, C. (1998), *The Rights Revolution: Lawyers, Activists, and Supreme Courts in Comparative Perspective* (Chicago: University of Chicago Press).

Galligan, B. (1995), *A Federal Republic: Australia's Constitutional System of Government* (Cambridge: Cambridge University Press).

Galligan, B. and McAllister, I. (1997), 'Citizen and Elite Attitudes towards an Australian Bill of Rights', in Galligan, B. and Sampford, C. (eds), *Rethinking Human Rights* (Sydney: Federation Press), p. 144.

Galligan, B., Trifiletti, G. and Roberts, W. (2001), *Australians and Globalisation: The Experience of Two Centuries* (Cambridge: Cambridge University Press).

Kinley, D. (1998) (ed.), *Human Rights in Australian Law: Practice and Potential* (Sydney: Federation Press).

Menzies, Sir R. (1967), *Central Power in the Australian Constitution* (London: Cassell).

New South Wales, Standing Committee on Law and Justice, NSW Legislative Council (2001), *A NSW Bill of Rights?* (Sydney: NSW Parliament).

Rosenberg, G.N. (1991), *The Hollow Hope: Can Courts Bring about Social Change?* (Chicago: University of Chicago Press).

Sampford, Charles (1997), 'The Four Dimensions of Rights', in Galligan, B. and Sampford, C. (eds), *Rethinking Human Rights* (Sydney: Federation Press), p. 50.

Sniderman, P.M., Fletcher, J.F., Russell, P.H. and Tetlock, P.E. (1996), *The Clash of Rights: Liberty, Equality, and Legitimacy in Pluralist Democracy* (New Haven, Connecticut: Yale University Press).

Tucker, D.F.B. (1997), 'Natural Law or Common Law: Human Rights in Australia', in Galligan, B. and Sampford C. (eds), *Rethinking Human Rights* (Sydney: Federation Press), p. 120.

Waldron, J. (1993), 'A Rights-Based Critique of Constitutional Rights', *Oxford Journal of Legal Studies*, 13: 18.

Williams, G. (1999), *Human Rights under the Australian Constitution* (Melbourne: Oxford University Press).

—— (2000), 'The Amicus Curiae and Intervener in the High Court of Australia: A Comparative Analysis', *Federal Law Review*, **28** (3): 365.

—— (2004), *The Case for a Bill of Rights* (Sydney: University of New South Wales Press).

Chapter 2

The Performance of Australian Legislatures in Protecting Rights

John Uhr

Introduction

My aim in this chapter is to reframe the discussion of the role of Australian parliaments as rights protectors, in part by reframing the influential concept of 'dialogue' now so prominent in the literature on relationships between parliaments and courts (consider Hiebert, 2003; Williams, 2003). I admit that the chapter is large on claims and light on evidence and that I do not provide a report card on the rights-protecting performance of all Australian parliaments. Part of the problem is that, from the perspective of elected members of parliament, 'rights' come in so many shapes and sizes that it is difficult to cover the field. I argue that parliaments are 'writing rights' on a regular basis when passing legislation and that much of this routine but quite fundamental rights-protection passes without note in much of the international rights-protection literature. We tend to think of rights in terms of the sort of rights covered by a bill or formal charter of rights, but many other bills or legislative proposals define or redefine many important rights and impose new obligations.

Citizenship itself is a striking example of rights generated by a parliament, with rights and obligations defined and redefined in many legislative enactments (consider Patapan, 2000, pp. 70–76; Galligan and Roberts, 2004). But a more routine example is voting rights (who may vote, for whom and how) which the Commonwealth Parliament has been defining and redefining for most of its institutional life (consider Uhr, 2003). This story of rights definition began with early enactment of the national franchise, which has been revised and redefined many times over the years since the original electoral legislation of 1902, with waves of new rights and obligations around compulsory voting, preferential voting and proportional representation. But over the same timeframe, new rights have emerged in electoral law: increasingly, rights for elected representatives and their political parties, typically to secure financial benefits from the Commonwealth through public funding schemes. This example illustrates one of the quite basic ways that parliaments contribute to politically important rights in an iterative but sustained way over many years, slowly but steadily reshaping the landscape of rights and obligations, with important implications for government and citizen alike. In other reviews of this legislative history, I have documented the typically messy performance of Australian parliaments in defining and promoting even core political rights, like voting rights. The theme here is 'party': parliamentary rights-protection is marshalled by political parties competing for the prizes of parliamentary power (Uhr, 2001).

But in this chapter I want to put this routine rights-writing in an appropriate institutional perspective, comparing the external constitutional framework establishing 'the parliament' with the most specialist internal framework for rights-protection associated with the Senate's two legislative scrutiny committees: the Regulations and Ordinances Committee established in 1932 and the Scrutiny of Bills Committee established in 1982. Party-ness is not everything: the Regulations Committee's impressive history illustrates the potential open to parliaments even in the absence of a bill of rights and even in the presence of ruling-party domination (the Committee predates the introduction of proportional representation). But the aim is not history: this section attempts to tease out lessons for any future strengthening of the capacity of Australian parliaments for rights-protection. This final section also returns to my reframing of the model of 'dialogue' in international discussions of parliaments as rights-protectors (see for example, Manfredi and Kelly, 1999; Hogg and Thornton, 1999a).

Internationally, interest in the topic of parliaments as rights-protectors emerges in the wake of interest in the relative capacity of the courts to use their powers of judicial review to provide citizens with greater rights protection than that provided by legislatures. Traditionally, leading politicians in systems of responsible government held that parliaments were the most reliable protectors of rights, but over recent decades this presumption has been challenged by judicial and other extra-parliamentary authorities (Patapan, 2000, pp. 41–47; see more generally Waldron, 1999). The Australian chapter in this international debate is quite underdeveloped compared to the international pacesetters, notably Canada which has begun to exercise influence over Australian discussions. But this very provisional quality of the Australian debate can be an asset: it is still possible to draw on the Australian situation in ways that can add fresh perspectives to the international debate. Australian accounts of parliamentary–judiciary relationships emphasize the separated responsibilities of the two sets of institutions – focusing more on the distance than any potential for dialogue (see for example, Campbell and Lee, 2001, pp. 240–46). But I suggest that we look in another direction. To anticipate: where much of the international literature maps out struggles for rights-protections between courts and parliaments, the Australian experience (largely without the benefit of a bill of rights, except for the Australian Capital Territory) reveals an added and largely unmapped dimension within the parliament itself, involving a version of the separation of powers story of struggling executive and legislative interests.

Not that Australia models best practice. The general absence of a bill of rights might make Australia outstanding, but not necessarily admirable. To say the least, there are many lessons to be learnt from Canadian and other experiences. My general orientation draws on the work of American political scientist Louis Fisher, whose *Constitutional Dialogues* (1988) is a model of politico-legal analysis of constitutional institutions. My more specific orientation draws on the defence of the roles of legislatures articulated by such Canadian scholars as Christopher Manfredi and Janet Hiebert, to name two prominent analysts of parliamentary capacities for rights-protection.[1] It is worth noting that both of these Canadian scholars, in their separate and distinctive ways, defend the roles of parliaments less by detailed reference to the *virtues* of legislative supremacy and more by reference to the *vices* of judicial supremacy, particularly the limitations of judicial power in resolving what are fundamentally matters of political judgment best left to the political branches of government. My analysis tracks a similar path, reflecting what might be called the perspective of a 'critical friend' of parliaments, hoping to help the parliamentary cause by reminding parliaments of their responsibilities as core constitutional agencies.[2]

The Framework of Responsible Government

This first section addresses the most general sense of parliamentary rights-protection, taking as my case in point the institutional design of the Commonwealth Parliament established under the *Australian Constitution*. This section attempts to provide a fresh perspective on parliamentary capacity missing from much of the conventional discussion of parliaments as rights-protectors. This section sets the tone for my reframing of the 'dialogue' model of parliamentary–court relationships through closer specification of what we mean by 'parliament': which could be the political executive using its political command of the legislative power; or the legislature, or even some constitutionally recognized component of the legislature, acting independently of the political executive (consider ACT Bill of Rights Consultative Committee, 2003, pp. 61–63 ('A "Dialogue" Model'); McDonald and Stone, 2003).

I suggest that the general properties of the Australian constitutional order are best illustrated through the instance of the federal *Constitution* of 1901. I will argue that this constitutional order itself reflects a larger constitutional commitment to a neglected model of rights-protection. This model is the one associated with the liberal separation of powers doctrine designed to promote a political regime of civil liberty, as distinct from (but not necessarily opposed to) more contemporary models of rights-protection designed to protect the civil liberties of individuals. I will also argue that at the national level where rights-protection by parliaments has probably been at its strongest, the Commonwealth Parliament's constitutional role in rights-protection has been overshadowed by the scholarly prominence given to the High Court.[3] This situation reflects a broader problem, which is a declining

---

1   See Manfredi, 1993; Hiebert, 2002. Also relevant and also Canadian is Morton and Knopff, 2000, especially ch. 2.

2   As in Uhr, 1998. See more generally Goldsworthy 1999, and Waldron, 1999. A good checklist of the limitations of parliamentary capacities is in Hiebert, 2003, pp. 236–38.

3   Compare Lindell and Bennett (eds), 2001 with Blackshield, Coper and Williams (eds), 2001.

understanding of the contribution of the older model of rights-protection informing the *Constitution.*

Civil Liberty and Individual Liberties

Consider the distinction between protection of many individuals' civil liberties and promotion of a political regime of civil liberty. I want to distinguish between two broad models of rights-protection, one dealing with civil *liberties* and one with civil *liberty*: the orthodox one associated with the protection of civil liberties and an older, more traditional and now often neglected one associated with the promotion of civil liberty. George Williams (1999), to take one impressive example, has analysed the general picture of the state of rights-protection under the Australian constitutional order. Williams' work reflects the best of the orthodox approach to rights protection, where rights are primarily understood in terms of the personal rights and liberties enjoyed by Australian citizens. In this usage, rights refer in their traditional sense to claims against government for private protection against the state, with some attention also to the contemporary turn to claims on the government for public assistance from the state.

But there is a second sense in which rights are secured through the constitutional order of a political regime of civil liberty. The call for bills of rights properly reflects the anxiety of civil libertarians about the unprotected nature of individual rights and liberties in the face of powerful government. This should be contrasted with an older anxiety about unconstitutional government, in the sense of the threat to civil liberty posed by unduly constituted government.[4] The particular gripe about governance represented by this anxiety were the threats to basic civil liberty posed by *concentrated* as distinct from *duly constituted* government. The Australian constitutional order is part of that development of what Manfredi calls 'liberal constitutionalism' associated with that classic liberal doctrine of the separation of powers (Manfredi, 1993, pp. 19–39; see also Morton and Knopff, 2000, pp. 149–54). Concentrated government in its classic form involved no separation of powers between the political and the judicial branches or indeed later within the political branches: that is, concentrated government involved no degrees of separation between legislative and the executive powers. By way of contrast, unconcentrated or dispersed government experimented with various forms of separated powers.

Take the *Commonwealth Constitution* as a case in point (Uhr, 1998, pp. 77–81). The *Constitution* identifies 'the Parliament' in the first of its eight chapters. The set of chapters one to three contains the constitutional provisions relating to the three core institutions of government: the parliament, the executive government and the judicature. The powers of government are presented according to these three formal institutions of government. Each section of each institution begins with a declaration that each institution is vested with a distinct *power*. Each institution

---

4   See Orwin and Pangle, 1984, pp. 1–22; and on bills of rights see Judge, 1993, pp. 207–9.

is identified in terms of 'the' definite article, as though each institution were definitely whole and one, with coherent capacity over its distinctive power. But this impression of institutional coherence is misleading. Parliaments are really quite fragmented: between government and opposition, between lower and upper houses, between frontbench and backbench, between big parties and small parties and so on. This situation of internally dispersed power is common to Westminster-derived parliaments. As a recent reform commission said of Westminster (Hansard Society Commission, 2001, para. 2.10):

> [t]here is little sense that Parliament owns its business or determines its own workload, nor much sense of Parliament acting collectively as an institution. In some respects, this atomises and individualises the works of MPs … Although Parliament has certain collective functions, its ability to deliver them is limited by the fact that it has no collective ethos.

The same expert commission went on to quote from evidence presented to it that '[t]he idea of Parliament' as 'a political force, or as a whole, is simply a myth. Parliament in this sense simply does not exist'.

The Parliament is the odd institution, because in its case the legislative power is vested in a body called 'the Parliament' but comprising two and possibly three distinctive component parts (crown, political executive, bicameral legislature), none of which has sole possession of legislative power. To be sure, at the practical level each of the other two constitutional branches has recognizable diversity of component parts: the executive government comprises members of the Federal Executive Council, including ministers of state who share executive power; and the judicature comprises the High Court 'and such other courts as the Parliament creates'. But only Parliament is recognized in terms of the formal 'parts' listed under the relevant constitutional chapter: Senate, House of Representatives, and both houses when called upon to act together.

Thus, although the *Constitution* speaks of 'the Parliament' (as in 'the powers of the Parliament' in part five of chapter one), the *Constitution* also acknowledges the two primary component parts: the Senate in part two and the House of Representatives in part three. For the most part, we tend to lean in the other direction and speak of 'the Parliament' having done this or that when what we really mean is that one component of the Parliament, typically the executive government, has used its control over Parliament to give effect to its particular will. That is, we speak of 'the Parliament' when we really mean the political executive using the formal powers of Parliament that are at the disposal of the executive by virtue of its political control of those components of the Parliament which, under the conventions of 'responsible government' (Uhr, 1998, pp. 58–77; see also Berns, 1983, pp. 51–66), trump the other components. In this way, we give an institutional coherence to 'the Parliament' which flatters the power and pretensions of the political executive and tends to legitimize the political executive's use of the legislative power which the *Constitution* shares among each of the component parts, albeit with certain specified limitations on the legislative powers available to the Senate.

Unpacking the Parliament

What is my point with this laboured rereading of the *Constitution*? It is the simple but neglected point that 'the Parliament' is potentially a less cohesive and less coherent constitutional agency than the other two branches (see Waldron, 1999, pp. 26–35). To be sure, the executive and judicial branches each comprise many public officials sharing responsibilities for the use of the executive and judicial power. The *Constitution* envisages that the executive and judicial branches will comprise a range of administrative entities, which could give rise to coordination problems. Putting to one side the rather elastic roles that the Queen/Governor-General have in the two political branches, we can say that practically each of the two non-legislative branches is under the leadership of a chief officer: the chief minister in the case of the executive branch; and the chief justice in the case of the judicial branch. By contrast, 'the Parliament' has no chief, except to the extent that the political executive marshals its majority to try to control the parliamentary process.

Of course, we know that neither chief minister nor chief justice has exclusive control over their branches. Chief ministers come and ago according to the political conventions of ruling political parties; and the judgments of chief justices count as one and no more than one of a number of judgments in most High Court decisions. But compared to 'the Parliament', the executive and judicial branches are quite cohesive and coherent. While 'the Parliament' might exist as a constitutional reality, it is worth emphasizing that the *Constitution* envisages a remarkable degree of institutional diversity in the legislative branch. To start with the obvious, the legislative branch is the most populous branch, if we can take note of the range of legislators recognized by the *Constitution*. While it is true that the political executive is drawn from the ranks of legislators, it is also true that the constitutional framers anticipated that 'the Parliament' would include a majority of non-executive members: not only pro-government backbenchers but also non-government and even anti-government members, including a publicly-recognized Opposition.

To add to the dispersed nature of 'the Parliament', legislators serve in one of two quite separate chambers, each with its own power to organize itself as a remarkably autonomous constitutional entity. At the time of Federation, there was considerable expectation that the House and Senate would deviate in their electoral systems, adding further to the complexity of 'the Parliament' through two distinct systems of parliamentary representation, which has since come to pass. The single-member system of preferential voting in the House now exists alongside the multi-member system of proportional representation in the Senate. My point here is that this diversity of electoral systems was anticipated by the framing generation, as was acknowledged at the time of the eventual introduction of Senate proportional representation in 1948 (Uhr, 1998, pp. 108–15).

Dispersed Powers

Putting all this together, we can begin to discern a model of rights-protection that tends to be neglected in contemporary debates over parliaments versus the courts as rights-protectors. The constitutional system of dispersed powers is informed by a version of the separation-of-powers doctrine, designed to place the powers of government in a range of public hands conducive to civil liberty. The framers' fear was that any system of concentrated powers would empower 'the government' and disempower the citizen and so nullify the prospects of self-government. The hope was that a constitutionally authorized dispersal of powers would distribute governmental powers within and among a variety of interrelated constitutional agencies, thereby empowering the citizen at the expense of a relatively disempowered or limited 'government'. In theory at least, systems of liberal constitutionalism take their bearings from liberal political doctrine, including liberalism's preoccupation with representative government based on the free consent of the governed. At the centre of this liberal project is constitutional protection for the rights of individuals to choose who represents them politically and for the corresponding obligations of elected representatives to govern constitutionally, ideally according to the forms and procedures of a written constitution.

In this construction, liberal constitutionalism promotes as one of its primary values a model of good (or limited or duly-processed or constitutional) governance designed to secure civil liberty, understood as a system of self-government with citizens freely determining how they are governed and who holds power in the two political branches of government. Where does a parliament fit into this picture? Centrally, as the necessary (even if insufficient) institution at the base of a system of good government. Parliament might have little to do with the detailed management of executive or judicial powers but, by virtue of its control over the legislative power, it is crucial to the maintenance of this civil-liberty model of rights-protection (consider Hiebert, 2003, pp. 234–41; cf. Knopff, 1989, ch. 1; and Patapan, 2000, pp. 150–77).

Thus it is not by accident that Parliament features as the first of the three branches of government outlined in the *Australian Constitution*. Parliament has a key role in maintaining civil liberty. Just as the consent of citizens is the basis of legitimate parliamentary representation, so too parliamentary consent is the basis of legitimate executive government. Civil liberty means that the civil realm is protected against arbitrary government through mechanisms that constitute government around a separation or, better perhaps, a division of responsibilities between the two political branches, with the executive power of 'the government' conditional on the legislative consent of 'the Parliament'. It is up to 'the Parliament' to specify these conditions of consent, including what information from government (and elsewhere) is required to satisfy proper standards of informed consent.

Thus the parliamentary contribution to a regime of civil liberty is or should be quite fundamental. What is distinctive about the Australian situation is the internally dispersed nature of legislative power which makes life difficult for executive governments. Because the Senate can reject even those bills that it may not initiate or amend, the two houses are virtually equal in respect of their legislative powers. Governments face two unequal tests of their command of 'the Parliament'. On one hand, governments find little difficulty in meeting the demands for informed consent made by one part of 'the Parliament' – the House of Representatives which they typically dominate. On the other hand, governments have found it quite difficult to meet the information demands of that other part known as the Senate, at least since the electoral system of proportional representation has consolidated to deny governing (or for that matter Opposition) parties the numbers to control the upper house – or at least until the historic double majority won by the Howard government at the 2004 election.

I do not have space to assess the record of parliamentary performance in relation to this model of rights-protection. Taking the Commonwealth Parliament as the leading type of Australian legislature, and based on other research,[5] I would tend to argue that the performance of 'the Parliament' is best assessed through separate evaluations of the performance of each chamber of the bicameral national Parliament. The evaluation of the contemporary record of the Senate would indicate considerable performance in securing accountable government, which is no small contribution to the civil-liberty model of rights-protection (cf. Tushnet, 2003, pp. 214–19).

Scrutinizing Rights Scrutiny

In this section, I focus on the conventional sense in which parliaments are considered as 'rights watchdogs'. This is the sense in which rights-protection is usually defined in studies of parliamentary capacities for the scrutiny of legislative provisions affecting the rights and liberties of individuals. Just as the previous section unpacked 'the Parliament' to reveal the many participating institutional components in the legislative process, so too the following section will unpack the influential concept of 'dialogue' used as the standard of 'best practice' in relations between courts and parliaments (consider Hogg and Thornton, 1999b; Morton, 1999). Following David Kinley (1999, pp. 167, 180–84), I want to draw on a case study of the Commonwealth Parliament's most experienced rights-protector, the Senate Regulations and Ordinances Committee, to show that effective parliamentary contributions to rights-protection can, and perhaps should, direct their primary dialogue to government rather than the courts. And just as 'the Parliament' can often mean a 'rights watchdog' along the lines of this distinguished Senate Committee, so too 'the government' can mean any number of dialogue partners (such as ministers, central agencies, line officials) whose roles escape much in the way of critical evaluation in the prevailing dialogue literature.

In contrast to many international accounts of parliamentary rights-dialogue, this account deals with a parliament operating without the benefit (or burden) of a bill of

---

5   Most recently Bach, 2003.

rights. This story of rights-protection demonstrates the potential open to parliaments even in the absence of a bill of rights, which is a primary feature of most 'dialogue' literature (see for example, Hiebert, 2003). Indeed, the rights dialogue of the Commonwealth Parliament might well be altered with the adoption of a bill of rights. This does not imply that a bill of rights is inappropriate for the Commonwealth but rather that a bill of rights should build on and not displace existing rights-protections established by Parliament.

Framework of Delegated Legislation

But back to basics, beginning with parliamentary scrutiny of delegated legislation. Parliamentary scrutiny of delegated legislation is a fertile ground for scholars of rights-protection. Further, delegated legislation is a good test case of parliamentary capacities more generally (see Page, 2001). Historically in Australia, political battles over the use and abuse of delegated legislation have been very much part of the mainstream story of party politics, as Gordon Reid has shown (1982, pp. 149–68; see also Reid and Forrest, 1989, pp. 172–74, 219–221; Pearce and Argument, 1999, pp. 23–30). The fact that it is now played out safely at the margins tells us much about a distinctive Australian contribution to the management of partisan difference. The origins and early development of the Senate Regulations and Ordinances Committee is part of a wider story about the spoils of party government and the performance of Parliament in 'spoiling the spoils' of executive decree by political executives. Importantly, in this case the spoiling agent was initially a parliamentary party dominated by government members, reflecting the general pattern of Senate party composition before the 1949 switch to proportional representation. Indeed, even after that momentous change, the Senate-delegated legislation committee continued to operate with a government chair and an effective government majority. Complementing the previous section, this section tells a story about the subordination of party-political interests to more fundamental parliamentary interests.

This is not the place to re-tell this history but it is worth remembering that it is a history of quite intense partisan dispute. The first and second Commonwealth Parliaments debated many proposals to allow Parliament greater say over the executive's regulatory power. Within three years of Federation, Parliament had enacted in the *Acts Interpretation Act 1901* (Cth) the provision specifying a limited period after the making of executive regulations for either house to disallow them (Reid and Forrest, 1989, p. 226; Walsh and Uhr, 1985, pp. 15–16). This is a classic example of legislative power over regulations being circumscribed to either confirmation or denial of executive initiatives, with no latitude for parliamentary amendment after the tabling of executive regulations. Parliament has the power to scrutinize and either silently approve or, through resolution of either house, veto government regulations.

The fate of the Scullin Labor government (1929–1931) demonstrates the partisan heat attached to this area of parliamentary scrutiny. The Scullin government was the first Labor government to win office since the Fisher government's conscription split during World War I. The Scullin Labor government faced a hostile Senate, dominated by opposition parties intent on using the powers of the Senate to obstruct and frustrate the Labor government. The issue of Senate hostility came to a head through a series of repeated Senate disallowances of union preference in waterfront regulations. The Scullin government tried to get round the Senate hostility by using its regulation-making powers, but even these were within reach of the Senate, thanks to the settlement arrived at in the early parliaments giving either house power to disallow government regulations. The Scullin government wore itself out in a cat-and-mouse game of making, then disallowing, then re-making regulations, with the Senate disallowing 17 of the 19 government waterfront regulations. The issue of the Senate's disallowance powers was challenged in the High Court, and the Senate in turn appealed (unsuccessfully) to Governor-General Isaacs to wind back ministerial reliance on regulatory powers (Sawer, 1963, pp. 30–31; Reid, 1982, p. 154; Walsh and Uhr, 1985, pp. 17–18).

During this escalating frustration, the Senate established a select committee in December 1929 (comprising among others two former state premiers) to inquire into and report on the feasibility of a new committee system 'with a view to improving the legislative work' of the Senate (Walsh and Uhr, 1985, p. 17; cf. Reid, 1982, pp. 152–55). As a result of this inquiry, the Senate agreed in principle to the priority of establishing a committee on delegated legislation, preferably as part of a committee system that would also deal with legislative scrutiny of primary legislation. The original idea was that the one legislative scrutiny committee might be able to tackle both types of legislation, primary and subordinate, particularly if it confined its scrutiny to what might be called 'legislative policy' (that is, a kind of civil liberties impact scrutiny, promoting appropriate protections against the misuse or abuse of powers conferred on government officials) as distinct from 'public policy' (that is, the policy merits or purpose).[6]

Nothing was done in practice before the election of the Lyons government in December 1931, with a majority in both houses. But early in the life of the new Lyons government, the Senate in March 1932 established the Standing Committee on Regulations and Ordinances. Apart from a comparatively restricted House of Lords Committee established in 1925, this was a pioneering chapter in legislative scrutiny across the Westminster world (Reid, 1982, p. 156; see also Evans, 2001, pp. 346–47). Few could predict that this new Committee would survive into the next century and even fewer thought that it would have any reason to. Typical of the sentiment at the time was the view put before the Senate inquiry by the legendary head of the Attorney-General's department, Robert Garran, who conceded that such a committee 'could scrutinize regulations' but argued that the work would not 'be very interesting or useful'. His basic premise was that the Committee 'would not discover very much to find fault with' (Walsh and Uhr, 1985, p. 17). Never was Robert Garran so wrong.

---

6   Sawer, 1963, p. 31. On the importance of parliamentary committees as rights-protectors, see Hiebert, 2003, pp. 242–43.

Senate Scrutiny Committee

The Regulations and Ordinances Committee has developed its own evaluative criteria which are reflected in the current Senate standing order establishing the Committee. The Committee uses these criteria (or terms of reference) to assess government regulations, testing each new regulation to see to what extent it complies with committee standards relating to (and here I simplify the real situation):

1. the protection of personal rights; and
2. the promotion of parliamentary propriety.

The 'rights' standard allows the Committee to ensure that regulations do not trespass unduly on personal rights and liberties or make rights dependent on unreviewable government decision making. The 'parliamentary propriety' standard allows the Committee to ensure that regulations are in accordance with their parent Act and are not more appropriately dealt with in primary legislation.

The standards relate to legislative policy rather than public policy as such, although this does not mean that the Committee steers away from controversial issues (Whalan, 1991, pp. 97–99; see also Evans, 2001, p. 361). Despite the self-confidence of successive governments, the Committee has seen its job as improving and not simply monitoring standards of 'best practice' across regulatory agencies. These standards have been devised by the Committee over many years of scrutinizing government regulation making. The standards have been adopted by the Senate, which overwhelmingly supports the Committee in its scrutiny strategy, which is to enter into private deliberation with the sponsoring minister before resorting to parliamentary deliberation over possible disallowance of offending regulations (Senate Regulations and Ordinances Committee, 2000, para. 3.11).

The general situation is that the Committee uses its powers carefully, holding back any recommendation for Senate disallowance until it has exhausted its deliberations with the sponsoring minister. The hope is that the threat of disallowance will convince ministers and interested agencies to undertake to amend and improve the regulation before the public shaming associated with a Senate debate on disallowance occurs. The Committee regularly records its satisfaction at the productivity of this process of cool committee scrutiny rather than heated public scrutiny.

There is no shortage of legislative scrutiny facing the Committee. The number of disallowable instruments annually initiated by executive governments grows steadily: for the Australian national government, more than trebling since the mid 1980s – executive instruments now exceeding annual Acts of Parliament around sevenfold, with 'about half of the law of the Commonwealth by volume (consisting) of delegated legislation rather than Acts of Parliament'.[7] The figures on increased Committee workload can look impressive. For instance, the number of instruments of delegated legislation made annually over recent years has been 1,888, 1,672 and

---

7   Evans, 2001, p. 346, with statistics at p. 345.

1,655; the number of instruments attracting the Committee's interest have been 175, 107 and 265; and the number of the Committee's notices for disallowance has been 25, 12 and 70 (Senate Regulations and Ordinances Committee, 2000, para. 3.11; see also Evans, 2001, p. 345). Very early in the history of the Committee, the Senate gave approval for an expert legal adviser to brief the Committee on suspect regulations. Over time, the Committee has come to point to the existence of impartial outsiders as proof of its own value and prestige, and of the merits of its recommendations to ministers, executive agencies and the Senate. Not that the Committee's effectiveness could not be improved, as the Administrative Review Council envisaged some years ago (Administrative Review Council, 1992, esp. paras 6.16–56 (pp. 47–56)).

Explaining Effective Rights Protection

Looking back over the 70 years of the Senate Committee's role in rights-protection, I can identify five factors which help explain the remarkable success of the Committee in forcing the hand of the political executive to amend and thereby improve defective regulatory instruments. I suggest that these factors can help explain parliamentary effectiveness more generally across the broad fields of rights-protection.

Real Parliamentary Power

The first issue from this Australian case study is that nothing very significant would have happened but for the pioneering work in the early parliaments establishing a regime of parliamentary disallowance of executive regulations. The Senate Regulations Committee would have had little or no leverage over the political executive if the *Acts Interpretation Act 1901* (Cth) did not contain an express provision allowing *either* house to disallow government regulations. The history shows that this provision had to be fought for, and that the Senate made its view very clear that it would not be marginalized. Parliament declared its will that the executive government could exercise delegated legislation but only on strict terms and conditions. Remembering that the *Australian Constitution* confers legislative power on Parliament and not the executive, perhaps it is not surprising that Parliament at a very early stage defined the terms and conditions of delegated power.

Bicameralism and Bargaining Power

Second, the Australian situation of bicameralism meant that the Senate enjoyed considerable power but somewhat diminished executive responsibility in the system of national governance. The political executive was located in the lower house, which from the beginning was expected to function as the house of government, with the Senate to function as a house of review. Although this widespread original understanding does less than justice to what the Senate is constitutionally capable of, responsible parliamentary government as it evolved in Australia has meant that the lower house has emerged as the home for the head of government. But the political executive is responsible, albeit in different ways, to *both* houses and not simply the lower house, which admittedly acts as the electoral college determining the party of government. This dual responsibility has allowed the Senate to carve out for itself an important scrutiny role in the Australian system of governance.

What was first experimented with over executive regulation making was later adapted to apply to executive budget making under a system of estimates committees, performing a scrutiny function in relation to the passage of a government's annual budget bills. In both cases, the achievement would have been less if the Senate did not contain government ministers, because in both cases the scrutinizing committees could deal with matters in terms of ministerial priorities. Both types of scrutiny committees have been able to speak the language of ministerial government, alerting Senate ministers to problems generally and trading on the Senate's undoubted power to deny ministers time and support for government priorities.

A Championing Chamber

Third, the Senate as an institution supported not only the establishment but also the subsequent development of the Regulations and Ordinances Committee, just as it did the eventual establishment of its companion legislative scrutiny committee, the Scrutiny of Bills Committee. A parliamentary committee is only as powerful as is its relationship to the house from which its members come and to which it reports. Over a period of many years, the Senate formed a view that the Regulations Committee was not simply an activity of a small group of senators but an institution performing a role on behalf of the Senate. The Senate turned the Committee from an interesting organization involving senators into an important institution involving the Senate. Senate support for the Committee's disallowance motions is one important piece of evidence of this institutional support.

Professional Expertise

Fourth, personnel issues rank high on the list of critical success indicators. Think here of the twenty-year period of Senator Wood as committee chair (1953–1973) and you begin to see what is required to bring sustained focus and drive to instruments of parliamentary scrutiny. The transition from an organization of senators to an institution of governance can be explained in large part by reference to the drive and determination of chairs like Senator Wood. The slow evolution of the system of legal advisers also deserves close attention, particularly in relation to the partnership open to chair and adviser to set the legislative policy agenda for the committee by using their time and energy to target particular issues.

Gurus within Government

Fifth, and I accept that this might surprise some, the role of the Attorney-General's Department cannot be underestimated. Similar comments can be made about the Attorney-General's Department in relation to the later Scrutiny of Bills Committee and indeed to the Finance department in relation to the estimates process. Effective scrutiny committees can get considerable support from interested central agencies of government which can help broadcast and defend the Committee's standards across government. This seems to have begun around 1937 at the urging of the Senate Committee (Walsh and Uhr, 1985, p. 20). Legislative drafting units within specific agencies look to central agency direction on evolving standards and policy. Scrutiny committees might be excellent articulators of such standards but much of the hard work of implementing those standards falls to central agencies within government, to the extent that the evolving system of governance looks to them for centralizing and standardizing functions. Those days might be declining now but the historical explanation for the effective scrutiny role performed by the Regulations and Ordinances Committee involves the support of legislative drafting units within executive government.

Remodelling the Rights Dialogue

A number of lessons emerge from this brief review of Australia's oldest parliamentary rights-protector. Conventional models of rights dialogue construct relationships between courts and legislatures, which serves the purpose of taking the sole focus away from the courts. But I think that effective parliamentary contributions involve an alternative relationship closer to the heart of the separation of powers story about the shared responsibilities of the two *political* powers and their institutions of government. Missing from conventional accounts is the importance of dialogue within 'the Parliament' itself, between legislative agencies and ministerial officers. The parliamentary-initiated dialogue goes further, of course: reaching into the administrative executive of public service officials responsible for so much of the routine management of executive discretion. It is notable that conventional accounts tend to downplay the very real initiative exercised by parliaments when committed to effective rights-protection. The role for parliaments in many conventional accounts is unduly reactive, confined to responding to policy preferences of courts. By contrast, the role on display here is one of policy initiative, setting the standards for executive compliance when rule making under the cover of delegated legislation.

My brief case study shows the importance of legislative–executive dialogue for effective parliamentary contribution to rights-protection. This is not to argue against legislative–judicial dialogues, which I have called for elsewhere (Uhr, 1998, e.g. pp. 244–45). But it is to argue that one of the secrets of institutional effectiveness of parliamentary rights-protectors is their capacity to set, and monitor compliance with, appropriate standards for executive decision-makers exercising legislative powers. The Senate case study shows the power of a legislative agency itself establishing the rules of the game of delegated legislation. Thus, one of the priorities of rights-protection dialogue with 'the Parliament' is for the appropriate legislative agency to fence in the political executive and prevent its potential abuse of delegated legislative powers. This involves a 'triangular' dialogue, if you will: between the parliamentary agency, ministers in the political executive *and the public service* (notably the relevant central agency responsible for legislative policy, but also line agencies), which can be enlisted to restrain the political executive when tempted to stray from parliament's duly authorized standards for the exercise of delegated powers. Executive use and abuse of legislative powers is a matter that is no less urgent than judicial use and abuse of policy-making powers; and many of the most effective instances of parliamentary rights-protections involve oversight of executive law-making rather than judicial policy making.

Turning from target to technique, what lessons might arise from this brief case study? Much of the literature on parliamentary democracy presumes that it is simply a fact of political life that executives dominate parliaments. The Australian experience shows the limits to this conventional wisdom. In general, the experience of this Committee suggests that parliamentary effectiveness in standards-setting and compliance-enforcement in rights-protection is strengthened to the extent that:

1. the scrutiny body can draw on real parliamentary power to veto executive action;
2. bicameralism encourages a review chamber to review core government law-making;
3. the review chamber actively supports the scrutiny body, in its outputs as well as its inputs;
4. the scrutiny body includes dedicated and expert personnel at political and advisory levels; and
5. support for public promotion of committee standards is provided from relevant central agencies within executive government.

What does this say about the design of rights dialogue? Taking in turn each paragraph above, we can say that:

1. effective parliamentary dialogue depends on possession of institutional power to veto the policy initiatives of the dialogue partner: nothing gets government talking so much as a parliament's power to disallow government measures;
2. internal divisions of legislative power such as those found in conditions of bicameralism greatly empower the voice of the legislature by giving legitimate holders of legislative power a safe harbour as a base to repair and maintain its legislative powers;
3. although dialogue requires a specialist parliamentary agency, that agency will be listened to more attentively when its sponsoring parliamentary chamber has demonstrated its institutional commitment to the relevant standards and

agenda of rights-protection;

4. dialogue within the parliamentary agency is no less important than dialogue across government agencies, and the best internal dialogue derives from a combination of political and policy professionalisms, with a committee of elected parliamentarians taking close advice from appropriate non-political professionals; and

5. dialogue between politicians sharing legislative powers can be strengthened by the participation of public service advisers: executive officials who often have a sense of the importance of due process that escapes their ministerial masters.

None of these institutional features is necessarily opposed to those found in many conventional models of parliamentary dialogue. But few of these features are as yet acknowledged in studies of effective parliamentary contributions to rights dialogue. My claim is not that these features are definitive but that their exposition here might serve to stimulate fresh consideration of parliamentary roles and responsibilities in rights dialogues (cf. Hiebert, 2001, pp. 161–72).

Conclusion

This chapter is no more than a provisional sketch of the topic. Evidence from the Commonwealth Parliament is limited, and there is none at all from the state parliaments. No reference has been made to the Commonwealth parliamentary debates resulting in the defeats of the three human rights bills so far introduced (see for example, Kinley, 1999, p. 159). But my aim has not been to document the state of legislative rights-protection in Australia. Instead, my aim has been to provoke fresh discussion over the general subject of parliaments as rights-protectors by reframing aspects of conventional approaches. This chapter will have served its purpose if it proves useful in reframing three aspects of the current debate: the family of rights in question; the nature of 'the Parliament' under examination; and the place of both parliaments and executive governments in the 'dialogue' model of rights-protection now circulating the world (consider Debeljak, 2003, pp. 154–46; see also Morton and Knopff, 2000, pp. 157–59).

At the end of the day, much turns on the meaning of 'the Parliament'. Defenders of the role of parliaments as rights-protectors tend to appeal to concepts of parliamentary supremacy to realign relationships between courts and parliaments (see for example, Goldsworthy, 1999, chs 2, 10; compare Manfredi, 1993, pp. 36–39, 205–10). I have suggested that pleas for the supremacy of 'the Parliament' can act as cloaks for the supremacy of the political executive, which might be a constitutional component of 'the Parliament' but enjoys no constitutional site-licence, as it were, over legislative powers. Executives are inherently no more trustworthy than the judiciary, making it important for defenders of the cause of parliaments to clarify precisely which parts of 'the Parliament' they mean when talking up parliamentary supremacy. Not all parliaments are the same. The Commonwealth Parliament differs in quite fundamental ways from, for example, the Parliament of Canada, through a more proportional electoral system, a greater array of checks on executive power, and most importantly a very powerful and publicly legitimate upper house.[8] It is a wonder, then, that rights-protectors have taken so long to take its contribution seriously.

References

ACT Bill of Rights Consultative Committee (May 2003), *Towards an ACT Human Rights Act: Report of the ACT Bill of Rights Consultative Committee* (Canberra: Publishing Services).

Administrative Review Council (1992), *Report no. 35: Rule Making by Commonwealth Agencies* (Canberra: Australian Govt Pub. Service).

Bach, S. (2003), *Platypus and Parliament: The Australian Senate in Theory and Practice* (Canberra: Department of the Senate Parliament House).

Berns, W. (1983), 'Taking Rights Frivolously', in MacLean, Douglas, and Mills, Claudia (eds), *Liberalism Reconsidered* (Totowa, N.J.: Rowman and Allanheld) ch. 4.

—— (1984), *In Defense of Liberal Democracy* (Chicago: Regnery Gateway).

Blackshield, T., Coper, M. and Williams, G. (eds) (2001), *Oxford Companion to the High Court of Australia* (Melbourne: Oxford University Press).

Campbell, E., and Lee, H.P. (2001), *The Australian Judiciary*, (Melbourne: Cambridge University Press).

Commonwealth, Senate Regulations and Ordinances Committee (September 2000), *Report 109* (Canberra: Parliament of Australia).

Debeljak, J. (2003), 'Rights and Democracy: A Reconciliation of the Institutional Debate', in Campbell, T., Goldsworthy, J. and Stone, A. (eds), *Protecting Human Rights: Instruments and Institutions* (Oxford: Oxford University Press), pp. 135–57.

Evans, H. (ed.) (2001), *Odgers' Australian Senate Practice*, 10th edn, (Canberra: Australian Government Publishing Service for Department of the Senate).

Fisher, L. (1988), *Constitutional Dialogues: Interpretation As Political Process* (Princeton, N.J.: Princeton University Press).

Galligan, B. and Roberts, W. (2004), *Australian Citizenship* (Carlton, Vic.: Melbourne University Press).

Goldsworthy, J.D. (1999), *The Sovereignty of Parliament: History and Philosophy* (New York: Oxford University Press).

---

8 Compare with the Parliament of Canada: Hiebert, 2003, p. 245. The wider debate is documented in Morton, 2002, ch. 13, pp. 571–625. The core principles are reviewed in Berns, 1984, pp. 29–62; cf. Waldron, 1999, pp. 63–91.

Hansard Society Commission on Parliamentary Scrutiny (2001), *The Challenge For Parliament: Making Government Accountable* (London: Vacher Dod Publishing).

Hiebert, J.L. (2001), 'A Relational Approach to Constitutional Interpretation: Shared Legislative and Judicial Responsibilities', *Journal of Canadian Studies*, **35** (4): 161–81.

—— (2002), *Charter Conflicts: What is Parliament's Role?* (Montreal: McGill-Queen's University Press).

—— (2003), 'Parliament and Rights', in Campbell, T., Goldsworthy, J. and Stone, A. (eds), *Protecting Human Rights: Instruments and Institutions* (Oxford: Oxford University Press), pp. 231–46.

Hogg, P.W. and Thornton, A.A. (1999)a, 'Reply', *Osgoode Hall Law Journal*, **37** (3): 529–36.

—— (1999)b, 'The Charter Dialogue Between Courts and Legislatures', *Policy Options*, April: 19.

Judge, D. (1993), *The Parliamentary State* (London: Newbury Park, Calif.: Sage Publications).

Kinley, D. (1999), 'Parliamentary Scrutiny of Human Rights: A Duty Neglected?' in Alston, Philip (ed.), *Promoting Human Rights through Bills of Rights: Comparative Perspectives* (Oxford: Oxford University Press), pp. 158–84.

Knopff, R. (1989), *Human Rights and Social Technology: The New War on Discrimination* (Ottawa: Carleton University Press).

Lindell, G. and Bennett, R. (eds) (2001), *Parliament: The Vision in Hindsight* (Annandale, NSW: Federation Press).

Manfredi, C.P. (1993), *Judicial Power and the Charter: Canada and the Paradox of Liberal Constitutionalism* (Toronto: University of Oklahoma Press).

Manfredi, C.P. and Kelly, J.B. (1999), 'Six Degrees of Dialogue: A Response to Hogg and Bushell', *Osgoode Hall Law Journal,* **37** (3): 513–27.

McDonald, L. and Stone, A, 'Planned Rights Act Won't Need "Twin" Code of Responsibilities', *The Canberra Times*, 19 November 2003.

Morton, F.L. (1999), 'Dialogue or Monologue?', *Policy Options*, April: 23–26.

Morton, F.L. and Knopff, R. (2000), *The Charter Revolution and the Court Party* (Peterborough, Ont.: Broadview).

Morton, F.L. (ed.) (2002), *Law, Politics and the Judicial Process in Canada* (Calgary: University of Calgary Press).

Orwin, C. and Pangle, T. (1984), 'The Philosophical Foundation of Human Rights', in Plattner, M.F. (ed.), *Human Rights in Our Time: Essays in Memory of Victor Baras* (Boulder: Westview Press), ch. 1.

Page, E.C. (2001), *Governing by Numbers: Delegated Legislation and Everyday Policy-Making* (Oxford: Hart Publishing).

Patapan, H. (2000), *Judging Democracy: The New Politics of the High Court of Australia* (Oakleigh, Vic.: Cambridge University Press).

Pearce, D.C. and Argument, S. (1999), *Delegated Legislation in Australia*, 2nd edn (Chatswood, NSW: Butterworths).

Reid, G.S. (1982), 'Parliament and Delegated Legislation', in Nethercote, J.R. (ed.), *Parliament and Bureaucracy: Parliamentary Scrutiny of Administration: Prospects and Problems in the 1980s* (Sydney: Hale and Iremonger), ch. 11.

Reid, G.S. and Forrest, M. (1989), *Australia's Commonwealth Parliament 1901–1988: Ten Perspectives* (Melbourne: Melbourne University Press).

Sawer, G. (1963), *Australian Federal Politics and Law, 1929–1949* (Melbourne: Melbourne University Press).

Tushnet, M. (2003), 'Non-judicial Review', in Campbell, T., Goldsworthy, J. and Stone, A. (eds), *Protecting Human Rights: Instruments and Institutions* (Oxford: Oxford University Press), pp. 213–29.

Uhr, J. (1998), *Deliberative Democracy in Australia: The Changing Place of Parliament* (Cambridge; Melbourne: Cambridge University Press).

—— (2001), 'Rules for Representation: Parliament and the Design of the Australian Electoral System', in Lindell, G. and Bennett, R. (eds), *Parliament: The Vision in Hindsight* (Annandale, NSW: Federation Press), pp. 249–90.

—— (2003), 'Measuring Parliaments Against the Spence Standard', in Orr, G., Mecurio, B. and Williams, G. (eds), *Realising Democracy: Electoral Law in Australia* (Annandale, NSW: Federation Press), pp. 66–79.

Waldron, J. (1999), *The Dignity of Legislation* (Cambridge: Cambridge University Press).

Walsh, R. and Uhr, J. (1985), 'Parliamentary Disallowance of Delegated Legislation: A History of the Basic Provisions in the *Acts Interpretation Act*', *Legislative Studies Newletter*, **10**: 11.

Whalan, D.J. (1991), 'Scrutiny of Delegated Legislation by the Australian Senate', *Statute Law Review*, **12** (2): 87–108.

Williams, G. (1999), *Human Rights Under the Australian Constitution* (Melbourne: Oxford University Press).

—— (2003), 'Constructing a Community-Based Bill of Rights', in Campbell, T., Goldsworthy, J. and Stone, A. (eds), *Protecting Human Rights: Instruments and Institutions* (Oxford: Oxford University Press), pp. 247–62.

Chapter 3

Improving Legislative Scrutiny of Proposed Laws to Enhance Basic Rights, Parliamentary Democracy, and the Quality of Law-Making

Bryan Horrigan

Overview

This chapter covers Parliamentary scrutiny of proposed laws to assess their potential implications for basic rights, the institutions of government, and good law-making, primarily through the institution of legislative scrutiny committees.[1] Written from an Anglo-Australian perspective, it is comparative on three different levels. That is, the chapter focuses on theory and practice; the national positions in Australia and the UK; and the sub-national positions across Australian jurisdictions. Popular debates about the protection of human rights often focus on the pros and cons of having a constitutional or statutory bill of rights. Yet the range of institutional mechanisms for protecting human rights extends beyond bills of rights (Webber, 2003, p. 173; Horrigan, 2003, ch. 7). Legislative scrutiny of proposed bills according to human rights yardsticks and other benchmarks for good legislation is an important and often undervalued and imperfectly understood form of institutional rights protection (Bayne, 2003, p. 2). Whether as part of a system enshrining a bill of rights or not, Parliamentary scrutiny of bills for human rights and other implications contributes to 'a culture of rights within Government, making them a mainstream element in decision making' (Feldman, 2004, p. 112).

---

1   The author acted as an academic consultant to the Scrutiny of Legislation Committee of the Queensland Legislative Assembly in the late 1990s. This chapter is informed by interviews conducted by the author and his colleague, Angus Francis, with Parliamentary chairs, members, and advisers of Parliamentary scrutiny committees in all of the following Australian jurisdictions – the Commonwealth of Australia, Queensland, New South Wales (NSW), Victoria, and the Australian Capital Territory (ACT) – and by discussions in a meeting between the author and members of the UK Parliament's Joint Committee on Human Rights in July 2004, as part of a research project funded in part by a University of Canberra research grant.

In its most common form, pre-enactment legislative scrutiny of proposed laws involves a Parliamentary committee making and reporting to Parliament its assessment of bills from a variety of perspectives, including but not limited to their human rights implications. Still, Parliamentary scrutiny committees are often seen as toothless tigers in the absence of a bill of rights and in the face of a government intent on sacrificing individual rights, liberties and freedoms to what the government perceives as a weightier collective need. In Australia, they are also seen as largely the province of Parliamentarians, unaided by input from the electorate and other non-government interests, at least in the core Parliamentary business of subjecting proposed laws to designated scrutiny requirements and reporting to Parliament on their assessment.

Accordingly, one theme of this chapter is that the business of Parliamentary scrutiny can be reconfigured in ways that reposition 'the people' in what is largely a legislator-centred exercise, at least in Australia. Another theme is that Parliamentary scrutiny work embraces more than just scrutiny of proposed laws for human rights implications and from more than just a law-based perspective of what does or does not amount to an infringement of rights. Yet another theme is that there are a number of ways in which Parliamentary scrutiny can be improved in its own right, and as part of an enhanced combination of mutually supportive rights-protection mechanisms.

Overall, the main theme of this chapter is that too narrow a focus in human rights debates on the respective merits of judges and politicians as guardians and enforcers of any bill of rights polarizes debate about institutional rights-protection and marginalizes those rights-protection measures (like Parliamentary scrutiny of proposed laws) which do not focus directly on who has responsibility for deciding questions under bills of rights. Moreover, Parliamentary scrutiny of proposed laws for human rights and other democratic implications has intrinsic value even without a bill of rights. It can complement other institutional mechanisms as part of an integrated multi-pronged approach to rights protection. It has a potential which is yet to be fully realized in all Australian jurisdictions.

Conceptual Framework – Connections between Scrutiny, Bills of Rights and Democratic Government

At the outset, Parliamentary scrutiny of proposed legislation needs to be positioned within a regime of rights-protection measures. That regime is not confined to rights-protection institutions within government, although they are obviously pivotal. It includes:

1. international human rights institutions, instruments, and norms;
2. domestic and transnational accommodation of human rights norms across regulation, policy and trade;
3. constitutional entrenchment or other protection of rights, including rights-based limits on legislative and executive power;

4. common law protection of rights;
5. statutory bills of rights;
6. rights-specific legislation (for example anti-discrimination laws);
7. rights-specific components of general laws;[2]
8. rights-protection agencies (for example anti-discrimination tribunals);
9. rights-orientated public roles (for example ombudsmen);
10. Parliamentary scrutiny of bills for human rights implications;
11. rights-based protocols for policy making;
12. administrative review mechanisms;
13. rights-orientated rules and presumptions of statutory interpretation;
14. corporate social responsibility and human rights management plans (for example Amnesty International (Australia), 2000); and
15. public human rights manuals, handbooks and guides.[3]

How is the wider bill of rights debate connected to legislative scrutiny of proposed laws for human rights and other implications? Canada and lately the United Kingdom have instituted bills of rights with different mechanisms for shared responsibility and institutional 'dialogue'[4] between courts and Parliaments about human rights interpretation and enforcement. If the fears of some critics of institutional dialogue on human rights matters are correct, giving complementary institutional roles to courts and Parliaments in deciding human rights questions solves some problems but creates others. While one of those institutions must still have the final say on human rights questions, what is done by the other institution still has some force politically and legally. This can result either in undue judicial deference to Parliament or, alternatively, in Parliamentary reluctance to exercise any legislative override of earlier judicial human rights decisions.[5]

Such an outcome might not be surprising in terms of the behavioural aspects of institutional relationships and interactions. Judges are key public officials and participants in the system of government. Their interpretation of laws is affected not only by the content of those laws but also by institutional considerations informing their public role and choice of interpretative strategy.[6] Courts spend their judicial capital notionally invested with the community (upon whose support for the rule of law their legitimacy and authority rests) when they rule that official actions and laws

---

2 For example, human rights dimensions of product disclosure statements for investment products under sections 1013D and 1013DA of the *Corporations Act 2001* (Cth).

3 For example Commonwealth, Department of Foreign Affairs and Trade, 2004; and Queensland, LCARC, 1998a. The author was a consultant to that committee in the preparation of the LCARC handbook.

4 For discussion of the strengths and weaknesses of the notion of 'dialogue' in conveying the institutional dynamics in play here, see, for example: Webber, 2003, pp. 135–36.

5 For example Webber, 2003; Goldsworthy, 2003; Hiebert, 2003; Klug, 2003; Clayton, 2004; and McDonald, 2004. See also the concerns identified by Robert Nagel and Christopher Manfredi in Chapters 9 and 10 of this volume.

6 For more on these institutional dynamics, see: Sunstein and Vermeule, 2002.

contravene legal yardsticks established for that politico-legal system. Legislatures *spend* their political capital notionally *invested* with the community (upon whose support their re-election or government membership depends) when they act to impose a limitation on rights which has been publicly identified and criticized by independent courts. As we shall see, members of legislative scrutiny committees also face choices of institutional strategy and interpretation.

Whatever its other pros and cons, a constitutional or statutory bill of rights for Australia would be likely to reinforce and enhance the role of pre-enactment scrutiny. As in the United Kingdom, a national bill of rights would give further force and backing to the work of a Parliamentary scrutiny committee. The two institutional mechanisms would reinforce each other, as the catalogue of rights in the bill of rights would provide the catalogue of rights against which proposed laws would be scrutinized for their potential impact, at least federally.

One of Australia's leading academic advocates of a bill of rights, Professor George Williams, highlights the interdependent connection between bills of rights and Parliamentary scrutiny work, in this way:

> A statutory Bill of Rights should establish a Parliamentary committee charged with determining, before a law is passed, whether it complies with the protected rights ... As part of an Australian Bill of Rights, a Parliamentary committee would serve two purposes. It would vet legislation before enactment, reducing the likelihood of Commonwealth legislation being found invalid by a court. It would also build Parliamentarians into the rights protection process, contributing to a greater understanding of rights issues by politicians and, through media coverage of committee deliberations, by the people. By inviting public submissions, it would also give individuals and community groups a means of contributing to the deliberative process.[7]

Human rights author and proponent Fr Frank Brennan SJ opposes a full-scale constitutional bill of rights but concedes the value of a statutory bill of rights (Brennan, 1998, pp. 178–81). Like Professor Williams, he too highlights the interdependent connection between legislative statements and bills of rights and Parliamentary scrutiny of bills.

Human rights advocate and chair of the ACT Bill of Rights Consultative Committee, Professor Hilary Charlesworth (Charlesworth, 2002, pp. 71, 73),

---

7   Williams, 2004, pp. 84–85. As this chapter focuses mainly upon legislative scrutiny of bills as a rights-protection measure, I shall save for another day any fuller examination of Professor George Williams' notion of a community-based bill of rights. Under his model, the community is more actively involved in framing a national bill of rights through Parliamentary committee processes and other institutional mechanisms. This leads to a statutory bill of rights with adequate mechanisms to create institutional dialogues of particular kinds between Parliaments and courts, thus giving them complementary interpretative roles on human rights matters. All of this is bolstered by judicial review to invalidate legislation, combined with an override clause which enables Parliament to have the final say, as distinct from simply having a judicial declaration of incompatibility: see Williams, 2003; 2004.

similarly combines a bill of rights with Parliamentary scrutiny in an integrated package of institutional rights protection, as follows:

> The most appropriate model for Australia may well be a version of the Canadian two-stage procedure: a statutory scheme of rights protection followed by constitutional entrenchment ... While I share the concern about the narrow perspective of the legal profession when it comes to social and moral questions, at the end of the day I nevertheless think that protection of rights is best overseen by a relatively independent judiciary, supported by a demanding system of Parliamentary scrutiny of draft legislation and the possibility ... of legislative override of judicial decisions.

For a country like Australia – a constitutional monarchy with a system of responsible government and representative democracy, as a liberal democratic nation governed by the rule of law – strong connections exist between democracy, basic rights and the rule of law (cf. Feldman, 2004, p. 92). The 'interdependence' (ibid.) of those three key things is reflected in Parliamentary scrutiny work: 'I take it to be axiomatic that, in a state that aspires to democracy, human rights can only be fully realised if they are taken as seriously in the law-making processes of the executive and the legislature as they are in the adjudicative work of the courts and tribunals', argues Professor David Feldman (ibid.).

As the inaugural legal adviser to the UK Joint Committee on Human Rights, Professor Feldman's assessment of the framework within which Parliamentary scrutiny work dovetails with oversight of a bill of rights like the UK *Human Rights Act 1998* (UK) has great weight. His comments that '(i)t is Parliament's responsibility to ensure, so far as possible, that it does not violate rights inadvertently or without proper consideration' (Feldman, 2002, p. 330) and that 'the object of scrutinizing legislation is to keep in check the tendency of governments to extend their powers, or the liabilities of citizens, too greatly, or for unacceptable purposes, at the expense of individual freedom' (p. 336), dovetail with jurisprudential notions of governmental responsibility and accountability founded on 'the core idea of trusteeship – that government exists to serve the interests of the people and that this has a limiting effect on what is lawfully allowable to government' (Finn, 1995, p. 13).

This conceptual framework, within which the importance of Parliamentary scrutiny work sits, arguably has other features too – some of which are still developing. Popular sovereignty, participatory democracy, citizenship and the exercise of public power in the public trust all place emphasis on the place and role of 'the people', both collectively and individually, in Australia's democratic system of government (cf. Finn, 1995, pp. 6–7). That development manifests itself variously in appreciation of rights protection as a key aspect of democracy; acceptance of the sovereignty of the people as the ultimate source of constitutional authority;[8] infusion of community standards and values into legal norms; recognition of individual-centred interests in limiting or conditioning the

---

8   For example *McGinty* v *Western Australia* (1996) 186 CLR 140, 275 (Gummow J); *Levy* v *Victoria* (1997) 189 CLR 579, 634 (Kirby J); and *Durham Holdings Pty Ltd* v *New South Wales* (2001) 205 CLR 399, 431 [75] (Kirby J).

exercise of governmental power; and – most directly, for current purposes – development of greater opportunities for engaging citizens and non-governmental actors in aspects of the law-making process such as Parliamentary scrutiny work.[9]

Viewed in that light, suggestions that governments should increase the use of public exposure drafts of legislation and develop more opportunities for public input into Parliamentary scrutiny work cannot simply be dismissed, for example, as suggestions which unnecessarily involve outsiders and increase delays in the law-making process in a system founded on rule by elected representatives. Rather, such suggestions have wider significance in meeting the point of the system of government, reconceptualized in a way which integrates all of its higher-order contemporary features (for example popular sovereignty, representative/participatory democracy, and civil society) (cf. Feldman, 2002, p. 333).

In other words, our conception of the importance of Parliamentary scrutiny work in our system of government, and our assessment of ways to increase public involvement and accountability in that process, must be informed by more than the status of Parliamentarians as elected representatives and the political realities and timelines of conventional Parliamentary law-making. The wider point simply is that Parliamentary scrutiny needs to be understood against the background of a wider conceptual framework about the system of government.[10] That framework provides a broader frame of reference for considering arguments about suggested changes and improvements to the mechanisms of Parliamentary scrutiny.

Rationale for Parliamentary Scrutiny of Proposed Laws

So far in the new millennium, Australian federal politics is yet to place debate about a national bill of rights at the top of the political agenda, notwithstanding valiant academic attempts to reawaken community support for a national bill of rights (for example Brennan, 1998; Williams, 2000; 2003; 2004; Harris, 2002; Charlesworth, 2002). In the past decade, both Queensland (Queensland, LCARC, 1998b) and New South Wales (NSW, SCLJ, 2001) have rejected the need for a State bill of rights, while the ACT has recently gone against this trend to become the first Australian jurisdiction with a legislated bill of rights, modelled heavily on bills of rights in other jurisdictions. In 2004, the Victorian Attorney-General stimulated public debate about rights protection and access to justice in Victoria with the release of a 'justice statement', which amongst other things canvassed the possibility of a charter of rights and responsibilities. Without a bill of rights, it is difficult but not impossible to create 'a culture in which government accepts the need to justify its measures

---

9 On some of these manifestations, see Finn, 1995, pp. 6–9. Further discussion of enhanced public input into the scrutiny process occurs in the outline of suggested reforms at the end of this chapter.

10 Here, I can only sketch parts of that underlying conceptual framework. Fuller analysis would require engagement with other dimensions of liberal democratic theory too; see, for example: Debeljak, 2003.

in terms of human rights', and in which the various stages of law-making, such as cabinet and departmental instructions to legislative drafters and departmental audits of legislative proposals, are all responsive to Parliament's obligation in the public trust to legislate responsibly on matters affecting individual rights and Parliamentary democracy (Feldman, 2002, pp. 347–48).

While all Australian jurisdictions have Parliamentary committees that scrutinize regulations and subordinate legislation, Parliamentary committees to scrutinize proposed laws at least for their impact on individual rights, liberties and freedoms are a relatively recent addition to the Australian Parliamentary landscape, starting with the Senate Committee for the Scrutiny of Bills and culminating in the recently created NSW Legislation Review Committee. Scholarship on legislative scrutiny generally and rights-orientated scrutiny in particular is a new and growing field in jurisdictions across the Commonwealth, especially since the commencement of the UK's *Human Rights Act 1998* (UK). This scholarship contains important theoretical, empirical and comparative assessments concerning the position of Parliamentary scrutiny work in the EU (for example Muylle, 2003), the UK (for example Kinley, 1999; Lester, 2002; Feldman, 2002; 2004; Oliver, 2004), Canada (for example Hiebert, 1998; 2003; and Webber, 2003), New Zealand (for example Iles, 1991; Taggart, 1998; Huscroft, 2003; and Morris and Malone, 2004) and Australia. (for example Bayne, 1992; Coghill, 1996; Uhr, 1997; 1998, pp. 126–27, 129, and 145; Brennan, 1998, pp. 177 and 181; Bayne and Stefaniak, 2003; Horrigan, 2003, pp. 246–51; Williams, 2004, pp. 84–85; and Francis, 2005). The scrutiny of proposed laws for potential human rights implications in Australia's first experiment with a statutory bill of rights in the ACT is likely to enhance the profile, significance and study of rights-based scrutiny of legislation.

At the outset, it must be recognized that Parliamentary scrutiny committees are not the only organ of government to undertake scrutiny of bills during the law-making process. Executive vetting of bills on human rights grounds is a feature in some jurisdictions across the wider Commonwealth, especially where ministers introducing government bills have an obligation to certify that bills are rights compliant (Hiebert, 2003, p. 241). Other Parliamentary committees and Parliaments engage in scrutiny and discussion of bills from a variety of constitutional, economic and other perspectives, none of which necessarily or systematically measure proposed laws against independent yardsticks grounded in human rights or anything else. Nor are Parliamentary scrutiny committees the only organ of government to scrutinize proposed laws for any adverse implications for basic rights, the institution of Parliament and the system of government and democracy. In different jurisdictions, organs including offices of legislative drafting, the attorney-general's department and cabinet itself can have a role in the stages of law-making which includes aspects of legislative scrutiny generally and Parliamentary scrutiny requirements in particular.[11]

---

11 In Queensland, for example, the Office of Parliamentary Counsel has a statutory role in advising departments of State on legislative drafting in compliance with 'fundamental

Professor David Feldman (2002, p. 328) refers to that aspect of Parliamentary scrutiny work involved in subjecting proposed laws to independent human rights, Parliamentary and democratic yardsticks in this way:

> Scrutiny [is] a rather more principled activity. Even if conducted in a somewhat unconstructive way, it has its own disciplines. The scrutineer tests the provisions of a measure against certain standards which are independent of the terms of subject-matter of the measure itself, and can and should be applied consistently to all measures which are scrutinized. The standards can, and should be, chosen and applied so as to be largely unaffected by political, or at any rate party-political, considerations.

This is the main sense of Parliamentary scrutiny which is discussed in this chapter, in terms of Parliamentary scrutiny work, Parliamentary scrutiny requirements and Parliamentary scrutiny committees.[12] According to Professor Feldman's (2002, pp. 332–33) summary of the scrutiny process, '(o)ne can therefore characterise the scrutiny process as being to examine legislation, to assess it against published criteria, and to report, leaving it to the [Parliament] to decide what to do about the report'. In the words of a former chair of the Australian Senate Scrutiny of Bills Committee, the role of a Parliamentary scrutiny committee is 'one of technical scrutiny in which it examines the justice, the fairness or the propriety of the way in which regulatory measures are determined and imposed', rather than 'the political acceptability of the policy being pursued'.[13] Nevertheless, the distinction is not always clear-cut between technical and legal scrutiny, on one hand, and political and policy-based scrutiny, on the other.

Of course, pre-enactment scrutiny of legislation against human rights yardsticks cannot always immunize legislation from breaching such standards, predict all of the specific contexts in which generally worded legislation might affect rights, or prevent governmental and statutory powers and discretions from being wielded in rights-damaging ways (ACT, ACT Bill of Rights Consultative Committee, 2003, p. 63). In addition, political, media and academic debate about the pros and cons of an Australian bill of rights has a higher profile than pre-enactment scrutiny of legislation for human rights, Parliamentary and democratic implications. This undervalues pre-enactment scrutiny. Like an audit committee of a corporate board, Parliamentary

---

legislative principles' (*Legislative Standards Act 1992* (Qld), s. 7(g)), and the 1995 Queensland Cabinet Handbook required Cabinet to approve any proposed legislation which departed from 'fundamental legislative principles': see Queensland, SLC, 1996a, p. 5.

12 Unless the context suggests otherwise, references here to 'pre-enactment scrutiny', 'legislative scrutiny' and 'Parliamentary scrutiny' all refer to this specific aspect of scrutinizing proposed laws against designated yardsticks. Many jurisdictions also have scrutiny of regulations and subordinate legislation. This chapter focuses primarily upon scrutiny of bills in the UK, Australia (at the federal level of government), Queensland, NSW, Victoria and the ACT.

13 Commonwealth, *Parliamentary Debates*, Senate, 4 June 1987, 3528 (Senator Cooney), quoted in: Commonwealth, Working Party of Representatives of Scrutiny of Legislation Committees throughout Australia, 1996, p. 4 [1.16].

scrutiny committees can assist their Parliaments with an audit function – namely, auditing proposed laws for human rights and other implications. Like regulatory impact statements and environmental impact statements, the scrutiny reports of Parliamentary scrutiny committees can serve both educational and functional purposes as human rights impact statements. Like an attorney-general acting as a legal adviser to the government, Parliamentary scrutiny committees can act as specialist advisers on human rights and other scrutiny matters to the Parliament as a whole (Oliver, 2004, p. 49).

Nature and Sources of Scrutiny Principles

'One can generalise by saying that scrutiny takes place at three main levels: scrutiny of policy or purpose; scrutiny of the mechanisms for achieving objectives; and scrutiny of drafting,' according to Professor Feldman.[14] Parliamentary scrutiny of bills has a number of potential functions, not all of which are expressly contemplated by the statutory and Parliamentary terms of reference of all Parliamentary scrutiny committees in Australia. In theory, those functions include assessing the extent to which proposed legislation is:

1. constitutionally valid;
2. fit for its stated purpose and a proportionate response to the stated need;
3. consistent with existing law and policy in the enacting jurisdiction;
4. adequately mindful of any impact on human rights;
5. adequately mindful of any impact on other individual rights and liberties;
6. adequately respectful of the institution of Parliament;
7. adequately respectful of the rule of law, the system of government and representative democracy;
8. well drafted; and
9. good policy.[15]

---

14 Feldman, 2002, p. 336. Of course, each of these scrutiny tasks is undertaken only to the extent necessary to fulfil the scrutiny brief. This does not justify a clean-slate review of the policy objectives of legislation, for example, as the benchmark is not the policy merits of the legislation on its own terms but rather the compatibility of the policy objectives with scrutiny yardsticks. Characteristically, scrutiny of policy objectives in proposed legislation is a political consideration for Parliament, except where the policy itself goes directly head to head with a rights-based scrutiny yardstick, such as a bill whose purpose is to reintroduce capital punishment, impose arbitrary detention without trial of any foreigner suspected of association with terrorists, or mandatory indefinite detention of visa-less people arriving in the country: cf. ibid., p. 337.

15 Professor David Feldman (2002, pp. 329–30), for example, identifies different sources of scrutiny standards in constitutional and public law, standards matching legislation to its purpose, requirements of the rule of law, and human rights jurisprudence.

Most Parliamentary scrutiny committees at least focus upon the impact of proposed legislation on the rights, freedoms and liberties of individuals.[16] Some of the Australian scrutiny criteria also focus on a proposed law's impact upon the system of democratic government generally and the institution of Parliament in particular. For example, laws which inappropriately delegate legislative powers offend that particular scrutiny criterion because of their inappropriateness for a system of democratic government with a separation of powers. Legislative scrutiny criteria can also focus upon the quality of legislative drafting. For example, the statutory list of examples of matters showing that a proposed law inadequately respects 'fundamental legislative principles' which protect individual rights and liberties, as outlined in Queensland's *Legislative Standards Act 1992* (Qld), is as drafting orientated as it is rights orientated, and certainly does not include a comprehensive and substantive set of human rights to be respected under law.

The scrutiny role might also embrace the regulatory impact of proposed laws. This could cover everything from financial impact statements to assessment of a proposed law's consistency or inconsistency with existing statutory and non-statutory law in the jurisdiction. Scrutiny might also focus upon the validity and constitutionality of proposed legislation. The responsibility of assessing bills legally and constitutionally does not necessarily fall only on Parliamentary scrutiny committees. Other committees might be assigned this role exclusively or concurrently, depending on the jurisdiction. At least one Australian Parliamentary scrutiny committee regards the constitutional validity of bills as a matter which implicitly falls within that jurisdiction's scrutiny requirements, but cautions that 'the lack of any mention of the issue of constitutional validity in the committee's report on a bill cannot be interpreted as an implicit statement that the committee is satisfied the bill is constitutionally valid' (Queensland, SLC, 1996b, p. 2 [3.8]). Finally, scrutiny could also focus upon the substantive merits of a proposed law as a matter of policy. Indeed, where the best governmental option is a policy solution rather than a legislative solution for a particular community problem, scrutiny principles can also provide a guide for good policy making (Sampford, 1994).

There are a number of important structural features of Parliamentary standing orders, scrutiny Acts, and other sources of legislative scrutiny obligations. These include:

1. the entrenchment of scrutiny obligations in law;
2. the scope of scrutiny beyond simply assessing any impact on rights;
3. the range of scrutiny criteria;

---

16 Of course, this simply leads to follow-up questions about the catalogue of rights against which proposed legislation might be measured – only human rights recognized under the laws of that jurisdiction; human rights protected under international human rights agreements which bind that jurisdiction's polity but which have not necessarily been enshrined in domestic law; rights and liberties beyond basic human rights but limited to those recognized under statutory and non-statutory law; or what?

4. the catalogue of matters relevant to human rights, the institution of Parliament, democratic government, the rule of law, and good legislative drafting;
5. the availability of internal/external expertise to assist Parliamentary committee members;
6. the timeliness of scrutiny reports for use in Parliament's business of making laws;
7. the availability of scrutiny reports to Parliament and the public;
8. the suitability of public consultation/input;
9. the obligation on other institutional actors (for example ministers) to consider and report on compatibility of bills with scrutiny principles;
10. the capacity for courts to use scrutiny reports as aids in statutory interpretation; and
11. the capacity for non-compliance with scrutiny requirements to invalidate resulting legislation.

In Australia, the catalogue of rights potentially available for consideration in Parliamentary scrutiny work is not limited either to human rights (as distinct from other kinds of individual rights, liberties and freedoms) or to individual rights, liberties and freedoms acknowledged and protected by existing statutory and judge-made laws. It includes:

1. rights, liberties, and freedoms which are explicitly or implicitly protected under the Australian Constitution;
2. human rights which are protected under legislation;
3. statutory rights;
4. common law rights;
5. rights that are necessary or desirable in a liberal democratic society with a system of responsible and representative government, whether or not such rights are fully acknowledged and protected under the law; and
6. rights that are recognized in international human rights instruments and jurisprudence, whether or not Australia is a party to those agreements and enshrines them in domestic law.

All of that is framed in terms of rights at large, including but not limited to human rights. The Queensland Scrutiny of Legislation Committee (2000, pp. 6–7 [2.12]), for example, takes a broad view of the range of potential rights which might need consideration:

> The committee, appropriately in its view, takes an expansive approach in identifying 'rights and liberties'. These of course include traditional common law rights, but the committee considers [that] they can encompass, for example, rights which are only incompletely recognized at common law (such as the right to privacy) and rights (especially human rights) which arise out of Australia's international treaty obligations.

However, as Professor George Williams (2000, p. 45) notes, current guidelines at both federal, State and Territory levels which refer simply to scrutinizing laws for their potential impact on 'rights and liberties' are inadequate, because they are 'too vague and imprecise to give Australians any clear indication of which of their rights are protected', including rights guaranteed under federal and State legislation like anti-discrimination laws. At the same time, guidelines for scrutiny need to extend beyond human rights principles, as it is also necessary to scrutinize new laws for constitutional implications, effects on Parliament and the system of government, consistency with principles of good legislative drafting and policy making, and compliance with other aspects of the rule of law. Currently, in the absence of agreed and extensive catalogues of basic rights and other scrutiny requirements, much turns on what Parliamentary committees and their expert advisers perceive as the rights worthy of consideration in each case.

Maintenance of ongoing bi-partisan support for the importance of Parliamentary scrutiny work and the fostering of relationships and communication channels between Parliamentary scrutiny committees and other actors in the law-making process (for example legislative drafters, key departmental advisers, ministers and other Parliamentarians) are both key institutional dynamics. The balancing act that Parliamentary scrutiny committees must perform here is well articulated by a former chairman of the New Zealand Regulation Review Committee in this way:

> Our task requires a difficult balance to be struck between losing the respect and support of colleagues and officials on whose cooperation we are ultimately dependent to have any effect and, on the other hand, being regarded either as a rubber stamp of the executive or a powerless irrelevance. (Caygill, 1993, quoted in NSW, Legislation Review Committee, 2004, p. *v*)

Scrutiny Terms of Reference and Other Guidelines

Australian Senate, New South Wales, and Victoria

The Australian Senate Scrutiny of Bills Committee has been operating for more than 20 years. Its role is outlined in Senate Standing Order 24 as follows:

> 24. (1)(a) At the commencement of each Parliament, a Standing Committee for the Scrutiny of Bills shall be appointed to report, in respect of the clauses of bills introduced into the Senate, and in respect of Acts of the Parliament, whether such bills of Acts, by express words or otherwise:
>
> i.   trespass unduly on personal rights and liberties;
> ii. make rights, liberties or obligations unduly dependent upon insufficiently defined administrative powers;
> iii. make rights, liberties or obligations unduly dependent upon non-reviewable decisions;
> iv. inappropriately delegate legislative powers; or
> v.   insufficiently subject the exercise of legislative power to Parliamentary scrutiny.

The role of the New South Wales Legislative Review Committee, as outlined in s. 8A of the *Legislation Review Act 1987* (NSW), is in similar terms. Equally, under s. 17 of the *Parliamentary Committees Act 2003* (Vic), the Victorian Scrutiny of Acts and Regulations Committee has a similar brief in scrutinizing bills, with additional rights-based functions to consider personal privacy and the privacy of health information.[17]

Queensland

The structure of Queensland's statutory regime for legislative scrutiny of proposed laws is slightly more elaborate than that in other jurisdictions. It is contained in the *Parliament of Queensland Act 2001* (Qld) ('*Parliament of Queensland Act*') and the *Legislative Standards Act 1992* (Qld) ('*Legislative Standards Act*'). The Scrutiny of Legislation Committee of the Queensland Legislative Assembly is established s. 80 of the *Parliament of Queensland Act*, which gives the Committee responsibility amongst other things for considering the application of 'fundamental legislative principles' (FLPs) to bills. Ministers can, but not must,[18] provide a response to a report of the Scrutiny of Legislation Committee about a proposed bill and, in practice, they mostly do so.

Section 4 of the *Legislative Standards Act* outlines a number of FLPs with which legislation must comply. The Act identifies two primary FLPs in s. 4(2) as follows:

> (2)   The principles include requiring that legislation has sufficient regard to—
>
> (a) rights and liberties of individuals; and
> (b) the institution of Parliament.

This list of FLPs is non-exhaustive, so it is possible that FLPs other than those relating to individual rights and liberties and the institution of Parliament might be put in issue by particular legislation. In addition, these two primary FLPs are inherently evaluative, in that they require an assessment of whether legislation 'has sufficient regard to' the relevant object of focus (that is, either individual rights and liberties or Parliament as an institution of government). That judgment is not always technical or purely legal in character. Whether or not a proposed legislative measure infringes or limits a right might essentially be a legal question, but the justification of that goes beyond purely legal judgments. That is the inherently evaluative nature of a requirement to have 'sufficient regard' to designated rights-based and institutional criteria.

---

17 The scrutiny role for this committee also extends to consideration of the impact of proposed legislation on the Supreme Court's jurisdiction and state constitutional laws. Legislative scrutiny of bills for human rights implications is enhanced further under the Victorian Government's proposed Charter of Human Rights and Responsibilities 2006 (Vic), especially Part 3.

18 *Parliament of Queensland Act 2001* (Qld) ss. 107(1), 107(2), and 107(10).

The *Legislative Standards Act* goes on in s. 4(3) to indicate a non-exhaustive list of indicators for the primary FLPs of adequately considering legislation's impact upon the rights and liberties of individuals, as follows:

(3) Whether legislation has sufficient regard to rights and liberties of individuals depends on whether, for example, the legislation—

(a) makes rights and liberties, or obligations, dependent on administrative power only if the power is sufficiently defined and subject to appropriate review; and
(b) is consistent with principles of natural justice; and
(c) allows the delegation of administrative power only in appropriate cases and to appropriate persons; and
(d) does not reverse the onus of proof in criminal proceedings without adequate justification; and
(e) confers power to enter premises, and search for or seize documents or other property, only with a warrant issued by a judge or other judicial officer; and
(f) provides appropriate protection against self-incrimination; and
(g) does not adversely affect rights and liberties, or impose obligations, retrospectively; and
(h) does not confer immunity from proceeding or prosecution without adequate justification; and
(i) provides for the compulsory acquisition of property only with fair compensation; and
(j) has sufficient regard to Aboriginal tradition and Island custom; and
(k) is unambiguous and drafted in a sufficiently clear and precise way.

Similarly, in s. 4(4), the *Legislative Standards Act* outlines a non-exhaustive list of indicators of the second primary FLP concerning a proposed law's impact upon the institution of Parliament, as follows:

(4) Whether a Bill has sufficient regard to the institution of Parliament depends on whether, for example, the Bill—

(a) allows the delegation of legislative power only in appropriate cases and to appropriate persons; and
(b) sufficiently subjects the exercise of a delegated legislative power to the scrutiny of the Legislative Assembly; and
(c) authorises the amendment of an Act only by another Act.

In terms of the hierarchy of institutional rights-protection mechanisms, which includes a constitutional bill of rights (with or without provision for legislative override), a statutory bill of rights (with or without provision for judicial declarations of incompatibility), and non-statutory statements of rights,[19] the Queensland model fits within the last category. However, it contains a highly selective and far-from-comprehensive list of substantive rights and drafting-based concerns. In terms of

---

19 On this hierarchy, see: Victoria, Department of Justice, 2004, pp. 54–55.

substantive rights, for example, the statutory list mentions things like protection against unwarranted self-incrimination, search and seizure, and compulsory acquisition of property, but nothing approaching the full set of rights to be found even in international human rights instruments binding on Australia. The fact that this list is only illustrative and that other substantive rights are included within the generic reference to individual rights and liberties is not a complete answer, because what is listed is far more likely to be considered than something which is not listed. Even if topics like search and seizure powers and reversing the onus of proof are the kinds of topics more likely to arise as issues in state-based legislative drafting than all of the human rights protected under international instruments, again that is not a complete answer.

The Committee's role under its statutory charter arguably embraces some assessments from perspectives that are not purely legal or technical, whatever other boundaries on the Committee's role might be necessary in terms of its wider function as a committee of the Legislative Assembly. Consider the structure of the legislative scrutiny regime as a whole. The basic role is to scrutinize proposed legislation according to FLPs. These FLPs are defined for Queensland's purposes as 'the principles relating to legislation that underlie a Parliamentary democracy based on the rule of law'.[20] So, the connection between scrutiny, democracy and the rule of law is legislatively made explicit.

One of the indicators concerning individual rights and liberties gives a flavour of the common structure of FLPs and their specified indicators. 'Whether legislation has sufficient regard to rights and liberties of individuals depends on whether, for example, the legislation ... has *sufficient* regard to Aboriginal tradition and Island custom', under s. 4(3)(j) (emphasis added). The key here is the sufficiency of the regard. This again reveals the evaluative judgment in play. Deciding, for example, that there is *appropriate* protection against self-incrimination,[21] *adequate* justification for reversing the criminal onus of proof,[22] and *adequate* justification for conferring an immunity[23] introduces an element of evaluation which is not always purely legal in character.[24]

Other features of the Queensland scrutiny regime support this basic structure. The fact that there is a statutory basis for scrutiny is itself a significant feature, particularly given the elaborate catalogue of matters for consideration. The *Legislative Standards Act* cannot be used to interfere judicially in the consideration of an arguably non-compliant bill during its passage through Parliament.[25] Absolute protection of rights is not mandatory, and failing to have sufficient regard for rights

---

20 *Legislative Standards Act 1992* (Qld) s. 4(1).

21 Ibid s. 4(3)(f).

22 Ibid s. 4(3)(d).

23 Ibid s. 4(3)(h).

24 The distinction between various kinds of legal, political and policy judgments in this context is discussed further below [see page 81–82].

25 *Bell* v *Beattie* [2003] QSC 333.

is not a basis for invalidity.[26] Explanatory notes accompanying government bills must include, amongst other things, 'a brief assessment of the consistency of the bill with fundamental legislative principles and, if it is inconsistent with fundamental legislative principles, the reasons for the inconsistency'.[27] The latter requirement enhances explanatory accountability, as distinct from simply asserting (without explaining and justifying) that, in a minister's and the government's view, the proposed bill is consistent with FLPs.

The Office of the Queensland Parliamentary Counsel has chief responsibility for drafting government bills,[28] advising government departments and other government entities on the application of FLPs,[29] ensuring that Queensland legislation is of the highest quality,[30] and advising ministers in writing if bills drafted outside the Office fail to meet 'an acceptable standard of legislative drafting'.[31] Non-compliance with the requirements for explanatory notes cannot be used to invalidate legislation.[32] However, the scrutiny reports of the Parliamentary scrutiny committee can serve as extrinsic evidence for the purposes of statutory interpretation in later court proceedings. This is because the set of 'extrinsic material' which judges can use in cases of legislative ambiguity includes relevant Parliamentary committee reports such as the Queensland Scrutiny of Legislation Committee's alert digests.[33]

Australian Capital Territory

The recent introduction of a bill of rights into the ACT has special significance for and interacts with Parliamentary scrutiny of legislation for human rights implications. The terms of reference for the Standing Committee on Legal Affairs in its performance of the duties of a scrutiny of bills committee include similar functions and rights-based

---

26 Section 25 of the *Legislative Standards Act 1992* (Qld) expressly indicates that non-compliance with the statutory requirements for explanatory material accompanying bills (including attention to any relevant FLPs) will not invalidate legislation. That section is probably enacted out of an abundance of caution. The absence of a specific section guaranteeing that a bill's substantive non-compliance with relevant FLPs invalidates the later Act is not strictly necessary. Constitutionally, such non-compliance cannot be used as a valid legal ground for invalidating duly passed legislation.

27 *Legislative Standards Act 1992* (Qld) s. 23(1)(f).

28 Ibid s. 7(a).

29 Ibid s. 7(g).

30 Ibid s. 7(j).

31 Ibid s. 8(2).

32 Ibid s. 25.

33 *Acts Interpretation Act 1954* (Qld) s. 14B. For examples of references to reports of the UK Joint Committee on Human Rights in a variety of contexts, see: *R v Chief Constable of South Yorkshire* [2002] EWCA Civ 1275; *A, X, and Y v Secretary of State for the Home Department* [2002] EWCA Civ 1502; *A v Secretary of State for the Home Department* [2004] UKHL 56; *R v Her Majesty's Coroner for the Western District of Somerset; ex parte Middleton* [2004] UKHL 10; and *R v Her Majesty's Coroner for the County of West Yorkshire; ex parte Sacker* [2004] UKHL 11.

concerns to those governing the Senate Scrutiny of Bills Committee and equivalent State Parliamentary scrutiny committees.

The Committee's published reports commonly include the following comment on the Committee's scrutiny role:

> The Committee examines all Bills and subordinate legislation presented to the Assembly. It does not make any comments on the policy aspects of the legislation. The Committee's terms of reference contain principles of scrutiny that enable it to operate in the best traditions of totally non-partisan, non-political technical scrutiny of legislation. These traditions have been adopted, without exception, by all scrutiny committees in Australia. Non-partisan, non-policy scrutiny allows the Committee to help the Assembly pass into law Acts and subordinate legislation which comply with the ideals set out in its terms of reference. (ACT, SCLA, 2003)

Like other Australian scrutiny committees, the ACT Committee is cautious about deciding and reporting unequivocally that a bill unduly trespasses on rights, preferring instead to comment in a way which 'generally seeks only to expose the potential for such a trespass, to state the competing arguments and to draw the issue to the attention of the Legislative Assembly' (Bayne and Stefaniak, 2003, p. 3). Like other committees, it too has limited resources – a factor which, when combined with the time constraints under which governments and Parliaments characteristically make such committees work during Parliamentary sittings, affects not only their current scrutiny work but also their capacity to engage in large-scale community consultation and solicitation of community submissions about bills:

> (T)he Committee is constrained in the extent of its examination of a bill by its resources. Often, it has but a few days to examine the bill and make a comment. In some situations, the rights issues are quite complex and all that can be achieved is an outline or indication of the competing considerations. (ibid.)

In addition, the *Human Rights Act 2004* (ACT) outlines rules affecting scrutiny of legislation for human rights implications in Part 5 of that Act. Section 37 says:

37   Attorney-General's statement on government bills

(1) This section applies to each bill presented to the Legislative Assembly by a Minister.
(2) The Attorney-General must prepare a written statement (the *compatibility statement)* about the bill for presentation to the Legislative Assembly.
(3) The compatibility statement must state—

(a)whether, in the Attorney-General's opinion, the bill is consistent with human rights; and
(b) if it is not consistent, how it is not consistent with human rights.

Note these features. The requirement for a compatibility statement is imposed for bills presented by a Minister, as distinct from opposition or private members' bills. The compatibility statement requires a conclusion about the extent of the bill's consistency with human rights, and the degree of detail will determine whether this provision is being complied with simply as a matter of form (in terms of announcing the Attorney-General's conclusion) or substantive accountability (in terms of providing a meaningful account of a bill's treatment of human rights issues). The effect of s. 37 and other sections[34] is to reinforce and enhance the pre-existing mechanisms for Parliamentary scrutiny, and to ensure that non-compliance with requirements for compatibility statements and committee scrutiny during passage of a bill cannot later be used to invalidate the resulting legislation.

Australian Similarities and Differences

There are many similarities and some differences in how Parliamentary scrutiny of proposed laws is conducted within Australia at federal, State and Territory levels. The similarities are quite striking and this at least reflects the common political and legal cultures within Australia across federal, State and Territory jurisdictions. It also reflects the network of communication between Australian Parliamentary scrutiny committees. They have the following things in common:

1. emphasis on individual rights and liberties;
2. focus on select liberty-based and drafting-orientated principles (as distinct from expansive human rights principles and catalogues of rights);
3. production and public availability of scrutiny reports and alert digests;
4. approaches to the timetable and management of scrutiny processes and work, particularly during Parliamentary sittings;
5. reliance on internal and/or external expertise to assist Parliamentary committee members in producing scrutiny reports;
6. all-party membership of Parliamentary scrutiny committees;
7. commitment to constructive and non-partisan approaches (as distinct from becoming an alternative policy forum to Parliament);
8. bilateral Parliamentary and governmental respect for the work of Parliamentary scrutiny committees;
9. extra-Parliamentary impact of scrutiny work;
10. constraints on resources for scrutiny work;
11. constraints on capacity for wider public input under current Parliamentary arrangements; and
12. ongoing mutual problems (for example national scheme legislation, and timeline pressures of Parliamentary sittings).

The nationwide differences are minor but possibly revealing. There are slight differences across Australian jurisdictions in the recourse to academic expert consultants. The Senate and ACT scrutiny committees each have one such consultant. At the outset, the Queensland committee used a panel of one general academic

---

34 *Human Rights Act 2004* (ACT) ss. 38 and 39.

consultant and up to three other academic consultants with specialist expertise in different areas of law. Victoria relies on the expertise of senior research officers. Other differences in the scope of reference to international human rights jurisprudence in scrutiny reports and alert digests, and in the kinds of scrutiny concerns which arise most frequently in those publications, might be more apparent than real. These differences can be affected by a range of dynamics, such as the nature of the subject matter of bills introduced in any given year.[35]

Comparative Australian and UK perspectives

This outline of the main terms of reference for pre-enactment scrutiny for the Commonwealth of Australia, Queensland, NSW, Victoria and the ACT shows that at least four important subjects for scrutiny dominate:

1. individual rights, liberties, freedoms, privileges and immunities, including (but not limited to) human rights;
2. roles and relationships between different parts of the system of government generally;
3. Parliament as an institution of government in particular; and
4. principles of good legislative drafting.[36]

These features of Australian scrutiny of bills committees can be compared and contrasted with the terms of reference of the UK Parliament's Joint Committee on Human Rights. It has responsibilities concerning remedial orders under the *Human Rights Act 1998* (UK) and a wide brief covering UK human rights issues which the Committee has interpreted 'as including a power to examine the impact of legislation and draft legislation on human rights in the United Kingdom' (UK, Joint Committee on Human Rights, 2001). In other words, its functions include a legislative scrutiny function similar to the function performed by Australian Parliamentary scrutiny of bills committees, bolstered by the presence of a bill of rights for that jurisdiction which has both scrutiny and non-scrutiny purposes.

The UK Joint Committee on Human Rights has a number of distinct features to its advantage in its rights-protecting scrutiny work. First, it has a wider brief than just scrutiny of proposed laws for human rights implications. Second, it is a joint committee of both houses of Parliament. Third, its scrutiny role is bolstered by the presence of a bill of rights in the *Human Rights Act 1998* (UK). Fourth, all of those involved in the law-making process (including the government of the day) know that both UK and European courts will have opportunities to comment and rule unfavourably if the UK Parliament legislatively breaches its human rights

---

35 Further research is needed on both the differences across jurisdictions which show up in committee publications and the dynamics which account for these differences.

36 See, for example: Feldman, 2002, pp. 330–31 (commenting on the Senate Scrutiny of Bills Committee).

obligations. In other words, No. 10 Downing Street and Whitehall need to keep an eye to Strasbourg as well as to the London courts precinct and to Westminster. Hence there are good institutional reasons for the government and the Parliament to work with this committee in its scrutiny work, as part of the mutual enterprise of minimizing the risk of producing rights-deficient legislation. Finally, this committee has relationships with external parties, especially non-government organizations (NGOs) and academic experts, which help to support, influence and legitimize its work.[37]

Based on his experience with the UK Joint Committee on Human Rights, Professor David Feldman identifies seven factors that affect a government's responsiveness to human rights critiques and concerns about its proposed legislation:[38]

- Ministers and departmental officials exhibit different degrees of willingness to discuss and respond to human rights queries about bills, depending on the institutional context. Opportunities for the government to illuminate its thinking occur in ministerial statements of compatibility with rights, select committee questioning, explanatory notes and ministerial correspondence. On this aspect, one correlative lesson for Australia lies in the adequacy of explanatory memoranda, second-reading speeches, regulatory impact statements, ministerial correspondence with Parliamentary scrutiny committees and ministerial compatibility statements.
- As a matter of policy and practical realities, human rights concerns and criticisms can often be more easily addressed in the earlier stages of the law-making process than in its latter stages, especially once a bill is introduced into Parliament. One lesson here lies in the greater use of public exposure drafts of bills, as 'the growing tendency towards public consultation, and particularly publishing bills in draft for consultation before finalizing them and introducing them to Parliament, increases the possibility of making influential contributions on the protection of human rights' (Feldman, 2004, p. 107).
- Conversely, the more that governments introduce new amendments with new policy imperatives during passage of a bill, the more political pressure which is then generated to pass a bill; the less time and opportunity there is for due scrutiny and comment; the less willing a government is to listen to critiques and suggestions at that late stage; and the more risk there is of legislation potentially infringing rights unjustifiably.
- Attacking the ends of a legislative proposal as rights-unfriendly is less likely to achieve changes to bills than attacking the undesirable means of an otherwise acceptable end and suggesting reasonable alternatives and safeguards.

---

37 These comments are based on discussions between the author and some members of the UK Joint Committee on Human Rights at a meeting in Westminster in July 2004. The author gratefully acknowledges the willingness of the Committee's members and advisers to meet and discuss their work. See also the factors identified in: Lester, 2002, p. 24.

38 On the summary and discussion which follow, see Feldman, 2004, pp. 105–15.

- Broad appeals in scrutiny work and submissions to general propositions about rights are not as useful or successful as arguments which are more focused, specific, and rigorous in nature.
- The source of any criticism of a bill can be just as important as the nature and quality of the critic's arguments, with criticisms from within Parliament itself usually carrying an inherent need for a governmental response and more weight than criticisms from those outside Parliament, such as academic experts, NGOs, lobby groups, and others with vested interests in the outcome.
- The design of the institutions and procedures for Parliamentary scrutiny critically affects the capacity for interplay between them, given the frequent interactions in the law-making process between departments, ministers, Parliamentary committees and the government of the day. Their mutual enterprise of ensuring that the Parliament and the government take seriously the business of avoiding unnecessary and unjustified departures from rights protection 'will be achievable only if the various institutions involved in legislation see themselves as working together, rather than against each other' (ibid., p. 113).

'Legal', 'Political' and 'Policy' Decisions in Scrutiny Work

Justification of limits on rights, or the balance to be struck in conflicts between rights themselves or rights and collective interests, are inherently policy-orientated questions. At a broad level, we can easily distinguish between Parliament's political decision about the merits of any proposed rights-infringing legislation and a lawyer's legal decision about whether and how a proposed law affects rights in terms of standards established in legal benchmarks like bills of rights and precedent. For this purpose, the decision that proposed legislation does or might infringe a right is the relevant *legal* decision. The decision that any such infringement is justified is the relevant *political* decision. As those engaged in Parliamentary scrutiny work themselves concede:

> Once a particular right is isolated, the issue is then whether the clause in the bill 'unduly' trespasses on it … In the end, however, any judgment about whether there has been a [justified] trespass on a right is a political judgment. (Bayne and Stefaniak, 2003, p. 2)

The question is whether all decisions by Parliamentary scrutiny committees fall into one camp, the other or a mixture of both. One might even try to colonize the other. For example, we might try to transform the purely political decision into a purely legal one, in the sense of making the political justification for any rights-limiting law wholly legal, as when we say that a measure is justified politically if it comes within an exception or limitation already accepted in human rights jurisprudence. Even then, making the legal benchmark the de facto sole justification for the political decision is itself part of the overall political decision. Conversely, Parliament might reconsider the justification for any limitation on rights at large, rather than simply defer to what courts have allowed.

Alternatively, take the constraint in some human rights instruments which imposes inherent limitations on specified rights based on what is necessary in a free and democratic society. Over time, courts develop jurisprudence on the meaning of such a limitation in a variety of contexts. To that extent, the question becomes legalized. Yet the content of that limitation is inherently controversial, both legally and politically. It is a *political* judgment in the sense that it involves value judgments and policy considerations of particular kinds, and cannot be made simply by reference to, and logical extrapolation from, existing legal rules. It can be viewed either in terms of what the legal system justifies or permits as a matter of good legal policy or alternatively as a political question at large in terms of good public policy. For this reason, the former *political* decision might be described as the relevant *legal policy* decision and the latter *political* decision might be described as the relevant *public policy* decision.[39] Parliamentary scrutiny committees and their academic legal advisers are more equipped to make evaluations and recommendations about legal policy matters than about public policy matters. In other words, a Parliamentary scrutiny committee's role can be conceptualized as one which always embraces the *legal* decision, often embraces the *political* decision in the form of the *legal policy* decision, and rarely (if ever) embraces the *public policy* decision.[40]

Institutional and Interpretative Strategies

Some people might criticize Parliamentary scrutiny committees for being too timid if they do not express concluded views about proposed rights-infringing laws and simply refer the issue of the proposed measure's merits and ultimate justification to Parliament. Yet there are also a number of institutional and role dynamics in play here. In terms of institutional and systemic dynamics, institutional studies remind us that institutional actors have institutional constraints and choices between interpretative strategies (for example Sunstein and Vermeule, 2002). They must spend their institutional capital wisely in making those interpretative choices, notwithstanding the particular substantive merits of the matter before them.

---

39 Here, I am not embracing, conflating or even contemplating Professor Ronald Dworkin's famous distinction between 'rules' and 'principles' (which judges do and should use in deciding the best legal answer as a matter of 'fit' and 'justification'/'soundness') and 'policy' (which is a matter only for legislatures): see Dworkin, 1978; 1986. If valid, those categories have validity and purpose not simply on their own but only within a particular jurisprudential account of law, and from a particular adjudication-orientated perspective. Neither of those contextual features applies here. The reality is that terms like 'political', 'legal' and 'policy' have different meanings in different contexts, as evidenced by the definitions and context here.

40 One rare exception might be where the means and ends of a proposed law both strike directly and clearly at rights unnecessarily.

In other words, the relationship and mutual respect between Parliamentary scrutiny committees and both Parliament as a whole and the government of the day are important institutional features that affect what these committees do and how they choose to do it. A committee might decide as a matter of policy or in particular circumstances that, while Parliamentary members of the committee have a concluded view on both the legal and policy merits, the best institutional course for a small committee without extensive resources, and without delegated authority to decide these matters for Parliament as a whole, is to refer all or at least controversial judgments on the policy merits of rights-infringing bills for Parliament's consideration. Alternatively, the committee might refrain from publicly expressing a concluded view on the policy merits in its report on the relevant bill, but at least identify and state what seem to the committee to be the relevant policy considerations on both sides of the argument, so that Parliament has the benefit of something which informs and guides its ultimate decision. Such a course of action does more than simply pass the scrutiny buck to Parliament unguided, and might even fulfil both the legislative and educative roles of these committees.

In his chairman's foreword to the 1995–96 *Annual Report* of Queensland's Scrutiny of Legislation Committee, Tony Elliot MLA describes the Committee's approach in this way:

> When raising issues about the fundamental legislative principles, it makes no political judgment about the policies incorporated therein nor about those introducing them. The Committee operates on a bi-partisan basis and avoids consideration of policy matters except where it is inevitable in the course of the Committee carrying out its responsibilities. (Queensland, SLC, 1996a)

This comment by someone involved in the business of Parliamentary scrutiny reflects a common sentiment – namely, that Parliamentary scrutiny committees should act in a bi-partisan way, refrain from making conclusions about the policy merits of legislation, and avoid undue conflict with the Parliament or government of the day. Yet none of that necessarily precludes these committees from doing more than simply assessing the *legal* question. In particular, it does not prevent them from dealing with the justification of a rights-infringing measure in terms of the relevant *legal policy* considerations. That still remains true to the scrutiny function of measuring bills against independent benchmarks from a rights-based perspective. However, that is very different from deciding that a bill as a whole, and its underlying policy thrust, amount to good or bad public policy.

Of course, the matter is often more complex than this. The Queensland Committee's *Annual Report* for 1995–96 admits that 'the dividing line is not always conveniently drawn' between the undesirable exercise of considering and deciding the policy merits of legislation on one hand and the necessary exercise of considering and deciding whether legislation satisfies designated scrutiny requirements on the other (Queensland, SLC, 1996a, p. 6). The *Annual Report* goes on to address the Committee's options for handling the mixture of legal, political and policy questions involved. It identifies four ways in which a potential conflict might arise between government policy and FLPs.[41] First, where there is a limited breach of FLPs by a bill with a clearly important policy objective and without any realistic alternative, the breach is justified and the bill can be reported as one which 'complies with FLPs'. Second, legislation that could achieve the same policy objective by a means which does not infringe relevant rights and liberties, but which instead chooses a means of fulfilling that objective which is not FLPs-compliant, can be criticized for being in breach of FLPs without that being taken as any judgment on the policy objective in question. Where depriving someone of their property interests is an incidental effect and not central to the policy being pursued, for example, an adverse scrutiny comment can be made about how this unjustifiably infringes rights, without taking issue directly with the underlying policy objective of the legislation (Bayne and Stefaniak, 2003, p. 3).

Third, in the case of a serious risk of a breach of FLPs because the proposed legislation generates legitimate questions about the impact on individual rights and liberties, the Committee is justified in flagging the concern, identifying the relevant issues, outlining the relevant arguments on all sides, referring all of this to Parliament for its consideration and leaving the ultimate judgment to Parliament as a whole. Finally, if compromising relevant rights and liberties is clearly not justifiable because they are 'too important to be sacrificed for the policy in question', the Committee's judgment that the legislation is not FLPs-compliant does not constitute a judgment on the policy of the legislation. In other words, Parliament as a whole might differ from its Parliamentary scrutiny committee in their respective judgments about the adequacy of legislation's respect for FLPs. However, the fact that the committee makes this judgment does not mean that the committee is usurping Parliament's ultimate responsibility for political judgments about legislation and does not mean that the committee is placing itself in conflict with government policy.

Cross-cutting Institutional and Behavioural Effects

We should not underestimate the systemic impact and ripple effect of pre-enactment scrutiny on institutional dynamics and behaviour elsewhere in the law-making process. Professor David Feldman perceives a 'growing sensitivity' to human rights considerations amongst various players in the law-making process since the UK *Human Rights Act 1998* (UK) became operative in 2000 (Feldman, 2004, p. 93). This includes government departments, legislative drafters, policy advisers, ministers and Parliament itself. For example, legislative drafters and departmental lawyers might consult Parliamentary scrutiny committees or their advisers in advance for some guidance on likely problems that these committees might have with particular

---

41 On these four items and the discussion which follows, see: Queensland, SLC, 1996a, p. 6.

legislative measures, and perhaps even modify proposed legislation during the drafting stages to remove potentially contentious measures (Oliver, 2004, pp. 48–49). The same effect is achieved when other official actors in the law-making process take account in advance of the kinds of scrutiny concerns which Parliamentary scrutiny committees habitually flag in their reports and alert digests. This is a positive and yet mostly hidden outcome of a good system of pre-enactment scrutiny, in which all participants in the law-making process take seriously the responsibility of helping Parliaments to do their best not to trespass on rights inadvertently or without adequate consideration and justification (cf. Feldman, 2002, p. 330).

Hence, even in routine pre-enactment scrutiny work, various lines of communication and accountability are in play. Legislative drafters and departmental lawyers take account of pre-enactment scrutiny requirements and concerns of Parliamentary scrutiny committees. Those committees communicate with ministers and Parliamentarians. Ministers and their departments communicate in response with those committees. Those committees then communicate with the public and other audiences in publishing their pre-enactment alert digests and other scrutiny reports. Courts interpret the legislative results. So we should not underestimate the importance of such cross-institutional dialogues and official interactions about human rights at various governmental levels (Webber, 2003, pp. 135–36).

Relevant institutional dialogue and official interactions therefore are not limited to courts and legislatures in the same jurisdiction focusing on a bill of rights. Occasionally, courts comment on the correctness of assertions in legislative preambles,[42] or direct the legislature's attention to weaknesses in the law and necessary reforms which become apparent in the cases before them. Conversely, legislatures might use public hearings, Parliamentary debate and legislative preambles to justify their legislative reversal of court decisions on rights (Hiebert, 2003, pp. 242–43). Ministers introducing government bills into Parliament might inform Parliament of the results of the executive's vetting of the legislation for human rights concerns, whether under a system of mandatory rights-compliant ministerial statements about proposed legislation or under a system of robust Parliamentary scrutiny of laws according to human rights standards. Systems of government that equally value responsible government, representative democracy and sovereignty of the people can create innovative mechanisms for public input into the law-making process, such as public hearings and submissions for Parliamentary committees examining bills. Parliamentary committees might produce reports on law-making topics that guide public servants within the executive arm of government in producing good legislation for Parliament's consideration. Occasionally, a Parliamentary committee might also even publish a report which responds to what the committee views as a misguided interpretation by courts of matters within the committee's oversight.[43]

---

42 For example *Wik Peoples* v *Queensland* (1996) 187 CLR 1.

43 See, for example, the disagreement between UK courts and the UK Joint Committee on Human Rights about the meaning of 'public authority' under the UK *Human Rights Act*

Where to from Here? Reform and Enhancement of Parliamentary Scrutiny

Legislative and Extra-legislative Statements of Rights

Historically, many Australian politicians and electors exhibit lukewarm support for entrenchment of a constitutional bill of rights. No overwhelming consensus exists about the need for a statutory bill of rights, let alone its desirable form and contents. Accordingly, an incremental and pragmatic approach towards reinvigorating both community and political interest in a bill of rights of any kind might start with a legislative statement of rights as a national benchmark for enhanced Parliamentary scrutiny of proposed laws for human rights implications.[44] This could be part of a joint community-based and Parliamentary initiative, akin to Professor George Williams' idea of a community-based process for developing a bill of rights (Williams, 2003). It is consistent with this suggestion by Fr Frank Brennan (1998, p. 181):

> I think we could have the best of both worlds were we immediately to legislate a Commonwealth Charter of Espoused Rights and Freedoms. This charter could be a precursor to a statutory bill of rights. It could be the benchmark against which a Senate Committee for Rights and Freedoms could scrutinize proposed legislation.

As Brennan notes, such a committee could complement or even replace the Parliamentary rights-protection scrutiny presently conducted by a variety of federal Parliamentary committees, including the Senate Scrutiny of Bills Committee. There is another possible benefit of an agreed catalogue of important rights, liberties and freedoms, whether or not it appears in a bill of rights, a legislative statement or charter, or simply designated scrutiny yardsticks, namely, the impact on public literacy about the system of government and citizenship. Moreover, using a nationally comprehensive catalogue of human rights principles for scrutinizing laws and policy-making, as a first step towards introduction of a legislative bill of rights and later a constitutional one, would also more easily meet widespread concerns about doing too much all in one hit.

Accordingly, we might start with a legislative statement of non-enforceable but nevertheless valuable basic rights. Accepting all of the usual problems which lawyers argue about legal lists (for example, that listing things involves the inherent possibility of leaving something out of the list, or that defining something in particular terms actually limits it), those who say that our rights are adequately protected should have no objection to being asked to catalogue those rights which they say are already adequately protected by law. If we cannot reach agreement on and state what many people say are our clearly and adequately protected rights, that itself would be a revealing reality check. This legislative statement of rights

---

1998 (UK), leading to the publication by the Committee of: UK, Joint Committee on Human Rights, 2004.

44 Some of the reform suggestions in the last part of this chapter amplify material in Horrigan, 2003.

would include but not necessarily be limited to the rights recognized in international human rights instruments which Australia has already signed. Despite criticisms of their biases and limitations, they nevertheless represent an international consensus on human rights and could act as a starting point for Australia. This could be part of a project of publicly agreed scrutiny criteria and guidelines for use across jurisdictions in scrutinizing bills which need to be uniform nationally or which otherwise result from intergovernmental and international agreements.

We should not underestimate the transformative effect of such a statement on the workings of government in terms of legislative drafting, policy making and official decision making. What is explicit, transparent and legislated is noticed and must be confronted one way or the other in the processes and decisions of government. I am presently agnostic on whether a legislative statement of rights should also include responsibilities, although I am cautious of the ulterior political motives behind some calls for individuals to accept their responsibilities as well as claim their rights.

Importantly, such a legislative statement of rights might serve a number of different institutional and public purposes. It certainly has a public awareness-raising and educational function, in terms of enhancing community legal literacy about human rights. It might at least serve as a guide for Parliamentary scrutiny of proposed legislation for human rights implications. It could operate federally but could also provide a uniform model for Parliamentary scrutiny in other Australian jurisdictions, to the extent that uniformity is necessary or desirable. It might serve as a model for good policy making, and might even exert a gravitational effect on both administrative and judicial decision making, at least in terms of being an authoritative legislative statement of weighty values and interests that warrant consideration in official decision making and adjudication respectively. It might help to familiarize the community with the kinds of issues and choices which are necessary in a follow-up bill of rights.

Uniform Catalogues of Scrutiny Criteria and Rights

Some might think it strange that those federal, State, and Territory governments which all confer briefs on their Parliamentary scrutiny committees to scrutinize proposed laws for their impact on rights and liberties cannot agree on even a uniform legislative template for Parliamentary scrutiny of bills, let alone a uniform catalogue of relevant rights and liberties to guide scrutiny work and ensure consistent approaches throughout Australia. Consider just one example, namely, the treatment of privacy. What important rights-related subjects in addition to privacy, for example, need to be considered by the Queensland Scrutiny of Legislation Committee as a matter of policy even though they are not explicitly enshrined in scrutiny criteria in the *Legislative Standards Act*? Why does personal privacy (particularly the privacy of personal health information) warrant specific legislative mention in scrutiny criteria in Victoria but not elsewhere? To what extent is privacy already implicitly covered by the general focus on individual rights and liberties in Parliamentary scrutiny criteria, notwithstanding that privacy's legislative protection is piecemeal and its common law recognition as a cause of action is not yet accepted throughout Australia?[45] What second-order scrutiny principles should guide assessment of privacy concerns in scrutiny work?

If any differences here are not marginal, can we justify them simply on the basis of different needs, political cultures and Parliamentary dynamics in different jurisdictions? If so, the terms of reference and basis for Parliamentary scrutiny need not necessarily be uniform throughout Australia. In practice, there is much uniformity in design, approach, culture and operations, not least because of the communication and networking between Parliamentary scrutiny committees and the reference to one another's scrutiny work on similar topics. At the same time, there are enough substantive differences in their accompanying legislative frameworks, terms of reference, range of scrutiny criteria and scope of considered rights in published reports to suggest that not every Australian government can claim to have the optimal conditions for Parliamentary scrutiny of bills enshrined in their jurisdiction's scrutiny requirements or practice.

Enhanced national cooperation and coordination between Parliaments and governments could assist in other ways too. The quality and consistency of Parliamentary scrutiny of cooperative and uniform national legislation could be enhanced by the promulgation of common scrutiny principles for such bills, developed and accepted by all Australian scrutiny of bills committees, as well as a mutually beneficial and consistent means of keeping all such committees adequately informed of domestic and international human rights developments (Bayne, 2003, pp. 1–2).

Towards a Reconceptualized Catalogue of Scrutiny Criteria

As shown by the existing terms of reference and scrutiny criteria used throughout Australia, we need to decide afresh (and perhaps from a cross-jurisdictional perspective) the full range and balance of liberty-based rights (for example free speech), opportunity-based rights (for example adequate education, housing and family life), group-based rights (for example respect for indigenous rights and culture[46]), procedural rights (for example natural justice and procedural fairness) and drafting-based interests (for example non-retrospectivity, non-ambiguity and non-conferral of unjustified immunity in legislative drafting) for any ideal catalogue of rights for reference in Parliamentary scrutiny work. Given the nature of Parliamentary scrutiny work, such a catalogue cannot properly be confined only

---

45 For discussion of the importance of privacy in Parliamentary scrutiny requirements, see: NSW, Legislation Review Committee, 2004, p. 4; and Queensland, SLC, 1996a, p. 4.

46 Under s. 4(3)(j) of the *Legislative Standards Act 1992* (Qld), '(w)hether legislation has sufficient regard to rights and liberties of individuals depends on whether, for example, the legislation ... has sufficient regard to Aboriginal tradition and Island custom'.

to substantive rights. Nor can it be confined to human rights standards or simply a catalogue of relevant human rights. It needs to embrace substantive, procedural and drafting concerns, even though human rights are still a core part of this catalogue. In terms of relevant human rights for scrutiny purposes, any starting list must include at least those human rights in international human rights agreements to which Australia is committed.

As illustrated by the published experiences of key players currently or previously involved with the UK Joint Committee on Human Rights, there is a need for political, public and academic understanding of pre-enactment scrutiny of bills for human rights implications to have deeper recourse to a core set of values grounded in requirements of the rule of law,[47] such as legal certainty, individual autonomy, independence of the judiciary,[48] and fundamental rights and freedoms.[49] The High Court is yet to develop fully what flows from the rule of law as a bedrock of our system of government and an underlying assumption on which the Australian Constitution is based.[50]

In Parliamentary scrutiny work too, much flows from the notion of Australia as a liberal democratic society governed by the rule of law which remains unarticulated in legislative scrutiny requirements. This remains so even though Queensland explicitly links its pre-enactment scrutiny principles to the notion of the rule of law.[51] In addition, some of Queensland's specific statutory scrutiny criteria embody notions conventionally associated with rule-of-law jurisprudence, such as the need for legislation to be clear, certain and generally non-retrospective.[52]

'Every society requires rulers, but not every society requires a system of rules to hedge in the rulers, as in our ideal of the rule of law, with due legislative procedures and impartial arbitration through a judiciary,' notes political scientist Dr John Uhr (1997, p. 54). A full catalogue of pre-enactment scrutiny criteria therefore would need to include such principles derived from the notion of the rule of law, as well as human rights standards, a list of important rights, bases for constitutional invalidity, principles of good legislative drafting and other criteria grounded in the system of democratic government and representative democracy.

In some contexts, first-order scrutiny criteria laid down in statutory or Parliamentary terms of reference for Parliamentary scrutiny committees can usefully be supplemented by official statements of second-order principles for guidance on particular topics. Something akin to this already happens, for example, in Australian federal governmental guidelines on the conditions under which the introduction of

---

47 Feldman, 2004, p. 92; and Bayne, 2003, pp. 6–7. For more detailed discussion of the attributes of the rule of law, see, for example: Mason, 1995.

48 *A (FC) and Others (FC)* v *Secretary of State for the Home Department* [2004] UKHL 56 [42].

49 For example Feldman, 2002, 2004; Lester, 2002; Lester and Taylor, 2004; and discussion of Feldman's and Lester's comments in Oliver, 2004, p. 48.

50 For example *Kartinyeri* v *Commonwealth* (1998) 195 CLR 337, 381 [89] (Gummow and Hayne JJ).

51 *Legislative Standards Act 1992* (Qld) s. 4(1).

52 Ibid s. 4(3)(g) and (k). See also: Feldman, 2002, p. 330.

an infringement notice regime is legislatively suitable. Official enquiries in the UK suggest second-order principles as a form of additional governmental institutional guidance for rights-protection issues in the context of terrorism legislation, namely, that:

- terrorism legislation should follow ordinary criminal law and procedure as much as possible;
- additional offences and powers are justified only if they meet the anticipated threat from terrorism and must strike the right balance between security needs and the rights and liberties of individuals;[53]
- additional powers need to be considered along with additional safeguards on the exercise of those powers in combating terrorism; and
- any counter-terrorism laws must comply with the UK's international legal obligations.[54]

There is scope for Parliamentary scrutiny committees and other public bodies to contribute to development of such second-order principles as follow-up guidelines for scrutiny in particular areas, beyond the general reference to rights and liberties at large in most Australian Parliamentary scrutiny requirements.

Scrutiny Timeframes and Resources

Further reforms and enhancements of Parliamentary scrutiny must address the practical realities and constraints confronting these committees. Parliamentary scrutiny of proposed laws is neither a full-time activity for Parliamentarians nor necessarily the most important one for them from a pragmatic and self-interested perspective (Feldman, 2002, pp. 324–25). The role, expertise and ready availability of expert academic consultants and senior committee staff to assist Parliamentary committee members in preparing Parliamentary scrutiny reports is a critical factor in the timely production and quality of Parliamentary scrutiny reports. It can also affect the range of rights highlighted for scrutiny.

Timelines for the introduction of bills and amendments could cater more for the need of Parliamentary scrutiny committees and their members and advisers to have sufficient time to produce Parliamentary scrutiny reports of sufficient quality on all proposed legislation to assist Parliamentarians in their primary task of law-making. Changes to Parliamentary procedures to increase the time period between

---

53 Note, however, that politicians such as Australian Attorney-General Philip Ruddock and Canadian Attorney-General Professor Irwin Cotler argue that counter-terrorism legislation should not be characterized in terms of a zero-sum competition between national security and civil liberties, because protection of rights is also part and parcel of protecting national security: see Ruddock, 2004.

54 Referred to in: UK, Privy Counsellor Review Committee, 2003. For more discussion of scrutiny in the context of counter-terrorism and national security laws, see: Lester, 2002; Feldman, 2002, 2004; Lester and Taylor, 2004; and Francis, 2005.

the introduction of a bill into Parliament (and any amendments) and the point in the law-making process where a Parliamentary scrutiny report is needed to assist Parliamentarians, as recommended previously in both Queensland and New South Wales, can make a big difference (Queensland, SLC, 1998; and NSW, Legislation Review Committee, 2004). So too can a move towards greater use of exposure drafts of important and uniform legislation, and their publication well in advance of Parliamentary sittings, to enable more time for research, reflective scrutiny and perhaps even some form of public consultation in advance of a bill's introduction into Parliament.

Effectiveness and Performance Measures

Without a national bill of rights or opportunities for citizens to engage with Parliamentary scrutiny committees in the law-making process, it is probably not surprising that Parliamentary scrutiny of proposed laws does not yet have the prominence which it deserves in the public consciousness and the news media. Better assessment is needed of the contribution which Parliamentary scrutiny committees make to the system of government and the law-making process. Of course, the performance measures for demonstrating the effectiveness and efficiency of commercial entities cannot simply be transposed without alteration to the public sector. To echo some of NSW Chief Justice James Spigelman's concerns about the indiscriminate application of some economic performance models to governmental institutions, legislation is not a *service* that Parliament provides to citizens as Parliament's *clients,* just as the administration of justice by courts is not a *service* provided to litigants or prosecuted people as *clients.*[55] Nevertheless, some assessment of the usefulness and impact of Parliamentary scrutiny work is possible.

What kinds of performance measures can we use to demonstrate the benefits of Parliamentary scrutiny work? The list of possible measures includes the following, not all of which are of equal importance:

1. the number of bills assessed;
2. the number of pages of bills assessed;
3. the range of rights considered and used as scrutiny benchmarks;
4. the number of clauses in bills which trigger the need for a scrutiny comment, and the proportion of comments relating to particular scrutiny concerns;[56]
5. changes over time in the number of clauses in bills which trigger a scrutiny comment, as a measure of a scrutiny committee's impact on legislative drafting;
6. the average turn-around time between introduction/publication of bills and

---

55 On the limitations of economic models and indicators in such contexts, see: Spigelman, 2001a; 2001b; 2002.

56 This measure is commonly reported in annual reports for some Parliamentary scrutiny committees.

publication of a scrutiny report on bills;

7. the number of meetings of Parliamentary scrutiny committees both during and outside Parliamentary sitting weeks;
8. the degree and frequency of unanimity in scrutiny reports;
9. the frequency of written queries to ministers concerning bills;
10. the frequency and nature of ministerial and departmental replies to committee concerns;
11. the citation of scrutiny reports in *Hansard*;
12. the number of Parliamentarians using scrutiny reports during passage of a bill;
13. the number of Parliamentarians reporting satisfaction with the content and timely publication of scrutiny reports;[57]
14. the number of occasions on which a scrutiny report frames and guides the subsequent Parliamentary discussion of relevant issues and concerns;
15. the number of occasions on which the government and the Parliament take account of reported scrutiny concerns in discussing, amending, rejecting or withdrawing bills;
16. the frequency of informal contact and discussions between legislative drafters, Parliamentary scrutiny committees and other actors in the law-making process, with a view to minimizing scrutiny concerns during the passage of legislation;
17. proportionate reductions in the number and range of proposed laws which are presented without features which have attracted adverse comment in previous scrutiny reports;
18. the number and range of published reports (other than scrutiny reports) and guides on legislative matters to educate the public and those within government about common or important issues in law-making and legislative scrutiny;
19. the frequency of citation of Parliamentary scrutiny reports in the work of courts, other Parliamentary committees in the same jurisdiction, Parliamentary scrutiny committees in other jurisdictions, law reform agencies, academic scholarship and other authoritative sources, as well as in public and media discussion of Parliamentary matters; and
20. benchmarking performance on these indicators against the performance of Parliamentary scrutiny committees in other jurisdictions.[58]

---

57 For example the survey of Parliamentarians conducted by the NSW Legislation Review Committee in 2004 and reported in: NSW, Legislation Review Committee, 2004, p. 12.

58 On some of these measures of effectiveness, see: Feldman, 2002, pp. 345–48.

Stimulating and Facilitating Greater Public Input

Governments and Parliaments could make more strategic use of public exposure drafts of significant legislation, and not just uniform national legislation based on intergovernmental agreements,[59] to facilitate better public involvement in the scrutiny process. Widespread public consultation on all bills by Parliamentary scrutiny committees is presently impossible, given their current resources and staffing as well as the tight time-frames within which much proposed legislation needs to be scrutinized in published reports available for use by Parliamentarians as bills proceed through Parliament.

Notwithstanding the weaknesses and impediments which surround any form of public consultation during pre-enactment scrutiny, some degree of specifically targeted extra-Parliamentary consultation by Parliamentary scrutiny committees, at least with individuals and groups with special expertise or interests, might better inform the current system of scrutiny by an elite group of Parliamentary committee members, academic consultants, committee staff and other public officials engaged in the law-making process.[60] It might also more precisely meet the needs of participatory democracy, citizenship engagement and civil society.

In addition to public consultation, another option is for Parliamentary committees that scrutinize bills to solicit and receive public submissions of proposed new laws, particularly in terms of their impact on individual rights. The timetable of many Parliamentary sittings currently allows inadequate time for this. Options like public consultation and submissions promote greater public involvement in the scrutiny process, so that testing of rights-based intrusions is not wholly governed by the analysis of public officials. This enhances educational, aspirational and democratic aspects of rights protection too.

Of course, opening up the law-making process to greater public consultation and input runs the risk of simply facilitating new ways for well-resourced interest groups to wield disproportionate influence upon the legislative process. The same argument is often used to warn against misuse of a bill of rights by well-resourced litigants. Nevertheless, in both contexts, the manipulation of legal and political avenues by those in a position to do so is not alone a good reason for not making such avenues available to all citizens.

If any other Australian jurisdictions follow the ACT's lead in introducing a bill of rights, which then becomes the benchmark against which all proposed laws in those jurisdictions are scrutinized, we can expect greater pressure from outside

---

59 For the views of scrutiny committees themselves on this important topic, see, for example: Commonwealth, Working Party of Representatives of Scrutiny of Legislation Committees throughout Australia (1996); and NSW, Regulation Review Committee of the NSW Parliament, 2001.

60 While the contexts and roles are slightly different, the UK Joint Committee on Human Rights occasionally receives some community submissions on bills under consideration and also consults with NGOs and academic experts on the human rights implications of bills: see Feldman, 2002, p. 333; and Lester, 2002, pp. 13–14.

government for public committee hearings and other forms of enhanced community input into the Parliamentary scrutiny process. Although it has some different roles from those currently enjoyed by most Australian scrutiny of bills committees, not least because its governing jurisdiction has a bill of rights, the experience of the UK Joint Committee on Human Rights has been as follows:

> The Committee's object is to develop ways of engaging Parliamentarians and Government in human rights discussions, and at the same time to give human rights specialists and NGOs, and members of society more generally, an additional, more systematic channel for involving themselves in the political engagement with human rights ... It also requires respect for the responsibilities and abilities of other bodies with complementary roles, whether in Government, in the courts, or among NGOs. No one body can establish a human rights culture. (Feldman, 2004, pp. 113–15)

At present, the views of many Australian Parliamentarians and voters would probably match this description:

> There is no expectation by the members of the [Scrutiny] Committee, the Parliament as a whole or the public that the opportunity of an open forum will be available to hear an explanation of the features of legislation, to receive submissions supporting, opposing or suggesting amendments and to question the minister, relevant officials and those making submissions. (Coghill, 1996, p. 28)

The knee-jerk reaction of some politicians and commentators might be to deride a more publicly open scrutiny process as unworkable, time-consuming, resource-intensive and corrosive of representative government. Whether it is ultimately right or wrong, such a reaction is predicated on assumptions about legislative roles, processes and practices which increasingly are under pressure, and not merely from the kind of conceptual framework outlined in this chapter, in which the business of Parliament generally and Parliamentary scrutiny in particular must be responsive to the higher-order demands of electoral engagement, participatory democracy and citizenship involvement.[61]

In what former key UK prime ministerial adviser, Dr Geoff Mulgan, once described as twenty-first-century knowledge-based democracy, there is an expansion of knowledge and information essential for democratic engagement across all community sectors, as well as opportunities and levels of entry for democratic participation and trust building between those governing and those governed in marrying the needs of a market economy, liberal democracy and civil society (Mulgan, 2003). This is fuelled by a series of developments like more ubiquitous and transparent public knowledge and information in the Internet age, evidence-based governmental policy development, power shifts from privileged official and professional elites to knowledge-empowered citizens, and a more aware, demanding and critical citizenry, all of which shape new forms of community participation in democratic government as well as governmental

---

61 Some of what follows on this point uses and amplifies material in: Horrigan, 2003, pp. 331–32.

responses to these pressures (ibid.). Meaningful engagement between public servants and the community is not immune from such developments, which create pressure for more than perfunctory stakeholder consultation in the course of developing government policy. Despite the differences between policy making and law-making, what will keep Parliamentary scrutiny mechanisms and processes totally immune from such developments in the long run?

Conclusion

Although most public debate about better ways of protecting human rights in Australia concentrates on the pros and cons of a bill of rights, it is a mistake to place all of the institutional rights-protection eggs in the bill-of-rights basket. A multi-pronged approach is needed to develop a better Australian rights-protection culture and regime. One possibility is a simultaneous seven-pronged attack on the human rights front domestically. Those seven prongs are:

1. bolstering rights-based Parliamentary scrutiny and policy-making measures;
2. introducing a statement or bill of rights in some legal form, with a strong correlation with scrutiny criteria;
3. developing targeted legislative rights-protection measures in specific areas of need beyond existing anti-discrimination regulation;
4. enhancing public mechanisms and institutions for human rights advocacy, representation and education;
5. improving rights-protection in judicial interpretation of constitutional and statutory law, and judicial development of non-statutory law;
6. encouraging better corporate and business rights-enhancing strategies; and
7. facilitating better citizenship education and community human rights literacy.

In an environment of post-2004 Australian federal politics where the government of the day has the numbers to control the Senate, perhaps the penultimate word about the preconditions for keeping pre-enactment scrutiny sustainable should go to Professor David Feldman, (2002, p. 347) who reflects on his experience with the UK Joint Committee on Human Rights in this way:

> In a Parliament where the government has a built-in majority and can take advantage of reasonably strong party discipline to get its legislative programme through the two Houses, the effectiveness of a scrutiny procedure has to be measured in terms of the influence which committees exercise, both with individual members of each House and, very importantly, with departments. The influence depends largely on the esteem in which the scrutineers are held, since committees have no power to force their views on an unwilling executive ... (W)hile a Parliamentary committee must always aim first and foremost to assist the work of Parliament, ministers and departments are likely to pay particular heed to a committee which is well regarded outside, as well as inside, [Parliament] as having a

good reputation among the relevant professions, interested academics, non-governmental organisations and the press.

In December 2004, the Australian Government publicly released an important new human rights statement and action plan. (Commonwealth, Attorney-General's Department, 2005) While it contains brief and general references to Parliamentary committees, it gives no special prominence to pre-enactment scrutiny of proposed laws against human rights benchmarks and other scrutiny yardsticks as a key means of Australian rights-protection. It is time to give this form of rights-protection a higher public and media profile, better tools and resources, and greater popular and academic study and engagement.

References

Amnesty International (Australia) (2000), *Just Business: A Human Rights Framework for Australian Companies* (Amnesty International Australia).

Australian Capital Territory (ACT), ACT Bill of Rights Consultative Committee (2003), *Towards an ACT Human Rights Act: Report of the ACT Bill of Rights Consultative Committee* (Canberra: ACT Bill of Rights Consultative Committee).

ACT, Standing Committee on Legal Affairs (Performing the Duties of a Scrutiny of Bills and Subordinate Legislation Committee) (SCLA) (2003), *Scrutiny Report No 33* (Canberra: Legislative Assembly for the Australian Capital Territory).

Bayne, P. (1992), 'The Protection of Rights – An Intersection of Judicial, Legislative and Executive Action', *Australian Law Journal*, **66**: 844.

——, 'Towards National Principles of Scrutiny Review: Paper for the Meeting of the Working Group of Chairs and Deputy Chairs of Australian Scrutiny of Primary and Delegated Legislation Committees of 3 February 2003', in ACT, Standing Committee on Legal Affairs (Performing the Duties of a Scrutiny of Bills and Subordinate Legislation Committee) (2003), *Scrutiny Report No. 28* (Canberra: Standing Committee on Legal Affairs), attachment 3.

Bayne, P. and Stefaniak, B. (2003), 'The Notion of Personal Rights in the Modern Era', paper prepared by Peter Bayne as legal adviser for Bill Stefaniak as chair of the ACT Standing Committee on Legal Affairs for the conference, 'Eighth Australasian and Pacific Conference on Delegated Legislation and Fifth Australasian and Pacific Conference on the Scrutiny of Bills', Hobart, Tasmania, 4–6 February 2003.

Brennan, F. (1998), *Legislating Liberty: A Bill of Rights for Australia?* (Brisbane: University of Queensland Press).

Caygill, D. (1993), 'Speech to Fourth Australasian and Pacific Conference on Delegated Legislation on Scrutiny of Bills', in Victoria, Parliament of Victoria (1993), *Proceedings of the Fourth Australasian and Pacific Conference on Delegated Legislation and First Australasian and Pacific Conference on the Scrutiny of Bills: 28–30 July 2003* (Melbourne: Parliament of Victoria).

Charlesworth, H. (2002), *Writing in Rights: Australia and the Protection of Human Rights* (Sydney: University of New South Wales Press).

Clayton, R. (2004), 'Judicial Deference and "Democratic Dialogue": The Legitimacy of Judicial Intervention under the Human Rights Act 1998', *Public Law*: 33.

Coghill, K. (1996), 'Scrutiny of Victorian Bills', *Legislative Studies*, 10 (2): 23.

Commonwealth, Attorney-General's Department (2005), *Australia's National Framework for Human Rights: National Action Plan* (Canberra: Attorney-General's Department), available at <http://www.ag.gov.au/agd/WWW/rwpattach. nsf/VAP/ (CFD7369FCAE9B8F32F341DBE097801FF)~18+NAP+17+FEB.pdf/ $file/18+NAP+17+FEB.pdf>.

Commonwealth, Department of Foreign Affairs and Trade (2004), *Human Rights Manual 2004*, 3rd edn (Canberra: Department of Foreign Affairs and Trade), available at <http://www.dfat.gov.au/hr/hr_manual_2004/ hr_manual.pdf>.

Commonwealth, Working Party of Representatives of Scrutiny of Legislation Committees throughout Australia (1996), *Scrutiny of National Schemes of Legislation*, Position Paper (Canberra: Working Party of Representatives of Scrutiny of Legislation Committees throughout Australia), available at <http:// www.aph.gov.au/senate/committee/scrutiny/ natschem/nat_schemes.pdf>.

Debeljak, J. (2003), 'Rights and Democracy: A Reconciliation of the Institutional Debate', in Campbell, T., Goldsworthy, J. and Stone, A. (eds), *Protecting Human Rights: Instruments and Institutions* (Oxford: Oxford University Press), p.135.

Dworkin, R. (1978), *Taking Rights Seriously* (London: Duckworth).

—— (1986), *Law's Empire* (London: Fontana Press),

Feldman, D. (2002), 'Parliamentary Scrutiny of Legislation and Human Rights', *Public Law*: 323.

—— (2004), 'The Impact of Human Rights on the UK Legislative Process', *Statute Law Review*, 25 (2): 91.

Finn, P. (1995), 'A Sovereign People, A Public Trust', in Finn, P. (ed), *Essays on Law and Government (Volume 1: Principles and Values)* (Sydney: Law Book Company), p. 1.

Francis, A. (2005), 'Parliamentary Scrutiny of Security and Asylum Bills' (forthcoming; copy on file with author).

Goldsworthy, J. (2003), 'Judicial review, Legislative Override, and Democracy', in Campbell, T., Goldsworthy, J., and Stone, A. (eds), *Protecting Human Rights: Instruments and Institutions* (Oxford: Oxford University Press), p. 263.

Harris, B. (2002), *A New Constitution for Australia* (London: Cavendish Publishing).

Hiebert, J. (1998), 'A Hybrid-Approach to Protect Rights? An Argument in Favour of Supplementing Canadian Judicial Review with Australia's Model of Parliamentary Scrutiny', *Federal Law Review*, 26: 115.

—— (2003), 'Parliament and Rights', in Campbell, T., Goldsworthy, J., and Stone, A. (eds), *Protecting Human Rights: Instruments and Institutions* (Oxford: Oxford University Press), p. 231.

Hope, Lord (2004), 'What a Second Chamber Can Do for Legislative Scrutiny', *Statute Law Review*, **25** (1), p. 3.

Horrigan, B. (2003), *Adventures in Law and Justice: Exploring Big Legal Questions in Everyday Life* (Sydney: University of New South Wales Press).

Huscroft, G. (2003), 'Is the Defeat of Health Warnings a Victory for Human Rights? The Attorney-General and Pre-Legislative Scrutiny for Consistency with the New Zealand Bill of Rights', *Public Law Review*, **14**: 109.

Iles, W. (1991), 'New Zealand Experience of Parliamentary Scrutiny of Legislation', *Statute Law Review*, **12** (3): 165.

Kinley, D. (1999), 'Human Rights Scrutiny in Parliament: Westminster Set to Leap Ahead', *Public Law Review*, **10** (4): 252.

Klug, F. (2003), 'Judicial Deference Under the Human Rights Act 1998', *European Human Rights Law Review*, **2**: 125.

Lester, A. (2002), 'Parliamentary Scrutiny of Legislation Under the Human Rights Act 1998', *Victoria University of Wellington Law Review*, **33**: 1.

Lester, A. and Taylor, K. (2004), in Lester, A. and Pannick, D. (eds), *Human Rights Law and Practice*, 2nd edn (London: LexisNexis UK), p. 599.

Mason, K. (1995), 'The Rule of Law', in Finn, P. (ed.), *Essays on Law and Government (Volume 1: Principles and Values)* (Sydney: Law Book Company), p. 114.

McDonald, L. (2004), 'New Directions in the Australian Bill of Rights Debate', *Public Law*: 22.

Morris, C. and Malone, R. (2004), 'Regulations Review in the New Zealand Parliament', *Macquarie Law Journal*, **4**: 7.

Mulgan, G. (2003), 'Government, Knowledge, and the Business of Policy-Making', paper presented to, *Facing the Future Conference*, National Institute for Governance and Australian Public Policy Research Network, Canberra, 23–24 April 2003.

Muylle, K. (2003), 'Improving the Effectiveness of Parliamentary Legislative Procedures', *Statute Law Review*, **24** (3): 169.

New South Wales (NSW), Legislation Review Committee (2004), *Operation, Issues and Future Directions*, Report No 1 (Sydney: Legislation Review Committee).

NSW, Regulation Review Committee of the NSW Parliament (2001), *Scrutiny of National Schemes of Legislation* (Sydney: NSW Parliament), available at<http://www.Parliament.nsw.gov.au/prod/parlment/committee.nsf/0/ f09f5fd653ffe7fcca256cfd002a517b/$FILE/Committee%20Report%2010%20N ovember%202000%20-%20Inquiry%20into%20General%20Matters.pdf>.

NSW, Standing Committee on Law and Justice of the New South Wales Legislative Council (SCLJ) (2001), *A NSW Bill of Rights*, Report No. 17 (Sydney: Standing Committee on Law and Justice of the New South Wales Legislative Council).

Oliver, D. (2004), 'Constitutional Scrutiny of Executive Bills', *Macquarie Law Journal*, **4**: 33.

Queensland, Legal, Constitutional and Administrative Review Committee of the Queensland Legislative Assembly (LCARC) (1998a), *Queenslanders' Basic Rights Handbook* (Brisbane: LCARC), available at <http://www.Parliament.qld.gov.

au/committees/view/committees/ documents/ lcarc/handbook/QBRhandbook-long%20version.pdf>.

—— (1998b), *The Preservation and Enhancement of Individuals' Rights and Freedoms in Queensland: Should Queensland Adopt a Bill of Rights?*, *Report No. 12* (Brisbane: LCARC), available at <http://www.Parliament.qld.gov.au/ view/committees/documents/lcarc/ reports/Bill%20of%20Rights%20report%20-%20Report%20No%2012.pdf>.

Queensland, Scrutiny of Legislation Committee of the Legislative Assembly in Queensland (SLC) (1996a), *Annual Report 1995–1996* (Brisbane: SLC), available at <http://www.Parliament.qld.gov.au/view/committees/ documents/ SLC/reports/95-96AnnRep.PDF>.

—— (1996b), *Scrutiny of Bills for Constitutional Validity*, Report No 26 (Brisbane: SLC).

—— (1998), *The Scrutiny of Bills within a Restrictive Timetable* (Brisbane: SLC), available at <http://www.Parliament.qld.gov.au/view/committees/ documents/ SLC/ reports/slcr07.pdf>.

—— (2000), *Annual Report 1999–2000* (Brisbane: Scrutiny of Legislation Committee of the Queensland Legislative Assembly), available at <http://www. Parliament.qld.gov.au/view/committees/documents/SLC/ reports/slcr017.pdf>.

Ruddock, P. (2004), 'A New Framework: Counter-Terrorism and the Rule of Law', address to the Sydney Institute, Sydney, 20 April 2004.

Ryan, K. (2000), 'Crises in Parliamentary Government', Occasional Lecture for the Queensland Supreme Court History Society, Brisbane.

Sampford, C. (1994), 'Fundamental Legislative Principles: Their Meaning and Rationale' *Queensland Law Society Journal*, **24**:531.

Spigelman, J. (2001a), 'Economic Rationalism and the Law' *University of New South Wales Law Journal*, **24**: 19.

—— (2001b), 'Quality in an Age of Measurement: The Limitations of Performance Indicators', paper presented to the Sydney Leadership Alumni Lecture, the Benevolent Society, Sydney, 28 November 2001.

—— (2002), 'Are Lawyers Lemons?: Competition Principles and Professional Regulation', Lecture for the St James Ethics Centre, Sydney, 29 October 2002.

Sunstein, C., and Vermeule, A. (2002), 'Interpretation and Institutions', University of Chicago Public Law Research Paper No 28, available at < http://www.law. uchicago. edu/academics/publiclaw/index.html>.

Taggart, M. (1998), 'Tugging on Superman's Cape: Lessons from Experience with the New Zealand Bill of Rights Act 1990', *Public Law*: 266.

Uhr, J. (1997), 'Keeping Government Honest: Preconditions for Parliamentary Effectiveness', in Commonwealth, Department of the Senate, *Parliaments in Evolution: Constitutional Reform in the 1990s: Papers on Parliament No. 29* (Canberra: Department of the Senate), p. 51.

—— (1998), *Deliberative Democracy in Australia: The Changing Place of Parliament* (Cambridge: Cambridge University Press).

UK Joint Committee on Human Rights (2001), *First Report: Criminal Justice and Police Bill* (London: UK Parliament), available at <http://www.publications. Parliament.uk/pa/jt200001/jtselect/jtrights/69/ 6907.htm>.

—— (2004), *The Meaning of Public Authority under the Human Rights Act: Seventh Report of Session 2003–04* (London: UK Parliament), available at <http://www. publications.Parliament.uk/pa/jt200304/jtselect/jtrights/39/ 39.pdf>.

UK, Privy Counsellor Review Committee (2003), *Anti-Terrorism, Crime and Security Act 2001 Review: Report* (London: UK Parliament).

Victoria, Department of Justice (2004), *Attorney-General's Justice Statement: New Directions for the Victorian Justice System 2004-2014* (Melbourne: Department of Justice).

Webber, J. (2003), 'Institutional Dialogue between Courts and Legislatures in the Definition of Fundamental Rights: Lessons from Canada and (Elsewhere)', *Australian Journal of Human Rights*, **9** (1): 135.

Williams, G. (1999), *Human Rights Under the Australian Constitution*, Melbourne: Oxford University Press

Williams, G. (2000), *A Bill of Rights for Australia*, Frontlines Series (Sydney: University of New South Wales Press).

—— (2003), 'Constructing a Community-Based Bill of Rights', in Campbell, T., Goldsworthy, J., and Stone, A. (eds), *Protecting Human Rights: Instruments and Institutions* (Oxford: Oxford University Press), p. 247.

—— (2004), *The Case for an Australian Bill of Rights: Freedom in the War on Terror*, Briefings Series (Sydney: University of New South Wales Press).

Chapter 4

The Performance of Administrative Law in Protecting Rights

Robin Creyke

There is a strong administrative review system in Australia to 'partially compensate for the absence of a Bill of Rights. (Liverani, 2001, p. 67)

So we say in the context where we have a system which is one of the best in the world and where we do not have any fundamental rights protections, the onus is on the government seeking to introduce change to prove that the situation will be improved.[1]

... the new system has contributed to a greater measure of administrative justice in its insistence on compliance with the rules of natural justice, its careful scrutiny of the reasons for decision, its emphasis on the justice of the case and its success in making the principles and procedures of review more uniform. These are the enduring benefits of independent review. No other system has been suggested that could provide them in the same measure. (Mason, 1994, p.133)

... we have inherited and were intended by our Constitution to live under a system of law and government which has traditionally protected the rights of persons by ensuring that those rights are determined by a judiciary independent of the parliament and the executive. But the rights referred to in such an enunciation are the basic rights which traditionally, and therefore historically, are judged by that independent judiciary which is the bulwark of freedom.[2]

There is already in place in Australia a complex of law, institutions and traditions operating to protect fundamental rights and freedoms. (Commonwealth, Senate Standing Committee on Constitutional and Legal Affairs, 1985, [2.1])

If these statements – by a legal practitioner, a senior politician, two High Court judges and a Senate Committee – were the report card on administrative law and its performance in protecting rights there would appear to be cause for congratulation, not alarm. However, the assessment needs to be tested more thoroughly.

There are a number of questions which need to be addressed. What do we mean by 'administrative law'? What 'rights' does administrative law protect? Are these the

---

1 Commonwealth, *Parliamentary Debates*, House of Representatives, 6 December 2000, 23496 (Robert McLelland, Shadow Attorney-General).

2 *R v Quinn; Ex parte Consolidated Foods Corporation* (1977) 138 CLR 1, 11 (Jacobs J).

rights which bill of rights proponents argue are unprotected in Australian law? And is administrative law a successful substitute for other forms of rights protection?

Administrative Law

It is common when describing administrative law to refer not just to the doctrines or standards imposed on the executive by courts, tribunals and other bodies, but to the plethora of institutions themselves. This approach reflects the array of administrative law bodies in Australia, each offering its own model of how the citizen can complain about government action. In total they constitute a comprehensive package of remedial options. The ability to make a complaint is, however, only one of the major purposes of administrative law. The other – to inculcate standards of lawfulness, fairness, rationality and accountability across public administration for the betterment of all those who deal with government – is equally important. (ARC, 1995, [2.10]) As the Administrative Review Council has pointed out: 'In an incremental fashion, review can also produce more fundamental effects, such as higher quality decision making, an altered commitment to reasoned decision making, improved program development, and administrative and legislative reform. (ARC, 1994, [2.41]) As the description earlier indicates, the administrative law package is multi-faceted. It comprises courts hearing appeals against tribunal decisions and testing whether administrative action complies with the law – their judicial review role.[3] There are tribunals providing review of the substantive merits of decisions, and investigative bodies such as the parliamentary ombudsman offices, privacy and other commissioners. Less formal channels include a complaint to the agency itself. Other investigative bodies – criminal justice and misconduct commissions – deal with crime and misconduct by government and, outside Australia, the United Nation Human Rights Committee may make recommendations to overturn or vary decisions by Australian public administration, or domestic laws or practices.

There is also a framework for seeking compensation for defective administration or wrongful government action. These include various forms of ex gratia payments, and court action to seek tortious or contractual remedies against government. Increasingly, too, the range of regulatory bodies controlling utilities and other essential services are being required to abide by administrative law standards.

Superimposed on these structures are certain rights, such as the right to obtain the reasons for an administrative decision, to access information held by government (subject to limited exemptions), and for the protection of personal information held by government. Administrative law, when described in these terms, is reminiscent of an Hieronymus Bosch painting in its richness and complexity. This chapter does not

---

3   The superior courts of each Australian jurisdiction have jurisdiction to exercise judicial review. The right for State and Territory Supreme Courts is an inherent power of these courts under common law principles but in the case of other courts (particularly the Federal Court and the High Court) is provided for by statute.

attempt to consider every facet of this intricate picture but is confined to the central domestic mechanisms for complaint or review.

The account would not be complete, however, without pointing out two key features of public law and public administration of significance for the protection of rights. The first is the principle of legality which requires that all action by the executive government must find authority in either legislation or executive power. The second is that decisions are made by officials, and there is a culture within public administration which impacts on the process.

The first of these features – the legality principle – is of growing importance. There is a rights-protecting aspect of the principle, namely, it ensures that government action must not be arbitrary or unlawful. At the same time, the courts, led by the High Court (Kirk, 2003), are paying increasing attention to the legislative framework in which decision making is conducted. This deference to the statutory context may mean that there are statutory limits on exploring rights options which foreclose any attempts under administrative law principles to expand rights protection.

The second feature is also capable of enhancing rights protection. Notions of public trust and accountability, which permeate the public sector, mean that decision-makers are expected to conform to standards of behaviour and probity in excess of those expected of the private sector. As Forsyth and Wade (2000, p. 357) note in their classic English text:

> The powers of public authorities are ... essentially different from those of private persons. A man making a will may, subject to any rights of his dependants, dispose of his property just as he may wish. He may act out of malice or a spirit of revenge, but in law this does not affect his exercise of his power. In the same way a private person has an absolute power to allow whom he likes to use his land, to release a debtor, or, where the law permits, to evict a tenant, regardless of his motives. This is unfettered discretion. But a public authority may do none of these things unless it acts reasonably and in good faith and upon lawful and relevant grounds of public interest. ... [U]nfettered discretion is inappropriate to a public authority, which possesses powers solely in order that it may use them for the public good.

This description of the range of remedial options offered by administrative law is not meant to suggest that the system is free of fault.[4] But as the ensuing discussion will indicate, there are firm grounds for asserting that the aggregation of options is effective in protecting the rights of the public.[5] To quote Sir Anthony Mason

---

4   For example, Commonwealth, Senate Standing Committee on Constitutional and Legal Affairs, 1985, pp. 15–23.

5   The effectiveness of the Australian system is supported by its being copied internationally, for example in South Africa (see, *Constitution of the Republic of South Africa 1996* (Act No. 108 of 1996) ss 32–34, 38, 181–84, 187 ('*South African Constitution*'); *Promotion of Administrative Justice Act 2000* (RSA)) and more recently, in the area of administrative tribunals, in the United Kingdom (see Leggatt's (2001), *Tribunals for Users One System One Service: Report of the Review of Tribunals*, a report which has been substantially adopted: see Great Britain, Lord Chancellor's Department, 2003. A UK Government White Paper

(1989, p. 133) again: 'No other system has been suggested that could provide [an administrative law framework of remedies] in the same measure.'

Rights

Rights Protected by Administrative Law

What are the 'rights' protected by administrative law? Rights for this purpose has a broad meaning. That is consistent with administrative law jurisprudence, which extends to matters beyond legal rights as such. For example, the right to natural justice – to put one's case – applies whenever government proposes to make a decision adverse to a person's interests. These interests which attract natural justice arise when a decision by government could adversely affect 'personal liberty, status, preservation of livelihood and reputation, ... proprietary rights and interests' and even a legitimate expectation – a legal interest of a lesser nature.[6] In other words, administrative law is capable of applying to mere interests of an individual rather than to rights per se. These interests include the opportunity for renewal of a licence, the option to tender for a government contract, as well as more substantive liberty, personal integrity, or reputational interests.

This is not to say that administrative law does not protect rights in the more conventional sense. Administrative law actions commonly relate to rights such as the right to the quiet enjoyment of property, to access the courts and not to incriminate oneself in a public inquiry. Even more frequently, complaints handled by the administrative law system relate to rights established by statute – to pensions, licences, income support, loans and other schemes for financial or commercial betterment. In addition, there are process rights – the right to a hearing by an unbiased decision-maker in accordance with evidence of sufficient probative value and a right to the reasons for a decision. These are all matters of considerable importance for people in their dealings with government.

The principal right protected by administrative law is the right to complain against government. That right has become increasingly important as government has become the main source of the rights and privileges which enable an individual to pursue a satisfying and productive life. Housing, education, health and welfare are a sufficient illustration, although government activities extend much further. Government also provides business and occupational licences, access to infrastructure such as roads, electricity and hospitals, and services which support individual enterprise. In other words, through funding or regulation, government has the final say on the provision to its citizens of fundamental financial, educational, health and infrastructure support.

---

has confirmed the commitment to the proposed amalgamation of tribunals: Great Britain, Department of Constitutional Affairs, 2004, ch. 6.

   6   *Kioa* v *West* (1985) 159 CLR 550, 582 (Mason J). The continued viability of the notion of legitimate expectation is currently under some threat as the High Court evaluates its utility: *Re Minister for Immigration and Multicultural Affairs; Ex parte Lam* (2003) 214 CLR 1.

Hence, if government neglects these tasks or falls into error when allocating these benefits or providing essential infrastructure, the consequences for individuals can be profound.

As Lord Scarman (1974, p. 75) described it in the 1974 Hamlyn Lecture, administrative law protections extend across 'the newly developed fields of administrative–legal activity upon which the quality of life in the society of the twentieth century already depends'. To be able to complain about these matters is critical. The signal contribution of those who have developed administrative law has been to establish institutions, to develop standards and to provide rights of redress against the loss or denial of such benefits – in other words, to provide administrative justice (Whitmore, 1989, p.117).

However, it is not only tangible or material interests which people are seeking to vindicate through administrative law. The various parliamentary ombudsman offices throughout Australia together handle over 60,000 complaints a year, making them the major avenue for redress against government (Commonwealth, Ombudsman, 2001, and Commonwealth, Parliamentary Commissioners, 2001). When the nature of those complaints is examined, although substantive matters are involved in roughly half these claims, often this is not the principal concern. As the 1991 Senate Standing Committee report on the Commonwealth Ombudsman pointed out:

- complaints predominantly are about delays, errors and misunderstandings;
- financial implications, where they exist, are typically small;
- relatively few of these complaints point to possibilities for systemic reform and the reforms that are indicated are typically minor (Commonwealth, Senate Standing Committee on Finance and Public Administration, 1991, [5.8]).

Moreover, given the broad remit or jurisdiction of the ombudsman, namely, to examine administrative action to see whether it is unlawful, unreasonable, unjust, oppressive or improperly discriminatory, or is wrong either legally or factually,[7] it is not the absence of authority to decide broader substantive matters which is the explanation for these findings.

The experience of the Human Rights and Equal Opportunity Commission also provides some measure of support for these views. A significant proportion of the remedies which are provided by that body amount to no more than an apology or the provision of a reference.[8] In review by tribunals, it is common for an explanation of the statutory basis for a decision to be sufficient for the applicant to leave the hearing satisfied that the decision against them was fair.

---

7   For example, *Ombudsman Act 1976* (Cth) s. 15. Other Australian Acts defining the role of the ombudsman or parliamentary commissioners have comparable provisions.

8   See annual reports of the various human rights and anti-discrimination bodies in Australia.

These findings that it is not necessarily a changed outcome which people are seeking when they complain about government are backed up by studies of psycho-legal researchers which have shown

> ... that it is *procedural justice* (the perception that the procedure is fair), rather than *distributive justice* (the perception that the outcome is fair), that is the most important factor in shaping disputants' overall perceptions of fairness, and in determining disputants' satisfaction with legal dispute resolution procedures, including mediation. (Howieson, 2002, p. 24. See also, Lind and Tyler, 1988, p. 3, cited in Fonacaro, 1995)

Are These the Rights which Should Be Protected?

The foregoing examples, many from the busier complaint-handling institutions, suggest that an emphasis on 'human rights'[9] in discussions on rights protection may be misplaced. It is not the right to liberty, to freedom of movement, to freedom of expression, electoral rights, to a fair trial, to equal treatment,[10] nor even the more fundamental social and economic rights – to food, to housing, to education and to basic health care – which occupies the minds of most Australians. That is not to say that these issues are not important, or that there is no poverty disadvantage, nor areas of Australians' lives which would not be improved by increased government assistance or regulation. It is to say that the emphasis on these rights has skewed the debate from the actual interests of Australian citizens in their dealings with government (Allan 2003, p. 176) and, against a democratic and social regime which already protects the civil, political and economic rights of its citizens, the focus of the administrative law system is generally not on these rights.

If this is too limited a description of rights for the purposes of this debate, the riposte is that there is a close relationship between administrative law and protection of rights in the more vernacular 'bill of rights' sense. That argument is promoted by those who suggest that rights conventions and charters are principally concerned with procedural justice, and it is procedural justice which is, in practice, protected by administrative law (Gearty, 1993).

In a close analysis of the *European Convention for the Protection of Human Rights and Fundamental Freedoms* and its exegesis by the European Court of Human Rights, Gearty concluded that although the primary concern of 'human rights' in its broader context is 'the full development of each individual being' (ibid, p. 93), this role 'has been inspirational and diplomatic rather than justiciable' (ibid, p. 94). In his view, 'the vast majority of the Convention's articles do not evoke substantive values' (ibid, p. 96) such as freedom from torture and slavery, or the right to marry or to privacy. Rather, he maintains, it is the notion of due process which is of central

---

9   It is often unclear what rights are intended to be covered by this expression.

10   See the civil and political rights listed in the *International Covenant on Civil and Political Rights* (opened for signature 19 December 1966), 999 UNTS 171, arts 2, 24 and 26 (entered into force 23 March 1976).

importance to the Convention and the jurisprudence of the European Court (ibid, p. 98).

Gearty's perceptions are based on three facets of 'due process'. First, due process is associated with judicial hearings; second, due process focuses on the 'protection of minorities and the political process itself' (ibid, p. 126). Both of these elements of due process are clearly a focus of administrative law. A classic illustration is that protection of natural justice interests has long been a central feature of its common law jurisprudence. In addition, equality rights are found in the common law's 'bill of rights'[11] and, more recently, in rights protection and anti-discrimination legislation. The third element, according to Gearty, is that the due process elements of charters or bills of rights provide 'limits to the activism of the Court' (Gearty, 1993, p. 126). Those limits are facilitated by judicial review standards which embody due process concepts. In other words, administrative law standards can curtail judicial creativity and provide a coherent theory to contain judicial activism.

The failure to establish such standards is, according to Gearty, 'to surrender intellectual interest in the vast area of judicial discretion that exists within the Convention' or similar rights-focused charters, conventions, or legislation (ibid, p. 96). To apply such standards is to avoid the dangers in the exercise of power which is unleashed by use of indeterminate notions such as proportionality, or the margin of appreciation as the sole benchmarks against which to measure whether rights infringement has occurred.[12] Administrative law clearly has a role to play in this task.

Performance in the Past

Administrative law has not always fulfilled these roles. Prior to the 1970s in Australia, there was little or no merits review to obtain a substantive change to a decision, there was no anti-discrimination or human rights body focused specifically on protection of equality interests or on civil or political, much less economic or social, rights. Crown privilege was exercised vigorously by government to deny access to information held by government including reasons for decisions, and court-based

---

11 The expression was coined by John Willis (1938, p. 17); see also Pearce and Geddes, 2001, p. 131.

12 Gearty, 1993, p. 97. Note that Gummow J firmly rejected the notion of proportionality as a benchmark which should be adopted in administrative law (*Minister for Resources* v *Dover Fisheries* (1993) 43 FCR 565, [46]–[47] (Gummow J); cf. Cooper J at [1]; Hill J not deciding at [4]). As Dawson J pointed out in *Cunliffe* v *Commonwealth* (1994) 182 CLR 272, although the proportionality test is useful in relation to purposive powers to make delegated legislation as in *SA* v *Tanner* (1988) 166 CLR 161, it does not provide a general ground of invalidity of administrative decisions. As Allars (1997, p. 485) comments: 'To accept that this is a general principle of administrative law would be to allow the courts in judicial review to trespass into the merits of administrative decisions'. Cf. *Behrooz* v *Secretary of the Department of Immigration and Multicultural Affairs* (2004) 208 ALR 271 (Kirby J dissenting). See also McMillan, 1999.

review was substantially limited to bodies exercising judicial power. In short, the system failed signally to provide protection for the interests of the citizens to pursue their legitimate claims against government.

Sir Anthony Mason (1998, p. 122), in a retrospective examination of the Kerr Committee report, the seminal report in the early 1970s which recommended the key elements of the current Commonwealth administrative law package, observed:

> Australian administrative lawyers have spoken in glowing terms about our federal system of administrative law. Certainly it is a vast improvement on what went before – technicalities associated with the prerogative writs, the arbitrary classification of functions according to a notion of separation of powers, and the struggle for judicial review in a world in which the administrator was entitled to give no reasons for a decision.

What went before, in terms of remedies, was described by the Queensland Electoral and Administrative Review Commission in its report in 1990, *Report on Judicial Review of Administrative Decisions and Actions*, in these terms: the common law remedies 'have become encrusted with technicalities and fine distinctions which have been dictated more by the course of their historical development than by logic' ([3.1]). The consequences, as the report noted,

> … are that even many practising lawyers are uncertain whether there is a remedy available for a person aggrieved by a government decision, the taking of proceedings is much more expensive than it ought to be, and it is fraught with the peril of shipwreck on the reefs of technicality. The scales are weighted against those who seek review. (ibid [3.2])

Another snapshot of the pre-Kerr Committee reform position was provided by former Justice Davies, then President of the Administrative Appeals Tribunal, when he commented:

> In Australia, as elsewhere, the common law did not expand to provide procedures and remedies suitable for the efficient control of administrative action. Why it did not develop in this area as in so many other spheres it did to meet changing needs is not clear. … But, whatever, the cause, the common law has been deficient. (Davies, 1981)

The Kerr Committee, in a masterly exposé in 1971 of the reasons for reform of administrative law, said:

> It is generally accepted that [the existing] complex pattern of rules as to appropriate courts, principles and remedies is both unwieldy and unnecessary. The pattern is not fully understood by most lawyers; the layman tends to find the technicalities not merely incomprehensible but quite absurd. A case can be lost or won on the basis of choice of remedy and the non-lawyer can never appreciate why this should be so. The basic fault of the entire structure is, however, that review cannot as a general rule, in the absence of special statutory provisions, be obtained 'on the merits' – and this is usually what the aggrieved citizen is seeking. (Commonwealth, Commonwealth Administrative Review Committee, 1971 [58])

The position outlined in these quotations changed for the Commonwealth in the 1970s and 1980s with the introduction of a package of measures designed to rectify the situation. The judicial review jurisdiction of the courts was expanded and codified by a statutory process for the exercise of review by the courts – the *Administrative Decisions (Judicial Review) Act 1977* (Cth).[13] Substantive protection of rights – the merit review function – was provided by an enhanced system of tribunals capped by the Commonwealth's Administrative Appeals Tribunal.[14] The Office of Ombudsman was established to conduct investigations of a range of complaints against government, including, but not confined to, administrative decisions.[15] In addition, statutory rights to access information held by government were provided through a right to obtain reasons for decisions,[16] and subsequently, to access information held by government through the *Freedom of Information Act 1982* (Cth).[17].

To cap off these developments, the Commonwealth's *Human Rights Commission Act 1981* (Cth) (as amended in 1986) made a significant contribution to the protection of individual rights. The Human Rights and Equal Opportunity Commission was to provide remedies for breaches of equality rights, and of civil and political rights including rights to life, to liberty and to security of person, to the protection of the courts, to freedom of movement and association, and to privacy.[18] More recently,

---

13 Forms of judicial review statutes now apply in Victoria (*Administrative Law Act 1978* (Vic)), the ACT (*Administrative Decisions (Judicial Review) Act 1989* (ACT)), Queensland (*Judicial Review Act 1991* (Qld)), Tasmania (*Judicial Review Act 2000* (Tas)), and a judicial review bill is being drafted in Western Australia.

14 Tribunals with wide rather than specialist, sole purpose jurisdiction, now exist in the ACT (*Administrative Appeals Tribunal Act 1989* (ACT)), NSW (*Administrative Decisions Tribunal Act 1997* (NSW)), Victoria (*Victorian Civil and Administrative Tribunal Act 1998* (Vic)), South Australia (*District Court Act 1991* (SA)), Tasmania (*Magistrates Court (Administrative Appeals Division) Act 2001* (Tas)), and a Bill for a State Administrative Tribunal has been introduced in Western Australia, and a similar body is being discussed in Tasmania.

15 Each Australian jurisdiction has passed laws establishing an ombudsman (known in Queensland and Western Australia as a parliamentary commissioner).

16 These are now widely available under statute, the move commencing with the *Administrative Appeals Tribunal Act 1975* (Cth) s. 28 and the *Administrative Decisions (Judicial Review) Act 1977* (Cth) s. 13.

17 Freedom of information legislation now exists in each Australian jurisdiction.

18 The *Human Rights Commission Act 1981* (Cth) had scheduled to it the *ICCPR*, the *Declaration on the Rights of the Child* GA Res 1386(XIV), 14 UN GAOR Supp (No 16) at 19, UN Doc A/4354 (1959) ('*Declaration on the Rights of the Child*'); the *Declaration on the Rights of Mentally Retarded Persons* GA Res 2856 (XXVI), 26 UN GAOR Supp (No 29) at 93, UN Doc A/8429 (1971), and the *Declaration on the Rights of Disabled Persons* GA Res 3447 (XXX), 30 UN GAOR Supp (No 34) at 88, UN Doc A/10034 (1975). The Act was upgraded and strengthened with the passage of the *Human Rights and Equal Opportunity Commission Act 1986* (Cth), the legislation currently in force. Equality rights in the Commonwealth have been facilitated by the passage of the *Racial Discrimination Act 1975* (Cth), the *Sex Discrimination Act 1984* (Cth), and the *Disability Discrimination Act 1992* (Cth) (incorporating provision

privacy legislation has been enacted to provide standards for the acquisition, storage, amendment and use of personal information held by government.[19]

These moves have clearly provided Australians with an array of measures through which to implement rights-protection. Nor has the Commonwealth been alone in these developments. Progressively, the States and Territories have enacted laws mirroring or adapting and extending the rights protected by the Commonwealth package.[20]

The question which arises is whether this system is sufficiently effective to be a response to those who argue that without a charter or bill of rights, Australian citizens are insufficiently protected? In other words, is the existing domestic system provided by administrative and other law adequate, or does the protection of rights need supplementation from a dedicated human rights instrument?

Current Performance

A preliminary but critical issue is how does one assess the adequacy of rights-protection in the current administrative law system? One set of measures to gauge the effectiveness of rights protection was suggested in a report in 1985 by the Senate Standing Committee on Constitutional and Legal Affairs on whether Australia needed a bill of rights. As the report noted:

---

for the Aboriginal and Torres Strait Islander Commissioner). There are State and Territory equivalent laws, each providing for core protections but exhibiting variations in the specific areas in which discrimination is prohibited.

19 *Privacy Act 1988* (Cth), as amended by the *Privacy Amendment (Private Sector) Act 2000* (Cth).

20 Every Australian jurisdiction has an ombudsman or parliamentary commissioner, an equal opportunity or anti-discrimination board or tribunal, and a freedom of information Act. NSW and Victoria have introduced their own forms of privacy protection legislation. However, since the *Privacy Act 1988* (Cth) applies nationally both to government agencies and to businesses in the private sector with a turnover in excess of $3 million, there is reasonably extensive privacy protection for Australians. ACT: has a modern administrative review regime mirroring that of the Commonwealth introduced on self-government in 1989; NSW: has not codified the NSW Supreme Court's judicial review jurisdiction, but has an embryonic multi-purpose tribunal, the Administrative Decisions Tribunal; Northern Territory: retains the common law, more complex, judicial review processes, has a mixture of specialist tribunals, but not a general jurisdiction body; Queensland: has a modernized judicial review jurisdiction, but no general jurisdiction tribunal; South Australia: retains the common law judicial review processes, and has an amalgamated tribunals body as a division of its District Court; Tasmania: has a modern judicial review Act and is in the process of developing an amalgamated tribunals body; Victoria: has a partially modernized judicial review jurisdiction, and a large super-tribunal – the Victorian Civil and Administrative Tribunal; Western Australia: retains the common law judicial review processes, but is in the process of setting up an amalgamated civil and administrative tribunal – the State Administrative Tribunal.

There are some distinct formal elements in our constitutional and political arrangements which relate to human rights such as:

- Constitutionally entrenched protections
- The courts and the common law
- The Human Rights Commission
- The Parliaments. (Commonwealth, Senate Standing Committee on Constitutional and Legal Affairs, 1985, [2.3])

It is not the function of a chapter on administrative law remedies to discuss how parliaments protect rights. Parliaments excepted, however, these constitutional and institutional mechanisms will be used to evaluate the effectiveness in rights-protection terms of the present administrative law package.

Notably absent from the list is any reference to the tribunal system and the Ombudsman, well established in most Australian jurisdictions by this time. Since these institutions have been seen as the sinews of administrative law rights-protection, this failure is surprising. No criticism can be made at that time of the absence of references to privacy and freedom of information legislation, internal review, codes of conduct, crime and misconduct commissions and other innovations since these were either yet to be introduced, or to make an impact.

Constitutional Protections

Reference to an issue in a constitution is always a clear signal of its importance. That signal is particularly bright in Australia given that Australia has a constitution that is difficult to change.[21] It is, therefore, significant to find the recognition of administrative law[22] in s. 75 of the *Constitution*.[23] That provision guarantees, as Zines noted, that 'there is an entrenched jurisdiction in which the Commonwealth and its officers can be made accountable for the observance of the law'. In effect s. 75 means that there is a right to access remedies to challenge actions by officials in proceedings in the High Court (Zines, 2000, p. 268), a jurisdiction that has emerged as a potent source of administrative law protection.

That potency was strikingly illustrated in *Plaintiff S157/2002* v *Commonwealth*[24] in which the High Court emasculated a comprehensively expressed privative (or ouster) clause in s. 474 of the *Migration Act 1958* (Cth) which had been designed to insulate certain migration decisions from most forms of judicial review. Had that provision been effective it would have substantially impaired access to the

---

21 *Australian Constitution* s. 128.

22 The only broadly equivalent protection to an administrative law remedy in Australia is found in the *Victorian Constitution* (*Constitution Act 1975* (Vic) s. 85(5), (6)).

23 It is not appropriate for this paper to consider the effectiveness of other constitutional protections of rights, such as the acquisition of property on just terms (s. 51(xxxi)), trial by jury (s. 80), freedom of religion (s. 116), which do not impinge directly on administrative law.

24 (2003) 211 CLR 476 ('*Plaintiff S157/2002*').

Australian court system by people within the migration system, including those claiming refugee status.

The ouster clause proved ineffective against s. 75(v).[25] In *Plaintiff S157* the High Court found, in Gleeson CJ's words, that '[t]he jurisdiction of the Court to require officers of the Commonwealth to act within the law cannot be taken away by Parliament'. Section 75(v), as His Honour expressed it, 'secures a basic element of the rule of law'.[26] In so saying, the High Court was also upholding the principle of legality which, as the introduction to this chapter indicates, ensures government cannot take away rights by unlawful or arbitrary government action.

The specific outcome in *Plaintiff S157/2002* was that the privative clause was ineffective to oust the High Court's jurisdiction for decision-making errors described as 'jurisdictional'. What is encompassed by jurisdictional error requires further elucidation by the Court, but the concept clearly includes a denial of procedural fairness or natural justice, the issue in *Plaintiff S157/2002*. More recent cases have concluded that a jurisdictional error is any significant error of law or process which is capable of impacting on a person's rights, interests or legitimate expectations.[27] In other words, a person can seek review by the High Court of any error by a decision-maker which materially affects decision making by the executive arm of government to the disadvantage of a person. This guarantee of fair process at the highest judicial level[28] is probably matched in only one other common law jurisdiction, namely, South Africa.[29]

The value of this right of access has not been lost, particularly on those in the migration jurisdiction. The clear evidence is the increase in the numbers of applications to the High Court. In 1999–2000 only 137 matters were filed in the original jurisdiction (which includes s. 75(v)), of which 65 cases (47 per cent) involved migration applications (Commonwealth, ALRC, 2001, [3.1]). By 2002–2003, there were 2,105 applications to the High Court in migration matters comprising some 99

---

25 The *Australian Constitution* s. 75(v) provides: 'In all matters – ... (v) in which a writ of Mandamus or prohibition or an injunction is sought against an officer of the Commonwealth ... the High Court shall have original jurisdiction.'

26 *Plaintiff S157/2002* v *Commonwealth* (2003) 211 CLR 476, 482. Chief Justice Gleeson's views were in accord with those of the majority judgment of Gaudron, McHugh, Gummow, Kirby and Hayne JJ.

27 *Minister for Immigration and Multicultural Affairs* v *SGLB* (2004) 207 ALR 12 , [48]–[57] (Gummow and Hayne JJ), Gleeson CJ agreed with their reasoning; Callinan J gave a separate concurring judgment; Kirby J dissented; *Re Minister for Immigration and Multicultural Affairs; Ex parte Lam* (2003) 214 CLR 1, 25 [77] (McHugh and Gummow JJ). See also *SDAV* v *Minister for Immigration & Multicultural & Indigenous Affairs; Minister for Immigration & Multicultural & Indigenous Affairs* v *SBBK* (2003) 199 ALR 43, 49–50 [27].

28 The right to judicial review is not constitutionally entrenched in the States or Territories, but protection of administrative law rights is provided by other means.

29 The constitutional right to administrative justice in the *South African Constitution* may give rise to a similar entrée but the ambit of this right is even more embryonic than the rights protected in Australia under s. 75(v): Lyster, 1999, p. 376.

per cent of the High Court's original jurisdiction and 82 per cent of all the matters filed with the Court (Commonwealth, HCA, 2003, p. 7). This constitutionally guaranteed avenue to challenge egregious error by government at the highest level of the country's court system is clear evidence of an effective administrative law system. Moreover, the usage figures show that the opportunity is being availed of by a minority group in Australia who generally have a lesser claim than citizens to enjoy access to the courts.

Common Law Protections

The second gauge of the efficacy of rights-protection by administrative law is found in those judicially developed standards which focus on individual rights and interests. Over the centuries the courts in common law jurisdictions, including Australia, have been creative in devising principles which operate to protect rights. These include, for example, use of international law standards to inform or to supplement domestic laws. An example is that rules of international law so notorious as to be part of the custom of nations (such as the prohibition of slavery, torture and genocide) are regarded as binding on all nations.[30] International law is also a legitimate and important influence on the development of the common law, especially when international law declares the existence of universal human rights.[31] Finally, in case of ambiguity in a legislative instrument, it has been accepted that courts should favour a construction of a statute which accords with the obligations of Australia under an international treaty.[32] These features of Australian public law open the door to use of international human rights norms in appropriate cases, particularly when they fill gaps in domestic rights protection.

The second major initiative by courts is the development of the so-called 'common law bill of rights'[33] or presumptions of interpretation. The value of these presumptions should not be underestimated. The list is capable of expansion but would commonly include: that legislation does not operate retrospectively; that penal provisions are strictly construed; that legislation does not lightly take away jurisdiction from the courts; that laws should be construed strictly in favour of the taxpayer; that property rights are not to be taken away without compensation; that parliament intends to legislate in conformity with international law; and that

---

30 *Koowarta* v *Bjelke-Petersen* (1982) 153 CLR 168, 234 [35] (Stephen J); *Applicant A* v *Minister for Immigration and Multicultural and Indigenous Affairs* (1997) 190 CLR 225, 272–75; *Minister for Immigration and Multicultural and Indigenous Affairs* v *Ibrahim* (2000) 175 ALR 535 [137] (Gummow J).

31 *Dietrich* v *R* (1992) 177 CLR 292, 321, 360; *Jago* v *District Court of NSW* (1988) 12 NSWLR 558, 569; *Chen* v *Minister for Immigration and Ethnic Affairs* (1994) 123 ALR 126; *Mabo* v *Queensland (No 2)* (1992) 175 CLR 1, 42 (Brennan J) (with whom Mason CJ, and McHugh J concurred); *Re Kavanagh's Application* (2003) 204 ALR 1, [11]–[13] (Kirby J).

32 *Lim* v *Minister for Immigration Local Government and Ethnic Affairs* (1992) 176 CLR 1, 38; *Re Kavanagh's Application* (2003) 204 ALR 1, [13] (Kirby J).

33 See above n 11.

parliament does not interfere with fundamental rights (Pearce and Geddes, 2001, ch. 5; Cook, et. al., 2001, [9.42]).

There are three reasons why these presumptions are valuable to administrative law. In the first place, administrative law is predominantly legislative in origin and these presumptions influence those who work with and interpret legislation. The second is the strong adherence of the courts to these presumptions.[34] No better evidence of the courts' use of the presumptions to protect rights could be provided than the decisions in the following cases.

Reference has already been made to the strongly promoted presumption against removal of the jurisdiction of the courts in *Plaintiff S157/2002*. Another notable example arose in *Coco* v *R*[35] in which the Court provided a sharp reminder of the weight attached to the presumption against removal of fundamental rights, in that case the right to protection of private property.[36] A third case, *Esber* v *Commonwealth*,[37] involved the presumption that legislation does not apply retrospectively. The decision was relied on to permit members of the armed forces to access the most advantageous legal regime for determining their entitlement to a disability pension on the basis that legislation should be interpreted as not interfering with accrued rights.[38]

Others have written at length about the impact in specific cases of these common law rights and their work is a valuable reflection on the operation of these principles in administrative law (Bayne, 1990, p. 203; McMillan and Williams, 1998, p. 63). Their writings and the cases they rely on cogently illustrate the observation that

> ... it is clear that the fundamental principles of our administrative law have their roots in the common law and that the jurisdiction by way of judicial review of administrative action is a jurisdiction that has been developed by the courts in accordance with the common law tradition. (Mason, 1994, p. 5).

An essential element of that common law tradition, as the High Court noted in *Plaintiff S157/2002,* is that 'courts do not impute to the legislature an intention to abrogate or curtail fundamental rights or freedoms unless such an intention is clearly manifested by unmistakable and unambiguous language'.[39]

---

34 *Attorney-General (Qld)* v *Australian Industrial Relations Commission* (2002) 192 ALR 129 [108], (Kirby J).

35 (1994) 179 CLR 427 ('*Coco*').

36 See also for cases on the presumption against removal of common law rights: *The Commissioner of Police* v *Tanos* (1958) 98 CLR 383, 395–96; *Malvaso* v *The Queen* (1989) 168 CLR 227, 233; *Durham Holdings Pty Ltd* v *New South Wales* (2001) 205 CLR 399, 414 [28]; cf. *Ackroyd* v *Whitehouse (Director of National Parks & Wildlife Service)* (1985) 2 NSWLR 239, 246–47; *Booker* v *SRA of NSW [No 2]* (1993) 31 NSWLR 402, 410.

37 (1992) 174 CLR 430 ('*Esber*'). The principle was *obiter* in that case but has been upheld in *Attorney-General (Qld)* v *Australian Industrial Relations Commission* (2002) 192 ALR 129, see [108] (Kirby J, who was agreeing with the majority). See also *Fisher* v *Hebburn* (1960) 105 CLR 188; *Rodway* v *R* (1990) 169 CLR 515.

38 *Repatriation Commission* v *Gorton* (2001) 65 ALD 609.

39 *Plaintiff S157/2002* (2003) 211 CLR 476, 492 [3] (Gleeson C.J).

The third reason for the importance of these common law presumptions of interpretation is that they relate to rights or interests which are of central importance to considerable numbers of Australians. This was recognized in *FAI Insurances Ltd* v *Winneke*,[40] a case concerning a company's licence to conduct workers' compensation insurance. A major consideration in the case was the finding that a statutory power will not ordinarily be interpreted to exclude consideration of the interests of individuals, in that case, not only the insurer but also policy holders and creditors. The presumption that a taxing law should be interpreted strictly in favour of the taxpayer, although now of less force,[41] is nonetheless of critical importance to millions of taxpayers. Numerous members of the military community benefit from the presumption against retrospectivity at issue in *Esber.*[42] Thousands of claimants of refugee status have taken advantage of the presumption against removal of the courts' jurisdiction involved in *Plaintiff S157/2002*. All property owners in Australia enjoy the protection of their property interests vindicated in *Coco.*[43] *Re Al Saeed and Secretary, Department of Social Security*[44] and *Re Ferguson and Secretary, Department of Employment, Education, Training and Youth Affairs*[45] illustrate the use of the presumption that statutory rights are presumed not to take away fundamental human rights – a presumption of considerable significance for the three to four million Australians receiving income support.[46] *Melbourne Corporation* v *Barry*[47] is an example of the Courts' protection of the right to freedom of movement, another freedom which is jealously guarded in Australia.[48] And hundreds of children subject to the welfare system have benefited from the High Court's decision in *Johnson* v *Director-General of Social Welfare (Vic)*[49] where the ancient *parens patriae* jurisdiction of the superior courts to protect the vulnerable in society, was held to be a right not lightly to be taken away by a statutory scheme.

These examples illustrate that common law rights cover matters of pivotal importance to people. Furthermore, the magnitude of the groups affected by these presumptions provides substance to the claim that the common law principles are a significant and practical source of rights-protection to large segments of the community.

---

40 (1982) 151 CLR 342.

41 *Federal Commissioner of Taxation* v *Westraders Pty Ltd* (1980) 144 CLR 55.

42 *Repatriation Commission* v *Gorton* (2001) 65 ALD 609.

43 See also *Clunies-Ross* v *Commonwealth* (1984) 155 CLR 193; *Anthony Lagoon Station Pty Ltd* v *Maurice* (1987) 15 FCR 565.

44 (1991) 22 ALD 675 (AAT).

45 (1996) 42 ALD 742 (AAT).

46 See also *Re Secretary, Department of Social Security and Clemson* (1991) 14 AAR 261.

47 (1922) 31 CLR 174, 206.

48 *Re Secretary, Department of Social Security and Clemson* (1991) 14 AAR 261.

49 (1976) 135 CLR 92. This is another decision in which the court refused to accept that its jurisdiction had been removed.

Human Rights Commission

The third institutional indicator of rights protection identified by the Senate Standing Committee on Constitutional and Legal Affairs (1985) was the Human Rights Commission (since 1986, the Human Rights and Equal Opportunity Commission).[50] The Commission promotes the rights found in the Conventions annexed to the *Human Rights and Equal Opportunity Act 1986* (Cth),[51] or which have subsequently been declared.[52] In addition, the Commission administers, through specialist commissioners, legislation that proscribes discrimination on grounds of sex, race, disability and age.[53] The Commission's functions are discharged in a variety of ways, including public education, investigation, conciliation, as well as reports to the Attorney-General on breaches of the standards in the legislation.[54] Other functions of the Commission and its specialist commissioners include to appear as *amicus curiae* in judicial actions concerning human rights or discrimination,[55] to examine legislation for consistency with human rights and equality standards, and to prepare guidelines designed to prevent breaches of these standards.[56]

These broad-based strategies for enforcement of rights protection, for the education of Australians about equality and other rights, and for the encouragement of non-discriminatory practices have the capacity to effect widespread normative change within the community. They have been implemented in a practical manner by the 'Commonwealth Disability Strategy' which encourages agencies to comply with the strategy, including by compliance with the 'Development of Disability Action Plans' and through a monitoring and reporting requirement. (Commonwealth, Commonwealth Disability Strategy, 2000)

---

50 *Human Rights and Equal Opportunity Commission Act 1986* (Cth).

51 These are the *Discrimination (Employment and Occupation) Convention 1958*, opened for signature 25 June 1958, 362 UNTS 31 (entered into force 15 June 1960); the *ICCPR*; *Declaration on the Rights of the Child*; the *Declaration on the Rights of Mentally Retarded Persons* GA Res 2856 (XXVI), 26 UN GAOR Supp (No 29) at 93, UN Doc A/8429 (1971); the *Declaration on the Rights of Disabled Persons* GA Res 3447 (XXX), 30 UN GAOR Supp (No 34) at 88, UN Doc A/10034 (1975).

52 For example, *Convention on the Rights of the Child*; *Declaration on the Elimination of All Forms of Intolerance and of Discrimination Based on Religion or Belief* CHR Res 1997/18, ESCOR Supp (No 3) at 81, UN Doc E/CN.4/1997/18 (1997).

53 *Racial Discrimination Act 1975* (Cth); *Sex Discrimination Act 1984* (Cth); *Disability Discrimination Act 1992* (Cth); *Age Discrimination Act 2004* (Cth). There are State and Territory human rights and anti-discrimination bodies which replicate in part the role of HREOC, although the State and Territory bodies, absent the constitutional restrictions identified in *Brandy* v *HREOC* (1995) 183 CLR 245, are able to offer successful claimants more effective remedies such as binding determinations of compensation, than their Commonwealth counterpart.

54 *Human Rights and Equal Opportunity Act 1986* (Cth) ss. 11, 20, 31.

55 Ibid ss. 11(1)(o), 31(j), 46PV.

56 Ibid ss. 11(1)(e), (n), 31(b),(h).

For constitutional reasons the Commission, unlike its State and Territory counterparts, does not have power to make conclusive determinations.[57] As a consequence, the remedial powers of the Commission are limited to making recommendations for redress.[58] Nonetheless, given the sensitivity of individuals and government agencies to adverse publicity, this reporting function is generally an effective way to encourage compliance with the human rights and anti-discrimination principles to which the legislation gives effect.[59]

Several characteristics of these bodies contribute to their efficacy. They apply not only to the public sector, but to those in the private sector as well, at least to the extent that these private sector bodies are breaching human rights standards, or are engaged in acts or practices which are discriminatory. That means the human rights and equality standards in the various instruments administered by these bodies apply to all Australians. Another of their beneficial features is that the institution takes over the inquiry and undertakes the investigation. In other words there is no cost, nor litigation burden on the applicant, a significant fillip to the achievement of rights-protection. This feature is shared with other administrative investigative bodies such as Ombudsman, privacy and health rights protection commissioners.

The success of the Commission is demonstrated by its continuing complaint-handling load. Since 1990 it has received nearly 30,000 complaints.[60] When to these figures are added the nearly 9,000 claims made annually to the equivalent State and Territory bodies,[61] it can be seen that for an Australian population of 21 million, a significant proportion – roughly 10,000 each year – are able to and do complain about breaches of equality and human rights standards.

---

57 *Brandy* v *Human Rights and Equal Opportunity Commission* (1995) 183 CLR 245.

58 *Human Rights and Equal Opportunity Act 1986* (Cth) ss 11(1)(f), 28, 29, 31(b), 34, 35. See too *Brandy* v *Human Rights and Equal Opportunity Commission* (1995) 183 CLR 245.

59 These rights and principles include not only those anti-discrimination rules in the Human Rights and Equal Opportunity Act 1986 (Cth) but also the rights which are annexed as schedules to the Act or which have subsequently been declared. The Human Rights and Equal Opportunity Act 1986 (Cth) s. 3 defines 'human rights' to mean 'the rights and freedoms recognised in the Covenant, declared by the Declarations or recognised or declared by any relevant international instrument' (emphasis added). Instruments have been recognized subsequently including on rights of the child.

60 The total number of complaints of 34,587 is taken from HREOC annual reports 1981–82 to 2002–03. In addition, the Commission responds to thousands of requests annually for information about the law and the complaint process. As an example, in 2002–03, around 9,000 people contacted the Commission for this purpose: Commonwealth, HREOC, 2003.

61 Over 8,000 complaints were handled in 2002–03 by the State and Territory human rights and equal opportunity bodies. They also received more than four times that number of inquiries. See Annual Reports for 2002-03 for State and Territory anti-discrimination and equal opportunity bodies.

Human Rights Act 2004 (ACT) v HREOC Act 1986

In this context, it is interesting to compare the provisions in existing human rights and equality legislation with those in the *Human Rights Act 2004* (ACT) ('HRA'). The HRA is the first legislation in Australia to be called a bill of rights. The Act is designed to ensure that Territory legislation is interpreted in a manner which protects the rights in the *International Covenant on Civil and Political Rights* ('*ICCPR*').[62] That protection is mainly effected in two ways: a Territory Act or subordinate law is to be interpreted consistently with the *ICCPR* unless to do so would be contrary to the purpose of the legislative instrument;[63] and in cases of doubt, the Supreme Court is authorized to declare that a law is incompatible with the HRA, but only when the issue arises in the context of a substantive claim being considered by the Court.[64] There is no invalidating effect of a declaration of incompatibility.[65] However, the Attorney-General must consider the declaration and within six months report to the Territory's Legislative Assembly on any action which has been taken in response to the declaration.[66] The Act is administered by a Human Rights and Anti-Discrimination Commissioner who has the functions of reviewing laws to ensure compliance with the Act, and providing public education and advice to the Attorney-General on its operation.[67] In interpreting the civil and political rights specifically referred to in the Act, decision-makers, tribunals and courts may, but are not required to, take account of relevant international law documents.[68]

It is difficult to see how the HRA is an advance on the present position. Currently ACT citizens are covered by the *Human Rights and Equal Opportunity Act 1986* (Cth) which, as already mentioned, provides for findings by the Commission that acts or practices are contrary to the *ICCPR*.[69] For the HRA also to provide for this right does not appear to add anything. At present, the Human Rights and Equal Opportunity Commission ('HREOC') also has the function of examining Acts and subordinate laws of both the Commonwealth and the Territory to ensure compliance

---

62 Initially, the draft bill annexed to the Report of the ACT Human Rights Consultative Committee was intended to cover social and economic rights as well, but the ACT Government has abandoned that element of the proposed package, presumably in the face of the financial implications.

63 *Human Rights Act 2004* (ACT) s. 30.

64 Ibid s. 32.

65 *Human Rights Act 2004* (ACT) s. 32(3). A declaration of incompatibility does not affect '(a) the validity, operation or enforcement of the law; or (b) the rights or obligations of anyone'. Section 39 of the *Human Rights Act 2004* (ACT) also provides that non-compliance with a statement by the Attorney-General as to the rights-compliance of bills and the consideration of such bills by the ACT Legislative Assembly does not affect the validity of the laws.

66 Ibid s. 33(3).

67 Ibid ss. 40, 41. See also Explanatory Statement to Human Rights Bill 2003.

68 *Human Rights Act 2004* (ACT) s. 31.

69 *Human Rights and Equal Opportunity Commission Act* 1986 (Cth) s. 4.

with the *ICCPR*.[70] So for the ACT Human Rights Commissioner, the ACT's Attorney-General and the ACT's Legislative Assembly also to have this function in relation to Territory laws appears to be otiose. Further, unlike the position under the HRA, HREOC is able to recommend an award of compensation for breaches of the *ICCPR*.[71] This must be an advantage over the HRA which simply provides for an unenforceable declaration of incompatibility. In addition, to obtain a declaration the individual or agency must go to the ACT Supreme Court and then only in the context of another substantive claim before the Court. At least HREOC can, in effect, make a declaration of incompatibility without the individual complainant facing any legal bills.[72]

The introduction of the HRA undoubtedly has symbolic significance, yet it is hard to see that it offers anything more. This assessment is borne out by a case decided early in the life of the new Act by the ACT Administrative Appeals Tribunal. The Tribunal was reviewing a decision not to award Priority Category 1 status for public housing to a single mother with young children living in a less than desirable location. The applicant relied on s. 30(1) of the Act, which requires that '[i]n working out the meaning of a Territory law, an interpretation that is consistent with human rights is as far as possible to be preferred'. The human rights referred to in her argument were the obligation on the state to give protection to the family as 'the natural and basic group unit of society',[73] and to give to a child 'the protection needed by the child because of being a child, without distinction or discrimination of any kind'.[74] The Tribunal found that none of these circumstances applied. There was no evidence that the children were not being protected, or that the issues being framed as human rights issues had not already been considered by the decision-maker both as a matter of policy and in reference to the facts of this individual case. Further, as the Tribunal noted, 'to grant [the applicant's] request would very likely have the consequence that some other family or child in more urgent need of accommodation was unable to be assisted, which could itself constitute a breach of obligations under the *Human Rights Act 2004*.'[75] In other words, the Act should not be used to advantage someone when there was already in existence an orderly system of prioritizing applications that was subject to independent review on the merits.

---

70 Ibid ss. 3,4 11(1)(e).

71 It has been estimated that about one third of HREOC recommendations are complied with by those in breach: Le Grand, 1997a, p. 1; Le Grand, 1997b, p. 9; Editorial, *The Australian*, 1997, p. 14.

72 The legal bills under the *Human Rights and Equal Opportunity Commission Act 1986* (Cth) only apply if a recommendation in favour of an applicant is not complied with by the wrongdoer and the person decides to seek an enforcement order from the Federal Court. The fee scale for the Federal Court is substantial.

73 *Human Rights Act 2004* (ACT) s. 11(1).

74 Ibid s. 11(2).

75 *Re Merritt and Commissioner for Housing* [2004] ACTAAT 37, [54].

Other Methods of Protecting Rights

Two key elements of the administrative law structure, namely, the ombudsmen and tribunals, were omitted from the institutions listed by the 1985 Senate Standing Committee on Constitutional and Legal Affairs report on whether Australia needed a bill of rights.[76] When it is appreciated that over a twenty-five year period, the number of Federal Court applications for administrative law matters is less than 10,000,[77] as compared, in the same period, with nearly 500,000 complaints to the Commonwealth Ombudsman alone,[78] and that the combined administrative review caseload of the major Commonwealth tribunals since they were established has been over 400,000 decisions,[79] the omission exhibits a seriously myopic view of what is encompassed by administrative law.

Ombudsman

The office of the Commonwealth Ombudsman is, according to the International Ombudsman Institute, among the busiest in the world. (Commonwealth, Ombudsman, 1988, p. 31; Commonwealth, Ombudsman, 1989, p. 20) The functions of the Ombudsman include investigating 'maladministration by government', a term which covers a wide spectrum of matters, either following a complaint or of its own motion.[80] The role for the Ombudsman envisaged by those introducing the office in Australia was to ensure public accountability and administrative justice for the individual (Creyke and McMillan, 1998, p. 2). Indeed, the Commonwealth

---

76 In that regard, the report is not alone. Administrative law watchers and commentators frequently limit their examination of the system to judicial review cases, that is, what emerges from the court room door. (eg., ACT, ACT Bill of Rights Consultative Committee, 2003)

77 Annual reports for the Federal Court and the Administrative Review Council. The statistics are not easily available in either place and there is an element of estimation about these figures.

78 Figures taken from the Commonwealth, Ombudsman, 1997–98, 1998–99, 1999–2000, 2000–01, 2001–02 and 2002–03, and for the period 1977–97, from Commonwealth, Ombudsman, 1997, insert following p. 25. If responses to inquiries are included, the figure is 708,507.

79 See the annual reports of the Veterans' Review Board (VRB) (and its predecessors) for 1973–74 and then continuously from 1979–80 (earlier figures are scarce); for the Social Security Appeals Tribunal (SSAT) from 1988–89; for the Migration Review Tribunal (MRT) from 1999–2000, and for the Refugee Review Tribunal (RRT) from 1993–94. Figures for the Immigration Review Tribunal (IRT), the body set up in 1989 which then became the MRT, are not included. Nor are those of the Taxation Relief Boards, the Public Service Promotions Appeals Boards, the Commissioner for Community Relations, the non-determinative recommendations of the SSAT prior to 1988, and the Student Assistance Review Tribunal, set up in 1974, which was folded into the SSAT in 1995. If figures for these bodies were included, it is clear that the figure for hearings by these tribunals, to 2003, would exceed 500,000.

80 *Ombudsman Act 1976* (Cth) ss 5, 10, 15. Each State and Territory has legislation containing standards in substantially similar terms.

office has been described as 'one of the main instruments of administrative review at the federal level' (Commonwealth, ARC, 1983, p. 24). Moreover, that office is not alone. There are now ombudsman officers or parliamentary commissioners in each State and Territory, as well as specialist national investigative bodies applying to significant areas of government such as tax and defence.[81] If the right to complain against government is one of the most significant of one's civic rights and freedoms, then the ombudsman offices are a pre-eminent source of protection of those rights.

A measure of the success of the concept of an ombudsman is the replication of the model in the private sector. There are now a myriad of private sector complaint-handling bodies, many labelled 'ombudsman'. These include the Banking Industry Ombudsman, the Telecommunications Industry Ombudsman, the Music Industry Ombudsman, the Legal Ombudsman (in Victoria), the Energy and Water Ombudsman (NSW), and even University Ombudsman.[82] If imitation is the sincerest form of flattery, then the private sector considers that the government ombudsman offices throughout Australia are indeed performing a valued role in our community.

It is no accident that the Commonwealth Ombudsman, for example, has been appointed as Defence Force Ombudsman, Tax Ombudsman and is proposed as the Postal Industry Ombudsman. This last-mentioned role involves dealing with complaints about postal service operators, including those in the private sector. Similarly, a report has recommended that the Commonwealth Ombudsman provides oversight of government conduct in Norfolk Island. The move is designed to combat allegations of misuse of political power, undue influence, bullying and corruption by a segment of the population, and to clean-up governance on Norfolk Island. (Commonwealth, House of Representatives, 2003) This is further evidence that the Office is regarded as an effective accountability measure to combat abuses affecting citizens and to ensure that individuals receive their entitlements according to law.

The value of the ombudsman is also illustrated by the recent history of the office in Victoria. A number of key institutions of government were under threat by the former Kennett Government. Restoration or securing of these offices became a key plank of the election campaign manifesto by the then Opposition. Following the election, the newly elected Bracks government set up an inquiry by a constitutional commission to report on these institutions, including the Ombudsman. The government accepted the recommendations in the report and amended the *Constitution Act 1975* (Vic) so that there is now constitutional entrenchment of these offices, including the office of

---

81 The Office of the Commonwealth Ombudsman is also the Defence Force Ombudsman and the Taxation Ombudsman – although there is also a complementary Commonwealth Inspector-General of Tax which handles systemic complaints about the operation of the taxation system, and an Inspector-General of the Australian Defence Force.

82 *Citipower Pty Ltd* v *Electricity Industry Ombudsman (Vic) Ltd* [1999] VSC 275 (Unreported, Warren J, 5 August 1999); *Re Telecommunications Industry Ombudsman* [1999] ATMO 82.

the Ombudsman.[83] The purpose of the entrenchment is, as the Premier said, to ensure 'that Victoria has the strongest possible democratic safeguards'.[84]

Several features of the mode of operations of the ombudsman have led to this popularity. Investigations by the ombudsman are inexpensive and informal.[85] This has enabled the expeditious resolution of a high volume of complaints. At the same time, the public sees the ombudsman as independent and fair – an office which assures public accountability and transparency in administrative decision making. Specific areas in which the offices have had particular success are complaints about police operations, a prime area of civil liberties, and in the effective handling of ex gratia payments. Ex gratia payments provide for compensation in circumstances in which, although government action has met the letter of the law, the outcome in an individual case has been inequitable or unjust. The ombudsman has a role in these areas which simply cannot be replicated by other administrative law mechanisms including judicial or tribunal review.

It is not only its primary, complaint-handling role which makes the ombudsman so successful. The production of whole-of-government reports is another feature of the ombudsman role which demonstrates admirably the dual focus of administrative law – providing appropriate avenues for individual complaints, while also encouraging systemic reform within public administration. The NSW Ombudsman has developed a manual of 'best practice' standards for the public service and the Commonwealth Ombudsman has produced reports which have been influential in developing benchmarks for administrative action and decision making. These include the making of oral reports to government and complaint handling by agencies. The implementation of reports such as these has the capacity to enhance fair and equitable treatment of individuals in their interaction with government, to the advantage of all who deal with government (Commonwealth, Ombudsman, 1997a; 1997b; 1999b).

The traditional high volume areas of the Commonwealth Ombudsman office, accounting for roughly 90 per cent of complaints, are Centrelink, the Australian Taxation Office, the Department of Immigration, the Child Support Agency, the Australian Postal Corporation, the Australian Federal Police, and the Australian Defence Force (Commonwealth, Ombudsman, 2003, pp. 121–26). It is clear that these are agencies which deal with issues of considerable moment to people. In the context of rights protection it is also significant to remember the comment of the Senate Committee referred to earlier, a comment confirmed by a recent annual report of the Commonwealth Ombudsman, that 'by far the most common remedial action in cases where complaints are found to be justified … is an adequate explanation by the agency' and '[t]he most common concrete outcome obtained is expedited

---

83 *Constitution Act 1975* (Vic) s. 94E.

84 Victoria, *Parliamentary Debates*, Legislative Assembly, 30 July 2003, 1 (Steve Bracks, Premier).

85 The Ombudsman Office takes over a complaint it agrees to investigate and conducts the inquiry.

action by the agency'.[86] The report also noted that in only about half the complaints finalized was a substantive issue involved (Commonwealth, Ombudsman, 2003, pp. 12–13). These findings reinforce the point made earlier that, in Australia, it is often not vindication of civil or political or even economic or social rights which are at the forefront of people's concerns.

As one of the three key public sector watchdogs – the others being the Auditor-General and the parliament – this snapshot indicates that the ombudsman is in a powerful position to foster people's rights against government, both at an individual level and by improving the quality of decisions and actions by government as a whole.

Tribunals

The other high-volume complaint-handling jurisdiction is administrative review by tribunals. The signal feature of tribunal review is that in most instances a person who is successful receives what they are seeking from government. Merit review enables them to obtain, for instance, the pension, benefit, or licence, the reduction in payment, waiver of a fine, the right to view a document, the reduction in charges, or the permission to import goods at a concessional rate of tariff. This means that merit review is a more effective response to individual complaints than review by the courts since a substantive outcome, rather than a pronouncement of illegality, 'is usually what the aggrieved citizen is seeking' (Commonwealth, Commonwealth Administrative Review Committee, 1971, [58]).

Although research by the present author and a colleague has indicated that denigration of judicial review on this ground is overstated, and that over two-thirds of applicants who are successful before the courts ultimately receive what they were seeking (Creyke and McMillan, 2004), this is not to detract from the pivotal position of tribunals in gaining satisfactory outcomes for people. After all, it is generally only those with deep pockets who can afford court proceedings.[87]

The statistics indicate that tribunal review is clearly a major source of protection of rights of Australians. A glance at the most common matters dealt with, for example, by the Commonwealth Administrative Appeals Tribunal (AAT), shows that the high volume areas of its jurisdiction are in tax, social security, veterans' affairs, compensation, immigration, and primary industry (Commonwealth, AAT, 2003, pp. 105–11). State and Territory tribunals deal with professional disciplinary

---

86 Commonwealth, Senate Standing Committee on Finance and Public Administration, 1991, [5.9]. These findings were confirmed in Commonwealth, Ombudsman, 2003, pp. 15, 16.

87 Although it is conceded that the average gross costs of a hearing before the Administrative Appeals Tribunal in 1997–98 of $3,594 as compared with Family Court costs of $1,693 or the costs of an Australian Industrial Relations Commission hearing of $2,242, are high: Commonwealth, A.L.R.C., 1999, p. 84 (table 4.7).

decisions, guardianship and property management for incompetent adults, conflict of interest issues for local governments, and consumer and tenancy matters.

Given that the number of Acts and regulations which authorize appeals to the AAT is now close to 400, it is not the narrowness of the jurisdiction of the Tribunal which has led to that concentration of complaints. The most commonly encountered matters are issues which do concern Australian citizens in their everyday lives, and affect rights or interests of sufficient moment for the individual to seek to have them vindicated.

There are a number of reasons for the prominence of tribunals. Not only is tribunal review relatively cheap, but tribunal members possess appropriate expertise for the matters they adjudicate. That expertise gives applicants and agencies confidence that the tribunal understands the issues and will bring an informed judgment to the decision-making task. Tribunal members are also chosen for their mix of skills, so that the dominance of the legally trained member is minimized. At tribunal hearings, the agency whose decision is being reviewed is often not represented, particularly before intermediate tribunals such as, at the federal level, the Veterans' Review Board, the Refugee Review Tribunal, the Migration Review Tribunal or the Social Security Appeals Tribunal. The absence of agency representation reduces the level of formality of the hearing, and minimizes stress for applicants appearing before an adjudicative body, often for the first time. In addition, hearings are generally required to be informal, rules of evidence are not required, assistance is provided with completion of application forms, interpreters are available, often free of charge, and alternative dispute resolution processes are used where mediated outcomes are possible. These features of tribunals contribute to their deserved reputation for accessibility by members of the public.

There also appears to be growing support for tribunals in Australia. In the States and Territories, five have established a tribunal with broad jurisdiction akin to the Commonwealth's AAT.[88] A sixth State, Western Australia, has introduced the State Administrative Tribunal Bill into the Parliament, leaving only Queensland and the Northern Territory to pick up this initiative. New Zealand has also made an in-principle decision to establish a tribunal to match the AAT, at least for the purpose of hearing appeals relating to decisions under a Trans-Tasman Therapeutic Goods Scheme operating in the two countries. There are also plans in New Zealand for a body with general merits review jurisdiction.[89]

That degree of satisfaction is apparent not only among users of the system, but also within government. Research by the author and a colleague involving over forty Commonwealth agencies has indicated that there is strong support for external review, including by tribunals. The close to 400 individual respondents involved in this research reported positively that tribunals meet administrative law objectives by focusing decision-makers' attention on their task, and enhancing accountability and compliance with the law. Approval was also expressed for the quality of the tribunals'

---

88 The ACT, NSW, South Australia, Victoria and Tasmania.

89 Judge Patrick Keane (2003), NZ Law Commission, has recommended a general jurisdiction tribunal for that country.

reasons, and the respondents substantially agreed that there were no drawbacks for agencies from either the philosophy or approaches of members of tribunals, nor did the review impact too heavily on agency resources, procedures or processes (Creyke and McMillan, 2002, pp. 163, 166–81, 185–90). It is notable, too, that it is tribunal, not court review, which has played the greatest part in interpreting agencies' legislation.

These developments reflect the growing awareness of the importance of tribunals in the system of administrative justice, and their ability to provide value-for-money adjudication. It also indicates a degree of satisfaction with merits review as an adjudicative option. Commenting on the Commonwealth AAT and its steady accretion of jurisdiction over its lifetime, Maher notes:

> As a matter of every day political reality, it is hard to accept that if, on balance, the external merits review system has been detrimental to the overall public good, this would have escaped the scrutiny either of politicians with a keen eye to satisfying their constituents, or of the organized groups which represent the interests of tribunal users especially those individuals who, in terms of the struggles of everyday life, are most at risk in their dealings with Commonwealth administrators. (Maher, 1994, p. 84)

Effectiveness of Administrative Law in Protecting Rights

Whether the administrative law system is an effective protector of individual rights and interests can be measured not only against constitutional and institutional mechanisms, but also against more general benchmarks. There has been considerable attention in the literature to such benchmarks.[90] What has emerged is an array of indicators. These include:

- clear and achievable standards against which rights can be measured;
- institutions and principles which make it possible for the individual to complain;
- processes in place to provide for the maximum precedential impact of rights jurisprudence;
- requirements for education programs to complement other measures;
- attention to equality principles;
- a prudential system to ensure that rights are protected.

How does the Australian administrative law system rate against these general criteria?

---

90 Barnhizer, 2001a. See also Barnhizer, 2001b; McCorquodale, 1999; Higgins, 1999; United Nations Committee on Economic, Social and Cultural Rights, 1993 (art. 2, para. 1, of the Covenant*)*; United Nations Committee on Economic, Social and Cultural Rights, 1998 (to include national human rights commissions through ombudsman offices, public interest or other human rights 'advocates' to 'defensores del pueblo'); Piotrowicz and Kaye, 2000, ch. 14; Rayner, 1998; Robertson, 1992; Johnston, 1992; Moss, 1992.

Standards

It is clear that there are standards which apply in Australian administrative law. Not all are directly referable to the particular rights commonly classified as human rights, but all do protect the broader rights, interests or legitimate expectations covered by this area of the law. In particular, the codification of the administrative law standards in the various judicial review statutes has had a beneficial impact on teasing out what processes must be complied with if government action is to be lawful.

There are some eighteen standards contained in the *Administrative Decisions (Judicial Review) Act 1977* (Cth) (and State counterparts).[91] These require, for instance, that decision making by public administration must proceed by way of fair process and not be biased, decision-makers must only take account of relevant matters and discard irrelevant matters, they must not be unduly swayed by government policy, nor be unreasonable, nor may decisions be made for an unauthorized purpose. The object of these standards is to ensure that the decisions which impact on the public are made in a manner which is lawful, impartial and fair.

The benchmark for tribunal review of administrative decisions – the decision under review must be 'correct or preferable' – ensures that government decision making affecting individuals must comply with the law and be factually and legally correct or defensible.

Specific human rights and equality standards are found in the package of human rights and anti-discrimination laws at Commonwealth, State and Territory levels. These embody international human rights norms as well as domestically shaped rights and equality laws, for example, gender or age-related discriminatory practices. Prominent among the internationally imported standards, as mentioned earlier, are the civil and political rights of the *ICCPR*, as well as the standards in the specialized declarations relating to people with particular disabilities.[92]

Common law rights-protecting standards have also been developed by the courts. These are capable, as mentioned earlier, of having a substantive impact on key aspects of public administration. Apart from the specific presumptions of interpretation which import common law rights standards into judicial decisions, the judiciary has long taken an approach to the interpretation of legislation which takes as its starting point the protection of the liberty of the individual.[93]

Finally, there are standards for information access in Australia. These enable the community to obtain information from government, particularly to correct personal

---

91 See for example, Cth: *Administrative Decisions (Judicial Review) Act 1977* (Cth); ACT: *Administrative Decisions (Judicial Review) Act 1989* (ACT); Queensland: *Judicial Review Act 1991* (Qld); Tasmania: *Judicial Review Act 2002* (Tas).

92 It is only the *Human Rights and Equal Opportunity Commission Act 1986* (Cth) which simply annexes international conventions to its human rights legislation or declares that such laws are to be recognized. In all other Australian jurisdictions, human rights norms are directly incorporated into the domestic legislation.

93 *George v Rockett* (1990) 170 CLR 104, [4] (the Court); *Harts Australia Ltd v Commissioner, Australian Federal Police* (2002) 49 ATR 427.

records, but also on matters connected with the probity, wisdom and lawfulness of government programs generally. As one commentator noted: 'Parliamentary scrutiny of the executive is fundamental to the Westminster system. For that scrutiny to be meaningful, all available information must be accessible' (Tanner, 2000, p. 2). At the same time, these standards are balanced against other legitimate interests. For example, exemptions to rights of access in freedom of information legislation are provided to protect essential confidentiality, security and other interests of government. Similarly, privacy laws protect from disclosure personal information supplied to government by individuals and companies. Both exemplify, in legislative form, necessary qualifications to rights protection principles.

Institutions and Principles

The structure of the administrative law system in Australia and its principles were discussed earlier under 'Current Performance'. As the prefatory extracts to this chapter indicate, there are those who consider that the Australian administrative law framework is the best-established and most sophisticated system of administrative law in any common law jurisdiction.[94] The earlier discussion illustrated that the system provides a wide variety of remedies, with different levels of access and costs for users. Judicial review of legality with its precedential value is matched by merits review and its ability to provide substantive outcomes. Alongside these adjudicative bodies are institutions which operate principally by means of investigation and recommendation, such as ombudsmen, information, privacy and other commissioners. Finally, there are particular rights – such as the right to reasons, to access information and to require government to keep to itself personal information supplied by an individual – which protect important interests. The system can be said to provide a comprehensive package of institutions and principles, each component designed to provide 'justice to the individual' (Commonwealth, Commonwealth Administrative Review Committee, 1971, [12]).

Precedential Impact of Rights Jurisprudence

Court and tribunal decisions undoubtedly have precedential value. They are clearly noted by agencies and often result in legislative or policy change. Similarly, reports of the ombudsman offices, and of other investigative bodies, serve as a vehicle to advise agencies of the offices' findings on policy issues and in relation to particular categories of complaints. Given agency sensitivity to public criticism, it can be hypothesized that these forms of publication are effective.

---

94 For example, the Foreword to the Sir Andrew Leggatt's *Tribunals for Users: One System, One Service* (2001) noted: 'The visit to Australia was valuable ... because it afforded an opportunity to inspect at first-hand the only tribunal system in any common law jurisdiction that is in important respects well in advance of our own': at 3.

The normative impact of administrative law is, however, under-explored, particularly by empirical studies. Research by the author and a colleague has indicated that there are deficiencies in the manner in which agencies receive, digest and disseminate decisions of courts and tribunals. Nonetheless, these areas need strengthening rather than the creation of new processes (Creyke and McMillan, 2002). The introduction of a formal mechanism for ensuring that adjudicative decisions are implemented and their principles incorporated into training and other material of agencies would rectify this deficiency (Creyke, 2004, pp. 13–14; see also, Fleming, 2000). Although dissemination does occur at an informal level (Commonwealth, ARC, 2004), arguably a more systematic approach to the process could be implemented. (Commonwealth, ARC, 1995, ch. 5)

Educational Measures

HREOC, the Privacy Commissioner, other specialist commissioners and the various ombudsman offices have developed strategies for public education. Public radio, media releases, official reports and organizational websites are used extensively in this process. Most agencies have public relations offices and seek platforms for speeches to publicize particular issues concerning rights. Other initiatives are the appointment of members of the public to reference groups or procedures sub-committees of tribunals, moves designed to enable the views of users to be reflected in tribunal procedures and practices.

An object of the Council of Australasian Tribunals (COAT), which was set up in 2002 to be the peak coordinating body for Australasian tribunals, is to provide training and support for members of tribunals, and to promote lectures, seminars and conferences about tribunals and tribunal practices and procedures. The work of other bodies such as the Australian Institute of Administrative Law, the Australian Institute of Judicial Administration, and the various University Centres with a focus on public law, also ensure that there are regular forums in which issues of relevance to rights protection and administrative law are aired.[95]

Equality Principles

Each Australian jurisdiction has anti-discrimination or equality legislation in place. Australians may access not one but two regimes specifically devoted to rights and equality protection. The anti-discrimination principles in the *HREOC Act* operate alongside and as an alternative remedy should an individual choose to access the Commonwealth, rather than a local State or Territory, institution for a remedy. Fine-tuning of the principles in the various Acts occurs regularly as society's ideas about what is acceptable behaviour develops.[96]

---

95 See for suggestions for improvements which can be made, Creyke, 2004, pp. 233–35.

96 For example, Cth: *Age Discrimination Act 2004* (Cth); ACT: *Human Rights Act 2004* (ACT); NSW: *Anti Discrimination Act 1977* (NSW) has added provisions proscribing racial

Prudential System

The Administrative Review Council was set up to perform a prudential function for the entire Commonwealth administrative law structure. The introduction of a similar institution has been mooted in several States, and been emulated in Tasmania with the establishment in 2004 of the Tasmanian Administrative Review Advisory Council. The value of the Australian monitoring model was also commended by the Leggatt Inquiry into tribunals in the United Kingdom, which recommended the setting up of a similar body in that country.[97] That recommendation has been accepted by the United Kingdom Government, which proposes to establish an Administrative Justice Council to be the supervisory body for the whole administrative justice sector (Great Britain, Department for Constitutional Affairs, 2004, ch. 11, esp. [11.12]).

For tribunals COAT also performs a prudential function. The objects of COAT include devising best practice or model procedural rules based on collective experience of what works; the development of standards of behaviour and conduct for members of tribunals; and the setting of performance standards for tribunals. The privacy commissioner and other specialist commissioners are also responsible for monitoring the operation of their domains.

In summary, the Australian administrative law system presently meets the performance indicators identified by writers as effective means for implementing rights-protection.

Future Performance

It is clear that in a dynamic area such as public administration, administrative law must keep in step with developments if it is to remain relevant as an accountability and rights-protection tool. There are two key drivers of change in this area of law in Australia: technology; and the fluid boundaries between the public and private spheres.

Technological change is currently being tackled with the introduction into high volume areas of government decision making of automated decision-assistance computer software. This development has the potential for more consistent but also less discretionary decision making. At a systemic level, the most significant effect is to shift the focus of administrative law from the *ex post facto* review stage, to the

---

vilification (Part 2, Div 3A), sexual harassment (Part 2A), and discrimination on transgender grounds (Part 3A).

97 Sir Andrew Leggatt (2001) noted: 'In the longer term, like the Administrative Review Council in Australia, the [UK] Council [on Tribunals] should be made responsible for upholding the system of administrative justice and keeping it under review, for monitoring developments in administrative law, and for making recommendations to the Lord Chancellor about improvements that might be made to the system': at [7.54]. That recommendation has been accepted: Footnote Department of Constitutional Affairs *Transforming Public Services: Complaints, Redress and Tribunals* (CM 6243, July 2004).

software development or input stage. It is when the software is being created, when decisions are made about what information should be included – from the legislation, case law, agency policy, and other material – that monitoring of the system should occur. Without it, there is the potential for databases to be set up which may curtail discretions or restrict rights. To avoid these outcomes, the processes of administrative law will need to be rethought, a task which is being essayed by the Administrative Review Council with a view to maintaining the traditional values which underpin administrative law.[98]

Another change is that greater attention is being paid by those monitoring the system to improving the quality of primary decision making. The advantages of such a move are the potential to benefit larger numbers of people than currently pursue administrative law remedies. To achieve this will require attention to quality assurance methodology, auditing and other prudential requirements which apply to initial decisions within agencies. Again this has hitherto not been the prime focus of attention for administrative law. However, it is significant that ombudsmen and other investigation offices, including the Auditor-General and regulators, have moved to institute regular auditing of action by government agencies.

Finally, it is clear that the boundaries of administrative law change to match the expansion or contraction of government. An ironic outcome of devolution, privatization and downsizing has been the commensurate increase in the reliance on regulatory authorities and independent statutory agencies to take up the supervisory function.

This phenomenon is particularly apparent in the regulation of utilities and essential services such as water, gas, electricity and transport. Increasingly, the courts are applying administrative law standards, for example, to gas and electricity suppliers. What is more, the objects clauses of the legislation relating to these utilities refer not just to economic efficiency objectives, but also to environmental and social objects which the regulators should seek to achieve.[99] So in addition to the imposition of administrative law standards, specific attention must be given by those supplying utilities to these statutory objectives. Given that the provision of adequate and affordable water, power and transport services significantly affect the day-to-day activities of the public, complying with these requirements is, therefore, of major benefit for Australians.

It is also notable, from a rights-protection objective, that alongside these regulatory bodies sit tribunals such as the NSW Independent Competition and Regulatory Tribunal, and the ACT's Essential Services Community Council. Their role is to protect individuals against harsh or unjust decisions or actions which may breach individual rights by the utilities providers. In other words, a new layer of administrative bodies is emerging to review the decisions of regulators in order

---

98 Commonwealth, ARC, 2003. The final report is expected in late 2004.

99 *TXU Electricity Ltd* v *Office of the Regulator-General* [2001] VSC 153 (Unreported, Gillard J, 17 May 2001); *Re Michael; Ex parte Epic Energy (WA) Nominees Pty Ltd* (2002) 25 WAR 511.

to ensure that administrative law and statutory standards applying to regulated industries are met.

Conclusion

In accordance with legality principles, the legislative matrix within which administrative law operates is determined by political and other imperatives. Within that legal framework, however, Australia is blessed with a system of administrative law which is well equipped to protect the rights and interests of concern to its citizens. To adapt a sentiment initially focused solely on judicial review: 'The fundamental contribution of [administrative law] to individual rights is to give reality to those rights by means of access to a forum where the lawfulness [and merits] of decisions and actions may be tested' (Robertson, 1992, p. 43).

The rights protected by Australian administrative law relate to interests of citizens which are of signal and practical importance to its citizens. In the current, highly regulated system for allocation of government largesse, having an effective means to call government to account, so that its citizens receive the benefits, goods and services to which they are entitled, is a major advantage. The Australian system of administrative review has gone at least as far as, if not further than, other western democracies in providing a practical and focused protection of rights – a phenomenon of which the administrative law community in Australia should be justly proud. It is doubtful whether charters or bills of rights would be able to achieve these practical objectives in the same measure.

References

ACT, ACT Bill of Rights Consultative Committee (2003), *Towards an ACT Human Rights Act: Report of the ACT Bill of Rights Consultative Committee* (Canberra: Publishing Services).

Allan, J. (2003), 'A Defence of the Status Quo', in Campbell, T., Goldsworthy, J. and Stone, A. (eds), *Protecting Human Rights – Instruments and Institutions* (Oxford: Oxford University Press, p. 1760.

Allars, M. (1997), *Australian Administrative Law: Cases and Materials* (Sydney: Butterworths).

Bayne, P. (1990), 'Administrative Law, Human Rights and International Humanitarian Law', *Australian Law Journal*, **64**: 203.

Barnhizer, D. (ed) (2001)a, *Effective Strategies for Protecting Human Rights: Economic Sanctions, Use of National Courts and International Fora and Coercive Power* (Aldershot: Ashgate).

—— (ed) (2001)b, *Effective Strategies for Protecting Human Rights: Prevention and Intervention, Trade and Education* (Aldershot: Ashgate).

Commonwealth, Administrative Appeals Tribunal ('AAT') (2003), *Annual Report 2002–03* (Canberra: Australian Government Publishing Service).

Commonwealth, Australian Law Reform Commission ('ALRC') (1999), *Review of the Federal Civil Justice System*, Discussion Paper 62 (Sydney, ALRC).

—— (2001), *The Judicial Power of the Commonwealth: A Review of the Judiciary Act 1903 and Related Legislation*, Report Number 92 (Sydney: ALRC).

Commonwealth, Administrative Review Council ('ARC') (1983), *Annual Report 1982–83* (Canberra: Australian Government Publishing Service).

—— (1994), *Review of the Commonwealth Merits Review Tribunals*, Discussion Paper (Canberra: Australian Government Publishing Service).

—— (1995), *Better Decisions: Review of Commonwealth Merits Review Tribunals*, Report Number 39 (Canberra: Australian Government Publishing Service).

—— (2003), *Automated Assistance in Administrative Decision Making*, Issues Paper (Canberra: Australian Government Publishing Service).

—— (2004), *Legal Training for Primary Decisions Makers: A Curriculum Guideline* (Canberra: Australian Government Publishing Service).

Commonwealth, Commonwealth Administrative Review Committee (1971), *Commonwealth Administrative Review Committee Report 1971*, Parliamentary Paper Number 144 of 1971 (Canberra: CGPS) ('Kerr Committee Report').

Commonwealth, Commonwealth Disability Strategy (2000), *The Commonwealth Disability Strategy: A strategic framework for inclusion and participation by people with disabilities in Government policies, programs and services*, available at www.facs.gov.au/disability/cds/cds/cds_index.htm> (accessed 4 May 2005).

Commonwealth, High Court of Australia ('HCA') (2003), *Annual Report 2002–03* (Canberra: Australian Government Publishing Service).

Commonwealth, House of Representatives (2003), 'Major reforms for Norfolk Island governance recommended', Press Release, 3 December 2003.

Commonwealth, Human Rights and Equal Opportunity Commission ('HREOC') (2003), *Annual Report 2002–03* (Canberra: Australian Government Publishing Service).

Commonwealth, Ombudsman (1988), *Ombudsman Annual Report 1987–1988* (Canberra: Australian Government Publishing Service).

—— (1989), *Ombudsman Annual Report 1988–1989* (Canberra: Australian Government Publishing Service).

—— (1997a), *A Good Practice Guide for Effective Complaint Handling* (Canberra: Australian Government Publishing Service).

—— (1997b), *Issues Relating to Oral Advice: Clients Beware* (Canberra: Australian Government Publishing Service).

—— (1997c), *Twenty Years of the Commonwealth Ombudsman 1977–1997* (Canberra: Commonwealth Ombudsman's Office).

—— (1998), *Annual Report 1997–98* (Canberra: Australian Government Publishing Service).

—— (1999a), *Annual Report 1998–99* (Canberra: Australian Government Publishing Service).

—— (1999b), *Balancing the Risks – Own Motion Investigation into the Role of Agencies in Providing Adequate Information to Customers in a Complex Income Support System* (Canberra: Australian Government Publishing Service).

—— (2000), *Annual Report 1999–2000* (Canberra: Australian Government Publishing Service).

—— (2001), *Annual Report 2000–01* (Canberra: Australian Government Publishing Service).

—— (2002), *Annual Report 2001–02* (Canberra: Australian Government Publishing Service).

—— (2003), *Annual Report 2002–03* (Canberra: Australian Government Publishing Service).

Commonwealth, Parliamentary Commissioners (2001), *Annual Report 2000–01* (Canberra: Australian Government Publishing Service).

Commonwealth, Senate Standing Committee on Constitutional and Legal Affairs (1985), *A Bill of Rights for Australia?* (Canberra: Australian Government Publishing Service).

Commonwealth, Senate Standing Committee on Finance and Public Administration (1991), *Review of the Office of the Commonwealth Ombudsman* (Canberra: Australian Government Publishing Service).

Cook, C., Creyke, R., Geddes, R., Holloway, I. (2001), *Laying Down the Law*, 5th edn (Sydney: Butterworths).

Creyke, R. (2004), 'The Special Place of Tribunals in the System of Justice. How Can Tribunals Make a Difference?', *Public Law Review*, **15**: 220.

Creyke, R., McMillan, J. (1998), 'Introduction: Administrative Law Assumptions … Then and Now', in Creyke, R. and McMillan, J. (eds), *The Kerr Vision of Australian Administrative Law – At the Twenty-Five Year Mark* (Canberra: Centre for International and Public Law).

——. (2002), 'Executive Perceptions of Administrative Law – an Empirical Study', *Australian Journal of Administrative Law*, **9**: 163.

——. (2004), 'Judicial Review Outcomes – an Empirical Study', *Australian Journal of Administrative Law*, **11**: 82.

Davies, Justice D. (1981), 'Administrative Law within the Australian Federal System', paper presented to the International Association of Law Libraries in Australia Conference, Sydney, 11 May 1981.

Editorial (1997), *The Australian* (Canberra), 16 September 1997.

Fleming, G. (2000), 'Administrative Review and the "Normative" Goal – Is Any Body Out There?', *Federal Law Review*, **28**: 61.

Fonacaro, M. (1995), 'Towards a Synthesis of Law and Social Science: Due Process and Procedural Justice in the Context of National Health Care Reform', *Denver University Law Review*, **72**: 303.

Forsyth, C.F. and Wade, H.W.R. (2000), *Administrative Law*, 8th edn (Oxford: Oxford University Press).

Gearty, C.A. (1993), 'The European Court of Human Rights and the Protection of Civil Liberties: An Overview' *Cambridge Law Journal*, **52**: 89.

Great Britain, Department for Constitutional Affairs (2004), *Transforming Public Services: Complaints, Redress and Tribunals*, White Paper Cm. 6243 (London and Norwich: Her Majesty's Stationery Office).

Great Britain, Lord Chancellor's Department (2003), 'Government Announces Modernised Tribunals Service in the Greatest Shake-up in 40 Years', Press Release, 11 March 2003.

Higgins, R. (1999), 'Role of Litigation in Implementing Human Rights', *Australian Journal of Human Rights*, **5** (2): 4.

Howieson, J. (2002), 'The Justice of Court-Connected Mediation', *Victorian Civil and Administrative Tribunal Mediation Newsletter*, Newsletter Number 6, p. 24.

Johnston, P. (1992), 'The Silence of the Books: The Role of the Administrative Appeals Tribunal in the Protection of Individual Rights', in McMillan, J. (ed.), *Administrative Law: Does the Public Benefit?* (Canberra: Australian Institute of Administrative Law).

Kirk J. (2003), 'Comment', a paper presented at the Australian National University Law Faculty's 'Public Law Weekend', Canberra, 7 November 2003.

Leggatt, Sir Andrew (2001), *Tribunals for Users: One System One Service* (London and Norwich: Her Majesty's Stationery Office).

Le Grand, C. (1997a), 'Justice doesn't pay in human rights', *The Australian* (Canberra), 15 September 1997.

—— (1997b), 'Rights and Wrongs', *The Australian* (Canberra), September 22, 1997.

Keane, Judge Patrick (2003), 'Statutory Tribunals in New Zealand – A Jungle of Different Jurisdictions', paper presented to the Legal Research Foundation, Auckland, 19 June 2003.

Lind, E.A., Tyler, T. (1988), *The Social Psychology of Procedural Justice* (New York: Plenum Press).

Liverani, Mary Rose (2001), 'Back to the Drawing Board for Tribunal Reformers', *Law Society Journal*, **39** (1): 67.

Lyster, R. (1999), 'The Effect of a Constitutionally Protected Right to Just Administrative Action' in Harris, M. and Partington, M. (eds), *Administrative Justice in the 21st Century* (Oxford: Hart Publishing), p. 376.

Maher, L. (1994), 'The Australian Experiment in Merits Review Tribunals' in Mendelsohn, O., Maher, L. (eds), *Courts, Tribunals and New Approaches to Justice*, Melbourne (La Trobe University Press), p. 84.

Mason, Sir Anthony (1989), 'Administrative Review: The Experience of the First Twelve Years', *Federal Law Review*, **18**: 122.

—— (1994), 'The Importance of Judicial Review of Administrative Action as a Safeguard of Individual Rights', *Australian Journal of Human Rights*, **1**: 3.

—— (1998), 'Reflections on the Development of Australian Administrative Law', in Creyke, R. and McMillan, J. (eds), *The Kerr Vision of Australian Administrative Law – At the Twenty-Five Year Mark* (Canberra: Centre for International and Public Law), p. 122.

—— (1999), 'Minister for Immigration v Federal Court', *AIAL Forum*, **22**: 1.

McMillan, J., Williams, N. (1998), 'Administrative Law and Human Rights', in Kinley, D. (ed.), *Human Rights in Australian Law* (Sydney: The Federation Press), p. 63.

McCorquodale, R. (1999), 'Introduction: Implementing Human Rights in Australia', *Australian Journal of Human Rights*, **5** (2): 1.

Moss, I. (1992), 'Human Rights Agencies and the Protection of Individual Rights', in McMillan J. (ed.), *Administrative Law: Does the Public Benefit?* (Canberra: Australian Institute of Administrative Law), p. 62.

Pearce, D.C., Geddes, R. (2001), *Statutory Interpretation in Australia*, 5th edn (Sydney: Butterworths).

Piotrowicz, R., Kaye, S. (2000), *Human Rights in International and Australian Law* (Sydney: Butterworths).

Queensland, Electoral and Administrative Review Commission (1990), *Report on Judicial Review of Administrative Decisions and Actions* (Brisbane: Queensland Government Printer).

Rayner, M. (1998), 'The Diminution of Human Rights in Australian Administration', in Kneebone, S. (ed.), *Administrative Law and the Rule of Law: Still Part of the Same Package?* (Canberra: Australian Institute of Administrative Law), p. 296.

Robertson, A. (1992), 'Judicial Review, and the Protection of Individual Rights', in McMillan J. (ed.), *Administrative Law: Does the Public Benefit?* (Canberra: Australian Institute of Administrative Law), p. 37.

Scarman, Lord (1974), *English Law − the New Dimension* (London: Stevens).

Tanner, L. (2000), 'Restoring Openness in Government', paper presented 2 November 2000, available at <http://www.lindsaytanner.com/Restoring%20openness%20in%20government.doc> (accessed 4 May 2005).

United Nations Committee on Economic, Social and Cultural Rights (1993), *General Comment 3 − The Nature of States Parties' Obligations (art 2, para 1 of the Covenant)*, Fifth session, 1990, UN Doc HRI\GEN\1\Rev.1 at 45 (1994).

—— (1998), *General Comment 10 − The Role of National Human Rights Institutions in the Protection of Economic, Social and Cultural Rights*, Nineteenth session, 1998, UN Doc E/1999/22 at 18.

Whitmore, H. (1989), 'Comment on "Administrative Review Before the Administrative Appeals Tribunal − A Fresh Approach to Dispute Resolution?"', *Federal Law Review*, **12**: 117.

Willis, J. (1938), 'Statutory Presumptions in a Nutshell', *Canadian Bar Review*, **16**: 17.

Zines, L. (2000), 'Federal, Associated and Accrued Jurisdiction', in Opeskin, B. and Wheeler, F. (eds*)*, *The Australian Federal Judicial System*, Melbourne: Melbourne University Press, p. 265.

Chapter 5

Australia's Constitutional Rights and the Problem of Interpretive Disagreement

Adrienne Stone[1]

Introduction

The rights found in the *Australian Constitution* are regarded as patchy, inconsistently interpreted and, in the case of 'implied' rights, obscure.[2] The inadequacy of Australia's constitutional rights is frequently one plank in an argument for an Australian bill of rights.[3] In this chapter, I subject Australia's constitutional rights to closer scrutiny. My point is three-fold. First, I seek to broaden the understanding of how rights pervade, or could pervade, Australian constitutional law. Secondly, I re-examine the critique of Australia's constitutional rights. I agree with the view that Australia's constitutional rights are especially weak, but I provide a more precise articulation of the source of that weakness. Finally, I briefly consider the implications of this analysis in deciding whether Australia should adopt a constitutional bill of rights.

I begin in the next part with a brief review of Australia's existing constitutional rights. The analysis extends beyond the express and implied rights that form the backbone of Australia's constitutional rights to less obvious means of rights protection found in apparently right-neutral contexts. In this latter section, I show how the High Court can pursue rights protection through the use of rights-sensitive interpretive devices and judicially created rules for the application of constitutional provisions.

In the following part I assess the claim that Australia's constitutional rights are an especially weak form of protecting rights. I will argue that a system of rights protection that depends so heavily on the implication of rights, on the incorporation of rights from extra-constitutional sources and other judicially created rules of constitutional law, is inevitably weak. The source of this weakness lies in the contested

---

1   This chapter has been previously published in the *Sydney Law Review*, **27**: 29.

2   For critiques of the express rights see, Zines, 1997, p. 410; Charlesworth, 2002, pp. 30–31; Williams, 1999, p. 245; Bailey, 1999. With respect to the 'implied rights' see, Williams, 1999, p. 259; and for a detailed critique of the freedom of political communication see Stone, 2001; 1998; and 1999.

3   See, for example, Williams, 1999, pp. 245, 257, 259; Wilcox, 1993, pp. 194–209, 230–31.

nature of constitutional interpretation itself. Because the methods of constitutional interpretation on which Australia's constitutional rights rely are themselves contested, many of these rights are subject to on-going disagreement as to their very existence. The doubt that attends the use of these methods is exacerbated when they are used in the context of a written constitution that deals primarily with non-rights concerns and was drafted without much consideration of rights. Arguments based on constitutional text and constitutional history will, therefore, tend to run counter to rights-protective readings of the *Constitution*.

In many cases, then, Australia's constitutional rights are likely to be accompanied by disagreement about the methods of constitutional interpretation on which they rely. Such rights are peculiarly vulnerable to judicial revision in the short term. Further, even when a right obtains a degree of acceptance over time, doubts surrounding its recognition will adversely affect its development.

I conclude with some brief reflections on the implications of these conclusions for the Australian bill of rights debate. It follows from my analysis in the previous part that an express bill of rights in the *Australian Constitution* would put to rest one important area of dispute, by providing an unarguable basis for the recognition of constitutional rights. However, I suggest that the settling of that interpretive controversy is not, itself, a reason to adopt a bill of rights, because such a reform would, overall, make constitutional adjudication considerably more complex and uncertain.

Rights under the *Australian Constitution*

Express and Implied Rights

The *Australian Constitution* is usually understood to contain express rights and rights implied from constitutional text and structure. Far more controversially, it has also been suggested that the *Constitution* contains rights implied from fundamental underlying doctrines.[4] Since these rights have received extensive treatment elsewhere (see Zines, 1997, chs 15 and 16; Winterton, 1996), I will deal with them only briefly before turning to another constitutional method of protecting rights.

Express rights   Despite the absence of a comprehensive bill of rights, a number of provisions in the Australian Constitution are often categorized as 'express rights' (Zines, 1997, 402–15; Williams, 1999, chs 5 and 6). The provisions most often placed in this category are s. 116, which in part prevents the Commonwealth acting to 'establish' a religion or to prohibit its 'free exercise';[5] s. 80, which provides for a jury trial when a Commonwealth offence is tried on indictment; s. 51(xxxi),

---

4   For a different, but very helpful, account of the 'schema' of constitutional rights see, Winterton, 1996, p. 121.

5   In these two respects s. 116 resembles the non-establishment and free exercise clauses of the First Amendment to the *United States Constitution*. Section 116 also prevents the

which qualifies the Commonwealth's power to acquire property with a requirement to provide 'just terms'; and s. 117, which prevents discrimination based on State residence.[6]

From a rights perspective, the High Court's interpretation of these provisions has been (with the exception of s. 117) disappointing. The rights that resemble traditional civil and political rights – such as ss. 80 and 116 – have been given very narrow fields of operation,[7] and criticism of their evisceration is heightened by charges of inconsistency. Commentators have complained of the Court's inconsistent preference for plain or literal meaning of constitutional text in some cases and for the framers' intent in others.[8] The narrowness of the Court's approach to these civil and political rights also contrasts unfavourably with those sections that seem to confer 'economic rights' (such as s. 51(xxxi) and s. 92), which have been given a relatively wide field of operation.[9] Though a thoroughgoing reinterpretation of the 'express rights' provisions is often advocated,[10] that argument has, with one notable exception (the interpretation of s. 117[11]), met with little success.

Commonwealth from 'imposing any religious observance' and provides that 'no religious test shall be required as a qualification for any office or public trust under the Commonwealth'.

6   The list of express rights sometimes also includes s. 41, which gives those who qualify as State electors the right to vote in federal elections; s. 92, which requires that interstate trade and commerce be 'absolutely free'; and s. 51(xiiiA), which precludes the 'civil conscription' of medical practitioners.

7   As interpreted by the High Court, s. 80 does not apply if Parliament provides that an offence is not to be tried on indictment: *R v Archdall & Roskruge* (1928) 41 CLR 128. The protection of religion by s. 116 is readily outweighed by other values: see for example, *Adelaide Company of Jehovah's Witnesses Inc v Commonwealth* (1943) 67 CLR 116 (holding that s. 116 did not prohibit laws prohibiting advocacy detrimental to the prosecution of war by the Commonwealth, even if that advocacy is undertaken in pursuit of religious conviction); *Attorney-General (Vic); Ex rel Black v Commonwealth (DOGS Case)* (1981) 146 CLR 559 (allowing government funding of the educational activities of religious schools). The 'right to vote' in s. 41 guarantees a right to vote only to those who qualified to vote in State elections at the time of federation: *R v Pearson; Ex Part Sipka (*1983) 152 CLR 254. See generally, Zines, 1997, pp. 402–05.

8   Williams (1999) contrasts the interpretation of s. 80 (in which the 'plain meaning' of the text has been said to preclude a substantive interpretation of 'trial on indictment') with the interpretation of s 41 (where historical material was used to limit the apparent plain meaning). He concludes '[i]t is hard to avoid the conclusion that until [the High Court's judgment in *Street v Queensland Bar Association* in] 1989 judges of the High Court have selectively used whatever tool was available ... to construe sections 41, 80, 116 and 117 as empty guarantees': at p. 128.

9   See generally, Bailey, 1990, pp. 84–86; Williams, 1999, ch. 6. Though, it should be noted that *Cole v Whitfield* (1988) 165 CLR 360 narrowed previous interpretations of s. 92.

10   See Bailey, 1990, p. 105; Williams, 1999, pp. 128, 249–50.

11   See *Street v Queensland Bar Association* (1989) 168 CLR 461, which transformed s. 117 into a real limitation on government that protects the individual from discrimination based on State residence.

Implied rights – text and structure A second form of constitutional right in the *Australian Constitution* arises from a method of interpretation known as 'implication from text and structure'. Two well-known kinds of implied rights in the *Australian Constitution* provide illustrations – the rights implied from representative and responsible government, and the rights implied from the separation of judicial power.

The first implication, drawn from representative and responsible government,[12] gives rise to a right of freedom of political communication (a limited kind of free speech right)[13] and, perhaps, to rights of freedom of movement and association.[14] Although the Court has occasionally been reticent about using the language of rights to describe the freedom of political communication,[15] the protection conferred by the freedom of political communication fits easily within the concept of a constitutional right.[16] Indeed the scope of the implied freedom overlaps with (though may be narrower than) the protection conferred by express free speech rights contained in other constitutions.[17]

A second set of constitutional rights is implied from the separation of judicial power.[18] In general terms, the separation of judicial power requires, first, that the judicial power of the Commonwealth be exercised only by the courts identified in

---

12 In *Lange* v *Australian Broadcasting Commission* (1997) 189 CLR 520, the Court emphasized that the freedom of political communication is derived from specific textual provisions implementing certain institutions of representative and responsible government rather than general principles. For a critique of that line of reasoning, see Stone, 1999.

13 *Lange* v *Australian Broadcasting Commission* (1997) 189 CLR 520.

14 The freedoms of movement and association are yet to be determined but have received some judicial recognition: *Kruger* v *Commonwealth* (1997) 190 CLR 1, 91 (Toohey J), 116 (Gaudron J), 142 (McHugh J), cf. 156 (Gummow J holding that there is no freedom of association for 'political cultural and familial purposes'). See also *R* v *Smithers; Ex parte Benson* (1912) 16 CLR 99, 109–110; *Higgins* v *Commonwealth* (1998) 79 FCR 528, 535. On the constitutional right of freedom of association see, *ACTV* (1992) 177 CLR 106, 232 (McHugh J); *Kruger* (1997) 190 CLR 1, 91 (Toohey J), 142 (Gaudron J) and *Mulholland* v *Australian Electoral Commission* [2004] HCA 41 (8 September 2004) [113]–[116] (McHugh J), [148] (Gummow and Hayne JJ with whom Heydon J agreed), [284]–[286] (Kirby J), cf. [334]–[335] (Callinan J).

15 *Mulholland* v *Australian Electoral Commission* [2004] HCA 41, [104], [182].

16 Albeit that the freedom is a 'negative' rather than a 'positive' right and therefore operates to prevent interference with political communication rather than facilitate its exercise. In addition the freedom applies 'vertically' against government action (including the judicial enforcement of the common law) rather than 'horizontally' against private action. See Stone, 1999.

17 On the kinds of communication covered by the freedom of political communication, see Stone, 2001, pp. 378–90; on the level of protection accorded to that communication, see Stone, 1999.

18 For an authoritative account see Zines, 1997, pp. 161–70, 202–12.

s. 71 of the *Constitution*;[19] and secondly, that courts established by or under the *Constitution* only exercise the judicial power referred to in Ch. III of the *Constitution* (together with incidental non-judicial powers).[20]

Those general principles give rise to a wide range of more specific rules too complex to be summarized here (see Zines, 1997, pp. 202–12). These rules can all, in some sense, be understood as protecting individual rights, because diffusing government power guards against the possibility of abuse of that power.[21] More specifically, the separation of powers promotes the independence and impartiality of the judiciary and thus the observance of important aspects of the rule of law. The implied separation of judicial power also gives rise to some rules that resemble rights commonly found in bills of rights. For example, because the adjudgment of criminal guilt is regarded an exclusively judicial task,[22] the High Court has recognized that the federal Parliament cannot enact a bill of attainder.[23] In addition, the Parliament cannot order detention (at least of a punitive nature) without the intervention of a court.[24] Finally, there is also a requirement that courts act consistently with judicial process which, though it has not lived up to the hopes of its most vigorous interpreters, has led some commentators to speak of a general right to curial due process.[25]

---

19 *New South Wales* v *Commonwealth* (1915) 20 CLR 54 (*Wheat Case*); *Waterside Workers' Federation of Australia* v *J W Alexander Ltd* (1918) 25 CLR 434.

20 *R* v *Kirby; Ex parte Boilermakers' Society of Australia* (1956) 94 CLR 254; affirmed on appeal to the Privy Council in *Attorney-General of the Commonwealth of Australia* v *The Queen* (1957) 95 CLR 529.

21 Wheeler, 2004. Blackstone stated that public liberty 'cannot subsist long in any State, unless the administration of common justice be in some degree separated both from the legislative and also from the executive power': see *Huddart, Parker and Co Pty Ltd* v *Moorehead* (1909) 8 CLR 330, 381 (Isaacs J).

22 *Chu Kheng Lim* v *Minister for Immigration* (1992) 176 CLR 1, 27; *Nicholas* v *The Queen* (1998) 193 CLR 173, 186, 208–09, 220. See also, *Wilson* v *Minister for Aboriginal and Torres Straight Islander Affairs* (1996) 189 CLR 1, 11.

23 *Polyukhovich* v *Commonwealth* (1991) 172 CLR 501, 536. For comparable express provisions, see *United States Constitution*, Article I ss. 9 and 10 (prohibiting Bills of Attainder); *Canada Act 1982* (UK), c. 11, sch. B, *Canadian Charter of Rights and Freedoms* s. 11 ('*Canadian Charter of Rights and Freedoms*') (requiring a trial according to law in a fair an public hearing by and independent and impartial tribunal); see also *New Zealand Bill of Right Act* (1990) s 25; and the *European Convention for the Protection of Human Rights and Fundamental Freedoms*, opened for signature 4 November 1950, 213 UNTS 222, art. 6 (entered into force 3 September 1953) ('*European Convention on Human Rights*').

24 *Chu Kheng Lim* v *Minister for Immigration* (1992) 176 CLR 1, 27–28. Those limitations do not, however, preclude the Parliament authorizing indefinite administrative detention: *Al Kateb* v *Godwin* [2004] HCA 37. Moreover, conditions of immigration detention are not relevant to the validity of that detention: *Behrooz* v *Secretary of the Department of Immigration and Multicultural and Indigenous Affairs* [2004] HCA 36.

25 According to Deane J the separation of powers gives rise to 'the Constitution's only general guarantee of due process': *Re Tracey; Ex Parte Ryan* (1989) 166 CLR 518, 580. See generally, Zines, 1997, pp. 202–212; Wheeler, 1997.

Fundamental Implied Rights

The *Australian Constitution* is sometimes understood to contain a third set of rights derived from fundamental doctrines that are said to be assumptions or foundations on which the *Constitution* is based. One form of this argument has it that the common law contains principles that are so fundamental that they limit parliamentary sovereignty.[26]

These rights are much more controversial than the rights implied from text and structure. Rights derived from fundamental doctrines or constitutional assumptions have only ever been recognized by a minority of the Court[27] and, in some contexts, they have met with explicit rejection.[28] Moreover, there are clear indications that the present High Court disapproves of this form of reasoning. Recent cases concerning immigration detention, which might have lent themselves to arguments based on fundamental common law rights,[29] were decided without any reference to the idea. Further, because these rights are derived with little direct appeal to constitutional text, their recognition seems to be precluded by the High Court's recent insistence that constitutional implications must have a firm textual base.[30]

However, these arguments cannot be entirely neglected in a study of Australian constitutional rights. The idea that common law notions might limit parliamentary sovereignty seems to underlie another argument that still influences the High Court. This idea is prominent in the constitutional understandings of Sir Owen Dixon (see generally Wait, 2001, pp. 67–68) and finds its most famous expression in his judgment in *Australian Communist Party* v *Commonwealth*:[31]

> [The *Australian Constitution*] is an instrument framed in accordance with many traditional conceptions, to some of which it gives effect ... others of which are simply assumed. Among these I think that it may fairly be said that the rule of law forms an assumption.

---

26 A view defended by Allan (2001). For a critical appraisal see Goldsworthy, 2003.

27 By Murphy J (see Winterton, 1996, p. 131) and Deane and Toohey JJ (who relied partly on the common law in advancing their argument that the *Constitution* contained 'a general doctrine of legal equality'): *Leeth* v *Commonwealth* (1991) 174 CLR 455, 486.

28 *Durham Holdings* v *New South Wales* (2001) 205 CLR 399 (rejecting the argument that a common law principle limited the power of a State parliament so that a statute of expropriation must provide for just compensation).

29 In *Behrooz* v *Secretary, Department of Immigration, Multicultural and Indigenous Affairs* [2004] HCA 36, a detainee charged with 'escaping' from detention asserted that the conditions in which he had been kept were inhuman and degrading. In *Al Kateb* v *Godwin* [2004] HCA 37, a stateless Palestinian who wished to leave Australia but would not be accepted by any other nation challenged the indefinite nature of his detention. Neither claim succeeded. See above n 23 and accompanying text. For an account of these cases noting the absence of any consideration of fundamental common law rights, see Kirby, 2004.

30 *Lange* v *Australian Broadcasting Corporation* (1997) 189 CLR 520.

31 (1951) 83 CLR 1, 193.

No doubt at least partly due to the personal prestige of Sir Owen Dixon, the idea that the 'rule of law' is a limiting principle in the *Australian Constitution* has retained some force, even despite doubts about the more general limiting power of the common law. It reappeared in the joint judgment of Gummow and Hayne JJ in *Kartinyeri* v *Commonwealth*,[32] who suggested that the power in s. 51(xxvi) of the *Constitution* (which confers legislative power with respect to 'the people of any race for whom it is deemed necessary to make special laws') might be limited by Dixon's idea.[33]

The precise content of this 'assumption' is unclear. The 'rule of law' is as complex and contested an ideal as there is (Fallon, 1997a) and its invocation in Australian constitutional law has been infrequent and sometimes tentative.[34] However, it is very likely that interpreting the *Constitution* to contain such an assumption would confer protection like that conferred by constitutional rights in other systems. A procedural conception of the ideal might impose limitations like those imposed by 'due process' guarantees[35] (thus overlapping with, or perhaps incorporating, implications drawn from the separation of judicial power) and by provisions requiring that limitations on rights be 'prescribed by law'.[36] A 'substantive' conception of the rule of law – which is unlikely though not entirely ruled out on current authority[37] – could be even more

---

32 (1998) 195 CLR 337.

33 (1998) 195 CLR 337, 381. Recently, the Court has sought to identify some textual basis for this doctrine. See *Plaintiff S157/2002* v *Commonwealth* (2003) 211 CLR 476, 513 (Gaudron, McHugh, Gummow, Kirby and Hayne JJ):

> The provision of the constitutional writs and the conferral upon this Court of an irremovable jurisdiction to issue them to an officer of the Commonwealth [in s 75(v)] constitutes a textual reinforcement for what Dixon J said about the significance of the rule of law for the Constitution in *Australian Communist Party* v *The Commonwealth*.

34 In *Kartinyeri* v *Commonwealth* (1998) 195 CLR 337, 381 Gummow and Hayne JJ say only 'the occasion has yet to arise for consideration of all that may follow from Dixon J's statement'.

35 The rule of law is commonly associated with the idea that a law must meet certain procedural requirements that ensure an individual is able to obey it; that it effectively guides the conduct of citizens; that it is reasonably stable; that legal authority governs the exercise of political power; and that it is impartially administered by independent courts: Raz, 1979, pp. 212–14. A 'procedural' interpretation of the rule of law would overlap with the guarantee of curial due process derived from the separation of judicial power.

36 Section 1 of the *Canadian Charter of Rights and Freedoms* provides that '[t]he *Canadian Charter of Rights and Freedoms* guarantees the rights and freedoms set out in it subject only to such reasonable limits *prescribed by law* as can be demonstrably justified in a free and democratic society' [emphasis added]. See also *European Convention on Human Rights*, arts 10(2) and 11(2).

37 The judgment of Gummow and Hayne JJ in *Kartinyeri* v *Commonwealth* may even contemplate such an understanding, because they seem to suggest that a law could possibly infringe the rule of law requirement because of its content (the conferral of a racially

significant. Requiring law to conform to some set of substantive moral criteria may entail protection resembling rights of equality or freedom of speech (Allan, 2001).

Rights Protection in Rights-Neutral Contexts

So far, I have advanced only the well-understood point that rights are protected under the *Australian Constitution* when there is constitutional language that refers (or is understood to refer)[38] to a right and secondly, when some general rights-protecting principle is given constitutional status (either because it is inferred from the text or, more tentatively, because it is considered to be assumed by the *Constitution*). But the recognition of express and implied rights does not exhaust the ways in which rights might enter Australian constitutional law. First, these methods might also be combined in quite complex ways. The dissenting Justices in *Leeth v Commonwealth,* Deane and Toohey JJ, demonstrate the point.[39] In that case, their Honours derived a right of 'equality before the law' relying both on fundamental principles of common law[40] and implications from other features of the *Constitution.*[41]

In addition, the High Court has incorporated rights into more discrete aspects of its interpretation of the *Constitution.* The Court has sometimes identified limitations that reflect a concern for rights in the course of deciding the extent of a particular power. In this way, considerations of rights may become relevant in what appear to be 'right-neutral' contexts.

To make this point, I need to make a few preliminary points about constitutional adjudication. Grants of legislative power (like many constitutional provisions) are usually expressed in general terms. Take, by way of illustration, the Commonwealth's power with respect to 'trade and commerce with other countries and among the

---

discriminatory burden). However, there are also indications that point in the other direction. In *Re Minister for Immigration and Multicultural Affairs; Ex parte Lam* (2003) 214 CLR 1, McHugh and Gummow JJ stated:

> In Australia, the observance by decision-makers of the limits within which they are constrained by the Constitution and by statutes and subsidiary laws validly made is an aspect of the rule of law under the Constitution. It may be said that the rule of law reflects values concerned in general terms with abuse of power by the executive and legislative branches of government. But it would be going much further to give those values an immediate normative operation in applying the Constitution: at 23 [72].

See also *Plaintiff S 157/2002* v *Commonwealth* (2003) 211 CLR 476, 513 [102]–[104] quoted at above n 32. I am grateful to Graeme Hill for this point.

38 The classification of a constitutional provision as a 'right' is sometimes controversial. See below nn. 87–89 and accompanying text.

39 (1992) 174 CLR 455. I am seeking here to demonstrate possibilities in constitutional interpretation rather than accepted propositions of law.

40 *Leeth* v *Commonwealth* (1992) 174 CLR 455, 487.

41 Ibid 486.

States'[42] and its power with respect to 'external affairs'.[43] In the context of individual cases, the courts are faced with very specific questions: Can the Commonwealth Parliament use its power over 'trade and commerce with other countries and among the States' to enact a law requiring that interstate traders obtain Ministerial approval before exporting a certain good?[44] Can the Commonwealth Parliament use its power over 'external affairs' to enact a law that implements obligations assumed under a particular treaty (the subject of which does not come within any other grant of legislative power)?[45]

One task for a court, therefore, is to transform the *Constitution's* general commands into rules that are capable of resolving specific disputes. To do this, the courts develop a body of rules or doctrines best known, at least in Australian constitutional law, as 'tests'.[46] Because judges have considerable latitude in the way they formulate these tests they may develop tests that allow them to take a rights-protective stance.

The rights-protecting potential of these tests is demonstrated by *Davis* v *Commonwealth*[47] and by the judgments of Mason CJ and McHugh J in *Nationwide News* v *Wills*.[48] In these cases, Commonwealth legislative powers[49] were held to be subject to limitations that prevented the Commonwealth from circumscribing freedom of expression. In *Davis*, the Court invalidated restrictions on the use of certain expressions (including the use of '200 years' in conjunction with '1988' or '88') that were imposed as part of the national commemoration of 200 years of white settlement in Australia.[50] In *Nationwide News*, some justices used a similar technique to invalidate a law[51] that prohibited criticism 'calculated ... to bring a member of the [Industrial Relations] Commission into disrepute.'[52]

These cases are usually taken to demonstrate that common law rights 'enjoy a weak form of constitutional entrenchment' (Goldsworthy, 1992, p. 157; see also Winterton, 1996). However, these cases also illustrate the importance, and the rights-

---

42 *Australian Constitution* s 51(i).

43 Ibid s 51(xxix).

44 See *Murphyores Incorporated Pty Ltd* v *Commonwealth* (1976) 136 CLR 1 (holding that such a law was within the Commonwealth's power with respect to 'trade and commerce with other countries and among the States').

45 See *Commonwealth* v *Tasmania* (1983) 158 CLR 1.

46 For extensive scholarly analysis of these and related kinds of rules as they arise in American constitutional law see, Fallon, 1997b; Sager, 1985; Berman, 2004; Strauss, 1988.

47 (1988) 166 CLR 79 ('*Davis*').

48 (1992) 177 CLR 1 ('*Nationwide News*').

49 In *Davis*, the so-called 'implied nationhood' power; in *Nationwide News*, the conciliation and arbitration power (s 51(xxxv)).

50 (1988) 166 CLR 79, 100 (Mason CJ, Deane and Gaudron JJ), Wilson, Dawson and Toohey JJ agreeing on this point.

51 *Industrial Relations Act 1988* (Cth) s 299 (1) (d)(ii).

52 (1992) 177 CLR 1, 34 (Mason CJ); see also 102 (McHugh J). Other Justices held that the law was contrary to the implied freedom of political communication.

protecting potential, of a particular kind of 'test of application' (proportionality) that drew attention to the effect of the law on rights.

For much of its history, the High Court has employed rather deferential tests of application in the interpretation of grants of legislative power. For example, when interpreting incidental powers,[53] the Court showed a high level of deference to the means employed by the Parliament to pursue ends within its power.[54] But for a period in the 1990s, the Court sometimes used a test of 'proportionality' (Zines, 1997, pp. 44–48) to apply closer scrutiny to Commonwealth legislation. Under this test, the Court considered whether alternative, less restrictive means could have been used and whether the end pursued by that law was worth the restriction imposed.[55]

In *Nationwide News* and *Davis*, the proportionality test drew attention to the adverse consequences of the law – the effect on freedom of expression.[56] In *Davis*, Mason CJ and Deane and Gaudron JJ described the law in question as 'grossly disproportionate to the need to protect the commemoration [of the Bicentenary of European Settlement]'.[57] The language of 'proportionality' was also employed in *Nationwide News* to similar effect.[58]

Thus, these cases demonstrate that rights-promotion need not be pursued only through doctrines understood as 'constitutional rights'. Even when considering the apparently technical question of whether a law was 'with respect to' a nominated head of power, the Court had latitude to incorporate rights concerns through closer scrutiny of the means chosen by Parliament to pursue a nominated end. Similar choices arise when framing the test for determining whether a Commonwealth law is contrary to a limitation on power (express or implied), such as the implied freedom of political communication. There is a continuing discussion of the proper test for

---

53 The Commonwealth Parliament has an express grant of incidental power conferred by s. 51(xxxix) of the *Australian Constitution*, which refers to 'matters incidental to the execution of any power vested by this Constitution in the Parliament'. In addition, each grant of enumerated power is taken, by virtue of the ordinary rules of construction, to authorize measures that are necessary to effectuate the main purpose of the power: *D'Emden* v *Pedder* (1904) 1 CLR 91, 109; *Grannall* v *Marrickville Margarine Pty Ltd* (1955) 93 CLR 55, 77.

54 See *Herald & Weekly Times* (1966) 115 CLR 418, 437 (Kitto J) for a famous statement of this approach. See generally Zines, 1997, p. 47.

55 The proportionality test as used by the Supreme Court of Canada and the European Court of Human Rights is usually understood to consist of three inquiries: (1) whether a law exhibits a 'rational connection' to its purported end; (2) the availability of alternative, less drastic means by which that same end could be achieved; and (3) whether the end pursued by that law is worth the restriction or costs imposed: Kirk, 1997, pp. 4–7; but see *Leask* v *Commonwealth* (1996) 187 CLR 579.

56 (1988) 166 CLR 79, 99–100.

57 (1988) 166 CLR 79, 100. (Mason CJ, Deane and Gaudron JJ); 116 (Brennan J). For Brennan J it was also relevant that the power was, on his analysis, an incident of the Executive power to 'advance the nation — an essentially facultative function' which made him especially reluctant to allow the creation of offences: at 112–13.

58 (1992) 177 CLR 1, 33 (Mason CJ), 101 (McHugh J).

the application of the freedom of political communication,[59] including discussion of the appropriate level of deference (if any) that courts should give to legislative judgments.[60] A test that is less deferential to legislative judgment will tend to give more protection to rights.[61]

Existing Constitutional Rights and an Australian Bill of Rights

I have so far sought to illustrate how the *Australian Constitution* has been interpreted to protect rights. In the next part of this chapter, I will identify why the *Australian Constitution* has proved to be an especially weak mechanism for the protection of rights.

The Potential Power of Non-Express Rights

To make that argument, I will first address a possible suggestion to the contrary. It might be argued that Australia's current system of constitutional rights is an especially *powerful* method for the protection of rights. Certainly some commentators have considered the existing express and implied rights to be at least functionally equivalent to a bill of rights. Following the early decisions recognizing the freedom of political communication, Michael Detmold optimistically heralded the arrival of 'The New Constitutional Law', stating 'we now have everything a written bill of rights could give us' (Detmold, 1994, p. 248).

The argument could perhaps be taken even further. Those who fear that articulating rights in textual form would undesirably limit rights,[62] or encourage technical legal argument about the meaning of text over substantive consideration of values,[63] might prefer a system in which rights are implied from constitutional structures or fundamental assumptions. After all, the point of these structural methods of interpretation is that they focus our attention on the nature of the *Constitution* and the institutions it creates.[64]

Viewed in that light, the interpretive methods just discussed can be viewed as instances of a potentially broader phenomenon.[65] The method of implication might give rise to a broad range of rights implied from various constitutional structures or perhaps

---

59 See Stone, 2001; *Coleman* v *Power* [2004] HCA 39, [95], [196], [211].

60 For a discussion of this in explicit terms, see *Mulholland* v *Australian Electoral Commission* [2004] HCA 41, [237] (Kirby J).

61 As argued in Stone, 2001.

62 Williams (2004) lists this as an argument put against an Australian bill of rights.

63 A possibility raised by Waldron (1999, p. 106).

64 Black, 1969. For Black, the great virtue of the structural method is that, 'it frees us to talk sense' when compared with '[t]he textual method [which], in some cases, forces us to blur the focus and talk evasively': at p. 13.

65   In a recent speech Kirby J (2004) has issued a reminder of the continuing significance of implied rights:

even the nature and existence of the *Constitution* itself (see Detmold). The reference to common law rights in *Nationwide News* and *Davis* might find analogous applications in the use of international law[66] or perhaps even by reference to developments in statute law.[67] Judges may also respond to uncertainty in constitutional meaning by incorporating their own conception of the appropriate protection of rights or by their assessment of community values (see Braithwaite 1995; Sadurski, 1987).

Detmold's declaration was, to be fair, intended as a statement of constitutional theory rather than as a prediction of the direction that the High Court would take.[68] However, its failure as a matter of prediction points to a deeper problem – the problem of interpretive disagreement. Most of the methods of constitutional interpretation on which Australian constitutional rights rely are contested, either generally or in their specific applications. Disagreement about constitutional rights thus stems from the highly contested nature of constitutional interpretation itself.

Interpretations of the *Constitution* will be most secure when an interpretation is clearly supported by one or more established methods and is not inconsistent with any of them. Established methods include textual argument, historical (or originalist) argument, argument based on precedent, and implications from constitutional text and structure. Although there are disagreements about the proper emphasis to be

---

At least in a country such as Australia, without a comprehensive and entrenched Bill of Rights, it is natural that courts should scrutinize cases of apparent or arguable injustice against the criterion of whether the written Constitution permits it – either in its text or in the implications derived from that text or the assumptions upon which it is drawn.

66 Prominently (and controversially) Kirby J interprets the *Constitution* by reference to international law. Justice Kirby adopted this approach in his interpretation of the constitutional guarantee of 'just terms' in s 51(xxxi) (*Newcrest Mining (WA) Pty Ltd* v *Commonwealth* (1990) 190 CLR 513, 657–58); in his interpretation of the Commonwealth's power to make laws with respect to 'the people of any race' (*Kartinyeri* v *Commonwealth* (1998) 195 CLR 337, 417–18); and, most recently, in his interpretation of the Commonwealth's power over aliens and limitations on that power implied from the separation of judicial power (*Al Kateb* v *Godwin* [2004] HCA 37, [150]).

67 This method is not widely advocated or even discussed. However, in an intriguing passage in *Street* v *Queensland Bar Association* (1989) 168 CLR 461, 566, Gaudron J appears to interpret the Constitution by reference to developments in legislation when, along with other members of the Court, she adopted a substantive and more rights-protective interpretation of the concept of discrimination (found in the s. 117 prohibition on discrimination based on State residence). In reference to the earlier cases on s. 117, she held: 'Those cases ... do not reflect recent developments within the field of anti-discrimination law which have led to an understanding that discrimination may be constituted by acts or decisions have discriminatory effect or disparate impact (indirect discrimination) as well as by acts or decisions based on discriminatory considerations (direct discrimination).' Her Honour referred to the Sex Discrimination Act 1984 (Cth) s. 5, the Anti-Discrimination Act 1977 (NSW) s. 7; the Equal Opportunity Act 1984 (Vic) s. 17: at ibid.

68 Detmold's (1994) argument is that the very idea of a constitution brings with it rights at least as extensive as those seen in a typical bill of rights.

given to these arguments in any given case, it is generally agreed that there is *some* place in constitutional interpretation for their use. By the same token, however, readings of the *Constitution* which rely on controversial modes of constitutional interpretation or which seem to run contrary to one of the established modes will be much less secure. The problem for many of the Australian constitutional rights is that there is at least one established form of constitutional argument (usually one based on constitutional text or constitutional history) that undermines them.

The Problem of Interpretive Disagreement

Reliance on a contested method of constitutional interpretation   The phenomenon of interpretive disagreement is most obvious in relation to the implication of rights based on fundamental doctrines of the common law or other unexpressed concepts. For this reason perhaps, the implication of such rights has never been fully accepted by courts,[69] and the recognition of rights implied in this manner has only ever sporadic and, except where supported by long-standing precedent, remains tentative.[70]

Reservations about this kind of interpretive method have thus prevented the realization of Michael Detmold's vision of 'The New Constitutional Law' which would recognize extensive implied rights, and in which the interpretation of the *Constitution* more generally would be infused by a commitment to equality and the rule of law. These reservations have also prevented the general acceptance of Kirby J's anti-originalist (Kirby, 2000) and internationalist approach[71] to constitutional interpretation.[72] That approach would allow for much greater protection of rights in the *Constitution*, because it renders irrelevant the framers' decision not to include

---

69   The method is regarded as relying on weak historical premises and as too imprecise to provide meaningful limit on government: Winterton, 1996, pp. 142–43.

70   As is the case with the 'rule of law' assumption recognized in *Australian Communist Party* v *Commonwealth* (1951) 83 CLR 1.

71   See above n. 65.

72   Despite Kirby J's opposition to the originalist method, other members of the Court continue to have regard to constitutional history, including the framers' intention, to determine the meaning of the *Constitution*. Among many examples, see *Grain Pool of Western Australia* v *Commonwealth* (2000) 202 CLR 479, in which a joint judgment of six judges interpreted the Commonwealth's power with respect to 'patents of invention' partly by reference to essential characteristics in 1900 and in which Kirby J declined to consider the historical meaning of the phrase: at 492–96, 515. On these cases see Hill, 2000. See also, *Singh* v *Commonwealth* [2004] HCA 43 in which all members of the High Court (including Kirby J) interpreted the Commonwealth's power with respect to 'aliens' by reference to the historical understanding of that concept; and Zines, 2004. For a critical assessment of Kirby J's anti-originalism, see Goldsworthy, 2000. For judicial rejection of Kirby J's approach to international law see, *Al Kateb* v *Godwin* [2004] HCA 37, [62]–[72]. See generally, Walker, 2002; Simpson and Williams, 2000.

rights in the *Australian Constitution*[73] and provides a mechanism for the incorporation of the growing international law of human rights.

Accepted method; contested application   Constitutional interpretation is further complicated by disagreements that arise as to the applications of a given method of interpretation. Thus, even when a method of constitutional interpretation is accepted, particular doctrinal developments are likely to remain disputed. That phenomenon is best illustrated by reference to implication of the freedom of political communication. The judgments first recognizing the freedom of political communication stressed the legitimacy (and prior use) of the method constitutional implication.[74] Nonetheless, the implication of a freedom of political communication was controversial, largely because it appeared to run contrary to originalist arguments as to the intention of the framers and because of doubts as to its textual foundation.[75] Even among those judges who have accepted that some form of implication exists, there are doubts – inspired by originalist and textualist concerns – about some of its applications. In particular, its application to the common law of defamation in *Theophanous* v *Herald & Weekly Times* was almost immediately subject to doubt[76] and soon after revised in *Lange* v *Australian Broadcasting Corporation*.[77]

The weakness that arises from this controversy has now been offset by the weight of precedent. The existence of the implied freedom of political communication was affirmed unanimously, though confined, in *Lange*. By virtue of the weight accorded to that decision, the existence of the implied freedom is probably beyond challenge for the moment. Nonetheless, the controversy surrounding the doctrine and its insecure textual and historical foundations may have on-going effects. The freedom of political communication still remains the subject of some judicial opposition,[78] and there may long be a temptation to revisit the foundational question of the doctrine's legitimacy.[79]

---

73 For accounts of the framers' attitudes with respect to rights, see Charlesworth, 2002, pp. 20–27; Campbell, 1970.

74 *Australian Capital Television* v *Commonwealth* (1992) 177 CLR 106, 133 (Mason CJ); *Nationwide News* v *Wills* (1992) 177 CLR 1, 41 (Brennan CJ), 69–70 (Toohey J., 209–10 (Gaudron J).

75 *Australian Capital Television* v *Commonwealth* (1992) 177 CLR 106, 186 (Dawson J). See also, Goldsworthy, 1997.

76 See, *McGinty* v *Western Australia*, (1995) 186 CLR 140, 235–36 (McHugh J); 291 (Gummow J).

77 (1997) 189 CLR 520, 566 ('*Lange*').

78 See *Lenah Game Meats* v *Australian Broadcasting Corporation* (2001) 208 CLR 199, 331 (Callinan J).

79 As has occurred with respect to the implied (or 'unenumerated') constitutional right of privacy and subsequent limits on State power to regulate abortion recognized by the United States Supreme Court in *Roe* v *Wade*, 410 US 113 (1973). Despite widespread doubts about the decision (see Ely, 1972; Ginsburg, 1985), *Roe* v *Wade* was affirmed (though modified) in *Casey* v *Planned Parenthood*, 505 US 833 (1992). However, there remains a real possibility

In addition, it seems that misgivings about the doctrine's foundation have had a continuing effect on its content. Doubts about the doctrine's textual basis were answered in *Lange* with an attempt to confine the doctrine to the necessary implications from the text and structure of the *Constitution*.[80] However, as I have argued at length elsewhere,[81] it is not possible to understand or articulate the extent of the freedom of political communication without reference to some ideas or values found outside constitutional text. By discouraging attention to these values, the High Court has deprived itself of the tools it needs to develop the freedom of political communication in a coherent manner.[82]

Text and context   A common thread in this discussion relates to the role of constitutional text. Rights implied from text and structure, rights implied from constitutional assumptions, and rights-sensitive tests of application all lack an obvious textual foundation in the *Constitution*. Reliance on constitutional text is a particularly powerful form of constitutional argument, at least where the text is sufficiently specific to resolve the question at issue.[83] Thus without clear textual recognition, rights-protective constitutional interpretations are vulnerable to later revision.[84] It is not surprising therefore to see a judicially created doctrine, like the doctrine of proportionality, revised and considerably confined.[85]

---

that it will one day be overruled. The views of potential Supreme Court Justices on the question are, therefore, closely scrutinized. See, 'Symposium: The Judicial Appointments Process' (2001) 10 *William and Mary Bill of Rights Law Journal.*

80 (1997) 189 CLR 520, 566.

81 Stone, 1999. For a judicial response, see *Coleman* v *Power* [2004] HCA 39, [84]–[90].

82 For example, the Court's commitment to 'text and structure' does not provide an adequate basis for determining the class of communication entitled to protection. On this see Stone, 2001, pp. 378–90.

83 As I have explained elsewhere reliance on constitutional text appeals to 'rule of law' values. Constitutional text is an ascertainable and generally applicable source of law and is the result (at least it is often argued) of a legitimate law-making process. See Stone, 1999, pp. 706.

84 Michael Dorf, (2004, p. 834) has made a similar observation about the use of structural argument in constitutional interpretation:

In our legal culture – by which I mean at least the legal culture of the common-law countries and probably something substantially broader – interpretive arguments unmoored from text are always vulnerable to being attacked as illegitimate ... structuralism in the absence of clear textual warrant is always vulnerable to retrenchment.

85 The High Court has since held that proportionality has a very limited role in determining whether a Commonwealth law is 'with respect to' a (non-purposive) head of legislative power: *Leask* v *Commonwealth* (1996) 187 CLR 579. There were differences, however, as to how that revision was expressed. Chief Justice Brennan's approach was to equate the test of proportionality with more deferential (and traditional) tests of application,

But text *alone* is also an insecure basis for the recognition of constitutional rights. Where constitutional text is read without reference to its context or its historical understanding, that interpretation is likely to be vulnerable to revision because aspects of context and historical understanding will be advanced as reasons to doubt that interpretation, even if that interpretation *could* be reconciled with constitutional text. Consider for example, the peculiarly open-textured s. 92. The injunction that 'trade, commerce and intercourse among the States shall be absolutely free' was once read as a guarantee of an individual right to engage in these activities.[86] However, that interpretation (at least in so far as it applied to interstate trade and commerce) eventually gave way to an interpretation, informed by the section's history, aimed at preserving free trade among the States.[87]

Are the express and implied rights really 'rights'?   The insufficiency of constitutional text, considered without reference to other sources of constitutional understanding, casts doubt on whether the so-called express rights are properly regarded as 'rights' at all. The chief reason for regarding these provisions as 'express rights' is that they appear to resemble rights found in constitutional bills of rights in other systems.[88] However, despite this superficial resemblance, there are some other matters – some contextual and some historical – that suggest an opposite conclusion. For one thing, these provisions are scattered through a document otherwise concerned with structures of government and the division of power between the central and State governments. Although that is not entirely unprecedented, their textual manifestation reflects the place they held in the framers' deliberation. At most, rights were an intermittent concern in a task overwhelmed with the more pressing task of forming a federation (see Charlesworth, 2002, pp. 20–27; Campbell, 1970).

The classification of many constitutional provisions as constitutional rights may therefore be open to challenge by reference to methods of constitutional interpretation that rely on historical meaning. Consider the protection of religion conferred by s. 116 of the *Constitution*. An interpretation informed by the history of that provision

---

finding that '[p]roportionality is another expression for "appropriate and adapted" ... [s]o used, proportionality has nothing to say about the appropriateness, necessity or desirability of the law to achieve an effect or purpose': ibid 593. Justice Dawson, on the other hand, declared that 'to introduce the concept of proportionality ... is to introduce a concept which is alien to the principles which this court has hitherto applied': ibid 602.

86 *Commonwealth* v *Bank of New South Wales* (1949) 79 CLR 497; *Hughes and Vale Pty Ltd* v *New South Wales (No 1)* (1954) 93 CLR 1. For an account of the complex history of s. 92 and its various interpretations see Zines, 1997, ch. 7 and Coper, 1983.

87 *Cole* v *Whitfield* (1988) 165 CLR 360; Zines, 1997, pp. 136–43.

88 Compare for example the text of s. 116 ('The Commonwealth shall not make any law for establishing any religion, or for imposing any religious observance, or for prohibiting the free exercise of any religion, and no religious test shall be required as a qualification for any office or public trust under the Commonwealth.') with the relevant parts of the First Amendment to the *United States Constitution* ('Congress shall make no law respecting and establishment of religion, or prohibiting the free exercise thereof').

(and perhaps also the context of the provision which is placed in a chapter headed 'The States') might interpret the provision (or at least its 'free exercise' and 'non-establishment' requirements) to be aimed only at preserving State independence with respect to the regulation of religion.[89] On this analysis, s. 116 would be devoted to dividing power among the States and the Commonwealth, like much of the rest of the *Constitution*.

Section 80 could be similarly reinterpreted. James Stellios has shown how such an argument could be made in relation to the jury trial requirement of s. 80, which he characterizes as 'an essential element of [the] federal structure' (2005, pp. 135–137). His argument is that s. 80 operates to qualify the power of State Parliaments over the constitution of State courts;[90] to empower a lay panel of a federal court to exercise the judicial power of the Commonwealth (in the form of jury trials); and to ensure that in federal criminal cases, accused persons face a jury drawn from their own State. Stellios's argument is important because it accepts the (undeniable) point that the reasons given for the current interpretation of s. 80 are unconvincing, but challenges the idea that a 'rights-promoting' interpretation would be the natural replacement. It remains to be seen whether such arguments are available with respect to other 'express rights', but the argument serves as a reminder that, even in this sphere, a rights-promoting interpretation may not be the only coherent alternative to the current interpretation.

At base the problem with Australia's constitutional rights is that in most cases, there are interpretive arguments that count against them (as well as some that count in their favour). So, many of Australian constitutional rights are likely to be mired in controversy not just as to their meaning, but also as to their existence. In this sense then they are particularly weak form of constitutional rights protection.

Conclusion

Like most other commentators on the *Australian Constitution*, then, I regard it as a weak institution for the protection of rights. In this chapter, I have located the source of that weakness more precisely in the interpretive controversy that inevitably attends rights-protective readings of a constitution that, in textual and historical terms, is so inhospitable to rights. Having reached that conclusion I will not, however, go on to argue for a constitutional bill of rights. Indeed, I regard the current state of Australia's constitutional rights as largely irrelevant to that question.

---

89 Such an analysis might rely on constitutional history. Delegates at the drafting Conventions appear to have been concerned that 'without the prohibition, the Commonwealth would have been in a position to regulate Sunday observance throughout Australia … it was clear that the mere prospect, however, remote of a federal government legislating in this area was on which most state representatives desired to avoid' Campbell, 1970, pp. 307–8. See also, Quick and Garran, 1901, p. 951.

90 By preventing them from abolishing jury trials when the federal Parliament has provided for a trial by indictment for an offence against Commonwealth law.

That conclusion might not be immediately obvious. At first glance, my argument could make an Australian bill of rights seem more attractive. An express bill of rights would, after all, settle interpretive controversies as to the existence of constitutional rights. An express bill of rights would provide judges with two good arguments for the existence of constitutional rights – constitutional text and a clear expression of 'original' intention.[91] If the *Australian Constitution* contained an explicit right of freedom of expression, a right of due process or an equality guarantee, there would be no point to a debate about whether one should be implied from text and structure or in some other manner. Similarly, an express guarantee of a right to a jury trial (without a requirement for indictment) would end the attempts to derive such a guarantee from s. 80, and an express freedom of religion (expressed in terms that made it generally applicable) would render irrelevant the limitation of s. 116 to Commonwealth laws.

The settling of these interpretive controversies, however, does not make the case for an Australian bill of rights. Certainty is an important legal value, but the adoption of a bill of rights would, if anything, make Australian constitutional law more complex and uncertain. The adoption of a bill of rights would settle interpretive controversies about the existence of rights, but interpretive controversies about the precise meaning of the rights adopted would remain.[92]

Importantly, controversies about the meaning of rights would not be reduced by their recognition in constitutional text. The text itself will provide only limited guidance.[93] Further, though a court interpreting a bill of rights would have various interpretive resources (such as international case law and scholarship on questions of rights), the guidance such resources could provide is also limited.

In each case, these resources are undermined by the prevalence of disagreement about the precise meaning of rights concepts. It is because rights are the subjects of such disagreement that bills of rights are expressed in general terms, leaving disputes about the limits of rights and their competing conceptions unresolved (Waldron, 1999, p. 220; Marmor, 1997). That same disagreement about rights would be reflected in other interpretive resources. Consider, for example, the suggestion that '[t]he social or political background to rights created [through a bill of rights formulated with wide popular involvement] may ... assist the High Court in its role by giving it the context necessary to balance rights against other community interests' (Williams, 1999, p. 259). Although the 'social and political background' may illuminate very

---

91 That is the enactment of a bill of rights would be taken as an expression of intention (by the framers of that bill of rights and by the people who ratified it) to protect rights.

92 In relation to the freedom of expression, I address some of these issues in Stone (1999) and Stone (2001).

93 It would, of course, be entirely naïve to suggest otherwise. Although rights can occasionally be expressed in a relatively specific form, most rights are expressed in general terms. Moreover, as McDonald (2004) points out, generality in the expression of rights is inevitable. In a diverse society, it is only because rights concepts are indeterminate (and the terms in which they are expressed consequently general) that a bill of rights can obtain general agreement.

general points of agreement (as may the text), it is difficult to see how it would yield much information useful in the rather precise process of determining 'the limits of a right'.[94]

And as a practical matter, a bill of rights would almost certainly expand the realm of constitutional rights. Therefore, even if (contrary to my earlier argument) a bill of rights could achieve greater certainty about the content of, say, constitutional freedom of expression, a bill of rights would give rise to many controversies surrounding rights that currently do not have constitutional status.

An argument for an Australian bill of rights does, of course, remain. By resolving interpretive disagreement about the existence of rights, an express bill of rights would limit the capacity of a court seriously to eviscerate or completely eradicate those rights. However, the weakness of the existing constitutional rights – including the possibility of their eradication – is only undesirable if stronger constitutional rights are desirable. Thus, we return to that fundamental question: whether constitutional rights are, in the final analysis to be preferred to other methods of rights protection.

References

Allan, T.R.S. (2001), *Constitutional Justice: A Liberal Theory of the Rule of Law*, Oxford: Oxford University Press.

Bailey, P. (1990), *Human Rights: Australia in an International Context* (Sydney: Butterworths).

Berman, M.N. (2004), 'Constitutional Decision Rules', *Virginia Law Review*, **90:** 2.

Black, C.L. (1969), *Structure and Relationship in Constitutional Law* (Baton Rouge: Louisiana State University Press).

Braithwaite, J. (1995), 'Community Values and Australian Jurisprudence', *Sydney Law Review*, **17:** 351.

Campbell, E. (1970), 'Civil Rights in the Australian Constitutional Tradition', in Beck, C. (ed.), *Law and Justice: Essays in Honor of Robert S. Rankin* (Durham: Duke University Press).

Charlesworth, H. (2002), *Writing in Rights: Australia and the Protection of Human Rights* (Sydney: University of New South Wales Press).

---

94 Williams (1999, p. 259) admits that these resources would not provide the courts with very precise guidelines for the resolution of particular disputes but maintains that they 'would assist a court in ascertaining the appropriate limits of a right and where it might draw the line between the judicial and political process.' But 'ascertaining the appropriate limits of a right' requires a precise determination of the nature of a right (what activity it covers, how much protection it confers on that activity) and its relative weight with respect to other rights and interests. If 'the social and political background' or 'context' cannot assist with that task then it is difficult to see what it adds to the process of applying rights and in particular how it renders that task more precise than the task of applying implied rights.

Coper, M. (1983), *Freedom of Interstate Trade under the Australian Constitution* (Sydney: Butterworths).

Detmold, M. (1994), 'The New Constitutional Law', *Sydney Law Review*, **16**: 228.

Dorf, M.C. (2004), 'Interpretive Holism and the Structural Method, or How Charles Black Might Have Thought About Campaign Finance Reform and Congressional Timidity', *Georgetown Law Review* **92**: 833.

Ely, J.H. (1972), 'The Wages of Crying Wolf: A Comment on *Roe v. Wade*', *Yale Law Journal*, **82**: 920.

Fallon, R. (1997a), 'The Rule of Law as a Concept in Constitutional Discourse', *Columbia Law Review*, **97**: 1.

—— (1997b), 'Supreme Court Foreword: Implementing the Constitution', *Harvard Law Review*, **111**: 54.

Ginsburg, R.B. (1985), 'Some Thoughts On Autonomy And Equality In Relation To *Roe* v *Wade*', *North Carolina Law Review*, **63**: 375.

Goldsworthy, J. (1997), 'Constitutional Implications and Freedom of Political Speech: A Reply to Stephen Donaghue', *Monash University Law Review*, **32**: 362.

—— (1992), The Constitutional Protection of Rights in Australia', in Craven, Greg (ed.), *Australian Federation: Towards the Second Century: A Work to Mark the Centenary of the Australasian Federation Conference, Held at Parliament House, Melbourne, 6-14 February, 1890*, Carlton: Melbourne University Press, p. 151.

—— (2000), 'Interpreting the Constitution in Its Second Century', *Melbourne University Law Review*, **24**: 677.

—— (2003), 'Homogenizing Constitutions', *Oxford Journal of Legal Studies*, **23**, p. 483.

Hill, G. (2000), '"Originalist" v "Progressive" Interpretations of the Constitution – Does it Matter?', *Public Law Review*, **11**: 159.

Kirby, Justice M. (2000), 'Constitutional Interpretation and Original Intent: A Form of Ancestor Worship?', *Melbourne University Law Review*, **24**: 1.

—— (2004), 'Deep Lying Rights – A Constitutional Conversation Continues', The Robin Cooke Lecture 2004, Wellington, New Zealand, 25 November 2004, available at <http://www.hcourt.gov.au/speeches/kirbyj/kirbyj_25nov04.html#f107>

Kirk, J. (1997), 'Constitutional Guarantees, Characterisation and the Concept of Proportionality', *Melbourne University Law Review*, **21**: 1.

Marmor, A. (1997), 'On the Limits of Rights', *Law and Philosophy*, **16**: 1.

McDonald, L. (2004), 'New Directions in the Australian Bill of Rights Debate', *Public Law*, **12**: 22.

Quick, Sir J. and Garran, Sir R.R. (1901), *The Annotated Constitution of the Australian Commonwealth* (Sydney: Angus and Robertson).

Raz, J. (1979), *The Authority of Law: Essays on Law and Morality* (Oxford: Clarendon).

Sadurski, W. (1987), 'Conventional Morality and Judicial Standards', *Virginia Law Review*, **73**: 339.

Sager, L.G. (1985), 'The Strategic Space between Norms and Rules of Constitutional Law', *Texas Law Review*, **63:** 959.

Simpson, A. and Williams, G. (2000), 'International Law and Constitutional Interpretation', *Public Law Review*, **11:** 205.

Stellios, J. (2005), 'Section 80 of the Constitution – "A Bulwark of Liberty"?', *Sydney Law Review*, **27:** 113.

Stone, A. (1998), 'Freedom of Political Communication, the Constitution and the Common Law', *Federal Law Review*, **26:** 219.

—— (1999), 'The Limits of Constitutional Text and Structure', *Melbourne University Law Review*, 23: 668.

—— (2001), 'Rights, Personal Rights and Freedoms: The Nature of the Freedom of Political Communication', *Melbourne University Law Review*, **25:** 374.

Strauss, D. (1998), 'The Ubiquity of Prophylactic Rules', *University of Chicago Law Review*, **55:** 190.

'Symposium: The Judicial Appointments Process' (2001), 10 *William and Mary Bill of Rights Journal.*

Wait, M. (2001), 'The Slumbering Sovereign: Sir Owen Dixon's Common Law Constitution Revisited', *Federal Law Review*, **29:** 57.

Waldron, J. (1999), *Law and Disagreement* (Oxford: Clarendon).

Walker, K. (2002), 'International Law as a Tool of Constitutional Interpretation', *Monash University Law Review*, **28:** 77.

Wheeler, F. (1997), 'The Doctrine of Separation of Powers and constitutionally Entrenched Due Process in Australia', *Monash University Law Review*, **23:** 248.

—— (2004), 'Due Process, Chapter III and the New High Court', *Federal Law Review*, **32:** 205.

Wilcox, M.R. (1993), *An Australian Charter of Rights?* (Sydney: Law Book Company).

Williams, G. (1999), *Human Rights under the Australian Constitution* (Melbourne: Oxford University Press).

—— (2004), *A Bill of Rights For Australia?* (Sydney: University of New South Wales Press).

Winterton, G. (1996), 'Constitutionally Entrenched Common Law Rights', in Sampford, C. and Preston, K. (eds), *Interpreting Constitutions: Theories, Principles and Institutions* (Leichardt, NSW: The Federation Press), p. 121.

Zines, L. (1997), *The High Court and the Constitution,* 4th edn (Sydney: Butterworths).

—— (2004), 'Dead Hands or Living Tree? Stability and Change in Constitutional Law', *Adelaide Law Review*, **25**:3.

PART II
Particular Human Rights Issues

Chapter 6

Rights and Citizenship in Law and Public Discourse

Helen Irving[1]

Introduction

In the discourse of rights, citizenship is never far behind. And for that of citizenship, rights are even closer. Indeed, we tend to think of the two as inextricably linked – with citizenship occupying a large subset of the field of rights. We talk freely of the 'rights of citizens' and of a person's 'rights *as* a citizen'. While we may recognize a class of rights that are not associated with citizenship (pre-eminently, those set out in the UN's *Universal Declaration of Human Rights*[2]), we seem to define citizenship, or speak of it, in such a way that assumes its attachment to rights. The title of Brian Galligan's and John Chesterman's book *Citizens without Rights: Aborigines and Australian Citizenship* (1997), for example, reflects the assumption of a connection between the two, as well as the idea that special explanation is needed where the connection is absent. To many people, the conflation of citizenship and rights would appear both natural and uncontroversial.

Yet rights and citizenship, I will argue, are far from inseparable. Indeed, historically and conceptually, they stand apart from each other in significant ways. Citizenship has rarely (if ever) conferred rights that are both automatic and inalienable. Even the most fundamental (one might think) of 'citizenship rights' – holding a passport, being able to return to one's country, and enjoying diplomatic protection while overseas – have all been lawfully denied to or withheld from legal citizens in Australia's history. Many other rights, such as voting, serving on juries and standing for parliament, have never been available to all who hold legal citizenship. The Australian record is not unique.

For some, this history may be an aberration. Others may regard the dissociation between rights and citizenship as regrettable, even intolerable; they may advocate its reversal. However, the relationship between rights and citizens is not as simple as this, either empirically or normatively. To begin with, many citizenship rights can, in practice, only be enjoyed by a subsection of citizens and most people would accept

---

1   Faculty of Law, University of Sydney.

2   GA Res 217A, 3 UN GAOR, 3rd sess, 183rd plen mtg, UN Doc A/Res/217A (III) (1948).

this, at least in some cases: voting, for example, is reasonably confined to adults, even with an otherwise broad franchise. Furthermore, many people (especially those who value rights) may agree that certain rights that are currently available only to legal citizens, and are therefore denied to non-citizens, might reasonably be extended to some classes of non-citizen: for example, a case might be made that the right to vote should extend to permanent residents, regardless of legal nationality.

In other words, to speak of citizenship rights suggests that there is a natural or automatic relationship between the status of citizen and the enjoyment of rights. But this is not demonstrable. Furthermore, it implies that non-citizens should be excluded from entitlement to certain rights, although these rights may have no *necessary* or essential (or even rational) association with legal citizenship.

There are few (if any) cases where a right has ever been historically available to all legal citizens without exception. Equally, there are few cases where it would be accepted that no exceptions should ever be made. The best we can say in regard to rights within one's own country is that historically, citizenship has been *required* in many instances as a precondition for taking part in certain things provided by the state; but, while citizenship has been necessary, it has not been sufficient for the exercise of certain rights. It has not, in itself, been the source of rights. And nor, I will argue, should it be.

An appreciation of this dissociation is important for understanding both the nature of rights and the way rights develop. It is significant in particular for debates about constitutionalizing rights. The conclusion, however, is not that we *should* tighten up the relationship and ensure that rights genuinely attach to citizenship. It is that we should recognize that these two concepts are different and that they serve different – and justifiably different – purposes. In other words, there is both an empirical and normative foundation to the separation of citizenship and rights.

The Historical Record

Citizenship is a matter for the law of a state. While the term 'citizen' is very frequently used loosely, and often rhetorically, to make certain normative claims about the character of, and opportunities for, participation in a political community, our point of departure must be the recognition that citizenship is defined by law. Many who write about citizenship simply ignore this. The result is the creation of an abstract model of citizenship (the 'good citizen', who is involved, for example, in the local community, or who works as a volunteer for worthy causes) that has only indirect relevance to the actual opportunities and constraints upon individual conduct.

The failure of our language in articulating the difference between legal and normative citizenship is part of the problem. Let us consider, first, the legal dimension. Certainly, it has been accepted at many stages in history, that particular entitlements should be available exclusively to a particular class of persons by simple virtue of their 'personhood', that is to say, rather than by association with their actions, or their office, profession, or title to property. This personhood has, in some historical examples, resided in the simple fact of birth in a defined territory. All free people born in ancient

Rome acquired citizenship, as all born in the United States (and other countries, albeit not Australia) continue to do. But citizenship, as a set of rights or entitlements, has rarely (if ever) extended even to all those who have been born within a state or territory. Citizens were included under the 'law of persons', in the classical threefold division: Law of Persons, Law of *Res* and Law of Actions (Buckland, 1963, p. 57). The law of persons also covered slaves, women and children, and these were further divided into freed and unfreed slaves, married and single women, legitimate and illegitimate children, and so on. Entitlement to rights, such as political participation and property-owning, was extremely variable, even for those born in the territory. Citizenship and rights, or legal entitlements, have not, historically, been co-extensive.

Australia's own history provides a closer example of differentiation of types of citizenship, and disassociation between citizenship and rights. Contrary to what is often believed, the definition of citizenship has very little to do with rights, or even obligations. The 1994 Preamble to the most recently amended version of the *Nationality and Citizenship Act*[3] seems to suggest that there is a link: 'Australian citizenship represents formal membership of the community of the Commonwealth of Australia; and Australian citizenship is a common bond, involving reciprocal rights and obligations, uniting all Australians, while respecting their diversity.' These assertions are, however, purely aspirational. What the Act goes on to do, notwithstanding the Preamble's generous words, is simply to set out the legal qualifications for citizenship by birth, descent or adoption. It does not confer rights or entitlements.

One has to look to other Acts to discover what it is, if anything, that 'unites all Australians' and what they get, if anything, from belonging to that category of person. When we look closely at these other sources of rights (using the term loosely, for the present), we find that certain of them *have* been treated as exclusive to legal citizens from time to time, or as incidents of citizenship, but in no cases has citizenship been treated as a *source* of rights, and nor have these rights been inalienable. Citizenship, that is, occasionally brings rights in its train, but guarantees none.

The guide to citizenship records in the National Archives of Australia begins its section entitled 'The Substance of Citizenship' with the statement:

> A chapter dealing with the rights and obligations attached to, or implied by, citizenship might be expected to be the most significant section of a guide to records on citizenship in Australia. However, researchers may be disappointed to learn that ... [c]itizenship in Australia has never been clearly defined by reference to a set of rights and corresponding obligations. (Dutton, 1999, p. 87)

Voting and Passports

What rights might the uninitiated readily expect to come with citizenship? More than one hundred years ago, in the (unsuccessful) attempt to reach a definition

---

3   *Australian Citizenship Act 1948* (Cth).

of 'citizenship' for inclusion in the *Constitution*, the founders of the Australian Commonwealth began with the idea that the right to vote might perhaps be the single, identifiable attribute of citizenship. However, they quickly recognized that there were many individuals whom they wanted to count as 'citizens' but who could not vote. To define a citizen as a person who could vote was to disqualify many who were both legal citizens (or British subjects, as was the legal expression at the time) and possibly also good citizens. The founders had in mind women, the majority of whom could not yet vote in the Australian colonies, but whom it would be unthinkable to define as 'non-citizens' (Irving, 1997, ch. 9).

Today, although many people, if asked, might also start to define citizenship along similar lines, they would get no further than the *Constitution*'s framers did. Voting and citizenship have never been co-extensive. Following the first *Nationality and Citizenship Act*,[4] from 1949, British subjects who were not Australian citizens but who met certain (minimal) residency requirements could vote, alongside Australians who were citizens (and also subjects) by birth or naturalization. This arrangement persisted until 1984, when legal citizens alone became entitled to enrol to vote. Citizenship also became exclusive, and Australian citizens no longer automatically had the status of subject. There was, however, a class of residents who were subjects before 1984 and therefore entitled to vote – mostly English nationals and New Zealanders – who remained on the electoral roll from that year, and who could therefore continue to vote in Australian elections, although they were not legally Australian citizens. The class of those entitled to vote is, thus, wider than the field of citizens.

This may, of course, be merely an accident of history, one that will come to its natural end sometime around the mid-twenty-first century at the latest. But it is not the only contrary example to be taken into account in attempting to establish a correlation between citizenship and voting. A large class of legal citizens – children – have never been entitled to vote. A smaller class – those who are 'by reason of being of unsound mind incapable of understanding the nature and significance of enrolment and voting'[5] – are similarly disenfranchised. Other citizens – prisoners serving a sentence of three years or more (for an offence in any Australian jurisdiction),[6] unpardoned traitors and Australian citizens residing overseas for more than six years[7] – lose the right to vote. This may, of course, seem fairly ordinary and even inevitable. After all, no right is absolute, and it is illogical to grant a right to a person who is incapable of (and some would say of prisoners, unworthy of) exercising it.

Throughout the Commonwealth's history, however, many fully competent, adult citizens[8] who have committed no prior illegal act and who have continued to live in

---

4 *1948* (Cth).

5 *Commonwealth Electoral Act 1918* (Cth) s. 93(8)(a).

6 *Commonwealth Electoral Act 1918* (Cth) s. 93(8)(b).

7 *Commonwealth Electoral Act 1918* (Cth) s. 94, defining 'eligible overseas electors'.

8 Using the term to refer both to 'subjects' and 'citizens' in law.

Australia, have been deprived of the vote. Most Aboriginal (and other native) citizens could not vote in Commonwealth elections until 1962.[9] In the First World War, under the Commonwealth *Crimes Act* of 1914, certain members of 'Unlawful Associations' were – in the same Act that rendered these associations unlawful – prohibited from voting.[10] In both cases, the disqualification arose from the sentiment that certain types of citizen did not deserve the vote, although (as with the case of permanent residents) these persons were affected by the law, which they were required to obey and under which they lived. The opportunity to take part in choosing representatives does not come, thus, as a right of citizenship.

What else might we imagine to be attached by right, automatically or exclusively, to the class of legal citizens? Holding a passport, one might think. But this is not a right. The grant or renewal of a passport is a matter for executive discretion. Apart from cases where a passport is withdrawn because a citizen is suspected of having committed an illegal act and is to be prevented from fleeing the jurisdiction, it may be denied or withdrawn for other reasons. The specific grounds for refusing a passport have changed throughout Australia's history, but the discretionary nature of the grant remains (Rubenstein, 2002). At various times passports have been refused for moral reasons. For example (under the *Passports Act* of 1934), the Minister for Immigration could deny a passport to a single girl who intended to accompany a man abroad, or intended to marry against her parents' wishes; to persons wishing to travel without a spouse's consent, or where an applicant was attempting to abandon his or her partner or children; as well as to persons of 'weak mentality'. Even where no pre-existing criminal action had been committed or suspected of being committed, and where the individuals in question were citizens by birth, a passport in these cases did not automatically come with citizenship.

An individual citizen may still be prevented from leaving, or even re-entering Australia, on political grounds. Under the current *Passports Act 1938* (Cth), the Minister for Immigration may refuse to issue a passport where the applicant is thought likely to engage in 'conduct prejudicial to the security of Australia or of a foreign country'.[11] A passport that has already been issued may be cancelled

---

9   The *Franchise Act 1902* (Cth) read 'No aboriginal native of Australia Asia Africa (*sic*) or the Islands of the Pacific except New Zealand shall be entitled to have his name placed on an Electoral Roll unless so entitled under section 41 of the Constitution.'

10   Unlawful Associations were defined as 'any body of persons ... which encourages the overthrow of the Constitution of the Commonwealth by revolution or sabotage; overthrow by force of violence of the government of Australia or of any other civilized country, or the destruction or injury of Commonwealth property' etc. Section 30FD of the Act provided that: 'Any person who, at the date of any declaration made ... declaring any body of persons to be an unlawful association, is a member of the Committee or Executive of that association, shall not for a period of 7 years from that date be entitled to have his name placed on or retained on any roll of electors ... unless so entitled under section 41 of the Constitution.' This disqualification was incorporated, as s. 39(5) into the *Commonwealth Electoral Act* 1918.

11   *Passports Act 1938* (Cth) s. 7E(1)(i).

on similar grounds. While this may occur relatively infrequently, it has played a significant role in Australia's history.

Citizen Burchett

Once the passport became essential for general travel from the time of the First World War on,[12] the Commonwealth used the denial of passports as a means of preventing the exit or entry of certain persons (in particular communists) – legal citizens who had not committed crimes – for political reasons. This did not occur merely during the war periods, but also during the inter-war years and the Cold War. With the denial of a passport, other rights were lost, or became unobtainable.

The case of the communist journalist, Wilfred Burchett, is a notable example, and it is worth describing, as an illustration in practice of the dissociation between citizenship and rights. Burchett was born in Melbourne in 1911, and thus acquired British subject status by birth and subsequently Australian citizenship under the *Nationality and Citizenship Act* of 1948. He began living overseas in 1940; for several decades thereafter, he was repeatedly denied an Australian passport. His three children, born during the 1950s in, respectively, Peking, Hanoi and Moscow, were denied registration of Australian nationality, despite provision in the *Citizenship Act* for obtaining Australian citizenship by registration where a child has a parent who is an Australian citizen. In the 1960s, Burchett's attempt to visit Australia (initially to appear as a plaintiff in libel proceedings against the Melbourne *Herald* newspaper) was repeatedly thwarted by the refusal of a passport.

The *Australian Citizenship Act 1948* (Cth), until amended in 2002, provided that an Australian citizen, who 'by some voluntary and formal act, other than marriage, acquires the nationality or citizenship of a country other than Australia, shall thereupon cease to be an Australian citizen.' The fact that Burchett (deprived of an Australian passport) travelled on a Cuban passport was potentially fatal to his claim to retain his Australian citizenship. However, Cuban law did not permit the acquisition of Cuban citizenship by any 'voluntary and formal act'. Commonwealth Cabinet documents from 1969, concerning submissions made on Burchett's behalf, reveal that the government was well aware that there was no legal basis for his losing Australian citizenship. A Cabinet note in 1968 indeed stated: 'To date his national status has not been the basis of decisions to withhold a passport from him.'[13]

Cabinet was also aware, following advice from the Attorney-General's department, that Burchett could not lawfully be denied entry if he arrived at an Australian port (although it was recognized that he might not be able to book a passage to Australia because he lacked evidence of freedom to enter).[14] It appears, however, that the government withheld this knowledge from Burchett and his solicitors; it is also clear that there was a deliberate misrepresenting of the legal advice concerning Cuban

---

12 Beginning with the *War Precautions Act* (Cth) 1914–15.
13 National Archives of Australia, 1969 Cabinet documents, submission 548.
14 Ibid, submission 345.

law, and that Cabinet adopted the strategy of openly suggesting that Burchett's citizenship status remained unclear.

Cabinet documents, including from the then Minister for Immigration, Billy Snedden, do disclose some concern about the prospect of embarrassment arising from the government's denial of a passport and the potential for this to be made, in Snedden's words, the 'basis of continued criticism of the Government for "denial of rights"'.[15] The government, however, chose simply to give no reason for its position, and declined to reveal information (provided, it is clear, by Australian Security Intelligence Organisation) about Burchett's propaganda work overseas as a pro-communist journalist.

Legally, some of this executive action was highly questionable; but the core remains. Burchett, while a citizen, had no right to be issued a passport; he, thus, had no right to return to his country, or as a consequence, to live in it. He was treated, effectively, in the same manner as Australian citizens by birth who have dual nationality and who serve in the armed forces of their other country during war with Australia, thus forfeiting their Australian citizenship.[16] Again, they lose what one might imagine as the right of a citizen to hold the citizenship of their country of birth. (Citizenship is no longer automatically acquired by birth in Australia.[17] However, the grounds for denying it – in cases where a person is born in Australia – are quite unrelated to the grounds for losing it.)

Other Rights

Printed on the first page of Australian passports is a statement that the Governor-General 'requests all those to whom it may concern' to, among other things, 'afford [the bearer] every assistance and protection of which he or she may stand in need'. However, the executive government does not automatically follow its own advice. It might be imagined that the citizen, bearing an Australian passport, has a right to Australian diplomatic representation and protection as they travels overseas. No such right has been established. To the extent that a connection between citizenship and diplomatic representation exists, it is more an international matter of state responsibility than a right inherent to citizenship. That is to say, states are (usually) required by other states to take responsibility for their citizens overseas. As the *Abbasi* case[18] in the United Kingdom recently demonstrated (a case which is likely to correspond to Australian law), citizens themselves have no legal right to require the government to make diplomatic representations on their behalf (although there

---

15 National Archives of Australia, 1969 Cabinet documents, submission 548. Such criticism, the Minister thought, might refer to the *United Nations Universal Declaration of Human Rights*: 'Everyone has the right to … return to his country'.

16 *Australian Citizenship Act 1948* (Cth) s. 19 (as amended).

17 Ibid, s. 10.

18 *R (Abassi)* v *Secretary of State for Foreign and Commonwealth Affairs* [2003] 3 LRC 297.

may be a 'legitimate expectation'[19] that the relevant executive decision-maker will give consideration to such a request. This, however, carries no corresponding duty except to 'consider').

What of jury duty? Only Australian citizens are entitled to, or required to serve on juries. But many citizens are disqualified from serving, or not required to serve, for a range of reasons depending upon the relevant state law (which determines jury qualifications, even for Commonwealth offences[20]). For example, in New South Wales, citizens are ineligible to perform jury duty if (among other things) they are legal practitioners, whether or not practising.[21] Under the *Juries Act* of South Australia, among others, the spouses of judges, Justices of the Peace, and members of the Police Force, are ineligible.[22]

Citizens alone can stand for Parliament, but a class of citizens – those holding dual nationality – cannot stand, because section 44 of the *Constitution* rules persons who are citizens of, or under allegiance to, a foreign power, to be ineligible. This has been interpreted by the High Court to apply to persons who are entitled to citizenship (paradoxically, indicated by entitlement to hold a passport) in another country, including Britain.[23]

What, finally, of the simple right to live in Australia if you are an Australian citizen? This is perhaps the closest we get to an inalienable (if not exclusive) right attached exclusively to legal citizens (or at least to native-born citizens). However, there are citizens like Wilfred Burchett, who cannot live in Australia because they are prevented from returning to Australia. There are also parts of Australia – notably Norfolk Island – in which Australian citizens have no rights of residence, not because of the classification of the land, but because of the Island's own migration policy, which requires visiting Australians from elsewhere in the Commonwealth to carry their passports to enter the Island, and prohibits them from buying property or residing there unless they are a descendant of the Pitcairn islanders, or otherwise get approval to take a place that has become vacant due to the departure of an approved resident. The Human Rights and Equal Opportunity Commission has found this regime to be in breach of international rights (HREOC, 1999), but it is not in breach of Australian law.

In sum, if we were constructing a definition of 'citizenship', we would not progress very much further in attempting to build it around rights than the *Constitution*'s framers did in the 1890s. If we said: a citizen is a person who has the right to vote, or to hold a passport, or to live in Australian territory, for example, we would have to qualify this definition and say: unless, that is, otherwise disqualified or excluded

---

19 The UK courts cited the Australian case of *Minister for Immigration and Ethnic Affairs* v *Teoh* (1995) 183 CLR 273, in reaching this conclusion.

20 The Commonwealth has its own exemptions for certain Commonwealth officers under the *Jury Exemption Act 1965* (Cth).

21 *Jury Act 1977* (NSW) s. 6.

22 *Juries Act 1927* (SA) s. 13.

23 *Sykes* v *Cleary* (1992) 176 CLR 77; *Sue* v *Hill* (1999) 199 CLR 462.

from exercising such a right. And then we would have a definition which did not, in fact, fit all those to whom the term being defined might be attached. A definition of a class that does not cover all the members of that class is a poor definition. We might simply say: 'A citizen is a person who holds citizenship under Australian law and who is, unless otherwise disqualified, entitled to exercise the rights and privileges available under law to Australian citizens.' But this, of course, is a circular definition, and it does not assist our understanding of the ways in which rights are, or should be, protected.

Those, however, who maintain that citizenship and rights *should* be inextricably or at least closely, connected, or that citizenship should be defined by rights, need to consider each of the rights discussed above. Should every citizen be entitled to enjoy them all? Should citizens alone be entitled to enjoy them? Should governments have no discretion to grant or withhold any of them? Are there no circumstances in which it is reasonable to deny a right to a legal citizen? We consider these questions further, below.

Citizenship as an Ideal

Perhaps all of the above is merely a storm in a teacup. After all, the majority of citizens these days are not deprived of the right to vote or hold a passport. A few exceptions do not necessarily undermine the rule that there is a close affinity between rights and citizenship. And perhaps what we are arguing about is actually an *ideal*, an aspirational or normative definition of a citizen. Such a definition might not correspond to practice at present, but in any case, the issue of whether rights derived from law fit the definition might be misplaced. Citizenship rights might be best associated with *duties and responsibilities*.

We might, thus, want to think of citizenship in terms of behaviour. In Australia in the postwar years, official citizenship initiatives have adopted this perspective. They have extended both to a review of the law and to measures for enhancing 'good citizenship'. There has been a long history of official programs – citizenship conventions for immigrants in the 1950s and 1960s, civics education, and the development and re-development of citizenship oaths and ceremonies. In mingling the two – legal citizenship and good citizenship – government has, however, failed to make clear what it considered to be cause and what it considered to be effect.

This assumption that good citizenship can be generated by official initiatives suggests a very limited appreciation of the historical relationship between law, behaviour and citizenship. To begin with, we need to recognize that all persons in Australia, regardless of their nationality, and however briefly they are here, are required to obey the law. There is nothing exceptional (or virtuous) in doing so. Obedience to particular legal duties, like voting and performing jury duty, might be desirable, but the law (as we have seen) does not in fact require all citizens to perform them; indeed it expressly prohibits some citizens from doing so. Other legal duties or responsibilities, like paying taxes, or performing military (or civilian) service, might be required of citizens, but these are required of all residents, not just citizens: under the *Defence Act*[24] resident aliens must perform military service when ordered. Thus, if we began by saying that good citizens must obey the law, we would not be saying very much.

What would it mean in practice to tie citizenship rights to particular duties? For example, might a person not be permitted to vote if they did not pay taxes? Setting aside the legal difficulties in enforcement, that would mean that people who were citizens would be subject to a double regime of penalties, whereas those who were not citizens but earned taxable income – since paying tax is not exclusive to legal citizens – would only be subject to the usual penalties for not paying taxes. (And what if a person refused to pay what they regarded as unjust taxes or taxes levied by an unjust regime? – as Thoreau, the modern pioneer of civil disobedience, advocated (Thoreau, c.1866). Would such an equation of voting with paying taxes serve to entrench unjust laws?)

Civic Duty

But, perhaps this is to place too much emphasis on legal duties (notwithstanding, as is argued above, that it is impossible to set aside the legal dimensions of citizenship). Might not rights, and thus citizenship, depend less upon law, and more upon the performance of certain *desirable* duties? Such a view is often found in discussions of rights, and is implied, as we have seen, in the Preamble to the *Citizenship Act.* What sort of other duties or responsibilities might one want to attach to citizenship which are not already required by law, and are not exclusive to citizens? What of all the civic duties or elements of civic virtue that are so often associated, loosely, with a normative or aspirational definition of the citizen? Should citizens, for example, be required to attend public meetings, join political parties or community organizations, or perform volunteer service? Should rights be granted subject to such service?

It would follow from the association between rights and desirable duties, that a withholding of rights would be a consequence of the failure to perform what we might broadly call 'community service'. It would, however, be absurd, and in many cases counter-productive to attach sanctions to such actions. Rewards may perhaps be productive – and we do have a system (albeit imperfect) of special rewards in Australia (such as the Australia Day and the Queen's Birthday Honours) – but a withdrawal or denial of rights would not. There are many citizens whose contribution to or membership of community organizations, for example, would not as a matter of course be fruitful or desirable; many others whose capacities are limited, or whose lives are already over-stretched; others who find just getting through the day to be an ordeal, for one reason or another. These people, already short on time or resources, would be doubly deprived if we chose to grant rights subject to performance of duties or the exercise of responsibilities.

---

24 *Defence Act 1903* (Cth) ss. 59, 60.

Aristotle's model of the citizen, as set out in *Politics*, was that of a man with the leisure and the capacity to understand political issues; those employed in manual work, as well as women, he concluded, were unsuited to the *Agora*. Similarly, among the arguments levied in the nineteenth century against women's right to vote, was that the privilege of voting was based upon political duties, pre-eminently the military defence of one's nation, something from which women were excluded. We do not need to reach either of these particular conclusions to see that the association between citizenship and service is problematic; if we are to define citizens as 'good citizens' and to attach rights accordingly, we do (as Aristotle did) invariably exclude from citizenship those who (for whatever reason) do not have the qualifications to perform.

In addition, the idea of citizenship as a practice, rather than a status, undermines the balance between tolerance and participation. In a liberal society, people should be free, as far as is compatible with the law, to decide how to fill their own days or devote their energies. Furthermore, the compulsion to perform good work *undermines* the concept of the good citizen, turning them into the compliant citizen. Community service may be required of persons convicted of offences, as an alternative to a prison sentence, but to require it of persons merely because it is considered desirable, is to alter the whole basis of the relationship between the individual and the state upon which our political system rests.

Those who advocate a correlation between citizenship and rights fail to account for exceptions that may be desirable or necessary. They also overlook the rights of aliens. Those who advocate a correlation between rights and duties do not account for what should follow (other than the sanction of the law, where a legal duty is shirked) from the refusal of some citizens to be good citizens.

Rights and the *Constitution*

For many advocates of citizenship rights, the ideal is to place them beyond the reach of government, entrenched in the *Constitution*. While rights may have a place in a constitution, to tie this to citizenship is undesirable. A constitutionalized and unqualified statement that every citizen has the right to vote, for example, may have the effect of preventing non-citizens from acquiring the vote, except through the difficult process of constitutional alteration, as such a statement is likely to be interpreted by the Courts (on the *expressio unius* principle) as confining the right to vote to legal citizens. A government that recognized the democratic logic that those who pay taxes and are subject to the law should have a say in choosing those who make the laws, could be prevented from enfranchising residents (something, for example, that member states of the European Union may do for residents). Similarly, such a constitutional provision might prevent a government from disenfranchising prisoners if this were thought desirable.

There may be many grounds upon which a government may, reasonably and legitimately, seek to restrict rights. There is, however, a class of rights, or freedoms, that should be immune from erosion: equality under the law, due process, freedom from arbitrary authority or arbitrary detention, dignity, freedom of conscience and freedom from servitude might all be desirably entrenched. These, however, are universal or human rights, and should not be confined to a particular category or class of person. Although international law does make distinctions between the rights enjoyed by nationals and non-nationals (Rubenstein, 2002, p. 179), fundamental rights as set out in the *Universal Declaration of Human Rights*, as well as the *International Covenant on Civil and Political Rights*[25] and the *International Covenant on Economic, Social and Cultural Rights*,[26] are meant to apply to non-citizens as well as legal citizens in any country.

Even instruments such as the 1985 *UN Declaration on the Human Rights of Individuals Who are not Nationals of the Country in which They Live*,[27] which specifically recognizes the distinction, are framed around the notion of equality of aliens with citizens in regard to legal and civil rights. Non-citizens, as this particular Declaration recognizes, need these protections just as much as citizens. In some respects the helpless, the stateless, the exiled and the alien need the protection of rights and freedoms even more than the legal citizen, the majority of whom have access at least *a priori* access to representatives, both political and diplomatic.

In Australia, the long denial of the franchise to Aborigines was not outrageous *because* they were legal citizens; it would have been outrageous even had they not been. Aboriginal Australians needed the vote because they were part of the Australian community, because they were required to obey laws and submit to policy, but were denied a direct opportunity to choose the law- and policy-makers.

Conclusion

So, what do we want to do with rights? Do we want people to have rights in common, as human beings, or only as legal citizens? Many people might want certain entitlements (such as the vote) to be available only to citizens, but to regard this as a right of citizenship adds very little. Unless it is to be available to all citizens without exception, it must stand as a qualified right; not a citizens' right, but a *class of citizens'* right, or indeed simply as an *electors'* right. Other rights we might wish to make legally enforceable must be available to non-citizens as well as citizens, either because they are human rights and the class of persons to whom they belong includes all human beings; or because they are the sort of right, such as residence, that could not be confined to citizens alone in any country which had an immigration

---

25   Opened for signature 19 December 1966, 999 UNTS 171 (entered into force 23 March 1976).

26   Opened for signature 16 December 1966, 999 UNTS 3 (entered into force 3 January 1976).

27   UN GAOR, UN Doc A/Res/40/144 (1985).

program of any sort, or which permitted its citizens to marry non-citizens but did not automatically confer citizenship upon the spouse.

Citizenship and rights should be dissociated for a further reason. As John Dryzek has argued in regard to pluralist claims for democratization:

> ... it is important to distinguish between inclusion in the state and inclusion in the polity more generally ... Because pressures and movements for democratization almost always originate in civil society rather than in the state ... a flourishing oppositional civil society is the key to further democratization. This sort of civil society is actually facilitated by a passively exclusive state. (Dryzek, 1996, p. 475)

The case of rights is both similar and related. Where rights are exhaustively (or effectively) defined by the state, then the avenue for contestation, for challenge and expansion of concepts of rights is narrowed, perhaps even closed. The concept itself is taken out of the hands of civil society, where, to paraphrase Dryzek, 'pressures and movements for' its expansion originate. As we have seen with instances of individual rights, the legal disqualification of citizens from exercising these rights has long been used for political control. This is not to say that this is always undesirable, nor that legal rights can somehow be set free from state control. It is to suggest that claims for citizenship rights tend towards this conclusion.

The active promotion of what is intended by good citizenship is certainly desirable as a field of human initiative and service, but it cannot be conflated with a collection of rights- or duties-bearing individuals. What many advocates of citizenship rights actually appear to want is, indeed, an active civil society, rather than an association between persons and legal rights. The state should not cover the field of what is intended by the language of citizenship and rights. Fortunately, although many would find this disturbing, it has not attempted to do so in Australia. And even more fortunately, it has not fully accomplished its normative or aspirational citizenship goals of creating (its approved version of) good citizens.

References

Buckland, W.W. (1963), *A Textbook of Roman Law from Augustus to Justinian*, 3rd edn (Cambridge: Cambridge University Press).

Chesterman, J. and G., Brian (1997), *Citizens without Rights: Aborigines and Australian Citizenship* (Cambridge; Melbourne: Cambridge University Press).

Dryzek, J.S. (1996), 'Political Inclusion and the Dynamics of Democratization', *American Political Science Review*, 90 (3): 475–87.

Dutton, D. (1999), *Citizenship in Australia: A Guide to Commonwealth Government Records* (Canberra: National Archives of Australia).

Human Rights and Equal Opportunity Commission ('HREOC') (1999), *Territorial Limits: Norfolk Island's Immigration Act and Human Rights* (Sydney: Human Rights and Equal Opportunity Commission).

Irving, H. (1997), *To Constitute a Nation: A Cultural History of Australia's Constitution* (Cambridge; New York: Cambridge University Press).

Rubenstein, K. (2002), *Australian Citizenship Law in Context* (Pyrmont, NSW: Lawbook).

Thoreau, H.D. (c.1866), *Civil Disobedience.*

Chapter 7

Chained to the Past: The Psychological *Terra Nullius* of Australia's Public Institutions

Megan Davis

There have been many sunsets since Gough Whitlam trickled a handful of red soil into the hand of the old man ... Have we seen consistent progress since that symbolic moment? Have we continued to advance? Have we 'gone forward together as mates?' as the old man wished at the time. Or do we still have to learn to follow his road; to learn to stand up for rights; learn to struggle for the achievement of real recognition; learn to go forward and to do it together. Do we still have to learn the meaning of mateship? Are we still chained to the past? (Dodson, 1999)

Institutional racism changes over time. Once people understand the facts they can see very clearly how Aboriginal people were continually subject to racism of the institutional type during the protection and assimilation periods ... now institutional racism is of a more subtle kind, not always obvious even to those involved. (Commonwealth, Royal Commission into Aboriginal Deaths in Custody, 1991 [12.1.28])

Indigenous peoples are the perennial footnote to Australia's record as a civil and humane liberal democracy. The conundrum of indigenous peoples' legal and political status within the Australian state fuels ongoing indigenous dislocation and exclusion from Australia's public institutions. Since 1788, indigenous peoples' relationship with Australia's national public institutions – the executive, the Parliament, the *Constitution*, the judiciary, the people – reflects a narrative of factual and ideological exclusion. Indeed the exclusion of indigenous peoples from Australia's institutional landscape has been described as Australia's institutional *terra nullius* (Behrendt, 2003, p. 3). The ambivalence to indigenous issues is never more evident than in relation to issues of the recognition of Aboriginal customary law, racial discrimination and appalling criminal justice statistics highlighting indigenous over-representation in prisons, recidivism rates and over-policing. These serious problems have meant that legislative and constitutional reform in federal and State realms is frequently suggested as integral to remedy indigenous exclusion from public institutions. Yet this reform has rarely been achieved despite the many inquiries into indigenous issues and campaigns for indigenous rights. Few of the recommendations of the Royal Commission into Aboriginal Deaths in Custody, for example, have been implemented.[1] Almost none of the recommendations from the Australian Law Reform Commission (1986) inquiry into recognition of Aboriginal customary law and few of the final recommendations of the Council for Aboriginal Reconciliation (2000, ch. 10) have been implemented. The report of the National Inquiry into the Separation of Aboriginal and Torres Strait Islander Children (Commonwealth, HREOC, 1997) continues to attract mean-spirited conservative comment (Pearson, 2005; Brunton, 1998; Marsh, 1999) and ambivalent federal government response to its recommendations (BBC, 1999; Buti, 2000). Moreover, contemporary campaigns for institutional reform such as advocacy for a bill of rights or for an Australian republic are often campaigns that make use of indigenous peoples' misfortune manifest in health and socio-economic exclusion in order to bolster advocacy for institutional reform, yet when it comes to the detail of that reform, indigenous peoples' specific demands are eschewed in favour of pragmatism and minimalism.[2] For example, in relation to an Australian republic, engagement with indigenous peoples and reconciliation is viewed as controversial as it could possibly derail a future referendum. In the case of a bill of rights, the inclusion of a specific indigenous right is eschewed in favour of a broad-based non-discrimination clause, which is considered more pragmatic and politically palatable to a racist electorate who, as in the case of the Australian Capital Territory ('ACT') bill of rights inquiry, 'would feel as if they did not have a stake in the rights regime' (ACT, ACT Bill of Rights Consultative Committee (2003), p. 102 [5.54]).

This chapter considers some of the dimensions of indigenous peoples' factual and ideological exclusion from Australian public institutions. The first part provides a general overview of indigenous exclusion because of the psychological *terra nullius* of Australian public institutions. The second part provides a case study specifically focusing upon institutional inertia in relation to the recognition of Aboriginal customary law. This case study highlights the exclusion of Aboriginal women in particular from the legal institutions, illustrating how the 'populist vision of the neutrality and fairness of the legal system' ignores 'the gendered and racialized biases that exist on the bench' (Shaw, 2003, p. 329). The conclusion of the chapter considers the future for indigenous Australia and proposals for a bill of rights.

The overarching concern of the chapter is that the simplistic dichotomy between the practical and the symbolic, as advocated by the current federal government has always been false, and serves only to prolong indigenous peoples' exclusion within the Australian state. 'Symbolism', also referred to as the 'rights' agenda is characterized by a raft of potential institutional changes: treaty, bill of rights,

---

1   Commonwealth, Royal Commission into Aboriginal Deaths in Custody, 1991; see, e.g., Cunneen, 1992; J. Behrendt and L. Behrendt, 1992; Sansbury, 2001; Ayres, 1994; Lavery, 1994; Kelly, 2001: 'To the casual observer, it would be surprising to learn that Aboriginal incarceration rates have actually increased rather than decreased since the publication of the final report of the Royal Commission into Aboriginal Deaths in Custody'.

2   See, McKenna, 2004; ACT, ACT Bill of Rights Consultative Committee (2003), p. 101 [5.52]: 'Reservations were expressed about the wisdom of identifying one group within the ACT community for special treatment in relation to a Bill of Rights'.

reconciliation, preambular recognition, constitutional amendment, and apology. Conversely, the practical approach distinguishes itself by emphasizing economic development, employment, banking and income management as its only priorities. Yet the practical and the symbolic are two sides of the same coin – egalitarianism, ANZAC, Kokoda, Gallipoli, the wattle on the lapel, the settler, the farmer, Don Bradman, war – these images define our nation and they are a mixture of both history and mythology. As a nation, Australians do not fail to understand the importance of symbolism for the Australian sense of nationhood, and therefore it is intriguing that the notion of symbolism in the context of indigenous Australia should be eschewed and that institutions cannot be re-imagined simply because there is no immediately identifiable economic benefit for indigenous communities. The fact that an artificial divide exists between the practical and symbolic in indigenous affairs illustrates ongoing and contemporary forms of institutional exclusion, subtle yet plainly obvious to indigenous peoples.

A History of Institutional Exclusion

Australia is the only Commonwealth nation to fail to negotiate a treaty agreement between its indigenous peoples and the state (Behrendt, Brennan, Strelein and Williams, 2005, p. 1; see also Williams, 2002, p.10). Many indigenous and non-indigenous commentators have attributed this failure to negotiate an agreement to the seemingly intractable contemporary problems of indigenous Australia (see, e.g., Dodson, 2003a, pp. 30–40; Mansell, 2003, pp. 5–17). Australia also stands alone as the only common law country without a legislated or constitutional bill of rights that protects the fundamental rights and freedoms of Australian citizens. As a result, indigenous people have suffered considerably as illustrated by the ease in which the federal Parliament was able to suspend the operation of the *Racial Discrimination Act 1975* (Cth) in relation to the 1998 *Native Title Amendments* (Cth). The situation of Indigenous Australians is often contrasted with those Aboriginal groups in other jurisdictions who have signed a treaty or have domestic human rights protections. Indigenous peoples in Canada benefited from agreement making early in Canada's history. Of those Aboriginal groups that did not benefit from negotiating a treaty from the outset, some have since participated in recent treaty negotiations with the state (as in the case of British Columbia). Moreover aboriginal groups in Canada have a specific indigenous constitutional protection in the *Canadian Charter of Rights and Freedoms*.[3]

The failure to adequately address the unresolved issue of Aboriginal sovereignty and thus indigenous Australians' place in the nation informs indigenous dislocation from Australia's legal and political institutions. It is a situation that has manifested itself in many ways. The lack of recognition of indigenous peoples' status within the state has meant that their rights are subject to the whims of the ideological fashions

---

3   *Canada Act 1982* (UK), c. 11, sch. B, s. 35.

and the governing political party of the day. There are a number of examples of this. In 1986, Australian Labor Party (ALP) Prime Minister Robert Hawke (11 March 1983 – 20 December 1991) abandoned the ALP land rights policy to save the Western Australian State government and, in 1988, promised a treaty that never eventuated. Legislation establishing the *Aboriginal and Torres Strait Islander Commission Act 1985* (Cth) was passed by the federal Labor government and came into operation on 5 March 1990 but was abolished in 2005 by the federal Coalition government, which was ideologically opposed to separate electoral systems (following an ALP policy announcement to do the same).[4] The *Racial Discrimination Act 1975* (Cth) enacted by a federal Labor government in 1975, was suspended in its application in 1998 so that the federal coalition government could amend the *Native Title Act 1998* (Cth) (originally a federal Labor government initiative) and derogate Aboriginal native title in response to the High Court decision in *Wik Peoples* v *Queensland*.[5] Up until 1996, federal Labor foreign policy at the United Nations Commission on Human Rights inter-sessional working group elaborating a draft declaration on the rights of indigenous peoples supported the indigenous right to self-determination.[6] Immediately after being elected, the incoming federal coalition government expressed its opposition and withdrew support for the indigenous right to self-determination in the working group (Forbes, 1998; Dodson and Pritchard, 1998). Then in 2004, immediately after signalling its intention to abolish ATSIC, the coalition government reinstated support for the right to self-determination. These examples highlight the insecurity of indigenous peoples' position within a party political system. Indigenous policy is inextricably linked to the goodwill of the governing political party of the day.

A corollary to this point is that advocacy of indigenous rights or reform in relation to indigenous policy is inextricably linked to political leadership. Of the 44 referendums held in Australia, those eight that have passed have succeeded because of bi-partisan support (Williams, 2002). The 1967 referendum is an example of a successful referendum because of bi-partisan support and can be sharply contrasted with the highly divisive republic referendum in 1999. The republic referendum illustrated the importance of bi-partisan political leadership in asking the Australian people to consider significant questions about the Australian state and its public institutions. Indeed, political leadership is even more influential in regards to the office of Prime Minister, whose advocacy on indigenous peoples issues often sets the tenor of public debate and attitudes. There have been few positive examples of the Prime Minister's office making a significant impact upon Australian citizens

---

4   Aboriginal and Torres Strait Islander Commission Amendment Bill 2005.

5   (1996) 187 CLR 1 ('*Wik*'); Triggs, 1999.

6   See, e.g., statement by Mr Bill Barker on behalf of the Australian delegation Geneva 21 November 1995: 'Since 1991, we have made statements in the WGIP in favour of the use of the term self-determination in the Draft Declaration. We have done so on the basis that the principles of territorial integrity of states is sufficiently enshrined internationally that a reference to self-determination in the Draft Declaration would not imply a right of secession', quoted in Pritchard (2001); see also Commonwealth, DFAT, 1995.

with regard to indigenous issues. Prime Minister Gough Whitlam (5 December 1972 – 11 November 1975) is one example, who in his first year articulated the need for land rights and played a role in the enduring national image of a Prime Minister of Australia pouring the red sands of Gurindji land through the hands of Gurindji elder Vincent Lingiari in 1975.

> In no field of government activity was Labor's slogan 'It's Time' more appropriate than in Aboriginal affairs. Whitlam, at the head of an energetically reformist government, came to power in December 1972 and almost immediately created the Department of Aboriginal Affairs … The government abolished the law which prevented Aborigines leaving the country without permission, established a commission to determine how (not if) land rights should be granted … dropped the charges against those arrested at the embassy, stepped up recruitment of Aborigines to the public service and froze uranium mining in the Northern Territory. (Read, 2001, p. 160)

Prime Minister Malcolm Fraser (11 November 1975 – 11 March 1983) oversaw the enactment of the *Aboriginal Land Rights (Northern Territory) Act 1976* implementing the recommendations of the Woodward Royal Commission established by Prime Minister Whitlam. It is perhaps the Redfern speech of Prime Minister Paul Keating (20 December 1991 – 11 March 1996) that is frequently used as a stand out example of the narrative of inclusion and has had a significant impact upon indigenous Australians:

> Imagine if ours was the oldest culture in the world and we were told that it was worthless. Imagine if we had resisted this settlement, suffered and died in the defence of our land, and then were told in history books that we had given up without a fight. Imagine if non-Aboriginal Australians had served their country in peace and war and were then ignored in history books. Imagine if our feats on sporting fields had inspired admiration and patriotism and yet did nothing to diminish prejudice. Imagine if our spiritual life was denied and ridiculed. Imagine if we had suffered the injustice and then were blamed for it. It seems to me that if we can imagine the injustice then we can imagine its opposite. (Keating, 1992)

This may be contrasted with current Prime Minister John Howard's (2000) speech at the Corroboree 2000 Reconciliation Conference where Aboriginal people turned their backs and heckled the Prime Minister. Under his leadership the dichotomy between symbolic and practical reconciliation was established. That leadership no doubt influences the reported rapidly decreasing numbers of reconciliation groups around Australia.

> The underlying issues confronting Australia regarding its race relations between indigenous and non-indigenous people will not go away. Many people thought that when half a million Australians marched across the bridge in support of reconciliation the momentum for substantive change was unstoppable. Since 2000, much of the wind has gone out of its sails. (Brennan, 2004, p. 160)

Yet it is the nature of liberal democracies that small and powerless groups struggle to influence public debate. Political interests that are defined as 'minority' interests can be damaged when they are defined in a pejorative sense. Indigenous peoples are a good example of this, though this can be juxtaposed with the powerful and wealthy rural minority of farmers and pastoralists who are treated differently. As a minority, they are particularly bolstered by enduring sentimental mythologies of the bush and the colonial frontier. This allows them to benefit from public funds, unscrutinized in a way that the 'undeserving Aboriginal' is not able to. During the aftermath of the *Wik* decision the Prime Minister said that

> Australian farmers, of course, have always occupied a very special place in our heart … They often endure the heartbreak of drought, the disappointment of bad international prices after a hard-worked season and quite frankly I find it impossible to imagine the Australia I love, without a strong and vibrant farming sector. (Howard, 1997)

Indeed, the culture wars and the contesting of Aboriginal history by conservative public commentators, supported by the federal government, has meant that the narrative of indigenous peoples as first peoples fails to provide sufficient basis for institutional reform, as in a treaty process or preambular constitutional acknowledgment. As the Prime Minister asserted in his 'black armband' speech,

> There is a challenge to ensure that our history as a nation is not rewritten definitively by those who take the view that Australians should apologise for most of it. This 'black armband' view of our past reflects a belief that most of Australian history since 1788 has been little more than a disgraceful history of imperialism, exploitation, racism, sexism and other forms of discrimination. I take a very different view. I believe that the balance sheet of our history is one of heroic achievement and that we have achieved much more as a nation of which we can be proud than of which we should be ashamed. (Howard, 1996).

It also does not assist indigenous peoples that failed structural reform, as in constitutional referenda, is equally attributed to poor civics knowledge in the Australian community (see Williams, 2000, pp. 496–98).

Liberal democracies like Australia tend to be majoritarian in that policies are formulated ostensibly on the basis of the greatest good for the greatest number. It is inevitable that indigenous peoples will be negatively affected. According to Hilary Charlesworth (2002, p. 39):

> [t]he utilitarian approach places the right of vulnerable minority groups at the mercy of the will of the majority as well as making particular rights subject to trading-off with others. A richer understanding of democracy involves acknowledging that there are some rights that are so basic to human dignity that they should be taken out of the political arena and given special protection.

The capacity of democracy to temper majoritarianism and, as Charlesworth asserts, to acknowledge that some rights should be taken outside of the political arena and given special protection, is confirmed by Alston and Steiner's (2000, p. 365) observations of liberal democracies, which they argue is 'hardly hostile to groups as such':

> It is not blind to the influence of groups (religious, cultural, ethnic) or of group and cultural identity in shaping the individual. Indeed the political life of modern liberal democracies is largely constituted by the interaction, lobbying and other political participation of groups, some of which are natural in their defining characteristic (race, sex, elderly citizens), some formed out of shared interests (labour unions, business associations, environmental groups). The liberal states, by definition committed to pluralism, must accommodate different types of groups and maintain the framework of rights within which they can struggle for recognition, power and survival.

Yet political interaction and participation has been severely hampered by the abolition of the peak indigenous representative structure, the Aboriginal and Torres Strait Islander Commission (ATSIC). Senator Amanda Vanstone said at the demise of ATSIC, that indigenous peoples now have the ballot box to influence political decisions like every other Australian, though the reality is that indigenous peoples constitute 2 per cent of the Australian population of 20 million.

Following the High Court decision in *Mabo* v *Queensland [No 2]*,[7] it had been hoped that such a watershed decision would signal a shift in the way in which Australia views its first peoples. Yet despite the promise of the *Mabo [No 2]* decision, indigenous peoples have had little success in forging a place within Australian institutions. The Prime Minister John Howard (1997) portended this in a statement he made during the *Wik* native title debate: 'We have clung tenaciously to the principle that no group in the Australian community should have rights that are not enjoyed by another group.' The Prime Minister's statement does encapsulate the prism through which indigenous policy is now viewed. It reflects the principle of formal equality that requires the same treatment for all Australians regardless of the exigencies of socio-economic status, despite such exigencies actually being the trigger for differential treatment under a variety of laws. It would be of greater advantage if indigenous Australians could move beyond being mere beneficiaries of 'special measures' to being recognized as a distinct cultural minority in their own right. This is a basic tenet of the *International Convention on the Elimination of Racial Discrimination*[8] and indeed it is a consideration that has not gone unnoticed by the High Court of Australia in a recent native title decision.[9]

The *Constitution*, the fundamental document of Australia's public institutions, originally expressly excluded indigenous peoples. This was addressed by the 1967

---

7   (1992) 175 CLR 1 ('*Mabo [No 2]*').

8   Opened for signature 21 December 1965, 660 UNTS 195 (entered into force 4 January 1969).

9   *Western Australia* v *The Commonwealth* (1995) 183 CLR 373, 483–84: 'If there were any discrepancy in the operation of the two Acts, the Native Title Act can be regarded either as a special measure under s. 8 of the Racial Discrimination Act or as a law, which, though it makes racial distinctions, is not racially discriminatory so as to offend the Racial Discrimination Act or the ICERD'.

referendum. However the historical records of the Constitutional Convention debates continue to imbue the *Constitution* with racism. Indeed it may be that the *Constitution* will still be used to discriminate against indigenous peoples on the basis of race in the twenty-first century. This argument was supported by the current federal government during *Kartinyeri* v *Commonwealth*,[10] when the Commonwealth Solicitor-General affirmed the 'direct racist content of this provision [s.51(xxvi) of the *Constitution*]'. In response to a question querying whether a law such as a Nazi race law would be beyond the Court's power to invalidate, the Solicitor-General responded: 'Your honour, if there was a reason why the Court could do something about it, a Nazi law, it would in our submission, be for a reason external to the races power. It would be for some wider over-arching reason.'[11] It is arguments such as these – the unresolved question of the races power; parliamentary sovereignty; the insecurity of rights – that inform campaigns for institutional reforms such as the renewed treaty debate, an Australian republic or a bill of rights.

The veneer of civility surrounding celebrations of Australia's federation in 2000 and the triumphal celebration without civil strife of Australia's settlement, belie the unsubtle exclusion of Aboriginal history and indigenous invisibility in the public institutions of the state. Indigenous Australia is even more excluded than they were 30 years ago when Lingiari symbolically accepted the red sands of his land from an Australian Prime Minister. The recent race riots in Redfern; the riots in Palm Island following a death in custody; the recently publicized systemic racism in the armed forces; the abolition of ATSIC; the 2005 Australian Medical Association report on Aboriginal health; are just some examples of the serious and unresolved business of race in Australia.

Aboriginal Customary Law and the Australian Legal System

Since colonization, the Australian legal system has had to deal with the existence of another legal system – Aboriginal customary law and its practice. It wasn't until *Mabo [No 2]* that these laws were formally acknowledged. However, in the context of criminal law[12] and Aboriginal sovereignty, they were apparently subordinated by the Australian legal system. The High Court held that the nature and content of native title will be shaped by the laws and customs of traditional landholders:

> Native title has its origin in and is given content by the traditional laws acknowledged by and the traditional customs observed by the indigenous inhabitants of a territory. The nature and incidents of native title must be ascertained as a matter of fact by reference to those laws and customs.[13]

---

10 *Kartinyeri* v *The Commonwealth* (1998) 195 CLR 337.
11 *Kartinyeri* v *The Commonwealth* A29/1997 (5 February 1998).
12 *Walker* v *New South Wales* (1994) 182 CLR 45.
13 *Mabo* v *Queensland* [No 2] (1992) 175 CLR 1, 58 [64] (Brennan J).

The High Court also found that Australian law can protect Aboriginal interests:

> ... in conformity with the traditional laws and customs of the people to whom the clan or group belongs and only where members of the clan or group acknowledge those laws and observe those customs.[14]

Yet the conundrum of the relationship between Aboriginal customary law and the common law has long been the subject of numerous State and federal law reform commission inquiries over the years, including a Northern Territory and Western Australia inquiry over the past two years (see Commonwealth, Australian Law Reform Commission, 1986; Northern Territory Law Reform Committee, 2003; Commonwealth, Senate Legal and Constitutional References Committee, 2002; see also Carrick, 2003). Aboriginal customary law is practised in different contexts in both rural and urban areas throughout Australia. It is the Aboriginal law practised in rural and remote areas of the Northern Territory and Western Australia that most regularly interacts with the common law and attracts occasional controversy (see generally, ABC Television, 2004; Barker, 2004; Bowling, 2004; Carrick, 2003; Lobez, 1995).

Aboriginal customary law covers a wide-ranging number of legal issues from marriage and adoption to land, native title and traditional knowledge or intellectual property. Moreover there are contemporary justice mechanisms such as circle sentencing and justice committees that are examples of how Aboriginal law is practised in both rural and urban settings. These law and justice programs are seen as modern configurations of Aboriginal customary law, and are viewed as heralding a transformation in the Australian legal system. Nevertheless there is widespread confusion about what constitutes Aboriginal customary law. The ignorance about this aspect of indigenous Australian culture informs the institutional inertia in legislating to address the more significant problems of inconsistency:

> Aboriginal law is popularly viewed as aboriginal communities reliving the halcyon days of aboriginal culture practicing brutal, traditional punishment such as wounding or tribal payback. The emphasis upon non-indigenous repulsion of payback spearing or child marriage tends to obfuscate the organic nature of customary law in aboriginal culture and the dynamic and shifting course of aboriginal law. Aboriginal law like all legal systems is complex and is not frozen in time but evolves and adapts. (Davis and McGlade, 2005, p. 13)

Aboriginal customary law is integral to Aboriginal cultures. It provides a framework of values and behaviour by which Aboriginal culture is practiced. The failure to adequately recognize Aboriginal law exacerbates indigenous dislocation from the Australian community. Historical Aboriginal political statements about sovereignty and self-determination such as the Barunga Statement (1998) and the Eva Valley Statement (2004) support this very fundamental reform. The HREOC Aboriginal

---

14 *Mabo* v *Queensland* [No 2] (1992) 175 CLR 1, 60 [66] (Brennan J).

and Torres Strait Islander Commissioner gave evidence of this to the Northern Territory inquiry:

> There is currently a crisis in Indigenous communities. It is reflected in all too familiar statistics about the over-representation of Indigenous men, women and children in criminal justice processes and the care and protection system; as well as in health statistics and rates of violence. Ultimately one thing that these statistics reflect is the breakdown of indigenous community and family structures. They indicate the deterioration of traditional, customary law processes for regulating the behaviour in communities. This is due in part to the interventions of the formal legal system through removal from country, historical lack of recognition of customary law processes as an integral component of the operation of Aboriginal families and societies in the Northern Territory. (Commonwealth, HREOC, 2003)

Indeed, Aboriginal leadership has always articulated the recognition of Aboriginal law as a key part of any reform package for indigenous communities.

> The long standing absence of meaningful official recognition of Aboriginal customary law has had a detrimental effect on all facets of Aboriginal community development and has substantially contributed to many of the social problems and varying degrees of lawlessness present today. The failure of successive governments to recognize customary law has resulted in the erosion of Aboriginal cultures. (O'Donoghue, 1995)

The important role that indigenous peoples can play in formulating solutions to their own community problems is often overlooked in discussion about recognition of Aboriginal law. Indigenous communities themselves can participate in the process of determining what elements of cultural practice are actually practiced and should be recognized in contemporary Aboriginal communities:

> Attempts to consign customary law to the time when Aborigines wore lap laps, used spears and stood on bended knee will result in the strengths of many Aboriginal communities being excluded from devising solutions to difficult, intransigent problems'. (Jonas, 2003)

The importance of this was also highlighted in the report of the Royal Commission into Aboriginal Deaths in Custody: 'the elimination of disadvantage requires an end of domination and an empowerment of Aboriginal people; that control of their lives, of their communities must be returned to Aboriginal hands' (Commonwealth, Royal Commission into Aboriginal Deaths in Custody, 1991).

According to a United Nations Seminar on Indigenous Peoples and the Administration of Justice, the subordination of Aboriginal law to national legal systems and the subsequent failure to implement procedures and mechanisms which would incorporate Aboriginal law into state legal systems contributes to the marginalization of indigenous peoples within the state (UNHCHR, 2004).

The manifestations of legislative inertia in the area of Aboriginal customary law, particularly in the context of criminal law, have been seriously detrimental to indigenous peoples. Indigenous women in particular have suffered because of the use of 'bullshit law' or distorted Aboriginal customary law to justify the crimes of Aboriginal men (Carrick, 2002; Chamber et. al., 2001). This has arisen for a number of reasons. First, the dysfunction and violence in many rural and remote Aboriginal communities has facilitated the rise of bullshit law. Secondly, the adversarial nature of the Australian legal system inevitably means that lawyers in Aboriginal legal services advocate the use of Aboriginal law to defend crimes against women. Thirdly, encouragement to use distorted customary law has been provided by the voluminous judicial pronouncements that have relegated Aboriginal women to a status lower than their non-indigenous counterparts. Fourthly, there has been a lack of legislative remedies in State and federal jurisdictions.

Aboriginal lawyer, Sharon Payne, has described bullshit law as:

... a distortion of traditional law used as a justification for assault and rape of women. It is ironic that the imposition of the white man's law on traditional law have resulted in the newest one. (Payne, 1993)

According to Audrey Bolger (1991, p. 50), bullshit traditional violence is 'the sort of assault on women which takes place today for illegitimate reasons, often by drunken men which they then attempt to justify as a traditional right'. Bolger believes that there are now three types of violence in Aboriginal communities: drunken violence, traditional violence and bullshit traditional violence (ibid, p. 188). This is supported by Professor Mick Dodson (2003b) who has argued that, 'Some of our perpetrators of abuse and their apologists corrupt these ties and our culture in a blatant and desperate attempt to excuse their abusive behavior.' The adversarial nature of the common law also makes it tempting for white legal counsel, in representing Aboriginal men, 'to employ distorted custom in defence' (Davis and McGlade, 2005, p. 13).

The most recent public controversy about Aboriginal customary law was the decision in *Hales* v *Jamilmira*.[15] The defendant Jackie Pascoe, a 50-year-old Aboriginal male, used Aboriginal law in defence of statutory rape (see for example, Bryant, 2003). In a recorded interview at Maningrida Police Station Mr Pascoe stated that '[s]he is my promised wife. I have rights to touch her body' and that 'its Aboriginal custom, my culture.'[16] In this particular case, the Court held that Mr Pascoe held a reasonably sophisticated knowledge of the criminal law, and reduced the original magistrate's sentence of four months to one day imprisonment. Justice Gallop stated: 'She didn't need protection from white law she knew what was expected of her ... It's very surprising to me [Pascoe] was charged at all' (Toohey, 2002, p. 2).

The use of distorted customary law and the derogatory comments made in *Hales* v *Jamilmira* is not novel in the Australian legal system. There are many examples of judges making such comments about Aboriginal women. In *R* v *Lane*[17] the judge

---

15 (2003) 142 NTR 1 ('*Jamilmira* v *Hales*'); see also *Jamilmira* v *Hales* [2004] HCATrans 18 (13 February 2004); A.B.C. Radio National, 2003.

16 Quoted in *Hales* v *Jamilmira* (2003) 142 NTR 1, 3.

17 [1980] 509 NTSC (Unreported, 29 May 1980).

stated that, rape was 'not considered as seriously in Aboriginal communities as it is in the white community'; that 'the chastity of women is not as importantly regarded as in white communities'; and the 'violation of an Aboriginal woman's integrity is not nearly as significant as it is in a white community'.[18] Interestingly, Audrey Bolger, who has written about the decision in *R v Lane*, said that the rape had resulted in the death of the woman, and that the defence counsel had suggested that 'by approaching the men and asking for a cigarette the woman may have been seen as inviting the men to join her' (Bolger, 1991, p. 86, cited in Cunneen, 1993. p. 128).

In *R v Narjic*, the defence submission argued that 'it is the custom ... for whatever reason, that wives are assaulted by their husbands', (cited in Cuneen, 1993, p. 128) and in *R v Mungkilli, Martin and Mintuma,* the Court stated that while rape was not acceptable in Aboriginal communities, it was not 'regarded with the seriousness that it is by the white people'.[19] Indigenous lawyers and commentators such as Professor Larissa Behrendt (2004) have condemned these judicial statements:

> Colonial notions that Aboriginal women are easy sexual sport have also contributed to the perception that incidents of sexual assault are the fault of aboriginal women. While the behaviour and treatment of aboriginal men is often contextualized within the process of colonization, no context is provided for the colonial attitudes that have seen the sexuality of aboriginal women demeaned, devalued and degraded. The result of these messages given to aboriginal women by their contact with the criminal justice system would only reinforce any sense of worthlessness and lack of respect that sexual assault and abuse have scarred them with.

It is ironic, given the emphasis in political rhetoric during land rights debates on equal treatment, and the notion that Australians cling tenaciously to the principle that all Australians should be treated equally, that for so long indigenous peoples have been treated so differently and that such injustice still fails to inspire legislative reform to protect the rights of indigenous women. Rather, such injustice towards Aboriginal women, as in the case of the controversy of Mr Pascoe, is used to argue for the wholesale abolition of the practice of indigenous law.

It is important to note that in the Pascoe case it was recognized on appeal that Aboriginal women must be protected from distorted customary law. Justice Riley stated that:

> Whilst proper recognition of claims to mitigation of sentence must be accorded and such claims will include relevant aspects of customary law, the court must be influenced by the need to protect members of the community including women and children from behaviour which the wider community regards as inappropriate.[20]

---

18 *R v Lane, Hunt & Smith* [1980] 509 NTSC (Unreported, Gallop J, 29 May 1980) ('*R v Lane*').

19 *Re Mungkilli, Martin and Mintuma* (Unreported, SASC, Millhouse J, 20 March 1991), cited in Beacroft (2003) p. 544.

20 *Hales* v *Jamilmira* (2003) 142 NTR 1, 22.

In *R* v *Daniel*, Fitzgerald P. observed that:

> It would be grossly offensive for the legal system to devalue the humanity and dignity of members of Aboriginal communities or to exacerbate any lack of self esteem felt within those communities by reason of our history and their living conditions ... Aboriginal women and children who live in deprived communities or circumstances should not also be deprived of the laws' protection ... they are entitled to equality of treatment in the laws' responses to offences against them, not to some lesser response because of their race and living conditions.[21]

In *R* v *Edwards*, Muirhead J commented that 'I am just not prepared to regard assaults of Aboriginal women as a lesser evil to assaults committed on other Australian women.'[22] In *Amagula* v *White*, Kearney J expressed the view that:

> The courts must do what they can to see that the pervasive violence against women in Aboriginal communities is reduced. There is a fairly widespread belief that it is acceptable for men to bash their wives in some circumstances; this belief must be erased.[23]

One of the implications of a bill of rights is how it may impact upon indigenous peoples' right to practice Aboriginal customary law. There is no doubt that the universal nature of individual rights has hampered the capacity of the world's cultural and ethnic groups to have their communal rights recognized. Nevertheless, international human rights law does provide considerable guidance as to how the rights of an individual may be reconciled with group rights, whether in the context of special measures[24] or legitimate recognition of cultural difference.

To resolve any potential conflict between Australia's human rights obligations and Aboriginal law, the notion of 'conflict' must also be resolved. The reality of universal rights is that they will conflict with some traditions of cultural and religious minorities, and when there is a conflict, an appropriate balance must be achieved between the right to practice culture and other rights. The fundamental principle must therefore be consultation. Yet Australian institutions have a poor history of consultation with indigenous peoples on the decisions that affect them. The United Nations Committee on the Elimination of Racial Discrimination held this in its controversial decision condemning Australia's breach of the *International Convention on the Elimination of Racial Discrimination*[25] in suspending the *Race*

---

21 *R* v *Daniel* (1997) 94 A Crim R 96, 127.

22 [1981] NTSC 155, 156 (Unreported, Muirhead J, 16 October 1981) cited in Beacroft (2003) p. 541.

23 [1998] NTSC JA92 (Unreported, Kearney J, 7 January 1998). Justice Angel expressed his agreement with this passage in *R* v *Chula* [1998] NTSC (Unreported, Angel J, 20 May 1998).

24 *Gerhardy* v *Brown* (1985) 159 CLR 70.

25 Opened for signature 21 December 1965, 660 UNTS 195 (entered into force 4 January 1969).

Discrimination Act 1975 (Cth) with respect to the *Native Title Amendment Act 1998* (Cth). The Committee recommended that

> members of Indigenous peoples have equal rights in respect of effective participation in public life and that no decisions directly relating to their rights and interests are taken without their informed consent.[26]

The negotiations leading to the amendments were problematic and attracted criticism from indigenous leaders such as Mick Dodson and Aden Ridgeway that they were not part of the crucial negotiations leading up to the *Native Title Amendment Act 1998* (Cth) and that they were 'not invited to the negotiating table' (McGlade, 2000, p. 97). The ease in which negotiations were conducted in the absence of true indigenous consultation is a classic illustration of the difficulties faced by a powerless minority group in influencing legislation, and indeed how they can be locked out. The experience prompted Mick Dodson to observe:

> What I see now is the spectacle of two white men, John Howard and Brian Harradine, discussing our native title when we're not even in the room. How symbolically colonialist is that? (Brearley and Nason, 1998, p. 25)

Such a claim for consultation with indigenous peoples on the recognition of Aboriginal customary law may appear straightforward or simple but the history of race relations between the Australian state and indigenous Australians clearly illustrate that consultation has not been a fundamental value defining relations between the two.

A second important approach in speculating about what aspects of Aboriginal customary law may conflict with community expectations of human rights or a bill of rights is to be aware of the changing and evolving nature of all cultures. Again, international human rights law provides a clear understanding of this:

> Historically, religion and culture have proven extraordinarily adaptive; most belief systems have been revised over time to accommodate new understandings and new values that emerge in human society ... Numerous cultures offer examples of traditions, including customs harmful to women, that have changed or died out. For generations, women (and some men) in Sudan endured mutilation to acquire face marks, a traditional sign of beauty as well as an indicator of tribal affiliation. In recent years, this tradition has rapidly disappeared. The binding of women's feet in China is another example of a nearly universal custom that is no longer practised. (UNIFEM, 1995)

Indeed the *Convention on the Elimination of All Forms of Discrimination against Women* also provides an obligation on all states parties to

> ... take all appropriate measures ... to modify the social and cultural patterns of conduct of men and women, with a view to achieving the elimination of prejudice and customary

---

26 Committee on the Elimination of Racial Discrimination, 54th Session, Decision 2(54) on Australia, 18 March 1999.

and all other practices which are based on the idea of the inferiority or the superiority of either of the sexes or on stereotyped roles for men and women.[27]

If Aboriginal women themselves are speaking out about bullshit law or other aspects of Aboriginal law as evidenced in the comments of Payne, Bolger and Behrendt, then it must be appreciated that this is evidence of an evolution in a culture. Not only does this mean modifying practice, which is not unusual in the context of culture, but it also requires assistance by institutions in concert with Aboriginal groups of addressing the use of bullshit law in an adversarial legal system. This information can only be determined, not through public sentiment or anecdotal evidence but through a measured consultation with those people who are affected by the cultural practice. Pru Goward, the Human Rights and Equal Opportunity Commission, Sex Discrimination Commissioner, shares this approach:

> HREOC considers that in situations where women's human rights are at risk, Aboriginal communities should be encouraged to develop their own solutions to these problems and to adapt traditional practices to ensure women's human rights. (Goward, 2003, [4.3])

Conclusion

Indigenous Australians remain the statistical irregularity for those who argue that Australia's myriad of State and Commonwealth human rights legislation, its inquisitive media, incorruptible judiciary and robust parliamentary system negate the requirement for an Australian bill of rights (cf., Howard, 2003). The perennially grave statistics of indigenous incarceration, of over-policing, of alcohol abuse, of domestic violence, of health and unemployment begs the question: how do these conditions exist in affluent Australia? One answer to this question is that these perennial statistics reflect a long established structural incapacity of Australian political and legal institutions to provide indigenous peoples with a space within the Australian nation.

Indigenous peoples are frustrated by the enduring yet archaic mythology that parliament is the best protector of human rights, because indigenous Australia cannot rely on Australian democracy to best protect their rights. As recent as 1998 the Australian federal Parliament, which according to the Prime Minister (2003) 'expresses the character of the Australian people', legislated to exempt the indigenous community from the statutory principle of non-discrimination on the basis of their race in the context of native title. Prior to that, the Deputy Prime Minister had announced after a significant Aboriginal native title win in the High Court that its next appointment to the High Court would be a capital 'C' conservative (Lane, 1997, p. 1).

---

27 Opened for signature 18 December 1979, 1249 UNTS art. 5(a) (entered into force September 3 1981).

In 2005, the poor track record of Australian political and legal institutions in addressing indigenous dislocation remains undiminished. Nevertheless it is not true to say that indigenous experience with Australian institutions has been a blanket failure. A balanced indigenous perspective would recognize the crucial role of the Australian people in some areas (the 1967 Referendum; reconciliation bridge walks), and the role of Australian courts as innovative in some (*Mabo [No 2]*; *Bulun Bulun v R & T Textiles Pty Ltd,*[28] *Milpurrurru* v *Indofurn Pty Ltd*[29]), important in others (*Koowarta* v *Bjelke Peterson;*[30] *Mabo* v *Queensland [No 1]*[31]), yet notoriously limited and hamstrung in others (*Cubillo* v *Commonwealth;*[32] *Kruger* v *Commonwealth;*[33] *Kartinyeri;*[34] *Western Australia* v *Ward*[35]). An indigenous perspective would also view the federal Parliament as instrumental in some areas (the 1967 Referendum), constructive and proactive in some (*Racial Discrimination Act 1975* (Cth); *Aboriginal and Torres Strait Islander Commission Act 1989* (Cth); *Human Rights and Equal Opportunity Commission Act 1986* (Cth); the Redfern Speech), and destructive in others (*Native Title Amendment Act 1998* (Cth)).

It does not require complex knowledge of indigenous issues in Australia to conclude that institutional reforms such as bills of rights, indigenous seats in parliament, a new preamble or an apology will not constitute an overnight panacea to infant mortality, truancy rates, alcoholism and nutritional problems. Indeed, there has been no indigenous or non-indigenous public commentator who has made such a claim. But neither is the answer to the crisis as simple as banning alcohol, pooling welfare, chlorine swimming pools, the promise of petrol bowsers or the enlistment of 'social entrepreneurs' to advise remote communities on economic developments.

In arguing that rights and the practical approach are not mutually exclusive, the only conclusion must be that the institutional symbolism of state actions such as a treaty, a bill of rights, an apology to the Stolen Generations or constitutional reform are unavoidable in addressing indigenous exclusion within the Australian state. Until then, the message remains for indigenous Australians: *we will legislate, but usually when it's against you.* The mixed messages of current public law reform are that not only should you not expect an entrenched and judicially enforceable right to non-discrimination because judges are undemocratic, but you shouldn't expect democracy to work for you either. Parliament won't legislate because you are perceived to be asking for something above and beyond what ordinary Australians are entitled to. These messages inform the implacable sense of detachment and mistrust among indigenous communities with Australian public institutions, and explains why inclusive measures, even minimalist measures such as an apology or

---

28 (1998) 86 FCR 244.
29 (1994) 54 FCR 240.
30 (1982) 153 CLR 168.
31 (1988) 166 CLR 186.
32 (2000) 174 ALR 97.
33 (1997) 190 CLR 1.
34 (1998) 195 CLR 337.
35 (2002) 213 CLR 1.

even an amended preamble, would have an enormous psychological impact upon indigenous Australians, who long ago dispensed with the fiction of the universality of human rights and the fiction that parliament can be trusted to protect the rights of a powerless and unpopular minority.

References

Australian Broadcasting Corporation (ABC) Radio National (2003) 'Aboriginal customary law/white law divide', *ABC Radio National, P.M.*, 16 April 2003, available at <http://www.abc.net.au/pm/content/2003/ s834003.html>.

ABC Television (2004), 'Tribal Payback Reduces Jail Time for Woman', *ABC Television, Messagestick*, 9 November 2004.

Australian Capital Territory (ACT), ACT Bill of Rights Consultative Committee (2003), *Towards an ACT Human Rights Act: Report of the ACT Bill of Rights Consultative Committee*, Canberra: Publishing Services.

Alston, P. and Steiner, H. (eds) (2000), *International Human Rights in Context: Law, Politics, Morals*, 2nd edn (Oxford: Clarendon Press).

Ayres, R. (1994), 'Way Our West: Implementation of RCIADIC Recommendations in WA', *Aboriginal Law Bulletin*, **29,** available at <http://www.austlii.edu.au/au/journals/AboriginalLB/1994/29.html >.

Backgrounder, **10** (1), available at <http://www.ipa.org.au/files/ IPABackgrounder10-1.pdf >.

Barker, A. (2004), 'Bail refused to man wanting to undergo tribal punishment', *ABC Local Radio, The World Today*, 17 February 2004, available at <http://www.abc.net.au/worldtoday/content/2004/s1046936.htm> at 8 October 2004.

'Barunga Statement' in Commonwealth, Council for Aboriginal Reconciliation (1998), *Documents of Reconciliation* (Canberra: Council for Aboriginal Reconciliation), available at <http://www.austlii.edu.au/au/orgs/car/docrec/policy/brief/attach.htm>.

Beacroft, L. (2003), *Indigenous Legal Issues: Commentaries and Materials*, 3rd edn (Sydney: LBC Information Services).

Behrendt, L. (2003), *Achieving Social Justice*, Annandale (NSW: Federation Press).

—— (2004), 'Law Stories and Life Stories: Aboriginal women, the law and Australian society', speech delivered at the 2004 Clare Burton Memorial Lecture, Hyatt Regency, Perth, 24 September 2004.

Behrendt, J., and Behrendt, L. (1992), 'Recommendations, Rhetoric and Another 33 Aboriginal Deaths in Custody: Aboriginal Custodial Deaths since May 1989', *Aboriginal Law Bulletin*, **50**, available at <http://www.austlii.edu.au/au/journals/AboriginalLB/1992/50.html>.

Behrendt, L., Brennan, S., Strelein, L., Williams, G. (2005), *Treaty* (Annandale, NSW: Federation Press).

Bolger, A. (1991), *Aboriginal Women and Violence* (Darwin: Australian National University, North Australia Research Unit).

Bowling, M. (2004), 'Aboriginal Traditional Law', *ABC Television, Stateline*, 20 February 2004, available at <http://www.abc.net.au/stateline/nt/content/ 2003/ s1049853.htm>

British Broadcasting Corporation, (BBC) (1999), 'Regret but No Apology for Aborigines', *BBC, BBC News*, 26 August 1999, available at http://news.bbc. co.uk/1/hi/world/asia-pacific/430512.stm at 25 July 2005

Brearley, D. and Nason, D. (1998), 'The Long Division, When can Black and White Australia Expect to be Reconciled?', *Weekend Australian*, 24–25 October 1998, p. 25.

Brennan, S. (2004), 'Reconciliation in Australia: The Relationship between indigenous peoples and the wider community', *Brown Journal of World Affairs*, **11**(1): 149.

Brunton, R. (1998), 'Betraying the Victims: The 'Stolen Generations' Report', IPA Backgrounder, Institute of Public Affairs Ltd, Melbourne.

Bryant, G. (2003), 'Promised Marriages – The Jackie Pascoe Case', *Indigenous Law Bulletin*, **20**, available at <http://www.austlii.edu.au/au/journals/ ILB/2003/20. html>.

Buti, A. (2000), 'Unfinished Business: The Australian Stolen Generations', *Murdoch University Electronic Journal of Law*, **7**, available at <http://www.murdoch.edu. au/elaw/issues/v7n4/buti74_text.html>.

Carrick, D. (2002), 'Customary Law and Sentencing', *ABC Radio National, The Law Report*, 22 October 2002, available at <http://www.abc.net.au/rn/ talks/8.30/ lawrpt/stories/s706299.htm>

Carrick, D (2003), 'Customary law and Anglo-Australian law – can they mix?', *ABC Radio National, The Law Report*, 29 July 2003, available at <http://www.abc.net. au/rn/talks/8.30/lawrpt/stories/s912416.htm>

Chamber, C., Keys, C., Memmott, P. and Stacy, R., (2001), *Violence in Indigenous Communities: Report to Crime Prevention Branch of Attorney-General's Department* (Canberra: AGPS).

Charlesworth, H. (2002), *Writing in Rights* (Sydney: University of New South Wales Press).

Commonwealth, Australian Law Reform Commission (1986), Report into the Recognition of Aboriginal Customary Laws, Report No 31 (Canberra: Australian Government Publishing Service).

Commonwealth, Aboriginal and Torres Strait Islander Social Justice Commissioner of the Human Rights and Equal Opportunity Commissioner (HREOC) (2003), Submission to the Northern Territory Law Reform Commission Inquiry into Aboriginal customary law in the Northern Territory (Sydney: Human Rights and Equal Opportunity Commission), available at <http://www.hreoc.gov.au/social_ justice/customary_law/ nt_lawreform.html>

Commonwealth, Council for Aboriginal Reconciliation (2000), *Reconciliation: Australia's Challenge* (Canberra: Council for Aboriginal Reconciliation), available at <http://www.austlii.edu.au/au/other/IndigLRes/car/2000/16/ text10.htm>.

Commonwealth, Department of Foreign Affairs and Trade ('DFAT') (1995), *Self-Determination: The Australian Position*, Working Paper, Canberra: DFAT

Commonwealth, Human Rights and Equal Opportunity Commission (HREOC) (1997), *Bringing Them Home: Report of the National Inquiry into the Separation of Aboriginal and Torres Strait Islander Children from Their Families*, Australian Government Publishing Service. <http://www.austlii.edu.au/au/special/rsjproject/rsjlibrary/hreoc/stolen/>.

Commonwealth, Royal Commission into Aboriginal Deaths in Custody (1991), *National Report* (Canberra: Australian Government Publishing Service).

Commonwealth, Senate Legal and Constitutional References Committee (2002), *Reconciliation: Off Track* (Canberra: Department of the Senate), available at <http://www.aph.gov.au/senate/committee/legcon_ctte/completed_inquiries/2002-04/reconciliation/report/report.pdf>

Cunneen, C. (1992), 'Aboriginal Imprisonment During and Since the Royal Commission into Aboriginal Deaths in Custody', *Aboriginal Law Bulletin*, **19**, available at <http://bar.austlii.edu.au/cgi-bin/disp.pl/au/journals/AboriginalLB/1992/19.html?query=%5e+rciadic>.

—— (1993), 'Judicial Racism', in Sandra McKillop (ed.), *AIC Conference Proceedings*.

Davis, M. and McGlade, H. (2005), *Background Paper on International Human Rights Law and the Recognition of Aboriginal Customary Law*, Background Paper No. 10 (Perth: Western Australia Law Reform Commission), available at <http://www.lrc.justice.wa.gov.au/Aboriginal/BackgroundPapers/P94-10_background_Davis-McGlade.pdf>

Dodson, M. (2003a), 'Unfinished Business: A Shadow across Our Relationships' in ATSIC and Australian Institute of Aboriginal and Torres Strait Islander Studies (AIATSIS), *Treaty: Let's get it right* (Acton, ACT: AIATSIS), p. 30.

—— (2003b), 'Violence Dysfunction Aboriginality', paper presented at the Telstra Address, National Press Club, Canberra, 11 June 2003.

Dodson, M. and Pritchard, S. (1998), 'Recent Developments in Indigenous Policy: The Abandonment of Self-Determination?' *Indigenous Law Bulletin*, **21**, available at <http://bar.austlii.edu.au/cgi-bin/disp.pl/au/journals/ILB/ 1998/70.html?query=%5e+sarah+pritchard>

Dodson, P. (1999), 'Until the Chains are Broken', speech delivered at the Vincent Lingiari Lecture, 1999, available <http://beta.austlii.edu.au/au/ special/rsjproject/rsjlibrary/car/lingiari/4dodson.html?>.

'Eva Valley Statement' in Agreements, Treaties and Negotiated Settlements Project (2004), *Agreements Database* (Melbourne: Indigenous Studies Program, The University of Melbourne), <http://www.atns.net.au/biogs/ A001286b.htm>.

Forbes, M (1998), 'Downer fears phrase will split Australia', *The Age*, 22 August 1998.

Goward, P. (2003), 'Submission to the Northern Territory Law Reform Committee Inquiry into Aboriginal Customary Law in the Northern Territory by the Sex Discrimination Commissioner of the Human Rights and Equal Opportunity Commission May 2003', available at http://www.hreoc.gov.au/sex_discrimination/customary_law/ submission.html

Howard, J. (1996) , 'The Liberal Tradition: The Beliefs and Values which Guide the Federal Government', Sir Robert Menzies Lecture, 18 November 1996

—— (1997), 'Address to the Nation', ABC Television, 30 November 1997, available at <http://www.pm.gov.au/news/speeches/1997/ wikadd.htm>.

—— (2000), 'Towards Reconciliation', address to Corroboree 2000, Sydney, May 27 2000, available at <http://www.australianpolitics.com/ news/2000/00-05-27.shtml>.

—— (2003), 'Address at the opening of the 13th Commonwealth Law conference', address given to the 13th Commonwealth Law Conference and 33rd Australian Legal Convention, Melbourne Convention Centre, Melbourne, 14 April 2003, available at <http://www.pm.gov.au/news/ speeches/speech89.html>.

Jonas, B. (2003), 'The recognition of Aboriginal customary law', paper presented at the Human Rights and Equal Opportunity Commission/International Law Association Seminar on Aboriginal Customary Law, Sydney Thursday 20 November, 2003, available at <http://www.hreoc.gov.au/speeches/social_justice/recognition_customary_law.html>.

Keating, P. (1992), 'Redfern Park Speech', in *Indigenous Law Bulletin* (2001) **57**, available at <http://bar.austlii.edu.au/cgi-bin/disp.pl/au/journals/ILB.20050121/2001/57.html?query=%5e+redfern+speech>

Kelly, L. (2001), '10 Years On: The Continuing Poor Health of Indigenous Prisoners', *Indigenous Law Bulletin*, **38**, available at <http://bar.austlii.edu.au/cgi-bin/disp.pl/au/journals/ILB/2001/ 38.html?query=%5e+rciadic>.

Kingston, M. (1998), 'Racing towards an election', The Sydney Morning Herald, 11 April 1998, p. 29.

Lane, B (1997), 'Conservative to fill High Court vacancy', *The Australian*, 13 August 1997.

Lavery, D. (1994), 'Empty Words – Queensland's Response to RCIADIC Recommendations 6 to 40', 26 *Aboriginal Law Bulletin* http://bar.austlii.edu.au/cgi-bin/disp.pl/au/journals/AboriginalLB/1994/ 26.html?query=%5e+rciadic at 27 July 2005

Lobez, S. (1995), 'Aboriginal law', *ABC Radio National, The Law Report*, 31 October 1995, available at <http://www.abc.net.au/rn/talks/8.30/lawrpt/ lstories/lr311001.htm>

Mansell, M. (2003), 'Citizenship, Assimilation and a Treaty' in ATSIC and AIATSIS, *Treaty: Let's Get it Right*, Acton, ACT: AIATSIS, p. 5.

Marsh, R. (1999), '"Lost", "Stolen" or "Rescued"? Australian policy towards part-Aboriginal children', *Quadrant* **40** (6): 15–18.

McGlade, H. (2000), 'Not Invited to the Negotiating Table: The Native Title Amendment Act 1998 (Cth) and Indigenous Peoples Right to Political Participation and self-determination under International Law', *Balayi*, **1**:. 97.

McKenna, M. (2004), *This Country: A Reconciled Republic?* (Sydney: University of New South Wales Press).

Northern Territory Law Reform Committee (2003), 'Towards Mutual Benefit: Report of the Northern Territory Law Reform Committee Inquiry into Aboriginal Customary Law' (Darwin: Northern Territory Law Reform Committee).

No. 21: Aboriginal Justice Issues : Proceedings of a Conference Held 23–25 June 1992, Canberra: Australian Institute of Criminology, available at <http://www.aic.gov.au/publications/proceedings/21/Cunneen.pdf>.

O'Donoghue, L. (1995), 'Customary Law as a Vehicle for Community Empowerment', speech delivered at the Forum on Indigenous customary law, Parliament House, Canberra, 18 October 1995.

Payne, S. (1993), 'Aboriginal Women and the Law', in P. W. Easteal and S. McKillop (eds), *Women and the Law* (Canberra: Australian Institute of Criminology).

Pearson, C. (2005), 'Conscience has the final say', *The Australian*, 23 July 2003, available at <http://www.theaustralian.news.com.au/common/ story_page/ 0,574 4,16013975%255E7583,00.html>.

Pritchard, S. (2001) *An Analysis of the United Nations Draft Declaration on the rights of Indigenous Peoples*, 3rd edn (Canberra: ATSIC), available at <http://www.atsic.gov.au/issues/indigenous_rights/international/ draft_declaration/default.asp>.

Read, P. (2001), *Charles Perkins: A Biography* (Ringwood, Victoria: Viking).

Sansbury, T. (2001), 'State and Territory Implementation of the Recommendations of the Royal Commission – Overview', *Indigenous Law Bulletin*, **29**, available at <http://bar.austlii.edu.au/cgi-bin/disp.pl/au/ journals/ILB.20050121/2001/29. html?query=%5e+rciadic>.

Shaw, W. (2003), 'Post-Colonial Encounters: Gendered Racialisations in Australian Courtrooms' *Gender Place and Culture*, **10**: 325.

Toohey, P. (2002), 'Victim Trapped Between Two Worlds: Tribal and White Law Clash Over Sex', *The Australian*, 9 October 2002, p. 2.

Triggs, G. (1999), 'Australia's Indigenous Peoples and International Law: Validity of the Native Title Amendment Act 1998 (Cth)', *Melbourne University Law Review*, **16**: 2.

United Nations High Commissioner on Human Rights (UNHCHR) (2004), *Report on the Expert Seminar on Indigenous Peoples and the Administration of Justice (Madrid, 12–14 November 2003)* (Geneva: UNHCHR).

United Nations Development Fund for Women (UNIFEM) (1995), 'Women, Culture and Traditional Practices' in *UNIFEM, CEDAW Advocacy Kit* (New York: UNIFEM).

Williams, G. (2000), 'Why Australia Kept the Queen', *Saskatchewan Law Review*, **63**: 477.

—— (2002), 'The Treaty debate, Bill of Rights and the Republic: Strategies and Lessons for Reform', *Balayi*, **5**: 10.

Chapter 8

Constitutional Property Rights in Australia: Reconciling Individual Rights and the Common Good

Simon Evans[1]

Introduction

Section 51(xxxi) of the *Australian Constitution* operates as one of the few rights-protecting provisions in the *Constitution*.[2] It is framed as a grant of power to the Commonwealth Parliament that enables it to make laws with respect to the compulsory acquisition of property on just terms.[3] However, it has been interpreted as a constitutional guarantee[4] that withdraws from the Commonwealth Parliament any powers it might have had to make laws with respect to the acquisition of property *other than* on just terms: it 'subject[s] the power of acquisition to an obligation to provide just terms'.[5]

Unfortunately, the proper interpretation of s. 51(xxxi) is unclear and contested and in some areas is close to incoherent.[6] I want to argue in this chapter that the

---

1   This chapter forms part of a project on Australian parliaments and human rights which I am pursuing with Carolyn Evans and Kristen Walker. I gratefully acknowledge funding received under the Australian Research Council Discovery – Project scheme for this research.

2   Provisions using the language of 'acquisition of property ... on just terms' appear in the self government legislation for the ACT, the Northern Territory and Norfolk Island. However, they operate only to withdraw legislative power from the Territory legislatures, not as grants of power.

3   The section provides:

The Parliament shall, subject to this Constitution, have power to make laws for the peace, order, and good government of the Commonwealth with respect to: ... (xxxi) the acquisition of property on just terms from any State or person for any purpose in respect of which the Parliament has power to make laws.

4   See, e.g., *Airservices Australia* v *Canadian Airlines International Ltd* (2000) 202 CLR 133, 193 ('*Airservices*'); see especially n.175 and the cases cited there.

5   *Smith* v *ANL Ltd* (2000) 204 CLR 493, 511 ('*Smith*').

6   Evans (2000, p. 184); cf. Ackerman (1977, p. 113) (discussing the Takings Clause).

complexity and contestedness is probably inevitable. Constitutional property clauses such as s. 51(xxxi) attempt to mediate 'the perennial' and, I would add, irreducibly moral, 'conflict between the need for stability of entitlements, on the one hand, and the need for flexibility and modification of entitlements in light of changed circumstances, on the other' (Merrill, 1987, p. 604). The spare text of such clauses provides no secure criteria for resolving the conflict[7] and the moral principles which might be called in aid are deeply contested. What is the High Court to do? Section 51(xxxi) is most unlikely to be amended or repealed. Most of the Court's options for dealing with s. 51(xxxi) are unattractive. However, there may be a way forward in an interpretive approach that directly recognizes the primacy of political institutions in resolving the conflict between stability and flexibility, coupled with measures that increase the capacity of those institutions to address property rights issues.

Acquisition of Property on Just Terms

Section 51(xxxi) is 'construed liberally as befits a constitutional guarantee'.[8] Nonetheless, it is construed and applied within the textualist tradition of Australian constitutional law. Members of the High Court disavow any suggestion that considerations of substantive fairness are involved in applying s. 51(xxxi).[9] Instead, whether a Commonwealth law falls within s. 51(xxxi) and requires just terms is determined by a process of characterization,[10] by asking whether it is a law with respect to the 'compound conception ... "acquisition-on-just-terms"'.[11]

This compound conception is largely a rhetorical device with two functions. First, it reinforces a commitment to formalism in the interpretation of s. 51(xxxi). Whether a law requires just terms is not determined by recourse to any moral principle underlying s. 51(xxxi) but by orthodox principles of characterization. Secondly, it helps support the view that there are acquisitions that are not 'acquisitions-on-just-terms' and which do not require just terms because they have nothing to do with s. 51(xxxi).[12] However, although the compound conception is routinely invoked to these ends, it is equally routinely dissected into its constituent elements. In practice, to determine whether a Commonwealth law falls within s. 51(xxxi) the Court will consider whether there is an acquisition, whether there is an acquisition *of property*,

---

7   Even prolix clauses like s. 25 of the *Constitution of the Republic of South Africa 1996* (Act No. 108 of 1996).

8   *Georgiadis* v *Australian and Overseas Telecommunications Corporation* (1994) 179 CLR 297, 312 (*'Georgiadis'*). See also the cases cited in *Smith* (2000) 204 CLR 493, 533 n. 160.

9   E.g., *Commonwealth* v *WMC Resources Limited* (1998) 194 CLR 1, 57 (*'WMC Resources'*).

10   E.g., *Airservices* (2000) 202 CLR 133, 181, 197, 246–248, 304; *Mutual Pools & Staff Pty Ltd* v *Commonwealth* (1994) 179 CLR 155, 171, 188 (*'Mutual Pools'*).

11   E.g. *Grace Brothers Proprietary Limited* v *Commonwealth* (1946) 72 CLR 269, 290 (*'Grace Brothers'*).

12   E.g. *Burton* v *Honan* (1952) 86 CLR 169, 180–81 (Dixon CJ).

whether the acquisition is for a purpose comprehended by s. 51(xxxi), and finally whether just terms are provided. I focus first on the 'acquisition' and 'property' questions, and return to 'just terms' below.[13]

Acquisition

At the core of the power conferred by s. 51(xxxi) is the power to acquire *title* to the property of a private person or a State. Section 51(xxxi) thus confirms that the Commonwealth possesses the power of eminent domain. When the power is exercised in this way, the Commonwealth acquires title to an item of property and the former owner suffers an exactly corresponding deprivation. The section also applies to acquisitions (and corresponding deprivations) of lesser interests.[14] However, a law is not within the scope of s. 51(xxxi) if it merely *deprives* an owner of property without resulting in some corresponding *acquisition* by the Commonwealth or some other person. In that respect it is distinguished from the Takings Clause of the Fifth Amendment to the *United States Constitution*.[15]

The significance for s. 51(xxxi) jurisprudence of the distinction between acquisition and deprivation has been progressively eroded. Extinguishment or modification of property rights may constitute an acquisition under s. 51(xxxi), even if no one acquires title to (or an interest in) the property rights that are extinguished or modified, so long as 'some identifiable and measurable countervailing benefit or advantage' accrues to some other person (whether or not that person is the Commonwealth).[16] This expansion in the scope of s. 51(xxxi) was probably inevitable once the section was read as a guarantee. The distinction between acquisition and deprivation is not salient if the purpose of the section is to guarantee individual property holdings against governmental interference. A law that merely prohibits use of property by the owner, or that requires that the property be destroyed, may produce the same effect on the individual and their property as a law that acquires title for the Commonwealth. The broad purpose of the guarantee stands in tension with any narrow interpretation that would confine s. 51(xxxi) to acquisitions that correspond exactly with deprivations.

---

13 The requirement that an acquisition be 'for any purpose in respect of which the Parliament has power to make laws' has not proven to be significant. But see *Clunies-Ross* v *Commonwealth* (1984) 155 CLR 193 (albeit in the context of a statutory power conferred on the executive).

14 See discussion below, Part II(B), 'Property'.

15 E.g. under a 'regulatory' taking, where a regulation restricts land use but results in no acquisition of title by the government. See, e.g., *Pennsylvania Coal Co* v *Mahon*, 260 US 393 (1922); *Lucas* v *South Carolina Coastal Council*, 505 US 1003 (1992). The Takings Clause provides, 'nor shall private property be taken for public use without just compensation'. Contrast *Mutual Pools* (1994) 179 CLR 155, 185 and the cases cited there. But see Callinan J's criticism in *Smith* (2000) 204 CLR 493, 545–47.

16 *Mutual Pools* (1994) 179 CLR 155, 185.

Property

Notwithstanding the breadth of the concept of acquisition, the distinction between acquisition and deprivation remains significant to the operation of s. 51(xxxi). Unless there is an acquisition *of property* there is no acquisition within the scope of s. 51(xxxi).[17] The Court, therefore, has not accepted the American regulatory takings doctrine.[18] That doctrine holds that a purely regulatory law that 'goes too far' can constitute a taking for which compensation is constitutionally mandated.[19] Under s. 51(xxxi), by contrast, there is no acquisition if the Commonwealth merely receives the satisfaction of its regulatory goals or if the economic position of the property owner is adversely affected.[20]

Again, however, the requirement is attenuated. The proprietary interest that is acquired may be 'slight or insubstantial'.[21] And the Court has given the widest interpretation to 'property'. Property includes 'innominate and anomalous interests',[22] 'any interest in property'[23] and 'every species of valuable right and interest'.[24] The result is that the acquisition of a bare right to possession,[25] of 'money and the right to receive a payment of money',[26] and of a chose in action;[27] relief from the Commonwealth's liability in debt or damages[28] and from a burden on the Commonwealth's radical title;[29] and 'the assumption and indefinite continuance of exclusive possession and control ... of any subject of property'[30] all fall within s. 51(xxxi) and require just terms. And again this expansion of s. 51(xxxi) was probably inevitable once a broad guarantee-based reading of the section was adopted.

---

17 *Australian Tape Manufacturers Association Ltd* v *Commonwealth* (1993) 176 CLR 480, 499–500 (*'Tape Manufacturers'*).

18 But see *Trade Practices Commission* v *Tooth & Co Ltd* (1979) 142 CLR 397, 414–15.

19 *Pennsylvania Coal Co* v *Mahon*, 260 US 393 (1922), 417.

20 *Federal Council of the British Medical Association in Australia* v *Commonwealth* (1949) 79 CLR 201, 270–71.

21 *Tape Manufacturers* (1993) 176 CLR 480, 499–500 approving *Commonwealth* v *Tasmania* (1983) 158 CLR 1, 145 (*'Tasmanian Dam Case'*).

22 *Bank of New South Wales* v *Commonwealth* (1948) 76 CLR 1, 349 (*'Bank Nationalisation Case'*).

23 *Minister of State for the Army* v *Dalziel* (1944) 68 CLR 261, 285 (*'Dalziel'*).

24 Ibid 290.

25 Ibid.

26 *Tape Manufacturers* (1993) 176 CLR 480, 509, cf. 527; *Mutual Pools* (1994) 179 CLR 155, 172–73, 184–185, cf. 195–97. The controversy on this point is mirrored in the United States: see *Eastern Enterprises* v *Apfel*, 524 US 498 (1998).

27 *Dalziel* (1944) 68 CLR 261, 290; *Georgiadis* (1994) 179 CLR 297, 303.

28 *Smith* (2000) 204 CLR 493.

29 *Newcrest Mining (WA) Ltd* v *Commonwealth* (1997) 190 CLR 513, 530 (*'Newcrest'*).

30 *Bank Nationalisation Case* (1948) 76 CLR 1, 349.

A Complex and Contested Provision

In short, s. 51(xxxi) is interpreted broadly and withdraws significant areas of legislative power to acquire property without just terms. Where then is the complexity and contestedness that I flagged at the outset? It can be seen already in the tension that I have just described between the constraining effects of the text of the section and the inflationary effects of reading the section as a guarantee. But it can be seen most clearly in the limiting principles that the High Court has identified to mark off those acquisitions that lie outside the scope of s. 51(xxxi). The section does not withdraw *all* Commonwealth legislative power to acquire property without just terms. As Holmes J said in *Pennsylvania Coal Co v Mahon*, '[g]overnment hardly could go on if to some extent values incident to property could not be diminished without paying for every such change in the general law.'[31] The Australian courts have concluded that the Commonwealth may, in exercise of its enumerated legislative powers, and without providing just terms:

- impose taxation and execute against the taxpayer's property;[32]
- confiscate enemy property;[33]
- confiscate the proceeds or instruments of customs,[34] fisheries[35] and other offences;[36]
- impose civil penalties for conduct that is not an offence;[37]
- sequestrate the property of bankrupts;[38]
- impose and enforce liens on the property of aircraft owners to secure charges incurred by the operators of the aircraft;[39]
- establish new intellectual property regimes under which existing lawful items become infringing items;[40]
- retrospectively reduce the amount of a rebate for medical services, initially payable to the patient but assigned to their doctor who provided the services in expectation of the rebate;[41]
- retrospectively impose a windfall tax to offset the Commonwealth's liability to make refunds of tax paid under an unconstitutional statute;[42]

---

31 *Pennsylvania Coal Co v Mahon*, 260 US 393, 413 (1922).

32 *Clyne v Deputy Commissioner of Taxation (NSW) (No 1)* (1982) 13 ATR 463.

33 *Attorney-General of the Commonwealth v Schmidt* (1961) 105 CLR 361.

34 *Burton v Honan* (1952) 86 CLR 169.

35 *Re Director of Public Prosecutions; Ex parte Lawler* (1994) 179 CLR 270 ('*Lawler*'); *Olbers v Commonwealth of Australia (No 4)* (2004) 205 ALR 432.

36 *Della Patrona v Director of Public Prosecutions (Cth) (No 2)* (1995) 38 NSWLR 257.

37 *R v Smithers; Ex Parte McMillan* (1982) 152 CLR 477.

38 *Schmidt* (1961) 105 CLR 361, 372; *Mutual Pools* (1994) 179 CLR 155, 170, 178, 188.

39 *Airservices* (2000) 202 CLR 133.

40 *Nintendo Co Ltd v Centronics Systems Pty Ltd* (1994) 181 CLR 134.

41 *Health Insurance Commission v Peverill* (1994) 179 CLR 226.

42 *Mutual Pools* (1994) 179 CLR 155.

- refuse consent to the export of items of cultural heritage;[43]
- provide for the Family Court to make orders that redistribute the property of the parties to a marriage;[44] and, it seems,
- impose a statutory obligation on non-custodial parents to pay to the Commonwealth the amount of child support previously owed to the custodial parent.[45]

The complexity and contestedness arises in attempting to explain and reconcile these various acquisitions that fall outside the scope of s. 51(xxxi). Members of the High Court have proposed at least six distinct limiting principles or tests:[46]

1. whether the legislation effecting the acquisition was a necessary or characteristic means of achieving an objective within the scope of Commonwealth legislative power, not being solely or chiefly the acquisition of property;[47]
2. whether the legislation was a genuine adjustment of competing rights and not directed at the acquisition of property;[48]
3. whether the legislation was enacted under a grant of power that 'clearly encompassed the making of laws providing for the acquisition of property unaccompanied by any quid pro quo of just terms';[49]
4. whether the legislation was 'clearly directed only to the prevention of a noxious use of proprietary rights';[50]
5. whether the right acquired (usually a statutory right) was one that was 'inherently susceptible of statutory modification or extinguishment';[51]
6. whether, in the context of the legislation, just terms were an 'irrelevant or incongruous' notion.[52]

The six limiting principles reflect substantive value judgments about the proper relationship between property rights and government power. In particular, they reflect substantive value judgments about how to resolve the competition between citizens' claims that they should be able to rely on their existing property holdings and government's claims that it should be able to reallocate existing property holdings in response to current needs. Moreover, the limiting principles can only be fully specified by reference to these underlying values. So, for example, what constitutes

---

43 *Waterhouse* v *Minister for Arts & Territories* (1993) 43 FCR 175.

44 *In the Marriage of Gould* (1993) 115 FLR 371; 17 Fam LR 156.

45 *Luton* v *Lessels* (2002) 210 CLR 333.

46 Analysed in greater detail and with further citations in Evans (2000).

47 *Airservices* (2000) 202 CLR 133, 180, 248–49, 252.

48 Ibid 298–99.

49 *Nintendo Co Ltd* v *Centronics Systems Pty Ltd* (1994) 181 CLR 134, 160–61.

50 *Trade Practices Commission* v *Tooth & Co Ltd* (1979) 142 CLR 397, 414–16. Cf. *Lucas* v *South Carolina Coastal Council*, 505 US 1003 (1992).

51 *WMC Resources* (1998) 194 CLR 1, 35.

52 *Airservices* (2000) 202 CLR 133, 251.

a '*genuine* adjustment of competing rights' that does not require just terms can only be determined in light of a substantive account of what sorts of government action are legitimate; if asking whether just terms are an 'irrelevant or incongruous' notion is not to be a circular question, the answer must make normative assumptions about which kinds of acquisition do not require compensation.

What are the substantive values that are reflected in the limiting principles? I want to highlight two contrasting sets of values, the first of which focuses on property as a mechanism for (efficiently) allocating resources to public or social ends and the second of which focuses on property as a mechanism for marking off individual rights and individual autonomy.

The first two limiting principles explicitly (and the third implicitly) distinguish between legislation that is directed at the acquisition of property and legislation that is incidental to some other legitimate governmental purpose. A similar distinction is implicit in the principle that generally speaking, a law will not be a law with respect to the acquisition of property if it provides for 'the creation, modification, extinguishment or transfer of rights and liabilities as an incident of, or a means for enforcing, some general regulation of the conduct, rights and obligations of citizens in relationships or areas which need to be regulated in the common interest'.[53] The substantive commitment reflected in these principles is basically Benthamite. Bentham wrote: 'Property and law are born together, and die together. Before laws were made there was no property; take away laws, and property ceases' (Bentham, 1911, p. 113).[54] On this approach, property is not a natural right but the result of consequentialist decision making by lawmakers. It is defined by law and redefined from time to time to accommodate changed circumstances or changed understandings of the common good: 'Property is nothing but a basis of expectation; the expectation of deriving certain advantages from a thing which we are said to possess, in consequence of the relation in which we stand towards it' (Bentham, 1978, p. 53). Accordingly, judges who have this view of property interpret s. 51(xxxi) narrowly and conclude that legislation that incidentally affects property rights while pursuing valued social objectives either does not infringe property rights or is justified by the social benefits it produces without the need for compensation to affected individuals. In 'the perennial conflict between the need for stability of entitlements, on the one hand, and the need for flexibility and modification of entitlements in light of changed circumstances, on the other', these judges take the side of flexibility and responsiveness (Merrill, 1987, p. 604).

The fourth limiting principle straddles this political and legal conception of property and a rival conception of property as a natural or pre-political right that favours stability over flexibility. The content of the fourth principle will depend on the extent of the individual judge's commitment to one of these conceptions. On the former conception, the legislature may determine that a particular use of property is 'noxious' and regulate it without compensation; on the latter, exemplified most clearly

---

53 *Mutual Pools* (1994) 179 CLR 155, 189–90.
54 Quoted in *Wily* v *St George Partnership Banking Ltd* (1999) 84 FCR 423, 426.

in the United States Supreme Court decision in *Lucas* v *South Carolina Coastal Commission*,[55] a use is 'noxious' and subject to regulation without compensation only if the common law of nuisance regards that use as noxious. (*Lucas* v *South Carolina Coastal Commission* makes the bold assumption, contrary to the lessons of twentieth-century jurisprudence, that common law rights are pre-political.) The latter conception may reflect a substantive commitment to a Lockean account of property.[56] That in turn may suggest an interpretation of the constitutional property clause that sharply limits the scope of government regulation (see for example Epstein, 1985).

The Lockean and Benthamite conceptions of property are both in play in the fifth principle but in a slightly different way. The fifth principle contrasts statutory rights 'not based on antecedent proprietary rights recognized by the general law' with common law rights. The former are 'as a general rule, ... inherently susceptible' to statutory modification or extinguishment without compensation, the latter are not. In broad terms, statutory rights are subject to the legislature's assessment of social needs and the social benefits that may be realised by modifying or extinguishing them (regardless of the owner's investment in his or her apparent rights),[57] whereas common law rights are regarded as vested individual rights not subject to reallocation by the legislature.[58] (Again, note the bold anti-realist assumption that common law rights are pre-political.)

Some judges appear to be quite directly influenced by the Lockean individually oriented conception of property rights. Justice Callinan, for example, has doubted the fifth limiting principle and commented 'that a right to compensation should [not] turn upon the way in which rights have originally arisen or have been created, whether by statute or otherwise'.[59] His interpretation of s. 51(xxxi) gives priority to individual property owners on both instrumental and rights-based grounds;[60] he

---

55 505 US 1003 (1992).

56 In broadest outline, Locke (1690) argued in the *Two Treatises of Government* that each man owns his own body, and therefore owns the product of his labour, including those things that he appropriates from the state of nature (II §27). The state is called into existence in order to regulate property (II §§3, 50, 89) but does not have any right to take property without consent (II §139). Mere utility does not justify infringing individual property rights. Those who rely on Locke's account of property and the state to argue for the minimalist libertarian state must explain away Locke's recognition that property may be subject to obligations to the needy: I §42, II §135.

57 *Peverill* (1994) 179 CLR 226, 237.

58 This is not the occasion to give a full account of the variants of this position or to pick apart the circularity in the reasoning that regards statutory rights as inherently susceptible of variation or extinguishment *and therefore* not requiring compensation under s 51(xxxi) when they are varied or extinguished.

59 *Smith* (2000) 204 CLR 493, 554.

60 Ibid. Compare his response to a violation of a land owner's exclusive right to possession in *Australian Broadcasting Corporation* v *Lenah Game Meats Pty Ltd* (2001) 208 CLR 199 (thanks to David Lindsay for this point).

appears to fear that an exception from the requirements of just terms for (rational) regulation and welfare policy will eat up the guarantee of individual rights. It is not surprising then that he doubts the first three limiting principles as well.[61]

The Lockean view of property that I outlined above is not the only natural rights account in play in the interpretation of s. 51(xxxi). In *Smith* v *ANL Ltd*, Gleeson CJ said:

> The guarantee contained in s 51(xxxi) is there to protect private property. It prevents expropriation of the property of individual citizens, without adequate compensation, even where such expropriation may be intended to serve a wider public interest. A government may be satisfied that it can use the assets of some citizens better than they can; but if it wants to acquire those assets in reliance upon the power given by s 51(xxxi) it must pay for them, or in some other way provide just terms of acquisition.[62]

Here Gleeson CJ echoes Black J's statement in *Armstrong* v *United States* that the Takings Clause of the Fifth Amendment to the *United States Constitution* is intended 'to bar Government from forcing some people alone to bear public burdens which, in all fairness and justice, should be borne by the public as a whole'.[63] The orientation of Gleeson CJ's remarks is basically Kantian. Section 51(xxxi) prevents the Commonwealth from using the property of an individual citizen as a means to the society's ends, even if doing so would maximize utility,[64] unless the Commonwealth does justice to the citizen by providing just terms.[65] Justice Callinan said in *Smith* v *ANL Ltd*:

> It is unthinkable that in a democratic society, particularly in normal and peaceful times that those who elect a government would regard with equanimity the expropriation of their or other private property without proper compensation. What the public enjoys should be at the public, and not a private expense. The authors of the Constitution must have been of that opinion when they inserted s. 51(xxxi) into the Constitution.[66]

Justice Callinan thus concludes that 'fairness and justice' almost always require that the public bear the cost of legislation that affects property rights. Justice Kirby has also observed, after surveying a collection of constitutional property clauses from diverse jurisdictions:

---

61 Ibid 551–52.

62 Ibid 501.

63 364 US 40, 49 (1960). See also *Tasmanian Dam Case* (1983) 158 CLR 1, 144–45, 247. Recently, however, some Justices have emphasized more overtly utilitarian rationales, in particular maintaining confidence in the Australian economy and the Commonwealth government as a contracting party: *WMC Resources* (1998) 194 CLR 1, 102 (Kirby J); *Smith* (2000) 204 CLR 493, 529–30 (Kirby J), 554 (Callinan J).

64 Even if the 'government [is] satisfied that it can use the assets of some citizens better than they can': *Smith* (2000) 204 CLR 493, 501.

65 Ibid.

66 Ibid 541–42.

In effect, the foregoing constitutional provisions do no more than reflect universal and fundamental rights by now recognized by customary international law. Ordinarily, in a civilized society, where private property rights are protected by law, the government, its agencies or those acting under authority of law may not deprive a person of such rights without a legal process which includes provision for just compensation. Whilst companies such as the appellants may not, as such, be entitled to the benefit of every fundamental human right, s. 51(xxxi) of the Australian Constitution must be understood as it commonly applies to individuals entitled to the protection of basic rights. It must be given a meaning and operation which fully reflects that application.[67]

These contrasting conceptions of property influence other aspects of s. 51(xxxi) jurisprudence as well, in particular, what constitutes 'just terms'. There are two broad approaches. The first, favoured by Dixon J, asks:

… whether the law amounts to a true attempt to provide fair and just standards of compensating or rehabilitating the individual considered as an owner of property, fair and just as between him and the government of the country.[68]

The second eschews the balancing of public and private interests and instead asks only whether the owner receives 'full compensation for what is lost'.[69] The diversity in utilitarian approaches can also be seen clearly in this context.[70] Some modern consequentialists in the law and economics movement would require compensation for a wide range of governmental regulations that affect property because, they argue, legislatures will overregulate unless forced to internalize the costs of their programmes. Some instead argue that compensation is required because citizens will *under*-invest in property unless they are assured (by a constitutional guarantee of just terms) that government will not take their property. Yet others draw the opposite conclusion: property owners will *over*-invest if they are guaranteed full compensation when government acquires their property, because under such a regime they are not forced to bear the social cost of their lost investment in the property.

In short, the interpretation of s. 51(xxxi) depends on fundamentally conflicting substantive commitments that are only occasionally explicitly articulated by the judges who hold them. It should not be surprising, therefore, that the interpretation of the section is complex and contested. Once s. 51(xxxi) was recognized as a constitutional guarantee, the High Court's jurisprudence came under the influence of the conflicting moral principles that drive that guarantee. As a result, almost all of the High Court's recent decisions on s. 51(xxxi) have been marked by sharp

---

67 *Newcrest* (1997) 190 CLR 513, 660.

68 *Grace Brothers* (1946) 72 CLR 269, 290. See also *Nelungaloo Pty Ltd* v *Commonwealth* (1948) 75 CLR 495, 569.

69 *Georgiadis* (1994) 179 CLR 297, 311 (Brennan J), approved in *Smith* (2000) 204 CLR 493, 500–01 (Gleeson CJ).

70 For a survey of these views, with citations, see Miceli and Segerson (2000).

division on the relevant principles and the application of the principles to the facts and predicting the result of s. 51(xxxi) cases is no simple matter.[71]

New Approaches

What then is to be done? The general record of constitutional change in Australia suggests that the prospects of any alteration to s. 51(xxxi) are bleak. In 1988, the people rejected a proposed amendment that would have extended s. 51(xxxi) to the States (see for example Williams, 1998–99). And the political symbolism of any attempt to limit the scope of s. 51(xxxi) makes it most unlikely that any such proposal would ever be made – the cultural and economic significance of property in a free-market political economy mean that broadly based property protection measures are likely to be irreversibly entrenched.[72]

In this section I consider three options for the High Court: to reconceptualize s. 51(xxxi) in light of its original intended scope and purpose, to adopt a process-oriented approach or to embrace a moral reading of the section.

Modest Originalism

The first option would be to cast off the rhetoric that labels s. 51(xxxi) as a constitutional guarantee and instead to embrace the much more limited purpose of s. 51(xxxi) that the Convention Debates reveal. Justice McHugh took the first step in *Commonwealth* v *WMC Resources Ltd*:

> Because s 51(xxxi) requires that any acquisition of property be on just terms, it has often been said (including by me) that it is a 'constitutional guarantee'. But that description is misleading ... Section 51(xxxi) is really a power hedged with a qualification. If the Commonwealth wishes to acquire property, its power to do so is ordinarily conditioned on the requirement that it pay just terms.[73]

The approach that McHugh J outlines here emphasizes the textualist and legalist elements in Australian constitutional interpretation. It moves as far as possible from interpreting s. 51(xxxi) as giving effect to a moral imperative. On this approach, the section's indirect protection for property rights stands in contrast with the direct guarantee effected by the Takings Clause.[74] Although conformity with an underlying norm may be welcomed it is not an independent aim for the interpreter:

---

71 Unsurprisingly, the divisions are not confined to the High Court. See, e.g., *Australian Capital Territory* v *Pinter* (2002) 121 FCR 509.

72 But cf. the Indian experience: see Van der Walt (1999a, pp. 188–228).

73 (1998) 194 CLR 1, 48.

74 Ibid 57–58. Cf. *Grace Brothers* (1946) 72 CLR 269, 285 (Starke J), 289–90 (Dixon J); but contrast *Bank Nationalisation Case* (1948) 76 CLR 1, 349 (Dixon J) (referring to the double aspect of s. 51(xxxi) as power and protection against governmental interference with property).

[W]hether or not the presence of s. 51(xxxi) in the Constitution prevents the Parliament using another head of power to acquire property without paying just terms cannot depend on the harshness of the result that the acquisition occasions. The question is one of constitutional power, not political morality.[75]

The second step in a modest originalist re-reading of s. 51(xxxi) would be to move away from the broad meanings ascribed to 'property' and 'acquisition' by the High Court and return to the apparently limited scope and purpose that the framers intended for s. 51(xxxi). The section was included in the *Constitution* to remove any doubts that the Commonwealth Parliament lacked the power of eminent domain and would instead have to negotiate with property owners to purchase land by agreement.[76] The framers referred to the likely need to acquire land for military facilities,[77] a federal court-house or a federal custom-house[78] or a leper station[79] and did not appear to contemplate the wider operation of s. 51(xxxi) as a constitutional guarantee.

Justice McHugh declined to take this second step, I think rightly (see generally Evans, 2001). I have previously argued that the examples given by the framers of the purposes for which property could be acquired under s. 51(xxxi) could not limit the generality of the purposes comprehended by the language of the provision: '[A]ny purpose in respect of which the Parliament has power to make laws'. Nor could their apparent assumption that the property to be acquired would be land, limit the generality of 'property' as the subject-matter of the section. I concluded, in any event, that it was too late to retreat to the narrower conception of the section that was apparently intended by the framers.

Even if these obstacles could be overcome, and the costs of such a radical break with the High Court's current approach could be reconciled with the limits on the judicial function, the gains are likely to be short-term. A non-purposive reading of s. 51(xxxi) such as that described here would stand in ongoing tension with deep-rooted cultural norms concerning private property. Those norms are not confined to land; and they are not confined to protection against governments attempting outright acquisition of title. The influences that produced the current wide 'guarantee' reading of s. 51(xxxi) would continue to operate and something like the current reading would almost inevitably return. Modest originalism is a doubtful long-term candidate for producing a coherent approach to s. 51(xxxi).

---

75 *WMC Resources* (1998) 194 CLR 1, 57.

76 See generally Evans (2001) where the argument and conclusions of this paragraph are expressed at greater length. The doubts appear to have stemmed from the suggestion that only sovereign legislatures possessed the inherent power of eminent domain.

77 Australasian Federal Convention (1898, Melbourne, Victoria) (1898), *Official Records of the Debates of the Australasian Federal Convention: Third Session, Melbourne, 20th January to 17th March, 1898*, vol. 1, Melbourne: R. S. Brain, Government Printer, p. 151 (John Quick).

78 Ibid p. 152 (John Quick).

79 Ibid p. 258 (John Cockburn).

A Process-Orientated Approach

Is there an approach that brackets the moral controversies of the current approach and offers more predictability? As a general matter, the existence of such approaches is a large and controversial question.[80] In the United States, process-oriented approaches were thought for a time to offer a neutral approach to rights adjudication. However, they are now widely criticized as inevitably involving moral choices of their own.[81] Further, there is a certain irony in suggesting a process-oriented approach to a constitutional property clause. After all, *United States* v *Carolene Products'* famous footnote 4, the inspiration of process-oriented approaches, advocated more searching scrutiny for legislation affecting the political process itself, and for legislation affecting 'discrete and insular minorities' who were excluded from the political process, than for 'regulatory legislation affecting ordinary commercial transactions'.[82] (But it is certainly possible for legislation to target the property interests of 'discrete and insular minorities'. The *Queensland Coast Islands Declaratory Act 1985* (Qld) and the *Hindmarsh Island Bridge Act 1997* (Cth) are examples.[83])

If these reservations were overcome, what might a process-oriented approach to a constitutional property clause look like? Treanor (1995, p. 784; see also 1988) argues in relation to the Takings Clause that:

> ... courts should mandate compensation only in those classes of cases in which process failure is particularly likely today – when there has been singling out or in environmental racism cases, where there has been discrimination against discrete and insular minorities. Outside of this realm, the Takings Clause should serve an educative function, but should not lead to court enforcement. Except where process failure is likely, the decision about whether to compensate should be left to the political process, even in cases involving government seizure of property. The political process is certainly capable of handling that responsibility.

Such an approach might attract the operation of a constitutional property clause in cases like *Durham Holdings Pty Ltd* v *New South Wales*,[84] where the three largest coal companies were singled out by the legislative cap on the compensation payable to them,[85] and *Mabo* v *Queensland*,[86] which considered the *Queensland Coast Islands Declaratory Act 1985* (Qld).[87] However, the focus on discrimination in this approach

---

80 See, e.g., Ely (1980) and the subsequent debate.

81 For a sympathetic reconstruction see Klarman (1991).

82 304 US 144, 152 (1938). Treanor (1995, p. 873) also notes the irony, but cf. Ely (1980, 97–98).

83 The insular references in the titles of the Acts are coincidental.

84 (2001) 205 CLR 399.

85 These companies may have been singled out, but it can hardly be said that they were excluded from the political process.

86 (1988) 166 CLR 186.

87 Assuming in both cases, of course, that the constitutional property clause extended to state legislation.

brings it squarely within one of the principal and compelling critiques of process-oriented approaches: they cannot fulfil their promise of a neutral approach because they depend on a substantive account of discrimination (see e.g., Klarman, 1991).

Moreover, such a direct borrowing from United States constitutional law would be unwise. The foundations of the American doctrine are controversial.[88] It is not an isolated doctrine that can be easily severed and transplanted but depends in complex way on many 'contextual variables' (Rosenfeld, 2001, p. 71). These include its textual foundation in the 14th Amendment (language explicitly rejected by the framers of the *Australian Constitution*); its development in the context of desegregation, an experience not duplicated in Australia despite our own history of institutionalized racism; its relationship to the 'specific prohibition[s] of the [United States] Constitution, such as those of the first ten Amendments';[89] and the myriad differences in the process by which the legislation is produced, including the presidential (rather than parliamentary) system of government, weak party allegiance and the committee and conference systems by which agreement is reached on legislative texts.

That is not to say that process theory has no insights for the interpretation of s. 51(xxxi). It accommodates respect for the outcomes of democratic processes with the need to consider the possibility of rights violations when democratic processes fail. However, a process-oriented approach cannot provide a solution to the problem of moral conflict in s. 51(xxxi) cases without an account of what constitutes a process failure in the context of the Australian legislative process.

Moral Reading(s) of s. 51(xxxi)

It seems inevitable, then, that some measure of reasoning based on moral values extrinsic to the *Constitution* will be required in interpreting s. 51(xxxi). Property disputes inevitably arise in conditions of scarcity and limited generosity: '[T]he "property" notion … is but a shadow of the individual and collective human response to a world of limited resources and attenuated altruism'(Gray, 1991, p. 307). In addition, legislatures and courts approach property disputes on the basis of incomplete information about many issues, not only about the distribution of resources and the behavioural consequences of any decision they make, but more importantly about whether the moral values at stake are incommensurable or whether in fact there is a 'uniquely correct resolution to problems of incompatible values' (let alone what that correct resolution might be) (Gutmann and Thompson, 1996, p. 25). The combination of these factors means that it is likely that the disputes that arise under s. 51(xxxi) are irreducibly moral disputes, that is, disputes that cannot be resolved in other than moral terms (unless there be resort to force or coercion) (ibid).

---

88 See, e.g., the searching criticism in Ackerman (1985).
89 *Carolene Products*, 304 US 144, 152 n. 4 (1938).

I have previously argued that in deliberating on s. 51(xxxi) cases, members of the Court should openly expose the moral values that drive the dispute.[90] They should acknowledge the public and private functions of property – as a socially constructed response to the problem of controlling access to scarce resources and as a mechanism for assuring stability and predictability for individuals. That will not of itself produce agreement on the appropriate interpretation of the section. Nor should it be expected to. As Gutmann and Thompson (1996, pp. 25–26) argue:

> We should not expect finally to resolve all or even most moral conflicts. If incompatible values and incomplete understanding are as endemic to human politics as scarcity and limited generosity, then the problem of moral disagreement is a condition with which we must learn to live, not merely an obstacle to be overcome on the way to a just society. We reach some resolutions, but they are partial and tentative ... [T]he principles and values with which we live are provisional, formed and continually revised in the process of making and responding to moral claims in public life.

Beyond Moral Reading(s)

Although judges interpreting s. 51(xxxi) should acknowledge the moral underpinnings of s. 51(xxxi), they should also recognize the Court's limitations as a site for moral deliberation. In particular, they should recognize that in all cases that arise under s. 51(xxxi), the Commonwealth Parliament has at least had the opportunity to engage in moral deliberation about the measure that is alleged to acquire property without just terms. This means that some measure of deference to legislative judgments is appropriate.

In practice, however, members of the High Court have rarely identified what standard of review should be applied when analysing whether a law falls within s. 51(xxxi). (That a standard of review is involved ought to be clear. Although just terms are required whenever there is an acquisition of property within the scope of the section, whether there *is* such an acquisition is a question that admits different answers.) Some justices have explicitly rejected proportionality and any balancing as a mode of analysis in s. 51(xxxi).[91] In applying the six limiting principles that I identified above, there is little explicit use of the language of deference or proportionality or consideration of whether legislation is 'reasonably appropriate and adapted' to some non-acquisitive purpose. (That language *is* used in identifying whether a law is supported by a head of power other than s 51(xxxi) and particularly in identifying whether a law falls within the scope of the power incidental to that

---

90 Evans (2000). I do not mean to suggest that courts should reason directly from moral principles in each case. But I would argue that my approach is compatible with a range of approaches to whether courts should develop and apply abstract moral theories (e.g. Stone (1998), reviewing Sunstein (1996)) and the kinds of reasons that are appropriate in public deliberation (e.g. Gutmann & Thompson (1996, ch. 1)).

91 *Georgiadis* (1994) 179 CLR 297, 310–11 (Brennan J).

other head of power; but that question only arises once it is determined that the law falls outside the scope of s 51(xxxi).[92])

By contrast, a rare acknowledgement that deference to the legislature may be appropriate under s. 51(xxxi) appears in the judgment of Dixon J in *Grace Brothers* analysing what constitutes just terms. He rejected an approach that required full compensation in every case in favour of asking:

> ... whether the law amounts to a true attempt to provide fair and just standards of compensating or rehabilitating the individual considered as an owner of property, fair and just as between him and the government of the country.[93]

He noted further that:

> In deciding whether any given law is within the power the Court must, of course, examine the justice of the terms provided. But it is a legislative function to provide the terms, and the Constitution does not mean to deprive the legislature of all discretion in determining what is just. Nor does justice to the subject or to the State demand a disregard of the interests of the public or of the Commonwealth.[94]

It would be consistent with the Court's approach to other rights protections (notably the freedom of political communication and the freedom of interstate intercourse[95]) if, for the reasons outlined above, the High Court were to recognize that some measure of deference were appropriate in s. 51(xxxi) cases.[96] It would not obviate the need for a substantive conception of the subject matter of s. 51(xxxi); but it would appropriately give primacy to the legislature's determination of the rights issues that are implicated by the legislation under review. Justice Callinan is correct to fear, however, that an approach to s. 51(xxxi) that merely assesses the proportionality of legislative means and ends would eliminate the rights-content of s. 51(xxxi).[97] It would not analyse the moral controversy within a deferential framework, but would resolve it in favour of one of the competing conceptions of property. A deferential approach must accommodate the rights-oriented conception of property by including

---

92 See, e.g., *Lawler* (1994) 179 CLR 270, 284–86; *Mutual Pools* (1994) 179 CLR 155, 219–22; *Peverill* (1994) 179 CLR 226, 259. These cases make plain that Andre van der Walt's (1999b, p. 133) descriptive claim (that the current approach to s 51(xxxi) is based on proportionality in anything other than a loose and impressionistic manner) is wrong. However, his normative claim is strong and is reflected in my text here (and also in Allen (2000, pp. 362–69)).

93 *Grace Brothers* (1946) 72 CLR 269, 290.

94 Ibid 291.

95 *Lange v Australian Broadcasting Corporation* (1997) 189 CLR 520, 562, 567; *AMS v AIF* (1999) 199 CLR 160.

96 Perhaps different measures of deference in different classes of case: see text following 80.

97 See above n. 60 and accompanying text.

something like the minimal impairment test (see also Allen, 2000, pp. 368–69) applied in *Canadian Charter of Rights and Freedoms* [98] cases in Canada.[99]

Property Rights in the Legislative Process

Given the pervasive problems with judicial interpretation of constitutional property clauses, and my proposal that the courts adopt a deferential stance to legislative judgments about property issues, it is appropriate to consider how parliaments can and do consider property issues in rights terms.

Parliaments and Courts

Gutmann and Thompson (1996, p. 45) rightly warn against a 'deductive institutionalism' that purports to decide on institutional competence to resolve moral issues without actually considering whether the empirical evidence supports common assumptions about the deliberative capacities of judges and legislators. But it certainly appears to be the case that some of the moral dimensions of property are better addressed by legislators than courts interpreting s. 51(xxxi), not least because of the greater deliberative capacity of legislatures and the epistemic advantages that they may enjoy. Moreover, there are significant moral dimensions to property that will not be reached by s. 51(xxxi) even on an overtly moral reading. For example, there is little, if any, scope for giving effect to the (positive) rights to have the property necessary for a healthy existence;[100] to be free from discrimination on grounds of property in the recognition of other rights;[101] and to be free from discrimination on grounds of race and sex in access to public property[102] and in ownership of property.[103] And, although the moral cogency of property claims will vary, there is little scope for selectivity about the types of property that fall within the scope of s. 51(xxxi): 'Courts can perceive whether or not an object has been taken, but cannot in the same way discern whether "too much" wealth has been taken'

---

98 *Canada Act 1982* (UK), c 11, sch B.

99 E.g. *R v Oakes* [1986] 1 SCR 103.

100 *International Covenant on Economic, Social and Cultural Rights*, opened for signature 16 December 1966, 999 UNTS 3, arts 9, 11–13 (entered into force 3 January 1976) ('*ICESCR*').

101 *Universal Declaration of Human Rights*, GA Res 217A, 3 UN GAOR, 3rd sess, 183rd plen mtg, UN Doc A/Res/217A (III) (1948) art 2; *International Covenant on Civil and Political Rights*, opened for signature 19 December 1966, 999 UNTS 171, arts 2, 24 and 26 (entered into force 23 March 1976); *ICESCR*, art 2(2).

102 *International Convention on the Elimination of All Forms of Racial Discrimination*, opened for signature 7 March 1966, 660 UNTS 195, art 3(2) (entered into force 4 January 1969) ('*CERD*').

103 *CERD*, art 5(d)(v); *Convention on the Elimination of All Forms of Discrimination against Women*, opened for signature 18 December 1979, 1249 UNTS 13, arts 13(b), 15(2), 16(1)(h) (entered into force 3 September 1981).

(Radin, 1993, p. 65; see also Treanor, 1997). And courts cannot discern whether the prevailing distribution of property rights is unjust and that an acquisitive law attempts to redistribute those rights more justly. Property rights may be unjustified under a historical account of justice in property holdings because of wrongs done to the former owners of that property. Property rights (for example, in weapons or in pornography or, at an earlier time, in slaves) may be unjustified and anachronistic under some critical moral accounts (Story, 1998). These issues were all addressed, to varying extents, in the parliamentary debates on the coal industry reform legislation that was ultimately considered by the High Court in *Durham Holdings Pty Ltd* v *New South Wales*[104] but inevitably formed no part of the Court's deliberation.

Equally, the text of s. 51(xxxi) does not easily accommodate those moral accounts that distinguish between property that is 'part of the way we constitute ourselves as continuing personal entities in the world' (Radin, 1993, p. 36, ch. 1 generally) and property that assumes a more fungible place in our lives.[105] Margaret Radin argues that the former type of property deserves greater protection than fungible property and may deserve immunity from government action (and not merely compensation for the effects of government regulation).[106] This non-economic, moral dimension of property is well caught in the parliamentary debates on the Victorian legislation that banned certain firearms. Members recounted their childhood and adolescent experiences with firearms and the importance of firearms to the identity of rural people and some ethnic communities; some referred to firearms that they had owned for a long period and with which they had strong associations or which were held as decorative objects; others bridled at the intrusion on the person and property of people who had not committed offences, especially as law abiding gun owners were likely to lose their registered weapons whereas unregistered weapons were unlikely to be surrendered or subsequently located and forfeited.[107]

The deliberative standards that parliaments should meet in debating rights issues are controversial (see for example Gutmann and Thompson, 1996; Dryzek, 2000); and it is unclear to what extent parliaments achieve those standards or what effect

---

104 (2001) 205 CLR 399. See, New South Wales, *Parliamentary Debates*, Legislative Assembly, 1 December 1981, 1175–226 (Coal Acquisition Bill 1981 (NSW)); Legislative Assembly, 16 May 1990, 3541–43; 23 May 1990, 4453–61, 4471–74; Legislative Council, 30 May 1990, 4757–68 (Coal Ownership Restitution Bill 1990 (NSW)); Legislative Assembly, 27 May 1997, 9252ff; Legislative Assembly, 14 May 1997, 8498–500 and 21 May 1997, 8915–19 (Coal Acquisition Amendment Bill 1997 (NSW)).

105 But cf. Alexander (2003, pp. 745–48) describing how the self-development conception of property affects constitutional adjudication in Germany.

106 Radin (1993, ch. 1) does not fully develop the argument that the importance of property to constituting personhood means that all persons should have minimum entitlements to the property necessary for autonomy. But cf. Waldron (1988, ch. 10) in his elaboration of Hegel's account of property.

107 See generally the debate on the Firearms (Prohibited Firearms) Bill 1996 (Vic): Victoria, *Parliamentary Debates*, Legislative Council, 25 June 1996, 702–21; Victoria, *Parliamentary Debates*, Legislative Assembly, 18 June 1996, 781–811.

they have on rights-outcomes. Those are questions for ongoing research. But there is no doubt that parliaments can recognize and debate property rights issues that arise in s. 51(xxxi) adjudication as well as issues that lie well beyond the view of the courts. The challenge is to ensure that parliaments are well equipped to carry out these functions. In what follows, I concentrate on two institutional mechanisms that already exist or have recently been proposed in Australia.

Scrutiny Committees

One of the parliamentary resources for rights-oriented deliberation is the committee system. Four Australian parliaments have committees that are responsible for the scrutiny of primary and delegated legislation against rights-based criteria.[108] However, only the Queensland Scrutiny of Legislation Committee is specifically directed to consider property issues, by considering whether proposed legislation 'provides for the compulsory acquisition of property only with fair compensation'.[109] The other scrutiny committees have the generic mandate to consider whether legislation:

- trespasses unduly on personal rights and liberties;
- makes rights, liberties or obligations unduly dependent upon insufficiently defined administrative powers; [or]
- makes rights, liberties or obligations unduly dependent upon non-reviewable decisions.[110]

In practice, property rights issues have not formed a significant part of the work of the Committees, apart from their consideration of Bills containing search and seizure powers.[111] That is not to say that the Committees regard property rights as unimportant. For example, the Senate Standing Committee for the Scrutiny of Bills has said: 'The Committee observes that there are some rights that are so fundamental that legislatures should not readily transgress them (for example, the confiscation of

---

108 There is a growing literature on the work of these Committees, not least the chapters by Brian Horrigan and John Uhr in this volume; see also Hiebert (1998).

109 *Parliament of Queensland Act 2001* (Qld) s. 103 requiring consideration of *Legislative Standards Act 1992* (Qld) s. 4(3)(i) (definition of fundamental legislative principles). Few Bills appear to have attracted scrutiny under this head; a rare exception is the Transport Legislation Amendment Bill 2001, noted in Commonwealth (2001, 37). Cheryl Saunders reminded me that the New South Wales Legislative Council Standing Committee on Law and Justice (2001, p.131) has rejected the checklist of rights approach for that State's Scrutiny Committee.

110 E.g. Senate Standing Order 24(1)(a).

111 Whether this is representative of the legislation that came before the Committee is an important question for an ongoing Australian Research Council funded project on Australian Parliaments and Human Rights in which I am involved with Kristen Walker and Carolyn Evans.

property rights without full and proper compensation).'[112] Although the Committees have been welcomed as contributing to the improvement of legislation and the rights record of Australian parliaments, they have also been criticized for not fully achieving their potential (see for example Kinley, 1999). This general critique holds true in the context of property rights issues. The Committees do not consider the merits of proposed legislation and so cannot consider whether the government's regulatory objectives justify the infringement of property rights or whether those objectives might be achieved with less impact on property rights. They do not trigger any veto points in the legislative process and their concerns may therefore be ignored in the course of parliamentary debate. Both of these problems are apparent in the Senate Committee's scrutiny of the legislation that the High Court later found to infringe s. 51(xxxi) in *Smith* v *ANL Ltd*.[113] The invalid provisions were contained in the transitional arrangements in a package of reforms to seafarers' workers' compensation entitlements. The legislation substituted a less generous statutory compensation regime for the previous common law regime, and did so even for existing but unlitigated claims. The Committee reported:

> The Committee noted that, in a sense, the Bill would not only take away rights but that it had the capacity to do so retrospectively. ... The Committee observed that, on its face, the Bill would appear to involve a serious trespass on the rights of persons affected by the Bill, as it proposed to take away certain long-standing common law rights ... The Committee noted that it was implicit that the proposed new scheme is intended to be beneficial to employees. However, the Committee concluded that whether or not this is, in fact, the case, was not appropriately a matter for judgment by the Committee ... The Committee drew Senators' attention to the provision, as it may be considered to trespass unduly on personal rights and liberties, in breach of principle 1(a)(i) of the Committee's terms of reference (Commonwealth, n. d., p. 523)

The Minister's response set out the Committee's report and simply drew attention to a six-month period afforded to injured employees in which they could bring proceedings under the old common law regime (ibid 524–25). That period, the High Court held, could not prevent the extinguishment of the old rights constituting an acquisition or constitute just terms for that acquisition.

It may not be practicable or desirable to have Scrutiny Committees engage on the merits of Bills or to trigger any veto points. But the Committees could do more to inform policy-makers and legislative drafters in the executive branch, and parliamentarians, about rights issues than is illustrated in the bland report of the Senate Committee on the seafarers' legislation. This chapter has shown that the moral dimension of property rights is considerably more complex than asking whether a Bill deprives a person of their property without providing compensation. The Committees could usefully conceive of their function in more educative terms,

---

112 Commonwealth (2000, p. 23). Note that the Committee acknowledges the ultimate power of the legislature to transgress even such fundamental rights.

113 (2000) 204 CLR 493.

not just to draw attention to rights issues but also to inform the executive and parliamentarians about the structure of the rights issues and the distinctively rights-oriented questions that they raise.

Property Rights Legislation

A further tool for improving parliamentary deliberation on property rights issues can be seen in the property rights legislation (commonly referred to as 'takings statutes') proposed, and enacted in some jurisdictions, in the United States, and now proposed in Queensland.[114] Takings statutes impose two requirements in relation to proposed legislation (primary or secondary) that affects property rights: first, that an executive agency (either an independent agency or the agency sponsoring the proposed legislation) prepare a statement that identifies and quantifies the legislation's impact on property rights; and, secondly, that the government pay compensation to affected property owners if the legislation diminishes the value of their property above some threshold amount. I focus here on the first requirement, that a legislative impact statement be prepared.

Legislative impact statements ostensibly aim to improve parliamentary deliberation about property rights issues by providing empirical information that is relevant to legislative decision making.[115] This is the apparent intention of the requirement in the *Private Property Protection Bill 2003* (Qld) ('Queensland Bill') that the government prepare 'private property impact studies' for legislation 'that has the effect of diminishing, removing or restricting a person's rights to the lawful use or enjoyment of the person's private property'. Impact studies are required to include:

- a clear and specific identification of the substance of the proposed legislation and the purpose and aims of the proposed legislation;
- an analysis of the extent to which the proposed legislation has the effect of diminishing, removing or restricting persons' rights to the lawful use or enjoyment of private property;
- an identification of the extent to which future development would be restricted by the proposed legislation;
- an analysis and quantification of the total financial cost to private property owners of the imposition of the proposed legislation;
- an analysis and quantification of the benefits of the proposed legislation, and an identification of the persons, or classes of person, to whom benefit

---

114 See, e.g., Folsom (1993). Oswald (2000, p. 541–42) reports that in 2000 approximately 17 states had enacted laws with similar requirements. See Cordes (1997), which classifies and analyses this legislation.

115 Other institutions perform a similar function: see, e.g., Commonwealth Productivity Commission (2003, esp. chs 2 and 8) which analyses the appropriateness of compensation for these regulations under an economic framework.

accrues;

- an examination of the alternatives to causing, through the proposed legislation, the rights any person has to the lawful use or enjoyment of the person's private property to be diminished, removed or restricted.[116]

However, the Queensland Bill's own superficial legislative impact statement shows the potential weakness of such requirements in the absence of effective mechanisms for ensuring compliance.[117] The Bill provides for a court to order that a private property impact study be redrafted 'to ensure that it includes the information required under this Act' and to direct the department, 'in redrafting the study, to have regard to particular evidence given by expert witness[es]'. This presents the risk of capture by the same organized groups that have significant access to the legislative process in any event; and the failure to afford standing to proponents of regulation heightens that risk. The epistemic value of these private property impact studies, therefore, cannot be predicted with certainty.

Legislative impact statements have moral implications as well as epistemic ones. They can shape (or constrain) the moral contours of parliamentary deliberation by including information that is relevant to decision making in accordance with some moral principles and not requiring other information. In most jurisdictions, takings statutes have been proposed by 'property rights advocates' who have been concerned that legislatures have adopted environmental regulations without adequately considering the costs that the regulations impose on property owners. As a result, in some cases at least, property rights legislation has required legislative impact statements that more fully articulate the impact of the legislation on property owners than they articulate the benefits accruing to property owners and the wider public.[118] Some commentators have reported that the result has been averseness by government

---

116 Queensland Bill s 7(1).

117 Queensland (2003), *Private Property Protection Bill 2003 (Qld): Explanatory Memorandum* <http://www.legislation.qld.gov.au/Bills/50PDF/2003/PrivPropProB03_PExp.pdf> at 19 April 2004.

118 Folsom (1993). Most jurisdictions have also set the compensation threshold at a substantially lower level than required under the Takings Clause or the otherwise applicable law. The most striking example is the Queensland Bill. It would have required compensation whenever legislation had the effect of diminishing, removing or restricting a person's rights to the lawful use or enjoyment of the person's private property. The amount of compensation payable would be 'the amount equivalent to any reduction in the fair market value of the property that, at the commencement of the legislation, is reasonably attributable to the impact of the legislation on the person's rights to the lawful use or enjoyment of the property': Queensland Bill s. 19(2). By contrast, United States takings legislation requires compensation only when the diminution in value of the property exceeds some trigger point, variously specified as between 10 per cent and 50 per cent or (in Florida) if the regulation imposes an 'inordinate burden' on the use of land (Oswald, 2000, p. 544).

even to propose regulatory measures.[119] The legislative impact statement provisions of the Queensland Bill are relatively neutral in this regard,[120] although there must be a risk that they will frame parliamentary deliberation about property rights purely in consequentialist terms.

Perhaps the most significant potential of legislative impact statements is to force the executive, the most powerful branch in modern government, to confront the rights-impact of its legislative proposals. But for that potential to be achieved even modestly, two further factors must be present. First, the legislative impact statements must (at least in part) be rights-oriented and not be purely consequentialist. Second, the process of preparing the legislative impact statements must be (again, at least in part) independent of the executive proponents of the legislative proposal. If not, as David Kinley observes in a slightly different context, 'one cannot help feeling uneasy at the prospect of political convenience trumping scrutinizing probity' (Kinley, 1999, p. 166). The Queensland Bill goes some way to meeting this requirement of independence by the provisions for court supervision of the drafting process but at the cost of introducing the courts into the legislative process. Other possible mechanisms for ensuring some measure of independence (or at least heightened accountability) in assessing the rights impact of legislative proposals include:

- scrutiny of legislative impact statements by an independent executive agency, perhaps modelled on the role of the Office of Regulation Review in reviewing Regulatory Impact Statements;[121]
- scrutiny of proposed legislation by a body that combines legislative, executive and judicial attributes, such as George Winterton's Australian Rights Council;[122]
- scrutiny of legislation and impact statements by the Justice Department or the law officers as in New Zealand;[123] or
- a requirement that Ministers certify *to Cabinet* that their legislative proposals

---

119 The automatic right to compensation in the Queensland Bill clearly implements a particular conception of property rights and has the potential to make government regulation averse *even if* a legislative impact study demonstrates that a regulatory proposal has net benefits.

120 It is possible to quibble with the requirement contained in s. 7(1)(c) of the Queensland Bill that impact statements identify 'the extent to which future development would be restricted by the proposed legislation', if this suggests that development is an intrinsic good, and with the failure to separately identify the property owner as a person to whom benefits accrue from legislation that in some respects adversely affects their land use (consider zoning legislation that restricts development but preserves local amenity for all owners).

121 Cf. the role of the Office of Management and Budget under United States Executive Order 12,630 (see Folsom, 1993).

122 See Chapter 13 by George Winterton in this volume (Cheryl Saunders reminded me of this point).

123 See New Zealand, Department of the Prime Minister and Cabinet (2001), *Cabinet Manual*.

comply with relevant rights standards.[124]

Each of these options has its own strengths and weaknesses. None would find the property rights issues to be uniformly straightforward. The problems are difficult and the moral choices are controversial. But these options would at least locate the problems and choices within an institutional framework that is more suited to addressing them than the courts are.

Conclusions

Improving the quality of deliberation on property rights issues requires changes both from the courts and from parliaments in the way they approach these issues. This chapter provides an outline of what the changes might be and of the challenges that remain. The courts should openly articulate the values that drive the interpretation of s. 51(xxxi) and they should settle on an explicit standard of review that incorporates a measure of deference to Parliament. Perhaps, in time, it will not be fair to characterize the interpretation of s. 51(xxxi) as close to incoherent, even though it will inevitably remain complex and contested. We can also hope that courts and parliaments together, mindful of their own comparative strengths and weaknesses, will be able to mediate the perennial conflicts that property produces without abandoning either the protection of individual rights or the pursuit of the common good.

References

Ackerman, B.A. (1985), 'Beyond *Carolene Products*', *Harvard Law Review*, **98**: 713.

—— (1977), *Private Property and the Constitution*, New Haven: Yale University Press.

Alexander, G.S. (2003), 'Property as a Constitutional Fundamental Right? The German Example', *Cornell Law Review*, **88**: 733.

Allen, T. (2000), 'The Acquisition of Property on Just Terms', *Sydney Law Review*, **22**: 351.

Australasian Federal Convention (1898, Melbourne, Victoria) (1898), *Official Records of the Debates of the Australasian Federal Convention: Third Session, Melbourne, 20ᵗʰ January to 17ᵗʰ March, 1898*, vol. 1 (Melbourne: R. S. Brain, Government Printer).

Bentham, J. (1978), *Principles of the Civil Code*, in C. B. Macpherson (ed.), *Property: Mainstream and Critical Positions* (Toronto: University Of Toronto Press), p. 51.

—— (1911), *Theory of Legislation* (London : Kegan Paul, Trench, Trübner).

124　E.g. ibid. 69–70.

Commonwealth, Productivity Commission (2003), *Impacts of Native Vegetation and Biodiversity Regulations,* Draft Report (Melbourne: Productivity Commission).

Commonwealth, Senate Standing Committee for the Scrutiny of Bills (n. d.), 17ᵗʰ Report of 1992, in *First to Twentieth Reports of 1992* (Canberra: Australian Government Publishing Service).

—— (2000), *Alert Digest No 13* (Canberra: Senate Standing Committee for the Scrutiny of Bills).

—— (2001), *Alert Digest No 9* (Canberra: Senate Standing Committee for the Scrutiny of Bills).

Cordes, M.W. (1997), 'Leapfrogging the Constitution: The Rise of State Takings Legislation', *Ecology Law Quarterly*, **24**: 187.

Dryzek, J.S. (2000), *Deliberative Democracy and Beyond: Liberals, Critics, Contestations* (Oxford; New York: Oxford University Press).

Ely, J.H. (1980), *Democracy and Distrust* (Cambridge: Harvard University Press).

Epstein, R.A. (1985), *Takings: Private Property and the Power of Eminent Domain* (Cambridge: Harvard University Press).

Evans, S. (2001), 'Property and the Drafting of the Australian Constitution', *Federal Law Review*, **29**: 121.

—— (2000), 'When is an Acquisition of Property Not an Acquisition of Property?' *Public Law Review*, **11**: 183.

Folsom, R.E. (1993), 'Executive Order 12,630: A President's Manipulation of the Fifth Amendment's Just Compensation Clause to Achieve Control Over Executive Agency Regulatory Decision-making', *Boston College Environmental Affairs Law Review*, **20**: 639.

Gray, K. (1991), 'Property in Thin Air', *Cambridge Law Journal*, **50**: 252.

Gutmann, A. and Thompson, D. (1996), *Democracy and Disagreement* (Cambridge: Belknap Press).

Hiebert, J.L. (1998), 'A Hybrid-Approach to Protect Rights? An Argument in favour of Supplementing Canadian Judicial Review with Australia's Model of Parliamentary Scrutiny', *Federal Law Review*, **26**: 115.

Kinley, D. (1999), 'Parliamentary Scrutiny of Human Rights: A Duty Neglected?', in Philip Alston (ed.), *Promoting Human Rights through Bills of Rights: Comparative Perspectives* (Oxford: Oxford University Press), p. 158.

Klarman, M.J. (1991), 'The Puzzling Resistance to Political Process Theory', *Virginia Law Review*, **77**: 747.

Locke, J. (1690), *Two Treatises of Government.*

Merrill, T.W. (1987), 'Public Contracts, Private Contracts, and the Transformation of the Constitutional Order', *Case Western Reserve Law Review*, **37**: 597.

Miceli, T.J. and Segerson K. (2000), 'Takings', in Boudewijn Bouckaert and Gerrit De Geest (eds), *Encyclopedia of Law and Economics*, vol. 6, p. 328 <http://encyclo.findlaw.com/6200book.pdf> at 19 April 2004.

New South Wales, Legislative Council Standing Committee on Law and Justice (2001), *A NSW Bill of Rights*, Parl Paper No 893 (Sydney: Standing Committee on Law and Justice).

New Zealand Department of the Prime Minister and Cabinet (2001), *Cabinet Manual* (Wellington: Cabinet Office, Department of Prime Minister and Cabinet), <http://www.dpmc.govt.nz/cabinet/manual/manual.pdf> at 5 April 2004.

Oswald, L.J. (2000), 'Property Rights Legislation and the Police Power', *American Business Law Journal*, **37**: 527.

Radin, M.J. (1993), *Reinterpreting Property* (Chicago: University of Chicago Press).

Rosenfeld, M. (2001), 'Constitutional Migration and the Bounds of Comparative Analysis', *New York University Annual Survey of American Law*, **58**: 67.

Stone, A. (1998), 'Incomplete Theorizing in the High Court', *Federal Law Review*, **26**: 195.

Story, A. (1998), 'Compensation for Banned Handguns: Indemnifying "Old Property"', *Modern Law Review*, **61**: 188.

Sunstein, C.R. (1996), *Legal Reasoning and Political Conflict* (New York: Oxford University Press).

Treanor, W.M. (1997), 'The Armstrong Principle, the Narratives of Takings, and Compensation Statutes', *William & Mary Law Review*, **38**: 1151.

—— (1988), 'Jam for Justice Holmes: Reassessing the Significance of *Mahon*', *Georgetown Law Journal*, **86**: 813.

—— (1995), 'The Original Understanding of the Takings Clause and the Political Process', *Columbia Law Review*, **95**: 782.

Van der Walt, A.J. (1999a), *Constitutional Property Clauses: A Comparative Analysis* (Lansdowne, South Africa: Juta and Company).

—— (1999b), 'The Constitutional Property Clause: Striking a Balance Between Guarantee and Limitation', in Janet McLean (ed.), *Property and the Constitution* (Oxford, Portland: Hart), p. 109.

Waldron, J. (1988), *The Right to Private Property* (Oxford: Clarendon).

Williams, G. (1998–99), *The Federal Parliament and the Protection of Human Rights*, Research Paper 20 (Canberra: Department of the Parliamentary Library).

PART III
International Perspectives

Chapter 9

American Judicial Review in Perspective

Robert F. Nagel[1]

Introduction

American style judicial review is certainly alluring. To judges it offers a prominent, sometimes even heroic, role. To the educated class it promises some direct influence over public policy (since lawyers and judges are members of this class) as well as the indirect advantages that arise from privileging relatively intellectualized forms of argumentation. To members of minority groups it raises the prospect of protection from majoritarian excesses. To everyone it provides some deeply reassuring possibilities, including not only public decision making that appears to be characterized by apolitical rationality but also mandated progress that comes clothed in the language of continuity. More specifically, at least if American theorists are to be believed, courts will identify and modernize deep political traditions, enforce attractive moral principles, improve democratic processes, teach the virtue of tolerance, shake up moribund public institutions, and – all the while – hold society together.[2] Even more exciting is the fact that such hopes and claims are to some degree substantiated by recent American history. No wonder, then, that judges in many countries, as well as in international tribunals, are edging closer to the American model.[3]

As the American model becomes internationalized, pressure intensifies on countries like Australia that have very different juridical traditions and practices. This pressure finds outlets in proposals to enact written bills of rights or in attempts to imitate American constitutional decisions, as well as in arguments for expansive

---

1   Ira C. Rothberger, Jr. Professor of Constitutional Law, University of Colorado School of Law

2   The literature I am referring to is vast. Illustrative works include: Bickel, 1962, 24–5 (court identifies and modernizes enduring values); Dworkin, 1977, ch.5 (moral principles); Ely, 1980 (democratic processes); Bollinger, 1986 (tolerance); Fiss, 1979 (public institutions); Burt, 1984 (social cohesion).

3   In *Coercing Virtue*, Robert H. Bork (2003) goes so far as to claim that we are well along on the road to a 'worldwide rule of judges'. He asserts, '[j]udicial imperialism is manifest everywhere, from the United States to Germany to Israel, from Scandinavia to Canada to Australia, and it is now the practice of international tribunals': at p. 11.

treatment of treaties and statutes.[4] At a more subtle level, the pressure is intellectual and psychological rather than operational. Those who resist what so many well-intentioned people are embracing find they must defend positions that increasingly seem out of step and niggardly.

The very attractiveness of the American practice of judicial review, however, signals the need for caution. This is powerful medicine. Once introduced, strong judicial review may be difficult to modulate or control. And it may have pervasive, perhaps, insidious consequences for politics and culture. At least, my suggestion in what follows is that these dangers, along with the more familiar advantages, also find considerable substantiation in the American experience. Whether the excesses experienced in the United States would necessarily be repeated in the different circumstances of Australia is, of course, a complex question, on which I shall offer some concluding speculations.

The Growth of Judicial Power in the United States

In the United States, theories of judicial review typically assert that the practice should be highly selective. Bickel's famous argument that the Court should examine political traditions to identify 'enduring values', for example, is coupled with Thayer's admonition that constitutional invalidation should be reserved for totally irrational and indefensible legislative acts. Dworkin's argument for judicial reliance on moral philosophy urges the Court to identify fundamental moral principles. Ely's 'representation reinforcing' model calls on courts to protect minorities from the kinds of cumulative disadvantages that make normal democratic redress impossible. Many theories apply only to 'preferred' constitutional provisions, such as the free speech clause, or to extraordinary circumstances, such as when the social fabric is threatened by irresolvable conflict.[5]

The various versions of exceptionality all mean that judicial interference with normal democratic processes and values can be conceived of as limited and specially justified. Moreover, they carry the bright promise of moral and political clarity. The animating model is the 'landmark case', such as *Brown* v *Board of Education,*[6] where the Supreme Court strikes a bold, cleansing stroke. Intervening in difficult circumstances on behalf of the highest and best principles, the judiciary rises above political struggle and inertia to achieve powerful lucidity. What was murky or forgotten or ignored or contested is made plain and compelling. Properly chastened and enlightened, political bodies can then carry on with the more ordinary affairs entrusted to them.

---

4   See Patapan, 1997; Bailey, 1995; Thomson, 1994.

5   The references in this paragraph are to the works cited above in n 2. The list could go on. For instance, Ackerman attempts to justify judicial enforcement of those select values accorded enhanced legitimacy by especially energetic and elevated political deliberation: Ackerman, 1991.

6   347 US 483 (1954).

Much of the inspiration for judicial review in America may have been the landmark case, but the practice certainly has not turned out to be exceptional. The descent of high constitutional judgment to prosaic coercion occurs in two basic ways. First, the landmark decision itself must be actualized – and this leads to what might be called vertical routinization. The Court made the grand pronouncement that racial segregation in public education is inherently unequal, but then it had to enforce that ruling in innumerable settings. While it is clear enough that segregation mandated by statute is unconstitutional, what of racial imbalances caused by parental choice? By residential segregation? By the school board's reluctance to bus students across town? By teacher training methods? By disparities in athletic programs? As judges are drawn into deciding such questions, they become embroiled in all the problems that face any public administrator – overcoming recalcitrance, sloth, self-interest and ineptness (Nagel 1984). Consequently, judges (or their special masters and monitors) must specify what is required with ever greater particularity. Training manuals must be written, budgets must be set. These same dynamics can be seen in other areas besides school desegregation, notably in the prison reform movement. Courts first announced the high principle that conditions of confinement can themselves amount to cruel and unusual punishment, but in operationalizing this principle they eventually descended to the level of mandating the number of feet of urinal trough to be made available to each inmate. Very similar dynamics were at play in the decades after the Supreme Court's landmark pronouncement that abortion in the first two trimesters of pregnancy cannot be made a criminal offence. Next was the question whether states could mandate hospitalization or two-doctor concurrence requirements or parental consent rules or spousal consent rules, and so on.

The second basic reason for the routinization of American judicial review is that the moral force of landmark decisions is difficult to contain – horizontally, so to speak – within the circumstances of the original decision. The principle, being attractive in one setting, naturally seems attractive in other, analogous settings. Equal protection principles, first invoked to determine the fundamental issue of racial segregation, are then applied to more peripheral matters such as gender separation in military academies, zoning rules that disadvantage the retarded, tuition burdens placed on non-citizens, and restrictions on contraceptive distribution to minors. This kind of legal osmosis explains why free-speech decisions control not only arguably pivotal issues, like prior restraints on newspaper coverage of the Vietnam War or defamation awards aimed at silencing a civil rights protest movement, but also a vast array of mundane and even tawdry issues arising from public efforts to regulate billboards, profanity, door-to-door solicitation, school dress codes and automobile licence plates. It explains why the fundamental right to privacy is first invoked to insulate married couples from the state but is later applied to contraceptive use by unmarried minors and then to homosexual behaviour. Indeed, privacy is used to protect the right of insolvent fathers to remarry and to oversee the provision of medical care to the dying. And the pressure for horizontal expansion explains why the procedures required by due process of law first are said to require legal representation at felony trials but then are used to determine the decision-making methods to be used to suspend a student from a public school or to deny public assistance benefits.

I am well aware that both the vertical and horizontal spread of constitutional decision making can be defended. Some or all of the specifications and applications of grand principle can be thought of as important in some way, especially to the individuals affected. It might be possible for a sensitive soul to see something significant in most or maybe even in all governmental contacts with citizens. My point is only that to the degree that courts recognize and respond to perceived injustices pervasively – in ordinary interactions – judicial review no longer can claim the advantages associated with exceptionality. To the degree that judicial interventions become routine, democratic values are correspondingly sacrificed and the potential for special clarity and force is lost.

In an odd way a country considering moving toward the siren call of American-style judicial review might be reassured by the costs of routinization. These costs, after all, might be expected to act as a self-correcting mechanism. If – for the sake of increasingly questionable values – judicial power begins to interfere a great deal with popular control over ordinary public policy, surely a dalliance with the American practice would be cut back or shut down altogether. In fact, American proponents of strong judicial review often argue (or assume) that the practice is correctable. Thus proponents note that judges are not completely unaccountable to democratic pressures.[7] Not only are federal judges human and, therefore, subject to normal cultural and political pressures, but they are appointed by the President and confirmed by the Senate. These connections to wider political life, it is asserted, constitute slow but reasonably effective methods of control. Moreover, it is assumed that judicial behaviour can be swayed by direct intellectual appeals, that is, by arguments addressing judicial philosophy, interpretive methods, democratic theory, and so on. American newspapers, books and professional journals burst with various kinds of advice and exhortations aimed at judges.

While there is no question that the American experience demonstrates that the exercise of judicial power can be affected by external pressures, both political and intellectual, the overall record suggests that judicial review in the United States is gradually and irreversibly growing. The general picture, at any rate, is quite clear.[8] At the time the American Constitution was ratified, judicial enforcement was controversial and generally regarded as far less important than popular resistance to unconstitutional measures. In the early decades of the American Republic, judicial review was utilized but usually in accordance with the widespread understanding that laws should be invalidated only when their unconstitutionality was beyond dispute. During the first half of the nineteenth century, two of the most prominent judicial decisions, *Marbury* v *Madison*[9] and *Dred Scott* v *Sandford*[10] both resulted in

---

7   For a fairly typical version of this argument, see Chemerinsky, 1989, p. 82.
8   A well-documented discussion of this history is Kramer, 2001.
9   5 US (1 Cranch) 137 (1803).
10 60 US (19 How) 393 (1856).

strong public criticism, and the latter seriously discredited the Court for twenty years. Nevertheless, the rate of invalidations increased towards the end of that century, and with some pulling and hauling, has been on the increase ever since.

The Court's record over the past hundred years is familiar, although its full significance is seldom recognized. During the first part of the twentieth century judicial power was used aggressively against economic regulation, especially New Deal reforms. Political opposition forced retrenchment in this area, but the Court moved its attention elsewhere. By mid-century the Warren Court was shocking and inspiring many with a series of, by now, legendary decisions protecting minorities and individual rights. By 1970 the political backlash had helped to install the so-called Burger Court, dominated by Republicans thought to be committed to a more restrained judicial role. That Court turned out in many respects to be bolder in its use of power than its predecessor. The Burger Court, for example, ordered unprecedented and costly school desegregation programs, undertook to restrict public subsidies to parochial schools, initiated a sweeping campaign against traditional distinctions between the sexes, announced the right to abortion, ordered the restructuring of disciplinary procedures used in public schools, and helped to force the resignation of the President responsible for appointing many of its members. Overall, such adventures, while popular in some instances and in some circles, did not entirely quiet the public's sense that the federal courts were out of hand. By 1986 President Reagan had appointed an even more conservative Chief Justice, William Rehnquist, and other conservative appointments soon followed. However, rather than reversing previous decisions that had been widely criticized as 'activist', this Court explicitly and emphatically reaffirmed some, such as *Miranda* v *Arizona*[11] and *Roe* v *Wade*,[12] and audaciously extended judicial power to new issues, including, for instance, flag burning, prayers at public ceremonies, protection of state sovereignty and homosexual conduct. Moreover, the Rehnquist Court made extraordinary claims for the exclusion of Congress, state governments and private citizens from participation in enforcing the Constitution.

This gradual but intensifying march towards the judicialization of American politics has proceeded in the face of relentless and powerful political opposition and vehement intellectual criticism. Indeed, it is not too much to say that for roughly the past thirty years the Supreme Court's decisions have amounted to an almost unbearable moral affront to major segments of the political party that is responsible for most of the Court's membership. And it is not too much to say that during that time, despite unending efforts by a host of brilliant thinkers, not a single satisfactory theory has been advanced to establish the legitimacy of the Court's use of power.

The history I have summarized does not at all demonstrate that the Court is insulated from the broader political culture. What it demonstrates, as I will attempt to explain next, is that the Court weakens the political culture in ways that encourage continuing and increasing reliance on judicial decision making.

---

11 384 US 436 (1966).

12 410 US 113 (1973).

Judicial Power and Political Culture

Centralization of Political Discourse

The horizontal spread of the definition of individual rights means, of course, that an increasing array of issues is subject to the Supreme Court's oversight and thus becomes the subject matter of its opinions. These issues include highly personal and sensitive matters that in the United States were once debated and decided at the state and local level. For instance, the Court's opinions now deal with the nature and significance of specific forms of sexual behaviour, with the relationship between husband and wife (as well as between parents and children), with a range of medical procedures (including the grotesque details of certain abortion procedures), and with the specifics of public education (such as the kinds of psychological pressures that exist for adolescents in classrooms and other settings). The issues also include highly dramatic and far-reaching matters of the sort that once would have been settled by national political institutions. The most prominent recent example, of course, is the Court's decision in *Bush* v *Gore*,[13] which helped to determine the outcome of the 2000 presidential election.

The increasing importance of federal judges on matters of immediate importance to people's personal and political lives means that lavish resources are devoted to national judicial discourse (see generally Nagel, 2001, ch. 10). Law schools emphasize national law, of course, and especially national constitutional law. All the best law schools, including those funded and controlled by particular states, define themselves as 'national schools'. The most successful graduates go to clerk for Supreme Court justices. Books, films, newspaper articles and editorials, and mountains of imaginative scholarship are all directed at evaluating and influencing federal judges. Skilled tacticians are brought in to prepare judicial nominees for their confirmation hearings before the Senate Judiciary Committee, while powerful organizations pour vast resources into investigating the unfortunate nominees' beliefs and personal backgrounds. Eventually, some justices take on celebrity status, either as heroes or villains.

The effect of this concentration of attention and resources is to reduce the vigour of both political and legal discourse at the local level. Suffering the loss of skills and respect that attends second-place finishers in a winner-take-all market, state judges imitate the opinion-writing style of the national judiciary. They often treat their state's own constitutional provisions as if they were indistinguishable from those of the federal Constitution. Similarly, state legislatures and executives recognize that they do not have the stature to challenge the Supreme Court's decrees on constitutional or even moral grounds and limply frame their positions as mere variations of policies imposed by the Court. Moreover, because virtually every decision is made against the backdrop of potential judicial review and invalidation, debate about even serious policy making becomes provisional in tone and subordinate in attitude. As decision

---

13 531 US 98 (2000).

making at the state and local levels becomes less interesting and important, even more attention is focused on the national institutions, including, naturally, the judiciary.

Judicial Methods and Political Self-confidence

Needless to say, the routine resolution of broad arrays of important public issues by the Supreme Court has led to certain adaptations in legal norms. Because the justices' decisions are expected to control the behaviour of thousands of public officials and lower court judges, one prevalent opinion-writing technique utilizes an elaborate doctrinal style that is an amalgam of the legalistic and bureaucratic (Nagel, 1989, ch. 7). These three- and four-part 'tests' are designed to signal how categories of cases should be treated and to impart at least the appearance of precision. Their rather bloodless terminology – 'rational relationship', 'less drastic means', 'legitimate interest' – is at once vaguely familiar and yet ultimately arcane. To those citizens who pay attention to the content of the Court's decisions, the doctrines suggest that the justices have access to specialized knowledge and superior methods of analysis. To some degree this impression filters out to the general public and further diminishes confidence in ordinary political decision making. In fact, to a surprising degree doctrinal phrases actually get picked up and used in public debate. Thus a commentator might criticize a proposed abortion regulation as serving only a 'legitimate' (as opposed to a 'compelling') public purpose, as if there were somewhere a known method for calibrating the importance of the objectives of public policy. Or a city official might fret that a proposed ordinance controlling advertising on city buses would create a 'content discrimination', as if it were obviously desirable for government to make no judgments about the value of different types of messages. Citizens, in short, are induced to utilize a language that is mostly foreign to them and to think in a way that is often counter-intuitive and unsatisfactory.

While constitutional doctrines come in many variations, they allow for the invalidation of legislation on the basis of two essential claims: that the public purpose behind the statute is not sufficiently important, or that the means chosen are not closely enough related to the purpose. Now, obviously both the importance and efficacy of a legislative scheme are normally highly controversial matters. In order to justify the authoritative invalidation of a statute that appears to be aimed at an arguably laudable goal, the Court often must resort to simplification, distortion and condemnation (Nagel, 1989, chs 5, 6). Thus, a law designed in part to protect the institution of heterosexual marriage is described by the Supreme Court as wholly unprecedented and inexplicable except on the ground of animosity towards homosexuals.[14] A policy that by its terms permitted both religious and secular invocations at a school event is described as a surreptitious effort to impose prayer.[15] Laws that are expressions of traditional beliefs and practices are disparaged as prejudiced or ignorant.

---

14 *Lawrence* v *Texas*, 539 US 588 (2003).
15 *Wallace* v *Jaffree*, 472 US 38 (1985).

A second opinion-writing technique that results from the constitutionalization of so much of American politics is unadorned interest balancing (Nagel, 2003b). This method, which is less common than doctrinalism but seems to be an emerging trend, abandons both the legalistic and the bureaucratic and substitutes bald, direct claims about instrumental efficacy, human psychology or morality. In these opinions the Court appears to be participating in ordinary political dialogue but implicitly (and sometimes explicitly) claims to know more than other decision makers. One side wins because, on balance, its interests are simply more important than the other's. Unadorned interest balancing is a reflection of the normalization of judicial oversight. There is little felt need to resort to established doctrines or other more conventional sources of legal authority because the public is so used to the exercise of judicial review that the justices believe no special justifications are required.

Because unvarnished interest balancing begins by acknowledging that there are legitimate interests on both sides of the case, the task of explaining why the authorities are constitutionally prohibited from favouring one set of those interests is daunting. One tactic is to dramatically elevate the interests favoured by the Court, thus exaggerating the dangers posed by the public policy at issue. In an everyday case involving a requirement that door-to-door solicitors register with the local officials before intruding on residents' privacy, the Court worked its concern into a near paroxysm. The offending ordinance, under which approval of the soliciting permit was automatic, was decreed to be offensive 'to the very notion of a free society'.[16] In even more spectacular language, the Court has famously described restrictions on both the right to abortion and the right to homosexual sodomy as threats to 'the right to define one's own concept of existence, of meaning, of the universe, and of the mystery of human life'.[17] Along with exaggerating the dangers posed by the governmental rule, the Court often deprecates the specific interests the rule protects. In the door-to-door solicitation case the Court recognized that in the abstract privacy in one's home is a significant interest but the specific problem represented by unwanted solicitors was, said the Court, only an 'annoyance'.[18] In the sodomy case, the justices admitted that many hold serious moral objections to homosexual conduct but suggested that those objections lose their force when applied outside an individual's personal ethical code.

What doctrinalism and interest balancing have in common, then, is a tendency to distort and belittle the public's understanding of its own objectives and traditions. This tendency is also characteristic of the third major non-traditional form of constitutional explanation, which is motive analysis. The characterization of legislative motivation was, in more innocent days, avoided on the grounds that the motives behind public

---

16 *Watchtower Bible and Tract Society of New York* v *Village of Stratton*, 536 US 150, 165–6 (2002).

17 *Lawrence* v *Texas*, 123 S Ct 2472, 2481 (2003) (quoting *Planned Parenthood of Southeastern Pennsylvania* v *Casey*, 505 US 833 (1992)).

18 *Watchtower Bible and Tract Society of New York* v *Village of Stratton*, 536 US 150, 168–9 (2002).

enactments are complex and obscure and that, in any event, judicial characterizations would involve undignified inquiries and judgments. However, in modern times, as judicial review has increasingly been seen as an essential protection against the constant dangers posed by political institutions, these objections have dropped away. Thus, it is not uncommon for the Court to assert that a public policy is motivated by prejudice or by a desire to establish an official religion or by an intention to suppress a particular point of view. In these cases, the public is rather directly accused of wanting to subvert important and attractive constitutional values.

Traditional sources of legal authority may have their drawbacks, but they have the advantage of permitting a certain antiseptic comity. Using traditional methods, the text of an authoritative constitutional provision might be said (regretfully) to require the invalidation of a perfectly sensible public policy, and the intent behind another provision – outmoded as it arguably is – might (sadly) require the invalidation of a brave piece of social experimentation. But traditional sources of authority have lost some of their force and, in any event, would never convincingly explain the routine application of constitutional law to every imaginable political choice. Consequently, the Court has moved to explanatory techniques thought to be more sophisticated and also adequate to the rather substantial task at hand. The difficulty is that these techniques often reflect back on the public a distorted and mean-spirited view of its values and purposes. To the extent that segments of the public dutifully accept this view, political self-confidence and self-respect are eroded. And many, distrustful of the foolish, dangerous people that are apparently in charge of political institutions, turn anxiously back to the Court.

Judicial Power and Political Struggle

To some extent, of course, segments of the public do not dutifully accept the Court's bleak depictions. Indeed, just about every kind of group on the political spectrum at one time or another expresses fury at the Court. It is an odd but true fact that when Americans are not marching hopefully towards the Supreme Court building for protection and vindication, they are likely to be loudly decrying the judiciary's hubris and illegitimacy. This distrust and anger takes many forms – from outraged academic and journalistic commentary, to laws aimed at inducing the Court to reverse itself, to sullen and sometimes violent street-level resistance.

The reasons for this vehement, if episodic and ambivalent, opposition go far beyond the distortive and contemptuous messages conveyed by modern constitutional decisions. One additional reason is that the more detailed and pervasive the application of constitutional law becomes the more implausible the underlying constitutional interpretations become. Supreme Court decisions are notorious for strained, if not downright inaccurate, accounts of American constitutional and political history, for wildly inconsistent applications of – as well as statements of – doctrine, for casual treatment of text, and for unsubstantiated assertions about highly contested matters. It is true that when judicial review was used more sparingly, even the occasional decision could be intellectually weak. But the task of credible explanation has become more difficult as the Court has had more to explain. Moreover, as long as Supreme Court decisions are exceptional, it is at least possible to draw on the mythic status of the fundamental law. But when that law is found to be relevant to everyday affairs, to that degree it cannot seem special or basic. Everything, after all, cannot be fundamental.

A second reason for public dissatisfaction is that the routine application of constitutional law makes possible whole programs of law reform litigation.[19] Indeed, the model for the modern practice of judicial review is the school desegregation litigation, which began by attacking provable inequalities in specific school systems and by degrees moved to an attack in principle on racial segregation in public schools and ended as a revolutionary assault on the whole system of racial caste in the American South. As laudable as this revolution was, the notion that grew out of it was that it is generally desirable for society to be vulnerable to revolutionary change imposed by distant and somewhat alien figures on the basis of rather inaccessible legal arguments and theories generated by academics and litigators. The possibility of this kind of sweeping, uncontrollable change comes to seem omnipresent because legal theories work from small victories to larger principles. Thus virtually any of the unexpected decisions that the Court hands down every year could eventually flower into a vast program of social change. For example, a few years ago the Court offered homosexuals what appeared to be an extremely narrow constitutional protection against discrimination. The law reform theories that went into this decision, however, were aimed at nothing less than cultural transformation, including eventually the transformation of the institution of marriage. This past term, posting another victory for these theories, the Court elevated homosexual sodomy to an exalted constitutional freedom – all the while sternly denying that this elevation threatened marriage or other important social institutions. No one, of course, can know whether this denial will hold. Segments of the public, however, already feel anxiously vulnerable to cultural transformations that they have not consented to and cannot control. For these people, whatever the Court finally decides on the right of homosexuals to marry, there is already a significantly enhanced sense of uneasiness and powerlessness that readily translates into anger.

Of course, profound dissension on issues like abortion, gay rights and public expression of religious belief would exist independently of the Court's constitutional decisions. But these decisions resolve such issues by imposing rules that are explicit, highly rationalized, uniform, ostensibly permanent, and national. Thus, the Court removes many of the opportunities that otherwise would exist for softening conflict. After the Court issues an opinion, it is more difficult for members of the public to ignore or suppress an issue. It is harder to construct compromises. It is virtually impossible for groups to find refuge in low-visibility localized rules. Consequently, those who were disinterested can be mobilized. Those who were interested become inflamed. Those who were inflamed become fanatical.

---

19 This dynamic is discussed more fully in Nagel, 2001, ch. 8.

It is against this turbulent backdrop that the justices decide how to react to opposition to their decisions. Consider their perspective.[20] They do not see their use of power as unusual or in need of special justification because they are by now used to settling highly contentious issues. Because they see their use of power as ordinary, they expect compliance. Moreover, through the decades of pervasive judicial review a massive outpouring from the most eminent law professors at the best national law schools attests to the importance and legitimacy of their actions. Elite opinion makers in the most respected newspapers and the most intellectual radio networks extol their landmark decisions as heroic, essential, path breaking. In contrast, the rhetoric of the justices' own opinions depicts political decision makers as irrational, prejudiced and dangerous to the Republic. The intellectual frame encouraged by their own work, therefore, tends to strip the positions of opponents of their moral seriousness. Conflict and disagreement become inexplicable or downright pernicious. The justices, therefore, are not only startled by opposition but deeply dismayed.

While the justices conceive of their decisions as representing a kind of enlightened progress, they also understand them to be interpretations of a permanent, fundamental law. Consequently, they resist seeing their work as destabilizing or anxiety provoking to those whose ways of life are being upset. The vociferousness of the opposition, as a result, seems even more puzzling and sinister. The protests, after all, are directed against what the justices depict as deep principles long central to the American system.

For all their certitude, the justices are beset by a certain kind of doubt as well. The reasoning in many decisions is, in fact, strained and unconvincing if not outright implausible. The justices not only know this but also know that the old idea of law as logically demonstrable deductions is entirely inadequate to their modern role. This means that even the best reasoning, as right as it may seem to the justices, is not ineluctable. Against their extreme sense of institutional importance, then, is set a sense of intellectual vulnerability and frustration. The opposition should be convinced, the justices feel sure, but ultimately there is no way to accomplish that. Where persuasion stops, brute authority must be invoked.

For a number of reasons, then, pervasive judicial review has generated angry criticism of the Supreme Court and sometimes opposition to its decrees. Paradoxically, however, this fervour seems on the whole only to encourage more extreme and strident claims of judicial authority (Kramer, 2001). This reaction is a result of the psychological and intellectual context created by the routine exercise of judicial power. That context causes the justices to perceive conflict in the political arena as profoundly dangerous, even anarchic (Nagel 2001, ch. 7). The Court's role, then, is understood to be profoundly important. The justices believe that their constitutional decisions prevent political and cultural chaos, and, accordingly, they see disagreement with those decisions as truly threatening. Therefore, they react to the resistance their decisions engender by exercising more power over public policy and by making more authoritarian demands for public compliance.

---

20 These ideas are more fully developed in Nagel, 2003a, 630–2.

The Applicability of the American Experience to Australia

There is no doubt that American judicial review has sometimes been a useful, even an admirable, practice. It has on important occasions vindicated high ideals. But the full picture should be troubling to Australians. Strong judicial review in the United States has accelerated other trends towards political centralization while it has subverted traditional legal norms. As a consequence, it has weakened and demoralized politics at the state and local level at the same time that it has exacerbated cultural and political divisions. More troubling yet, the cultural and political damage done by judicial review works in a way that only fuels greater and more authoritarian uses of judicial power. This ratchet-like effect is not as perverse as it might at first seem. The judiciary is, after all, a part of the political culture and ultimately expresses the character of the people in that culture. Dependence on problem solving by the courts is an indication of the American people's simultaneous perfectionism and self-doubt. To the extent that judicial review operates to enhance these traits it is generating the conditions for its own expansion.

Precisely because judicial review both reflects and shapes a culture, it is difficult to know whether the American experience would be repeated if Australia were to move further toward strong judicial review. The Australian Constitution, like the American, was designed in an optimistic, rationalistic age (Irving, 1997). It may be, nevertheless, that judicial behaviour in Australia is more influenced by common law practices and norms and that these might cause Australian jurists to qualify their enthusiasms more than American jurists have or, at least, to act more slowly and prudently. As James Stoner has shown (2003), however, common law standards have been a significant influence on American constitutionalism, and in the United States the valuable instincts that inhere in those standards seem to have been overwhelmed by other influences.

In any event, the relevant aspects of political culture go far beyond legal philosophy. American devotion to judicial power is, in my view, traceable in significant part to two historical events – the Civil War and the closing of the American frontier (Nagel, 1984, pp. 10–11). The war affirmed certain crucial utopian ideals at the same time that it planted deep seeds of fear and distrust. And, as odd as it may sound, I cannot escape the suspicion that the practice of American judicial review – the self-assertion and creativity of forceful legal argument, the individualism evident in endless claims of autonomy and right, the perfectionism revealed in constant appeals to fundamental principles – is a deflected version of the driving force that once found its outlet in westward expansion. It is, needless to say, far too simple to attribute all the excesses of American constitutionalism to the Civil War and the closing of the frontier. Nevertheless, to pretend that these great events do not still help to shape the character of the American people, as well as their political institutions, would be unrealistic.

Australia, like the United States, has a history of vast frontiers that has helped to shape a people who are independent, energetic and hopeful. In both countries there is, at least to some degree, the underlying tension and insecurity created by a history of racial division. But Australia never suffered through anything like the American Civil War. And it may be that today Australia is in general a more homogenous, less polarized country. In any event, Australia has the advantage that whatever bitter social conflicts it must endure, its disputes do not have to be carried on against the lingering memory of bloody national disintegration. And it still has room for the energy and forcefulness of its people to be directed outward onto the land.

It is tempting to conclude from this brief and simplistic comparison that Australia might be able to establish and then maintain what the United States has not – a moderately strong form of judicial review. My doubt that this will be possible arises from one undeniable difference between the two countries: Americans invented their style of judicial review as they went along. With no clear model to follow, Americans discovered the deep appeal of strong judicial review only gradually and in spite of periods of significant opposition. The Australian flirtation is taking place with the example of the American model fully in place. This model provides not only the cautionary story that I have tried to tell but more prominently the potent allure of judicial heroism, the endless attractions of high-toned institutional and jurisprudential theories, and evidence of real advantages for the intellectual elite. To the extent that Australia is moved by these temptations, the slide to excessive dependence on the judiciary could be (in historical terms) fast. Once established, strong judicial review could create in Australia some of the same kinds of damage to her political culture that it has in the United States. Even if Australian society is less driven and anxious than is American society, this damage could cumulate. The commitment to judicial power might then be irrevocable.

References

Ackerman, B. (1991), *We the People, Volume 1: Foundations* (Cambridge: Harvard University Press).

Bailey, P. (1995), '"Righting" The Constitution Without a Bill of Rights', *Federal Law Review*, **23**: 1.

Bickel, A.M. (1962), *The Least Dangerous Branch* (Indianapolis: Bobbs-Merrill).

Bollinger, L.C. (1986), *The Tolerant Society: Freedom of Speech and Extremist Speech in America* (New York: Oxford University Press).

Bork, R.H. (2003), *Coercing Virtue: The Worldwide Rule of Judges* (Washington D.C.: AEI Press).

Burt, R.A. (1984), '*Constitutional Law and the Teaching of the Parables*', *Yale Law Journal*, **93**: 455.

Chermerinsky, E. (1989), 'Foreword: The Vanishing Constitution', *Harvard Law Review*, **103**: 43.

Dworkin, R. (1977), *Taking Rights Seriously* (London: Duckworth).

Ely, J.H. (1980), *Democracy and Distrust: A Theory of Judicial Review* (Cambridge: Harvard University Press).

Fiss, O.M. (1979), 'Foreword: The Forms of Justice', *Harvard Law Review*, **93**: 1.

Irving, H. (1997), *To Constitute a Nation* (New York: Cambridge University Press).

Kramer, L.D. (2001), 'Foreward: We the Court', *Harvard Law Review*, **115**: 4.

Nagel, R.F. (1984), 'Controlling the Structural Injunction', *Harvard Journal of Law and Public Policy*, **7**: 395.

—— (1989), *Constitutional Cultures: The Mentality and Consequences of Judicial Review* (Berkeley: University of California Press).

—— (2001), *The Implosion of American Federalism* (Oxford: Oxford University Press).

—— (2003), '*Marbury* v. *Madison* and Modern Judicial Review', *Wake Forest Law Review*, **38**: 613.

—— (2003), 'Six Opinions by Mr. Justice Stevens: A New Methodology for Constitutional Cases?', *Chicago-Kent Law Review*, **78**: 509.

Patapan, H. (1997), 'Competing Visions of Liberalism: Theoretical Underpinnings of the Bill of Rights Debate in Australia', *Melbourne University Law Review*, **21**: 497.

Stoner, J.R. (2003), *Common-Law Liberty: Rethinking American Constitutionalism* (Lawrence: University Press of Kansas).

Thayer, J.B. (1893), 'The Origin and Scope of the American Doctrine of Constitutional Law' *Harvard Law Review*, **7**: 129.

Thompson, J.A. (1994), 'An Australian Bill of Rights: Glorious Promises, Concealed Dangers', *Melbourne University Law* Review, **19**: 1020.

Chapter 10

The Unfulfilled Promise of Dialogic Constitutionalism: Judicial–Legislative Relationships under the *Canadian Charter of Rights and Freedoms*

Christopher P. Manfredi[1]

In 1998, Frank Iacobucci J chastised those who argue that Canadian courts are 'wrongfully usurping the role of the legislatures' for misunderstanding 'what took place and what was intended when our country adopted the *Charter* [*of Rights and Freedoms*]'.[2] Rather than posing a danger to 'democratic values,' as these critics and commentators alleged, Iacobucci J argued that the *Canadian Charter of Rights and Freedoms* (the '*Charter*')[3] promotes a 'dialogue between and accountability of each of the branches' that has 'the effect of enhancing the democratic process, not denying it'.[4] In making this assertion, Iacobucci J gave the Court's imprimatur to the idea that the *Charter*'s structure provides an ingenious solution to the problem of judicial supremacy. According to this 'dialogue metaphor', or theory of 'dialogic constitutionalism', the presence of sections 1 (reasonable limits clause) and 33 (legislative override clause), in particular, ensure that courts cannot use 'rights talk' to have the last word on public policy.

To many foreign observers of the *Charter*, the dialogue metaphor suggests that Canada has succeeded in discovering the legal holy grail of a constitutionally entrenched, judicially enforceable bill of rights that avoids judicial supremacy. In this chapter, I offer a more sceptical view of the dialogue metaphor and suggest and provide an alternative understanding of the judicial–legislative relationship under constitutionally entrenched bills of rights. My counterargument has two components:

---

1   Department of Political Science, McGill University. Prepared for: 'Workshop on Protecting Human Rights in Australia: Past, Present and Future, Monash University, Melbourne', Australia, 10–12 December, 2003. This paper represents the elaboration, expansion and synthesis of ideas I have explored in various places, including: Manfredi, 2001a; Manfredi, 2002, 147–67; Kelly and Manfredi, 2001, 323–46; Manfredi, 2001b, 331–40; Kelly and Manfredi, 1999, Kelly and Manfredi, 1999, 513–27.

2   *Vriend* v *Alberta* [1998] 1 SCR 493, 563 [130].

3   *Canada Act 1982* (UK), c 11, sch B.

4   Ibid, 566 [139].

first, that the *Charter's* structure is not as robust a remedy for judicial supremacy as the dialogue theorists suggest; and second, that the empirical evidence in support of the theory is not as strong as it might appear. I then suggest that courts and legislatures should be understood as competing political institutions, each with an interest in maximizing its influence over the development of public policy. In order to achieve this objective, the paper is divided into three parts. First, I summarize the case for the dialogue metaphor and dialogic constitutionalism. Second, I present my counterargument. Finally, I offer an alternative to the theory of dialogic constitutionalism.

The Theory and Structure of Dialogic Constitutionalism

The dialogue metaphor to which Iacobucci J alluded in *Vriend* v *Alberta*, has its extra-judicial origins in an article by Allison Bushell and Peter Hogg (1997, pp. 75–124). Although the Hogg and Bushell article is as well known as any in recent Canadian legal scholarship, it is nevertheless useful to summarize its argument. The article's purpose is to confront critiques of the *Charter* 'based on an objection to the legitimacy of judicial review in a democratic society' (p. 77). Their strategy is to pursue an 'intriguing idea ... raised in the literature ... [but] left largely unexplored. That is the notion that judicial review is part of a 'dialogue' between the judges and legislatures' (p. 79). The essence of dialogue is the ability of legislatures to reverse, modify or avoid judicial nullification of statutes by enacting alternative laws (p. 80). Although there are some instances where dialogue is precluded, Hogg and Bushell argue that structural features of the *Charter* ensure that the 'normal situation' is one in which 'the judicial decision to strike down a law can be reversed, modified or avoided by the ordinary legislative process' (pp. 92–6 and 80).

The structural features to which Hogg and Bushell refer, and which Iacobucci J affirmed, are fourfold (pp. 82–92; *Vriend* v *Alberta* [1998] 1 SCR 493, 565 [137]). First, section 33 gives legislatures the ultimate power of legislative override. Second, section 1 allows legislatures to implement and defend alternative means of achieving important objectives following judicial nullification. Third, some rights are internally qualified and therefore do not constitute an absolute prohibition on certain actions. Finally, the *Charter* contemplates a variety of remedial measures, especially under section 15, short of nullification. Taken as a whole, these features of the *Charter* mean that it 'can act as a catalyst for a two-way exchange between the judiciary and the legislature on the topic of human rights and freedoms, but it rarely raises an absolute barrier to the wishes of the democratic institutions' (p. 81). To Hogg and Bushell, the theory and practice of dialogue meant 'that the critique of the *Charter* based on democratic legitimacy cannot be sustained' (p. 105).

As Hogg and Bushell recognized, the idea of dialogue in constitutional interpretation was not particularly novel.[5] So why did their particular version of the

---

5　Bushell and Hogg, 1997, p. 79 n. 12. Putting modesty aside, I might also point out that in 1993 I wrote the following: '... section 33 can have a positive impact by encouraging a more politically vital discourse on the meaning of rights and their relationship to competing

argument attract Iacobucci J's attention? The answer to this question lies in their empirical analysis of 'legislative sequels', which they defined operationally as 'some action by the competent legislative body' following judicial nullification (pp. 82, 98). Examining 65 cases in which a court struck down legislation on *Charter* grounds, they found that 80 per cent of those decisions had evoked a legislative response (p. 97). In addition, the exercise of judicial review encouraged legislatures to engage in '*Charter*-speak' by incorporating the language of *Charter* review ('pressing and substantial objectives'; 'reasonable limit') into statutory preambles (pp. 101–4). Finally, they found dialogue in judicial deference, as legislatures identified flaws in statutes that required correction in the process of defending them, even where courts did not detect a *constitutional* violation (pp. 104–5; *Thibaudeau v Canada* [1995] 2 SCR 627). In some ways, Hogg and Bushell suggested that Canadian courts had fulfilled the *Charter's* promise of transforming 'rights-talk' into 'democratic conversation'.[6] Where others had discussed dialogue as an abstract possibility, they argued that it had become a concrete reality.

Kent Roach (2001) took up the dialogue metaphor a few years later in *The Supreme Court on Trial*. Like Hogg and Bushell, Roach was responding to charges that the Canadian Supreme Court had become dangerously active under the *Charter*. In his view, the Court's critics were mired in a dead-end American debate rendered moot by the *Charter's* structure. According to Roach, the *Charter* is a product of a 'creative compromise that combined the virtues of both legislative and judicial activism' (Roach 2001, p. 54). Again like Hogg and Bushell, Roach emphasized the importance of sections 1 and 33 to this compromise. To quote him at length:

> The requirement in section 1 of the *Charter* that limits on rights be prescribed by law followed common law traditions of demanding clear statements for the infringements of rights. It enhances democracy by requiring legislatures to articulate, and presumably to debate, the limits they place on rights. Section 33 similarly requires legislatures expressly to declare that legislation will operate notwithstanding certain *Charter* rights. It also requires the legislature to revisit the matter in calmer times when the override expires after five years. Section 1 and section 33 remain distinctive features of the *Charter* that would be unthinkable to most Americans, who believe that rights are absolute and that courts should have the last say on rights. (Roach 2001, p. 59)

These distinctive features of the *Charter*'s approach to judicial enforcement of rights, Roach continued, have made it highly appreciated in other legal systems (pp. 60–5).

---

constitutional visions than what emanates from the judicial monologue that results from a regime of judicial supremacy ' (Manfredi, 1993, pp. 207–8). Interestingly, in an article that purports to defeat the democratic critique of *Charter* review, Hogg and Bushell cite only one work in Canadian political science, where much of this critique has originated. For a recent discussion of the failure by Canadian legal scholars to engage with political science see Sujit Choudhry's (2003) review of the second edition of *Judicial Power and the Charter*.

6 See Hutchinson 1995, pp. 184–220. Hutchinson, of course, was highly sceptical about whether the Charter could achieve this transformation.

The key to dialogic constitutionalism, then, is that, '[u]nder the *Charter* and other modern bills of rights, legislatures can still respond to court decisions by limiting or overriding the rights the Court has proclaimed' (p. 239). Roach's preferred theory of democratic dialogue is one in which courts and legislatures perform distinct but complementary roles. The role of courts is to 'bring to the attention of legislatures and society important values, such as fairness and minority rights, that politicians and bureaucrats would often prefer to ignore' (p. 251); the role of legislatures is to expand and refine the terms of the debate and to make clear 'why rights have to be limited in particular contexts', or even overridden in exceptional circumstances (p. 250). The result is 'a process in which all of us in a democracy can struggle together for the right answers, without relying on the monologues and concentrated power produced by either judicial or legislative supremacy' (p. 251). Roach ends his discussion of dialogic constitutionalism with several practical examples of dialogue under the *Charter*. All of his examples are in the criminal law field, and the three most interesting involve sexual assault law.

The two most potentially powerful examples of dialogue are the *Seaboyer*–Bill C-49–*Darrach* and *O'Connor*–Bill C-46–*Mills* sequences. In *R v Seaboyer*[7] the Court struck down section 276 of the *Criminal Code*, which narrowed the circumstances under which defendants could question sexual assault complainants about their sexual activity with third parties. The majority judgment, by then McLachlin J, did not advocate the removal of all restrictions on such questioning, but held that the exceptions to these restrictions in section 276 were insufficient. Parliament responded to *Seaboyer* with Bill C-49, which adopted McLachlin J's broader list of exceptions, redefined consent, and limited the defences available to sexual assault defendants.[8] In *R v O'Connor*,[9] the Court did not strike down any legislation, but unanimously defined a new right for sexual assault defendants (access to medical and therapeutic records held by third parties), and adopted a particular process to govern the exercise of that right by a vote of 5–4. Parliament responded to *O'Connor* with Bill C-46, which accepted the basic right articulated by the Court, but adopted the process articulated by the minority.[10] In both instances, the Court would review these legislative responses and uphold their constitutionality: Bill C-49 in *R v Darrach*,[11] and Bill C-46 in *R v Mills*.[12]

The third example involves outright legislative reversal of the Court's decision in *R v Daviault*.[13] At issue in *Daviault* was the availability of the common law defence of voluntary intoxication in sexual assault cases. A six-justice majority led by Peter Cory J held that the common law rule against intoxication as a defence for general

---

7   [1991] 2 SCR 577 ('*Seaboyer*').
8   Bill C-49, 3d Session, 34th Parliament, 40 Elizabeth II, 1991.
9   [1995] 4 SCR 411 ('*O'Connor*').
10   Bill C-46, 2d Session, 35th Parliament, 45-46 Elizabeth II, 1996-97.
11   [2000] 2 SCR 443 ('*Darrach*').
12   [1999] 3 SCR 668 ('*Mills*').
13   [1994] 3 SCR 63 ('*Daviault*').

intent offences infringed sections 7 and 11(d) (presumption of innocence) of the *Charter*. According to Cory J, *mens rea* is an integral part of any crime, and the Crown's obligation to prove its existence is a principle of fundamental justice. In his judgment, the existing rule substituted intent to become drunk for intent to commit sexual assault as the mental element of the offence. An individual might intend to become intoxicated, Cory J implied, without thereby intending to commit prohibited acts. Indeed, a person's state of intoxication might make it impossible for them to form any intent at all, even if they retained the physical capacity to act. In such instances the act would not be voluntary, and to convict where reasonable doubt exists that the 'mental element of voluntariness' is present would violate both sections 7 and 11(d). Cory J conceded that ordinary levels of drunkenness would not negate *mens rea* for general intent offences like sexual assault. Indeed, he averred, 'only those who can demonstrate that they were in such an extreme degree of intoxication that they were in a state akin to automatism or insanity' might raise a reasonable doubt as to the voluntariness of their actions.[14]

Parliament responded to *Daviault* by amending the *Criminal Code* to remove the defence of self-induced intoxication 'where the accused departed markedly from the standard of reasonable care'. The amendments defined such departure as 'in a state of self-induced intoxication that renders the person unaware of, or incapable of consciously controlling their behaviour, voluntarily or involuntarily interferes or threatens to interfere with the bodily integrity of another person'.[15] Parliament found general support for its response in John Sopinka J's *Daviault* dissent, which saw no reason to jettison the existing rule even while offering a positive assessment of policy recommendations to create a new offence of 'dangerous intoxication'.[16] In essence, Parliament agreed with the dissenting judgment that there was no conflict between the existing rule and the *Charter*, but it saw no need to take the additional step of creating a new offence. The legislative response simply codified and clarified the existing rule, directly reversing the majority judgment at the level of fundamental constitutional interpretation.

Roach is highly critical of the Court's deference in *Mills* and of the legislative response to *Daviault*, not so much on substantive grounds (although he is sceptical about these, as well), but because Parliament acted in both instances without invoking the section 33 override. In his view, explicit legislative reversal of the Court without an override 'diminishes respect for the Court as an institution, trivializes the Court's precedents, and allows the rights of the most unpopular people to be defined by elected politicians – all without the special safeguards and sober second thoughts of the override' (Roach, 2001, pp. 276–7).

To summarize, according to the theory of dialogic constitutionalism (or the dialogue metaphor, by which it is better known) sections 1 and 33 provide significant opportunities for legislatures to modify or reverse even rights-based

---

14 Ibid, 99.

15 Criminal Code, s 33.1(2).

16 [1994] 3 SCR 63, 131-2.

judicial decisions. In modifying a *Charter* decision, legislatures accept a decision's fundamental constitutional holding but reject all or part of the decision's section 1 analysis with respect to reasonable limitations. Legislative reversal of a *Charter* decision is the most aggressive response to judicial nullification. In my view, reversal entails legislative rejection of a decision's fundamental constitutional holding that there is a conflict between the impugned action and the *Charter*. Where the Court has nullified an existing statute, Roach is undoubtedly correct that the path to reversal must go through the section 33 override. However, where the conflict involves existing or new common law rules, one can argue that simple legislation is sufficient. Indeed, to legislate and invoke section 33 where no statute existed before would pre-empt judicial review of the new statute and undermine any opportunity for dialogue. As I have argued elsewhere, when used preemptively, section 33 does become an instrument of legislative supremacy rather than of constitutional supremacy (which includes an important review function for courts) (Manfredi, 2001a, ch. 7).

The case for Canada's unique contribution to rights-based constitutionalism with the practice of judicial review thus rests on the robustness of sections 1 and 33 as instruments for inter-institutional dialogue. In the next section of the paper I question just how robust these provisions really are in serving this function.

Unfulfilled Promises

Section 1 and Legislative Modification

Section 1 of the *Charter*, which provides that the rights and freedoms set out in the document are 'subject only to such reasonable limits prescribed by law as can be demonstrably justified in a free and democratic society', recognizes that constitutionally guaranteed rights cannot be absolute in a functioning society. In this respect, section 1 resembles the 'giving reasons' requirement that animates judicial review of administrative decision making in the United States and other jurisdictions. Under this requirement, rule-making discretion is mildly constrained by the obligation to 'inform the citizens of what [decision makers] are doing and why' (Shapiro, 2002, pp. 228–57). In fact, much of the Canadian Court's interpretation of section 1 is consistent with this resemblance. Of the provision's four distinct elements – 'reasonable limits', 'prescribed by law', 'demonstrably justified', and 'free and democratic society' – two have raised fewer interpretive questions than the others.[17] The Court has interpreted 'prescribed by law' to mean that any limitation of *Charter* rights must be expressly contained in legislation, regulations or (under certain circumstances) court orders. Consequently, actions by government officials (for example, law enforcement officers) that infringe *Charter* rights are not salvageable under section 1 unless those actions are expressly authorized by a law or regulation. The Court has defined 'demonstrably justified' to mean that governments

---

17 For a review of the early jurisprudence interpreting section 1, see Hogg, 1985, pp. 678–90.

bear the burden of proving that the *Charter* infringements they seek to uphold are justifiable. In this respect, limitations on rights must be systematic and purposeful rather than ad hoc and random.

If this were all that section 1 entailed, then it would only provide the basis for procedural review of government action. However, as Martin Shapiro argues, it is very difficult to prevent the 'giving reasons' requirement from becoming a substantive standard of review. The reason for this 'inevitable and peculiarly easy' conversion, according to Shapiro, is that the requirement to give reasons forces decision makers 'to give a fairly full account of the factual basis for [their] decisions, making it far easier for judges to second-guess those decisions' (Shapiro, 2002, p. 235). It is relatively easy, Shapiro argues, for courts to move from 'did not give reasons' to 'did not give *good* reasons' to 'did not give *good enough* reasons'. This distinction between 'good enough reasons' and 'good enough policy', he asserts, is 'non-existent in many instances'. 'Indeed,' Shapiro concludes this point, 'in rejecting various offered reasons, a court can usually signal what substantive policy it would accept' (p. 248). In fact, one can see this conversion in the Court's interpretation of the third and fourth elements of section 1.

At one level, the term 'free and democratic society' has been interpreted to mean that legislation limiting *Charter* rights should be compared to similar measures operating in other free and democratic societies. At another level, Dickson CJ suggested in 1986 that this term means that *Charter* limitations should be measured against the 'values and principles essential to a free and democratic society', which include 'respect for the inherent dignity of the human person, commitment to social justice and equality, accommodation of a wide variety of beliefs, respect for cultural and group identity, and faith in social and political institutions which enhance the participation of individuals and groups in society'.[18] Limitations on rights, in other words, must serve a set of substantive principles. The obvious difficulty is that these 'values and principles' are both indeterminate and often internally irreconcilable. For example, reasonable people can disagree about the practical consequences of respecting the inherent dignity of the human person, just as this value can conflict with respect for cultural and group identity. The result is that 'free and democratic society' licences judicial discretion rather than constraining it.

The same can be said for 'reasonable limits'. The Court offered its first definitive interpretation of this term in *R* v *Oakes*.[19] This '*Oakes* test', as it came to be known, contains two elements. First, the government seeking to defend the limit in question must show that its legislative objective relates 'to concerns that are *pressing and substantial* in a free and democratic society'.[20] Second, the limit itself must be proportionate to the legislative objective, which courts determine according to a three-pronged proportionality test. To pass the first prong of this test, the limit must be rationally connected to the legislative objective. Next, the government must show

18 *R* v *Oakes* [1986] 1 SCR 103, 136 ('*Oakes*').

19 Ibid, 138-40.

20 Ibid, 138–9 (emphasis added).

that, by impairing the relevant right or freedom as little as possible, the limit in question represents the least restrictive means of achieving this objective. Finally, it must be clear that the collective benefits of the limitation outweigh its individual costs. Although superficially procedural, proportionality and minimal impairment analysis represent strong forms of substantive review because they imply that a court can envision a better law than the one under review in the sense that the court's alternative would achieve legislative goals at less cost to competing rights claims (Shapiro, 2002, p. 253).

This problem is apparent in the Court's attempt to vary the application of the *Oakes* test according to the type and intended beneficiaries of a public policy. The Court began to articulate this principle in *Edwards Books and Art* v *The Queen*,[21] where it cautioned against the adoption of 'rigid and inflexible standards' of review in circumstances where legislatures limit rights in order to promote the interests of otherwise disadvantaged groups.[22] Three years later, in *A-G Quebec* v *Irwin Toy*,[23] Dickson CJ elaborated this principle by stating his belief that the Court 'must be cautious to ensure that [the *Charter*] does not simply become an instrument of better situated individuals to roll back legislation which has as its object the improvement of the condition of less advantaged persons'.[24] For the first time in *Irwin Toy*, the Court drew an explicit distinction between policies that mediate the claims of competing groups and those where government 'is best characterized as the singular antagonist of an individual'.[25] For policies of the first type, Dickson CJ suggested, the Court should be circumspect in assessing legislative objectives and means. By contrast, the second type of policy frees the Court to exercise its review function more aggressively. However, as I argue below, this distinction is both untenable and non-binding.

The most obvious example of the second policy type, according to Dickson CJ, is an infringement on legal rights. In this context:

> ... the state, on behalf of the whole community, typically will assert its responsibility for prosecuting crime whereas the individual will assert the paramountcy of principles of fundamental justice. There might not be any further competing claims among different groups. In such circumstances, and indeed whenever the government's purpose relates to maintaining the authority and impartiality of the judicial system, the courts can assess with some certainty whether the 'least drastic means' for achieving the purpose have been chosen, especially given their accumulated experience in dealing with such questions.[26]

The justification for judicial activism, or at least a lesser degree of deference, in the legal rights field rests, therefore, on a general distinction between socio-economic

---

21 [1986] 2 SCR 713 (*'Edwards Books and Art'*).

22 Ibid; see also Hiebert 1996, 64, 76.

23 [1989] 1 SCR 927 (*'Irwin Toy'*).

24 Ibid, 993.

25 Ibid, 994; see also Dassios and Prophet 1993, 289-91.

26 Ibid, 994.

policy and criminal justice policy, and on a distinction within criminal justice policy itself between criminal *law* and *procedure*. At first glance, the Court's approach to these distinctions appears both consistent and unproblematic. Where legislatures have sought to balance competing claims in complex areas of socio-economic policy, or where the criminal law is alleged to violate rights that are not essential to the criminal process itself, the Court exercises restraint. Only in procedural matters, where courts have an important responsibility to protect individuals from state coercion, and also possess a unique expertise, is judicial activism unequivocally legitimate.

As a general constraint on judicial activism, however, this policy distinction is extremely unsatisfactory. Even where the state is engaged in balancing competing claims in complex areas of socio-economic policy, the outcome will produce winners and losers. In some limited cases, the losers will be no worse off than if the government had not made a particular policy choice, and their *Charter* claim may simply stem from an assertion that a different choice might have made them better off. In most other cases, however, once the government strikes a balance in favour of one interest over another it becomes the adversary of the losing interest. This is particularly true where either provincial regulatory statutes or federal criminal law is the vehicle for striking that balance.

Edwards Books and Art, Irwin Toy, R v Keegstra[27] and *R v Butler*[28] provide an excellent illustration of the difficulty. Although each case involved government attempts to protect vulnerable groups, each also involved enforcement through provincial penal law or criminal prosecution. Consequently, the Court's deference to legislative policy choices in these cases cannot be explained by the absence of an adversarial relationship between the individual and the state. In the final analysis, the distinction between socio-economic balancing and adversarial infringement of individual interests is not sufficiently tangible to provide the foundation for a principled guide to judicial action. Indeed, the Court has been inconsistent in its willingness to follow the implications of its apparently general rule of judicial deference in socio-economic policy cases. For example, in order to enhance the Court's ability to exercise review beyond the realm of legal procedure, Lamer CJ restated the third prong of the *Oakes* proportionality test in *Dagenais* v *Canadian Broadcasting Corporation* to require that there 'be a proportionality between the deleterious effects of the measures which are responsible for limiting the rights or freedoms in question and the objective, *and ... a proportionality between the deleterious and the salutary effects of the measures.*'[29] Similarly, in *R J R Macdonald* v *A-G Canada*, it stated that '[t]o carry judicial deference to the point of accepting Parliament's view simply on the basis that the problem is serious and the solution difficult, would be to diminish the role of the courts in the constitutional process and to weaken the structure of rights upon which our constitution and our nation is

---

27 [1990] 3 SCR 697.
28 [1992] 1 SCR 452.
29 [1994] 3 SCR 835, 889 (emphasis in the original).

founded.'[30] In both cases, the result was a strict rather than deferential application of the *Oakes* test in policy areas where deference should have been the guiding principle. In sum, the Court is unwilling to follow even self-imposed limits on its judicial review function, and its control over the interpretation and application of section 1 allows it to expand and contract those limits to suit its immediate policy preferences.

Thus, the potential range of legislative responses under section 1 is extremely limited. For example, it is questionable whether Bills C-49 and C-46 actually modified the judicial decisions to which they were directed. To be sure, Bill C-49 added elements to Canada's sexual assault law that were not implicated in *Seaboyer*, especially with respect to the definition of consent.[31] However, it is unclear whether it *modified* McLachlin J's judgment. The Court's own view is perhaps best reflected in *Darrach*, in which it chose not to invoke the dialogue metaphor to justify its approval of the amended section 276. Instead, Gonthier J characterized it as a 'codification by the Parliament of the Court's guidelines in *Seaboyer*'.[32] Similarly, the process governing access to third-party records introduced by Bill C-46 is taken almost word for word from the minority judgment in *O'Connor* (Kelly and Manfredi, 2001, pp. 334–5). Although one might argue that the legislature 'modified' the decision by adopting the minority's position, Bill C-46 nevertheless gave the last word on access to records to the judicial branch. These two sequences may mean that 'slavish conformity'[33] is not the standard legislatures must meet, but they also seem to fall short of democratic dialogue.

The same might be said of the legislative response to *R J R MacDonald*. In this case the Court struck down the labelling regulations and restrictions on advertising of the *Tobacco Products Control Act*[34] as an unreasonable limit on freedom of restriction. The five-justice majority found the labelling regulations too restrictive because they required unattributed health warnings. The advertising restrictions failed because they did not distinguish between 'lifestyle' and 'brand preference' advertising. Given the rather strong statement of the Court's supervisory role (quoted above) the federal government took no chances (even with four justices supporting the statute's constitutionality) and responded to this decision in 1997 by passing the *Tobacco Act*,[35] which imposed an absolute ban on lifestyle advertising, regulated brand preference advertising and allowed tobacco companies to attribute health

---

30 [1995] 3 SCR 199, 332–3 [136] (McLachlin J) ('*R J R Macdonald*')

31 The Court upheld this element of Bill C-49 in *R v Ewanchuk* [1999] 1 SCR 330.

32 [2000] 2 SCR 443, 459 [20]. Roach (2001, p. 273) argues that this characterization understates the degree of difference between the *Seaboyer* guidelines and Bill C-49.

33 *R v Mills* [1999] 3 SCR 668, 710 [55] (McLachlin and Iacobucci JJ); *R v Darrach* [2000] 2 SCR 443, 466 [34] (Gonthier J).

34 SC 1988, c 20.

35 SC 1997, c 13.

warnings to Health Canada.[36] Implementation, rather than modification, properly characterizes the response.

Rather than encourage a dialogue between equals, section 1 elevates judicial policy preferences to the status of constitutional principle. Consequently, legislatures are placed on the defensive in formulating any response to judicial nullification. A rational legislature, interested in maximizing the likelihood that its legislative sequel will be found constitutional, will choose a policy alternative that deviates minimally (if at all) from the Court's preferred position. Of course, the legislative override in section 33 permits legislatures to reject the Court's position outright, but as I argue below that option is increasingly difficult to implement.

Section 33 and Legislative Reversal

The legislative override clause in section 33 of the *Charter* provides that both Parliament and the provincial legislatures may expressly declare that legislation shall operate 'notwithstanding' the *Charter's* constitutional protection of fundamental freedoms (section 2), legal rights (sections 7 to 14) and equality rights (section 15). Although legislative declarations to this effect automatically expire after five years, they may be renewed indefinitely.

Section 33 was the product of hard political bargaining and compromise. When the First Ministers met on 2 November 1981 for a final round of constitutional negotiations, eight provinces still opposed the federal government's patriation plan. During the course of those negotiations, Saskatchewan Premier, Allan Blakeney, argued forcefully for a legislative override provision that would apply to everything in the *Charter* except language rights, democratic rights and fundamental freedoms.[37] This proposal attracted the attention of other dissentient provinces, and they also pushed for the extension of the override provision to include fundamental freedoms. Sensing the opportunity for agreement, Prime Minister Trudeau indicated his willingness to accept this proposal subject to the premiers agreeing to a five-year time limit on any specific override clause. In what Roy Romanow and two other participants would describe as a 'classic example of raw bargaining' (Leeson, Romanow and Whyte 1984, p. 211), the federal government and nine provincial governments agreed to this provision without which the negotiations might have failed (also p. 211). The circumstances that produced section 33 inhibited the public development of a coherent theoretical justification for the legislative override. The most extensive public discussion of this provision occurred on 20 November 1981

---

36 The *Tobacco Act*, SC 1997, c. 13, s. 22(4) defines 'lifestyle advertising' as 'advertising that associates a product with, or evokes a positive or negative emotion about or image of, a way of life such as one that includes glamour, recreation, excitement, vitality, risk or daring'. Brand-preference advertising is 'advertising that promotes a tobacco product by means of its brand characteristics'.

37 The details of these negotiations are set out in Leeson, Romanow and Whyte, 1984, pp. 193–215.

when then Justice Minister Jean Chrétien introduced the constitutional resolution containing the *Charter* into the House of Commons. Even then, Chrétien's remarks on section 33 covered only 11 paragraphs and were aimed primarily at assuring the House that it did not 'emasculate' the *Charter*. The only theoretical point that Chrétien stressed in these remarks was that section 33 would be an infrequently used 'safety valve' which would ensure 'that legislatures rather than judges would have the final say on important matters of public policy.' Section 33, Chrétien argued, would allow legislatures 'to correct absurd situations without going through the difficulty of obtaining constitutional amendments.'[38]

Contrary to Chrétien's explanation of the circumstances that might lead to the use of section 33, the first government to invoke the notwithstanding clause did so with quite different purposes in mind. On 23 June 1982 the Québec National Assembly passed legislation (Bill 62) amending all existing Québec statutes to include a notwithstanding clause.[39] The Québec government thus used section 33 to make a pre-emptive strike against an agreement to which it had refused to give its assent.

Despite this unexpected use of section 33, most observers still considered it a viable part of the *Constitution*. Nowhere is this more evident than in the Supreme Court's January 1988 abortion decision.[40] The political context of the decision meant that there was at least the possibility that the conservative government of the day could find public support to override a judicial declaration of a constitutional right to abortion. This possibility presented the Court with a strategic dilemma. On the one hand, maintaining its *Charter*-based institutional authority to participate in controversial policy debates meant that the Court could not simply avoid the abortion issue, as it had in 1976. On the other hand, faced with uncertainty about whether judicial nullification of the federal abortion policy would trigger a legislative override, the Justices confronted the possibility that the Court might 'lose' its first direct confrontation with Parliament over a highly visible policy issue. In the long term, this outcome could have seriously undermined any future claims the Court might make to constitutional supremacy.

Chief Justice Dickson's solution to the dilemma was to nullify the existing law while maximizing the set of alternatives to legislative override. He did this by discovering administrative flaws in the operation of the abortion law while making it quite clear that it was 'neither necessary nor wise ... to explore the broadest implications' of liberty in analysing the abortion provisions.[41] One plausible explanation for this cautious approach was the viability of section 33. That viability would suffer a significant blow less than one year after the abortion decision.

---

38 Parliament of Canada, *Debates of the House of Commons,* 20 November 1981, 13042-43 (Jean Chrétien).

39 The legislation was Bill 62, *An Act respecting the Constitution Act, 1982.* See Arbess 1983, pp. 117–19; Greschner and Norman, 1987, pp. 161–2.

40 *Morgentaler, Smoling and Scott* v *The Queen* [1988] 1 SCR 30 (*'Morgentaler'*).

41 Ibid, 51.

After the Supreme Court struck down the commercial signs provisions of Quebec's Bill 101 in December 1988,[42] Robert Bourassa announced his intention to enact new language legislation (Bill 178) that would be insulated from judicial review by a notwithstanding clause. The decision had important consequences. It cost Bourassa three members of his cabinet; it undermined political support for the Meech Lake Accord outside Québec (dealing a fatal blow to the chances for its ratification) (Monahan, 1991, p. 165); and it led Prime Minister Brian Mulroney to attack the notwithstanding clause's legitimacy. Speaking before the House of Commons, the Prime Minister called section 33 'that major fatal flaw of 1981, which reduces your individual rights and mine'. Section 33, Mulroney continued, 'holds rights hostage' and renders the entire *Constitution* suspect. Any constitution, he concluded, 'that does not protect the inalienable and imprescriptible individual rights of individual Canadians is not worth the paper it is written on'.[43]

This sequence of events severely undermined the political legitimacy of section 33, and no government has used it in major legislation since.[44] Indeed, in March 1998 the Alberta government learned a very hard lesson about the politics of section 33. On March 10 the province of Alberta introduced a bill to compensate victims of eugenic sterilization laws that were in effect from 1929 to 1972. One element of the Bill was a provision to prohibit victims from suing for additional compensation, and the government proposed to shield that provision from judicial review through the notwithstanding clause. In purely legal terms there was nothing particularly unusual about this provision. For example, provincial workers' compensation and no-fault automobile insurance regimes also prohibit individual lawsuits as a *quid pro quo* for a simplified system of guaranteed compensation. On an emotional level, however, wielding the notwithstanding clause against this vulnerable group smacked of mean-spiritedness. As a result, one day after introducing the Bill, the provincial Attorney General withdrew it under intense political pressure. Alberta's Premier, Ralph Klein, explained the decision to withdraw the Bill in the following terms: 'It became abundantly clear that to individuals in this country the *Charter of Rights and Freedoms* is paramount and the use of any tool ... to undermine [it] is something that should be used only in very, very rare circumstances' (Jeffs, 1998, A1).

The recent debate in Canada over same-sex marriage appeared for a time to revive interest in section 33. In fact, in March 2000 a private member's bill – the *Marriage Amendment Act* – passed in Alberta that defined marriage exclusively as an opposite sex union and contained a notwithstanding clause to protect that definition from *Charter* review. Although undoubtedly unconstitutional on federalism grounds, the Bill indicated the possibility that a social innovation as fundamental as changing the legal definition of marriage might provoke sufficient political resistance to revitalize

---

42 *Ford* v *Quebec (Attorney-General)* [1988] 2 SCR 712.

43 Canada, Parliament, *House of Commons Debates*, 6 April 1989, 153 (Brian Mulroney).

44 For a review of all instances of the override's use, see Kahana 2001, 255ff.

the legislative override. Ironically, it was precisely this possibility that may have made the notwithstanding clause even more difficult to invoke.

On 16 September 2003, the federal Official Opposition introduced a motion in Parliament 'to reaffirm that marriage is and should remain the union of one man and one woman to the exclusion of all others, and that Parliament take all necessary steps within the jurisdiction of the Parliament of Canada to preserve this definition of marriage in Canada'. The motion presented members of the governing Liberal party with a dilemma: most of them had supported an almost identical motion in 1999, but the government's new policy was that the definition of marriage should be changed to include same-sex unions. The Prime Minister suggested that those members could vote differently in 2003 in good conscience because a vote for the motion would be a vote against the *Charter of Rights and Freedoms*. Why? Because 'all necessary steps' might include invoking the notwithstanding clause, and to invoke the notwithstanding clause would undermine the *Charter*. The Prime Minister's gambit worked: by the narrowest of margins (the Speaker casting the tie-breaking vote against it) the House of Commons rejected an amendment to remove the reference to 'all necessary steps', leading to the rejection of the main motion by a vote of 137–132. The successful transformation of a motion about the definition of marriage into a *de facto* referendum on the notwithstanding clause affirms earlier views of a growing constitutional convention that it should never be invoked by any legislative body (Heard, 1991, p. 147).

To base a theory of dialogic constitutionalism on the mere existence of section 33 is thus an overly simplistic, ahistorical and apolitical type of legal formalism. Of course legislatures *could* reverse by override, but the advocates of judicial power – if not of supremacy – have altered the political context to put the presumptive advantage in debates about rights squarely in the hands of the Supreme Court. Indeed, the very idea that section 33 involves legislatures *overriding* rights enhances the judicial advantage. Under these circumstances there cannot be inter-institutional dialogue in any real sense. The judicial–legislative interaction must therefore be of a different form.

A Strategic Model of Judicial–Legislative Interaction

If sections 1 and 33 are not robust enough to support the kind of dialogic interaction between courts and legislatures envisioned by theorists like Roach and Hogg and Bushell, how might we understand this interaction? The first step is to recognize that final courts of appeal are political institutions: they make policy not as an accidental by-product of performing their legal functions, but because their individual members believe that certain rules will be socially beneficial. For almost sixty years the dominant paradigm for explaining individual decision making in these courts has been the attitudinal model (Segal and Spaeth, 1993). This model rests on two assumptions. One is that judges, like other political actors, are goal-oriented and seek to advance their goals through legal judgments. Second, the model assumes that judicial goals include policy preferences that have been shaped by the personal background and experiences of individual judges. According to the attitudinal model, judges, particularly those on national high courts, are free to decide disputes according to their attitudinally and experientially determined policy preferences because of the ambiguity of legal rules and institutional provisions like security of tenure and formal independence from legislatures and executives. From this perspective, changes in legal doctrine are the product of attitudinal shifts caused by changes in judicial personnel.

However, as James Gibson has argued, judicial decision making is not just a 'function of what [judges] prefer to do', it is also 'tempered by what they think they ought to do, [and] constrained by what they perceive is feasible to do' (Gibson, 1991, p. 256). Consequently, since at least the mid 1960s scholars have also explored the strategic elements of judicial decision making (Murphy, 1964). Strategic models of judicial behaviour assert that the freedom of judges to advance their interests through legal decisions is subject to institutional constraints. These constraints – which force judges to consider other actors' preferences, the choices they expect others to make, and the context in which they operate (Epstein and Knight, 1998, p. xiii) – produce strategic behaviour on two distinct levels. First, judges are constrained internally by rules that govern their interactions with colleagues. Most obviously, the successful transformation of individual policy preferences into law on multi-member appellate courts requires coalition building to produce majority support for particular decisions. Second, judges are constrained externally by rules that govern the relationship between courts and other political institutions. In other words, since the achievement of immediate policy goals depends to a significant degree on a court's institutional power and prestige (Baum 1997, p. 123), courts must minimize threats to their institutional legitimacy in the process of maximizing their policy preferences. They must therefore be cognizant of the capacity of other institutions to negate specific policy decisions or to challenge the legitimacy of the court itself. These internal and external institutional constraints generate a wide range of strategic behaviour, including internal bargaining, prospective thinking, agenda manipulation and strategic opinion writing (Epstein and Knight, 1998, pp. 59–107).

From this perspective, the Canadian Supreme Court is a strategic player in the policy-making game. In high-profile cases the Court must balance the pursuit of immediate policy objectives against long-term institutional legitimacy. More precisely, it must ask itself the following question: How far can we intervene before provoking a negative reaction from other political actors that might undermine our constitutional authority? In particular, the Court must avoid provoking the legislative override because it represents a double blow to achieving judicial goals. On the one hand, it negates the effects of the Court's immediate intervention in the policy process. On the other hand, it challenges the Court's long-term institutional authority by immunizing an issue from judicial review.

Let me therefore borrow a different metaphor – the 'separation of powers game' (Segal, 1997, pp. 28–44) – to understand the judicial–legislative relationship under the *Charter*. According to this metaphor, the relationship is one of strategic interaction between different political actors, which can be modelled, although in an obviously simplified way, in game-theoretic terms (see Figure 10.1).[45] In brief, the game begins when a group or individual challenges the constitutionality of legislation. The game's first move belongs to the Court, which has a choice among three options. It can defer to the legislature, uphold the legislation, and leave the status quo (SQ) intact. Alternatively, it can declare the legislation unconstitutional and either nullify it under section 52 or impose a different policy, either directly through section 24(1) or indirectly through the instructions contained in its section 1 analysis. If the Court nullifies or imposes, the next move belongs to the legislature. In the event of nullification, the legislature can defer to the Court, pass an alternative law or override the Court's judgment by invoking section 33. Legislative deference produces a policy vacuum (V); alternative legislation produces a new status quo (SQ') that could be challenged later; and an override produces a reinforced status quo (SQ!) that is immune to *Charter* review for at least five years. In the event of judicial policy imposition, legislative choice is reduced to two: deference or override. The first choice produces the Court's ideal policy (CI), while the second produces a reinforced status quo (SQ!).

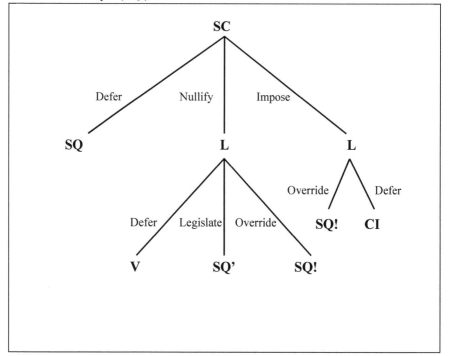

Figure 10.1

45 I thank Tom Flanagan for assisting me in working out the details of this game.

In *Charter* cases the Court has unlimited discretion to defer to, nullify, or replace the challenged policy. Like other political actors, its decisions 'represent a complex individualized judicial calculus enveloped by external and social forces' (Haynie, p. 177). Judges, this approach argues, pursue their personal and institutional goals in an environment characterized by uncertainty over outcomes. Although they must justify their decisions in legal terms, their choice among a wide array of alternative legal outcomes and justifications is the product of strategic considerations. Their most important calculation concerns the potential likelihood of successful legislative resistance to the Court's judgments. Judicial activism, in the form of increasingly intrusive remedies, increases when the Court perceives fewer institutional constraints on its ability to assert constitutional supremacy.

In the context of strategic interaction, sections 1 and 33 (particularly the latter's declining legitimacy) play an important role, but one that differs significantly from the role envisioned by dialogue theorists. Section 1 allows the Court to mask its substantive policy decisions under the cover of procedural review.[46] The genius of the first prong of the *Oakes* test (the 'pressing and substantial' objective standard) is that judicial policy making can occur even in the apparent absence of any judicial disagreement with the legislature's desired results. By focusing primarily on the means by which legislatures pursue their objectives, the *Oakes* test allows the Canadian Court to undertake policy making not by questioning the social desirability of the legislature's ends, but the effectiveness of the means to those ends. The result, as Mark Tushnet points out, is nevertheless policy distortion, as 'legislators choose policies that are less effective but more easily defensible than other constitutionally acceptable alternatives' (Tushnet, 1995, p. 250), or act 'within the range of policies it believes is available to it, mistakenly believing that the policy [it prefers] is outside the available range' (p. 270).

The importance of the decline of the legislative override's legitimacy lies in its effect on judicial and legislative preferences with respect to the various outcomes in each case. As Figure 10.2 indicates, the players' most preferred outcome remains stable in both cases. The most valuable outcome for the justices is always CI; for legislatures, the SQ always trumps all other alternatives. The justices' least preferred outcome – SQ! – also remains stable in both cases. The most important phenomenon indicated by Figure 10.2, however, is the change over time in the least preferred legislative outcome. In 1988, CI was the legislatures' least preferred outcome, but by 1998 SQ! had taken its place. The explanation for this change is clearly the decline in the legislative override's political legitimacy described above. As that discussion suggests, the political cost of invoking section 33 is perceived to be so high that legislatures are willing to defer to judicial policy preferences.

---

46 For a similar evaluation of the 'giving reasons' requirement, see Shapiro 2002, p. 236.

Pre-1988
Court: CI > SQ' > V > SQ > SQ!
Legislature: SQ > SQ' > V > SQ! > CI

Post-1988
Court: CI > + SQ' > SQ > V > SQ!
Legislature: SQ > SQ' > CI> V> SQ!

CI: Court's Ideal
SQ: Status Quo
V: Vacuum
SQ': New Status Quo
SQ!: Reinforced Status Quo

Figure 10.2 Preference orderings

The dialogue theorists are correct to suggest that the inclusion of a legislative override provision in the *Charter* generated an element of uncertainty about the institutional locus of constitutional supremacy. For a Supreme Court vested with newly expanded powers of judicial review, this uncertainty created the conditions for the strategic use of those powers to avoid a political confrontation that might undermine its long-term institutional status. However, the unfolding of events after December 1988 gradually shifted the balance of power toward the courts. The decreasing likelihood that section 33 would be used to reverse a judicial decision has emboldened the Canadian Supreme Court. To be sure, the Court – and the Chief Justice in particular – have been careful to use its power judiciously in order not to disturb the political status quo. Nevertheless, the Court has much greater freedom to pursue its collective policy preferences now than it did fifteen years ago.[47]

Conclusion

Constitutionally entrenched bills of rights inevitably shift power to final courts of appeal. According to Canadian dialogue theorists, the *Charter* contains structural features to ensure that this shift produces two institutions with roughly equal power to determine the content of public policy. I have argued in this paper, however, that neither sections 1 nor 33 are sufficiently robust constraints on judicial decision

---

47 Sujit Choudhry (2003) has, with some justification, criticized me for not providing sufficient empirical evidence to support this assertion. I provide some empirical evidence with respect to the different approaches to abortion and sexual orientation in *Morgentaler* and *Vriend* (see Manfredi 2002). See also the following exchange over judicial activism in the *McGill Law Journal*: Choudhry and Hunter (2003); and Kelly and Manfredi, (2003).

making discretion. Once courts are seen as the source of rights, and legislatures as the source of limitations or overrides, the rhetorical advantage shifts to the judicial institution. The fact that even dialogue theorists are unwilling to question this functional paradigm indicates the theory's limitations.

It is much better to recognize the inherently political nature of rights-based adjudication. It is about redistributing power among society-based actors and between different components of the state. The judicial–legislative relationship is a struggle over which institution controls the levers of redistribution. This struggle takes place in a changing strategic environment that constrains both institutions to some degree. However, the current strategic context of judicial–legislative interaction in Canada strongly favours courts. No amount of legal formalism can change the fact that, where the judicial will exists to trump legislative policy preferences, the judicial capacity to do so is uncontestable.

References

Arbess, D.J. (1983), 'Limitations on Legislative Override Under the *Charter of Rights and Freedoms*: A Matter of Balancing Values', *Osgoode Hall Law Journal*, **21** (1): 113.

Baum, L. (1997), *The Puzzle of Judicial Behavior* (Ann Arbor: University of Michigan Press).

Bushell, A.A. and Hogg, P.W., 'The *Charter* Dialogue Between Courts and Legislatures (or Perhaps the *Charter of Rights* Isn't Such a Bad Thing After All)', *Osgoode Hall Law Journal*, **35** (1): 75.

Choudhry, S. (2003), 'Book Reviews: *Judicial Power and the Charter: Canada and the Paradox of Liberal Constitutionalism*, Christopher P. Manfredi, 2d ed., Toronto: Oxford University Press, 2001. xvii, 276pp', *International Journal of Constitutional Law*, **1** (2): 389.

Choudhry, S. and Hunter, C.E., (2003), 'Measuring Judicial Activism on the Supreme Court of Canada: A Comment on *Newfoundland (Treasury Board)* v *NAPE*', *McGill Law Journal*, **49** (3): 525.

Dassios, C.M. and Prophet, C.P. (1993), 'Charter Section 1: The Decline of Grand Unified Theory and the Trend Towards Deference in the Supreme Court of Canada', *Advocates' Quarterly*, **15**.

Epstein, L. and Knight, J. (1998), *The Choices Justices Make* (Washington DC: CQ Press).

Gibson, J.L. (1991), 'Decision Making in Appellate Courts', in Gates, J.B. and Johnson, C.A. (eds), *The American Courts: A Critical Assessment* (Washington DC: CQ Press).

Greschner, D. and Norman, K. (1987), 'The Courts and Section 33', *Queen's Law Journal*, **12**.

Haynie, S., 'Judging in Black and White: Decision Making in the South African Appellate Division, 1950-1990', unpublished manuscript on file with the author.

Heard, A. (1991), *Canadian Constitutional Conventions: The Marriage of Law and Politics* (Toronto: Oxford University Press).

Hiebert, J.L. (1996), *Limiting Rights: The Dilemma of Judicial Review* (Montreal and Kinston: McGill-Queen's University Press).

Hogg, P.W. (1985), *Constitutional Law of Canada*, 2nd edn (Toronto: Carswell).

Hutchinson, A. (1995), *Waiting for Coraf: A Critique of Law and Rights* (Toronto: University of Toronto Press).

Jeffs, A. (1998), 'About Face; Massive outcry forces Klein to back down on controversial move to limit sterilization settlements', *Edmonton Journal*, A1, March 12.

Kahana, T. (2001), 'The Notwithstanding Clause and Public Discussion: Lessons from the Ignored Practice of S.33 of the *Charter*', *Canadian Public Administration*, **44**.

Kelly, J. and Manfredi,, C.P. (1999), 'Six Degrees of Dialogue: A Response to Hogg and Bushell', *Osgoode Hall Law Journal* **37** (4): 513.

—— (2001), 'Dialogue, Deference and Restraint: Judicial Independence and Trial Procedures', *Saskatchewan Law Review*, **64**.

—— (2003), 'Misrepresenting the Supreme Court's Record? A Comment on Sujit Choudhry and Claire E. Hunter, 'Measuring Judicial Activism on the Supreme Court of Canada', *McGill Law Journal* **49** (3) (forthcoming).

Leeson, H., Romanow, R. and Whyte, J. (1984), *Canada Notwithstanding: The Making of the Constitution, 1976-1982* (Toronto: Carswell/Methuen).

Manfredi, C.P. (1993), *Judicial Power and the Charter: Canada and the Paradox of Liberal Constitutionalism* (Norman: University of Oklahoma Press).

—— (2001a), *Judicial Power and the Charter: Canada and the Paradox of Liberal Constitutionalism*, 2nd edn (Toronto: Oxford University Press).

—— (2001)b, 'Judicial Power and the Charter: Three Myths and a Political Analysis', *Supreme Court Law Review (2d)*, **14**.

—— (2002), 'Strategic Judicial Behaviour and the *Canadian Charter of Rights and Freedoms*', in James, P., Abelson, D. and Lusztig, M. (eds), *The Myth of the Sacred: The Charter, the Courts and the Politics of the Constitution in Canada* (Montreal and Kingston: McGill-Queen's University Press).

Monahan, P. (1991), *Meech Lake: The Inside Story* (Toronto: University of Toronto Press).

Murphy, W.F. (1964), *Elements of Judicial Strategy* (Chicago: University of Chicago Press).

Roach, K. (2001), *The Supreme Court on Trial: Judicial Activism or Democratic Dialogue* (Toronto: Irwin Law).

Segal, J. (1997), 'Separation of Powers Games in the Positive Theory of Congress and Courts', *American Political Science Review*, **91**.

Segal, J.A. and Spaeth, H.J. (1993), *The Supreme Court and the Attitudinal Model* (New York: Cambridge).

Shapiro, M. (2002), 'The Giving Reasons Requirement', in Martin Shapiro and Alec Stone Sweet (eds), *On Law Politics and Judicialization* (Oxford: Oxford University Press).

Tushnet, M. (1995), 'Policy Distortion and Democratic Debilitation: Comparative Illumination of the Countermajoritarian Difficulty', *Michigan Law Review*, **94:** 245.

PART IV
Strategies for Institutional Reform

Chapter 11

A Modest (but Robust) Defence of Statutory Bills of Rights

Jeremy Webber

Introduction

Arguments over statutory bills of rights tend to mimic arguments over entrenched bills of rights.[1] Those in favour of statutory bills generally support them *faute de mieux*. They therefore advance precisely the same arguments that they use to support constitutionally entrenched bills. For them, statutory bills are merely a fallback – a regrettable compromise when an entrenched bill is unachievable.[2] Those who oppose statutory bills often fall prey to the converse phenomenon. They too echo the constitutional arguments. They oppose what they characterize as a wholesale and open-ended transfer of decision making to the courts. They point to the contentious nature of the judgments that are required when applying rights guarantees and decry the lack of democratic participation in these judgments.[3] This is true, for example, of the writings of the most prolific opponent of statutory bills, James Allan. He relies overwhelmingly on arguments that are most telling when directed against entrenched bills and either inapplicable or of much less force when directed against statutory bills.[4]

---

1   There are exceptions. Among supporters see: Lord Irvine of Lairg, 2003, pp. 310–11 (as then Lord Chancellor, Lord Irvine was the chief promoter of the *Human Rights Act 1998* (UK) c. 42); Frank Brennan, 1998a. Among opponents see: Tom Campbell, 2001.

2   In the Australian context see: Williams, 2000; Davis and Williams, 2002. In New Zealand, the government first sought to enact an entrenched bill, and only when this was resisted fell back upon a statutory bill: Palmer, 1992, pp. 51–58; Rishworth, 1995, pp. 13–25; Joseph, 1999, pp. 286–89.

3   See the reasons of the New South Wales Legislative Council Standing Committee on Law and Justice regarding the proposal for a statutory bill, reported in Davis, 2002.

4   See Allan, 2000; 2001a; 2001b; 2002a. When Allan directly poses the question as to the difference a lack of entrenchment might make, his reasons become very thin indeed; he cites only 'judicial activism' (specifically the creation of a civil remedy not contemplated by the New Zealand Bill's promoters and the New Zealand courts' assertion of the right to make declarations of incompatibility) and a likely lack of political support for any attempt by a legislature to overturn the effect of a bill of rights judgment: Allan and Cullen, 1997, pp. 185–88; Allan, 2001a, pp. 327–28; 2002b, pp. 284ff; 2003, p. 188. This may in part be

To the extent that the parties do distinguish between statutory and entrenched bills, they tend to invoke the idea of 'dialogue'. Statutory bills, it is said, allow the courts and legislature to enter into a dialogue about rights, each contributing its own views.[5] Dialogue is indeed useful as a means of emphasizing that every system for protecting rights (even an entrenched bill) is best approached as a relationship among institutions, where neither operates unencumbered and effective protections rely on a careful structuring of the institutional interaction (Webber, 2003). But the notion of dialogue, as it is usually deployed in support of statutory bills, is deficient. The justification for and even the characteristics of dialogue are left very vague. Why should each institution have a say about rights, and who should have the predominant say? What counts as dialogue? Without answers to these questions, it is impossible to determine what arrangements provide an appropriate balance – or even whether one should aim for a balance. In fact, it often seems that the idea of dialogue is used simply to fend off critics of entrenched bills or, on the other side, to encourage advocates of judicial supremacy to acknowledge the legitimacy of some legislative role in rights protection. The argument is reactive, a tactical response in a struggle between opponents who fundamentally support either judicial or legislative determination.[6]

As a result, the discussion over statutory bills tends to be a pale imitation of the debate over entrenched bills. This is a great pity, for the two types of instrument are substantially different in institutional structure and role. In this paper, I argue the positive case: that there are good reasons to adopt a statutory bill of rights even if one accepts many of the arguments against the adoption of constitutionally entrenched bills (as I do).[7]

What are Statutory Bills of Rights?

By statutory bills of rights I mean instruments, enacted by ordinary legislative process, that articulate rights and subject governmental action to some form of judicial review. As statutes, statutory bills do not constrain, at least not in any absolute manner, the legislature. Their protections can always be amended or overridden by later statutes. They lack, then, the principal characteristic of constitutional guarantees – the

---

a reaction against arguments used to support statutory bills. Those arguments have often failed to distinguish statutory from entrenched bills, especially in New Zealand, and the bills' promoters may well harbour hopes of upgrading them to something like entrenched status. Allan may, then, be reacting in kind. But that does produce a shadow debate that fails to join issue on the specific merits of statutory bills of rights.

5   See, for example: ACT, 2003, pp. 54ff. For an insightful critique, see: McDonald, 2004.

6   This ambiguity in dialogue theory, and its tendency to undermine standard justifications for bills of rights, is acutely explored in Petter, 2003.

7   There are contexts in which entrenched bills of rights make very good sense, such as when it is necessary to establish a new ethic after a long history of rights abuses (e.g. post-apartheid South Africa) or when an entrenched bill is an essential element of a constitutional settlement in a divided polity. But entrenched bills are rarely appropriate in countries with strong rights traditions. See: Webber, 1993; 2000; 2003; 2006.

characteristic that dominates debates over entrenched bills – namely the imposition of absolute limits on legislative action. That raises the question of how they can be effective. One of the purposes of this section will be to canvass means by which the drafters of statutory bills have sought to secure their aims.

The first prominent example of a statutory bill of rights in the common law world was the *Canadian Bill of Rights*, SC 1960, c. 44 (*'Canadian Bill of Rights'*) adopted at the initiative of the Progressive Conservative government of John G. Diefenbaker in 1960 (the province of Saskatchewan had enacted its own bill of rights in 1947,[8] although with less prominence and impact).[9] Indeed until recently Canada remained the most active practitioner of the art. Statutory bills were also adopted at the provincial level in both Alberta (1972) and Quebec (1975).[10] These instruments had considerable effect in Canada prior to and even after the adoption of the entrenched *Canadian Charter of Rights and Freedoms*[11] in 1982 (although judicial conservatism and a lack of experience with rights instruments are generally considered to have undermined decision making under the 1960 Act).[12] The adoption of the *Charter* did mean, however, that active discussion of statutory bills in Canada was largely confined to the period before 1982.

In Australia and New Zealand, rights instruments of various kinds were discussed during the 1980s. Labour governments promoted, in New Zealand, the adoption of an entrenched bill, and, in Australia, the enactment first of a statutory bill (in 1985) and subsequently the entrenchment of selected rights guarantees (Palmer, 1992, pp. 51–58; Williams, 2000, pp. 30–33). All those initiatives failed, however, and with that failure discussion in both countries shifted back to statutory bills. That development coincided with an increasing debate over statutory bills in the United Kingdom, where concern over the rights record of the Thatcher government, combined with embarrassment over adverse rulings by the European Court of Human Rights, led many to seek some form of domestic rights protection.

The first such bill to be adopted was the *New Zealand Bill of Rights Act 1990* (NZ). Hong Kong and Israel enacted statutory bills in 1991 and 1992 respectively, although for reasons peculiar to each jurisdiction these bills were, in effect, entrenched.[13] The UK adopted a statutory bill in 1998: the *Human Rights Act 1998* (UK) c. 42 (*'Human Rights Act 1998* (UK)'), which forms an important element in the Blair government's constitutional reform program and incorporated the provisions of the *European*

---

8 *Saskatchewan Bill of Rights Act*, SS 1947, c. 35.

9 For the background to the *Canadian Bill of Rights*, see Egerton, 2004.

10 *Alberta Bill of Rights*, AS 1972, c. 1(*'Alberta Bill of Rights'*) and *Individual's Rights Protection Act*, AS 1972, c. 2 (*'Individual's Rights Protection Act'*); *Charter of Human Rights and Freedoms*, RSQ c. C-12 (*'Charter of Human Rights and Freedoms'*).

11 *Canada Act 1982* (UK), c. 11, sch B (the *'Charter'*).

12 For experience under the *Canadian Bill of Rights*, see: Tarnopolsky, 1975; Hovius, 1982; Hogg, 1992ff, ch. 32.

13 *Hong Kong Bill of Rights Ordinance 1991* (HK); *Basic Law: Human Dignity and Liberty* (Israel), 1992, S.H. 1391. See Ghai, 1997; Kretzmer, 1999.

Convention for the Protection of Human Rights and Fundamental Freedoms[14] into British law. Only one Australian jurisdiction, the Australian Capital Territory (ACT), has enacted a comprehensive statutory bill (in 2004). But instruments serving many of the functions of statutory bills – notably the *Racial Discrimination Act 1975* – have existed at the Commonwealth level for several years.[15]

How do these bills have any impact, given their purely statutory character? There are a number of ways in which such statutory bills advance a rights agenda.

Three are beyond the scope of this paper, although they are well worth noting. First, the very declaration of rights raises the profile of rights in the community, providing a touchstone for future arguments and performing an educative function. Second, many statutory bills require the prior vetting of legislation, either by a member of the executive or by a legislative committee, to ensure that the legislation complies with rights guarantees.[16] Rights are injected, then, into the very process of legislative drafting and enactment. Third, in some jurisdictions the courts have held that they should develop the common law in a manner that is consistent with rights.

These dimensions are important, but they do not speak to the principal focus of this paper. Here, I concentrate on the judicial review of executive or legislative action. This is the heart of the dispute over bills of rights. Most advocates want judicial review and most opponents – opponents, that is, of both statutory and entrenched bills – want to prevent it. The assessment of statutory bills depends primarily on the form of judicial review they provide and the justification for that review.

Now, statutory bills do commonly provide at least some role for the courts in reviewing executive and legislative action. To begin, they generally subject the conduct of the executive – and indeed, to some extent, the courts themselves – to review on grounds of rights, as long as the rights-limiting aspect of the conduct has not been specifically authorized by legislation.[17] They thus govern important features of the criminal process – the behaviour of police, the conduct of prosecutors, and

---

14 Opened for signature 4 November 1950, 213 UNTS 222 (entered into force 3 September 1953) (*'European Convention'*).

15 *Human Rights Act 2004* (ACT); *Racial Discrimination Act 1975* (Cth). The latter has had a substantial impact within Australian law, an impact broadly analogous to that of a statutory bill. Among other things, it formed an essential foundation for the High Court's recognition that Aboriginal title had survived, and could still survive, efforts by the states to extinguish it: *Mabo v Queensland [No 1]* (1988) 83 ALR 14 (HCA). It also played an important role in the Howard government's attempt to amend the *Native Title Act 1993* (Cth) in the wake of the High Court's decision in *Wik Peoples v Queensland* (1996) 187 CLR 1: Brennan, 1998b, pp. 69–71, 73–74, 85.

16 See in Canada: *Canadian Bill of Rights* s. 3; Tarnopolsky, 1975, pp. 125–28; Hiebert, 2002, pp. 3–19. In New Zealand: *New Zealand Bill of Rights Act 1990* (NZ) s. 7; Fitzgerald, 1992; Taggart, 1998, pp. 269–74. In the UK: *Human Rights Act 1998 (UK) s.* 19. In the A.C.T.: *Human Rights Act 2004* (ACT) ss. 37–38; Evans, C., 2004.

17 This is an area in which the *New Zealand Bill of Rights Act 1990* (NZ) has had a significant impact, especially with respect to criminal investigation and trial: Taggart, 1998, pp. 274–80; Butler, A., 2000, pp. 270ff. But there have also been criticisms of alleged

those parts of criminal procedure that are not specified by statute. They also apply to government action that occurs under the Crown prerogative, under the powers that the executive derives from its possession of legal personality, and under statutorily conferred powers and discretion (again as long as a statute does not specifically authorize the rights-limiting conduct). Of course, in these areas the law already takes rights concerns into account, at least to some degree. This is true of such fundamental features of the criminal process as the presumption of innocence or the rules with respect to the admissibility of confessions. Statutory bills augment this protection by expressly enunciating rights and authorizing judicial review directly upon them. They help to overcome the sometimes awkward and partial fit between rights concerns and the inherited categories of criminal and administrative law.[18]

This review of executive action should not be underestimated. Its scope is wide, covering a large number of traditional rights concerns. When the court finds that a violation has occurred, the judgment is just as effectual as it would be under an entrenched bill (although the legislature can overturn the judgment). Indeed, the tendency of the bill of rights debate to concentrate exclusively on legislation neglects the fact that rights-limiting conduct is much more likely to emanate from the executive. The very representativeness of the legislature, and its reliance on open debate and justification, create in-built protections against rights infringements.

But a second type of judicial role does affect legislation. Statutory bills universally require that courts interpret legislation in a manner consistent with the rights set out in the bills.[19] What this means in practice is a matter of vigorous debate in all jurisdictions.[20] It cannot mean that courts impose a rights-protecting meaning in complete disregard for the language of the statute. The bills themselves qualify the obligation: the *Human Rights Act 1998* (UK), for example, states that legislation must be read in a way that is compatible with the *European Convention* rights, but only '[s]o far as it is possible to do so.'[21] And the fact that the bills are not entrenched, but merely have the status of ordinary Acts, requires that they be applied in a manner that preserves some reality to parliamentary sovereignty. Any exercise of the interpretive obligation has to be consistent with that ultimate legislative responsibility.

---

backsliding: Schwartz, 1998; Optican, 1999. See, in the UK: Klug and O'Brien, 2002, pp. 657–61; Starmer, 2003, pp. 20–21.

18 For explorations of the gap between administrative law and human rights review in the context of statutory bills of rights, see *R (Daly) v Secretary of State for the Home Department* [2001] 2 WLR 1622 (HL) (Lord Steyn); McLean, Rishworth and Taggart, 1992, p. 62.

19 *Canadian Bill of Rights* s. 2; *New Zealand Bill of Rights Act 1990* (NZ) s. 6; *Human Rights Act 1998 (UK)* s. 3; *Human Rights Act 2004* (ACT) ss. 30–31.

20 See in Canada: Hovius, esp. p. 54. In New Zealand: Taggart, pp. 280–85; Butler, A., 2000; 2001. This debate led to the enactment of section 3(2) of the *Supreme Court Act 2003* (NZ) which expressly affirms 'continuing commitment to the rule of law and the sovereignty of parliament': Butler, P., 2004, pp. 341–42. See in the UK: Klug and O'Brien, 2002, pp. 650–54; Gearty, 2002; Starmer, 2003, pp. 16–18; Marshall, 2003; Debeljak, 2003, pp. 199–209.

21 *Human Rights Act* (UK) s. 3.

Even when the legislation is, in the courts' view, incapable of a rights-respecting interpretation, some statutory bills provide a remedy. The most basic of these is a 'declaration of incompatibility,' which is expressly permitted under the UK and ACT statutes and which the New Zealand courts have said may be available under their bill (indeed New Zealand recently amended its legislation to expressly permit such declarations, but only in cases of discrimination).[22] These declarations do not affect the operation of the impugned legislation. Their impact is purely moral (unless combined with some other sanction). But they undoubtedly apply pressure on the government either to justify the measure or to change it.

This is the full extent of the remedies available under some statutory bills. They are significant: they govern executive conduct, shape statutory interpretation, and specifically authorize courts to declare that legislation violates rights. But some bills go further, directly affecting the force of the legislation in question.

First, statutory bills are undoubtedly able to invalidate legislation that was passed prior to the enactment of the statutory bill itself. Here, the doctrine of parliamentary sovereignty works in the bill's favour: the later legislation (the statutory bill) takes precedence over the previous legislation, repealing the latter to the extent of the inconsistency. This potential impact has, however, been expressly excluded in some statutory bills (notably those of New Zealand and Israel), either because of the asymmetrical impact the bills would otherwise have on prior as opposed to subsequent legislation, or because of a general desire to limit the effect of the bill.[23]

Second, in some federal jurisdictions, centrally enacted bills take precedence over state-enacted laws by virtue of federal paramountcy. This depends on the federal legislature having power to enact a bill of rights applicable to the states. In Australia this authority exists under the external relations power (when the bill implements international human-rights obligations). The Commonwealth's chief human rights statute, the *Racial Discrimination Act 1975* (Cth) (which incorporates the *International Convention on the Elimination of All Forms of Racial Discrimination*[24]) has been used to render state legislation inoperative.[25] There is no general treaty implementing or other relevant power in Canada, however. There, the impact of statutory bills has been confined to the sphere of the enacting legislature.

Outside of these situations the effect of statutory bills is limited by the doctrine of parliamentary sovereignty. Parliament remains sovereign at every moment. Its latest word is law. Thus, if later legislation is inconsistent with a statutory bill, it is the later

---

22 *Human Rights Act* (UK) s. 4; Starmer, 2003, pp. 18–20; *Human Rights Act 2004* (ACT) ss. 32–33; *Moonen v Film and Literature Board of Review* [2000] 2 NZLR 9, 17 (CA); *Human Rights Amendment Act 2001* (NZ) s. 9, enacting new sections 92J and 92K.

23 *New Zealand Bill of Rights Act* s. 4; *Basic Law: Human Dignity and Liberty* s. 10; Kretzmer, 1999, pp. 85–87.

24 Opened for signature 7 March 1966, 660 UNTS 195 (entered into force 4 January 1969).

25 See above n 15.

legislation, not the bill, that takes precedence. But legislatures have nevertheless found two ingenious means for giving effect to statutory bills.

Under the UK Act, when there has been a declaration of incompatibility (or a decision of the European Court of Human Rights that a legislative provision is incompatible with the *European Convention*), ministers are given the power to amend the legislation to remedy the defect, by executive order.[26] This does not directly contradict the doctrine of parliamentary sovereignty, for parliament has conferred the power to amend on the ministers; the impugned legislation, though inconsistent with the rights set out in the statutory bill, has done nothing to set aside this power. But such a clause does severely qualify parliament's role, permitting unilateral executive action to change a law adopted by parliament. Such 'Henry VIII clauses' have generally been considered legally valid but constitutionally suspect, subject at least to special justification. Here, the UK Act uses them to permit a rapid response to an adverse judgment without the further involvement of parliament.

In Canada a second device has been common: 'manner and form requirements' are used to give statutory bills precedence over later legislation. The principle behind this approach is that although parliament cannot bind its successors as to substance, it can as to procedure. Parliament therefore drafts its bills so that only a procedural requirement is imposed: later parliaments are free to derogate from the rights, but only if they use a particular form of words, generally stating expressly that the later Act's provisions apply 'notwithstanding' the bill of rights. Because, in the end, the bill only requires that a particular procedure be followed, Canadian courts have held that its stipulations are applicable to later legislation. Later statutes can be ruled inoperative if they infringe a right without complying with the procedural requirement.[27] The *Canadian Bill of Rights* uses this approach, as do the Alberta and Quebec Bills.[28]

The binding force of manner and form requirements has been questioned from time to time outside Canada,[29] and indeed even within Canada there was considerable

---

26 *Human Rights Act* (UK) s. 10.

27 *Singh* v *Minister of Employment and Immigration* [1985] 1 SCR 177; *MacBain* v *Lederman* [1985] 1 FC 856 (CA); *Ford* v *Quebec* [1988] 2 SCR 712; *Devine* v *Quebec* [1988] 2 SCR 790.

28 *Canadian Bill of Rights* s. 2; Hovius, 1982; *Alberta Bill of Rights* s. 2; *Individual's Rights Protection Act* s. 1(1); *Charter of Human Rights and Freedoms* s. 52.

29 An early version of a bill of rights for the UK, the Human Rights and Fundamental Freedoms Bill 1985 (UK), contained a manner and form requirement roughly along the lines of the Canadian models, but this was replaced with an interpretive obligation on second reading. In debate in the House of Lords, at least one Law Lord expressed the opinion that Parliament could not bind itself in the manner contemplated in the Canadian models. See: Clapham, 1999, p. 118. There has been debate over whether such provisions would be binding at the Commonwealth level in Australia, although the better view is that they would be binding: Winterton, 1980. The 1985 Australian Bill of Rights Bill would have adopted this mechanism.

debate over the effect of the *Canadian Bill of Rights*.[30] The Canadian debate has now been settled in favour of their binding force.

It is important to note that some interpretive approaches can have an impact very similar to Canadian-style manner and form requirements. They can require such a clear expression of parliamentary intention that, in effect, courts will only interpret legislation in a way that restricts rights when parliament has expressly, not impliedly, stated its intention to do so. Anything less and the court will read the statute so that rights are preserved, even if this means that the statute is effectively rendered inoperative. The British courts have taken a position very like this with respect to the primacy of European law. At least one Law Lord has suggested that a similar approach be adopted with respect to the *Human Rights Act 1998* (UK).[31]

Statutory bills can, then, have a significant impact on governmental action. All statutory bills directly control executive action and shape the courts' interpretation of legislation. Statutory bills in the UK, New Zealand and the ACT permit courts to issue declarations of incompatibility, holding that legislation contravenes rights. In the UK ministers can respond to such declarations by amending the legislation by executive order, without further reference to parliament. And in Canada, statutory bills can be used directly to strike down inconsistent legislation.

These are significant recourses. They differ from remedies available under entrenched bills primarily in the role that legislatures continue to play under statutory bills. First, the legislatures are the authors of the bills. They remain their authors throughout. They confer the powers that the courts or other officials exercise. They can amend the bills or repeal them entirely. Second, legislatures are able to override the effect of the bills. At the very least they can do so expressly. Indeed, under many bills they can do so impliedly, by using language that is inconsistent with any other interpretation. Those are crucial differences between statutory and entrenched bills.

Arguments against Statutory Bills

Many of the standard arguments against entrenched bills are either inapplicable or much less convincing when applied to statutory bills, even when those bills employ the strongest remedies canvassed above.

---

30 Tarnopolsky, 1975, pp. 131ff; Hovius, pp. 34 and 48. Prior to the adoption of the *Canadian Charter of Rights and Freedoms* only one provision was struck down, and that was in a statute that predated the *Canadian Bill of Rights*: *R v Drybones* [1970] SCR 282.

31 For examples in the UK where the approach to interpretation comes very close to requiring an express intention to derogate, see (with respect to the *Human Rights Act* (UK)) *R v A (No 2)* [2001] 2 WLR 1546, 1563 (Lord Steyn) (HL); and (with respect to European law) *Garland v British Rail Engineering Ltd* [1983] 2 AC 751, 771 (Lord Diplock) (HL); *Thoburn v Sunderland City Council* [2003] QB 151, 185ff (Laws LJ). For an example in Canada (with respect to provincial human rights legislation) see *Winnipeg School Division No 1 v Craton* [1985] 2 SCR 150.

This is true, for example, of the common concern with pre-commitment in bill of rights debates, because statutory bills, because of the possibility of statutory revision, tend not to bind future generations to past decisions. It is also true of criticisms of the distorting effect of rights discourse, which in entrenched bills can a) generate a deep gulf between rights concerns and all other considerations, impeding trade-offs between them, and b) systematically prefer private interests over public action by imposing prominent one-sided constraints on the latter. Statutory bills allow the legislature to remain involved in the definition of trade-offs and foster a more nuanced definition of rights. Some statutory bills apply comparable restrictions to both the public and the private sectors.[32] Moreover, the fact that statutory bills remain ordinary statutes, not part of the fundamental-values-of-the-nation-that-we-all-hold-dear, means that there is less likelihood of a highly abstract and symbolic discourse taking precedence over other legitimate public concerns. And finally under statutory bills, legislatures are not painted implicitly as the enemies of rights whose influence has to be kept at bay. Instead, they become a partner in the definition of rights, avoiding the simplistic, anti-democratic and caricatured contrast between a forum of principle (the courts) and a forum of interest (the legislature).

Many common grounds for criticism of constitutionally entrenched bills of rights are therefore attenuated in statutory bills – to such an extent that many of the arguments advanced by opponents seem very thin indeed. Opponents of statutory bills are forced to depend on a much more contentious and questionable set of claims. I can think of five:

1. *A very strong position on the illegitimacy of open-ended normative decision making by courts, so that any adjudication of human rights guarantees is inappropriate, even if it occurs at legislative direction and even if the results can be overturned by legislative action.*

This is most likely to take the form of a strong objection to courts making 'political' or 'moral' decisions.[33] There appear to be two variants of this position. One focuses on the potential undermining of the courts' legitimacy as they are drawn into more 'political' and less tightly bounded forms of decision making. The other objects to judicial engagement in 'moral' or 'political' decision making on philosophical grounds. The precise basis for this second variant is unclear. One strong objection against entrenched bills – the displacement of democratic by judicial determination of fundamental moral issues – applies with much less force to statutory bills, for

---

32 See, for example: *Individual's Rights Protection Act*, adopted simultaneously with the *Alberta Bill of Rights*; *Charter of Human Rights and Freedoms*.

33 See, for example, Allan and Cullen, 1997, pp. 175–76 and 185–88; Campbell, 2001; Allan, 2001a, pp. 328–29. According to Hovius (1982, pp. 52–57), this was the principal reason for the Supreme Court of Canada's deferential interpretation of the *Canadian Bill of Rights* in the 1960s and 1970s, although he also argues that most members of the Court resisted the idea that individual rights should take priority over the general good.

the legislature can always override judicial decisions. The objection therefore has to rely on more difficult claims of incompatibility with the judicial function or problems posed for social coordination because of legal uncertainty – arguments largely shorn of their pro-democratic dimension.[34] But whatever form the objection takes, it necessarily assumes that a clear distinction exists between legal decision making and moral or political judgment, and objects to courts having any role in the latter. Indeed, some commentators seem affronted that judges should express any opinion whatever on contestable issues of rights, especially an opinion that might be different from that adopted by the legislature.[35]

2. A special concern with uncertainty in the interpretation of the statutory bills themselves due to an unresolved tension between judicial review and parliamentary supremacy in statutory bills.[36]

This is closely aligned to the first objection, for it too assumes that adjudication should be founded on clear, relatively precise and authoritatively declared norms. The difference here is that the objection focuses on the terms of statutory bills themselves, and especially on the divergence of views that exists as to the interpretive stance courts should adopt under such bills. Should they be deferential toward legislative judgments, or should they actively pursue their understanding of rights?

3. A thorough-going opposition to rights as a useful category of legal analysis, so that any move towards the protection of rights is seen as regrettable, detracting from attention to the general good, obscuring interests other than rights, and/or impairing the interests of the collectivity.[37]

This is rarely the principal ground advanced against statutory bills, perhaps because few commentators want to claim that they are opposing rights, given the widespread hegemony of rights discourse. One suspects, however, that this objection plays a

---

34 Tom Campbell's (1996) analysis is the best equipped to maintain the critique, grounded as it is in his theory of ethical positivism. But his criticisms of bills of rights also rely heavily on democratic concerns, and in any case his theory exaggerates (in my view) the value of legal certainty and our capacity to achieve it. This is not the place to respond to his theory as a whole. I address the relative balance in the claims of certainty versus utility, in the context of statutory bills, below.

35 See, for example, Allan, 2002a, p. 569, or Allan's (2001a, p. 329) and Huscroft's (2002, p. 15) criticism of judges' supposed 'threat' that legislation's failings might be brought to the attention of the UN Human Rights Committee, which they find to be implicit in judicial declarations of incompatibility.

36 See Allan, 2000, pp. 624–27, although Allan's objections go much deeper than this.

37 Tomkins, 2001, pp. 8–9. This appears to be a strong, though understated, element in James Allan's position. See, for example: Allan, 2002b, p. 284. Tom Campbell (1996, pp. 164ff) also expresses strong scepticism about the language of rights, although he does recognize some utility in a substantially reformulated conception.

larger role than generally appears, providing much of the drive behind the opposition to rights adjudication.

4. A strong opposition to adjudication as a procedural mechanism for dealing with such issues, perhaps based on the unrepresentative character of the judiciary, the cost of litigation, or adjudication's retrospective nature and the consequent uncertainty of the law on the books – an opposition that goes so far as to suggest that adjudication's defects outweigh any potential benefits (Tomkins, 2001, pp. 9–10).

This objection has significant force when applied to entrenched bills. It is much less persuasive when applied to statutory bills, again because the legislature has the last word. Perhaps the branch of this objection that retains the most force is the last – the potential for uncertainty in the law prior to adjudication – and this objection tends to collapse into the first: the resistance to open-ended judicial interpretation.

5. The fear that a statutory bill of rights is likely to evolve into de facto *entrenchment, as courts make of it what they will.*[38]

This last objection is commonly advanced but misleading. The critics seldom claim that courts will in fact find that a statutory bill is entrenched so that legislatures cannot amend or repeal it.[39] Instead, the critics emphasize three things: a) that courts tend to interpret the terms of statutory bills broadly; b) that courts use statutory bills to interpret statutes in a manner that departs from those statutes' ordinary interpretation; and c) that legislatures may find it politically impossible to overturn judicial decisions. The first two concern the interpretive latitude that courts may assume under a bill of rights; they are variants of the first objection above. The third does raise a different argument, but one that sits uncomfortably with a commitment to legislative supremacy. If a bill of rights is adopted by ordinary legislation, and if the legislature remains free to amend it, repeal it or legislate an interpretation that differs from that adopted by the courts, what is the problem if it declines to do so?

---

38   This appears to be James Allan's principal concern: *supra*, note 4. See also Campbell, 2001, p. 87 (although Campbell (2001, pp. 81–82) does qualify his comments, given that under a statutory bill the legislature remains able to overturn judgments with which it disagrees).

39   Something like this has occurred in Israel, however. There, the Supreme Court has suggested that the Basic Laws adopted by the Knesset bind the Knesset itself and that the Court can rule legislation invalid in consequence. The basis for the holding is unique, for it is founded on the continuing status of the Knesset as a constituent assembly. See '*United Mizrachi Bank plc* v *Migdal CooperativeVillage* (1995) 49(iv) P.D. 221 [English translation with annotation]' (1997) 31 Israel Law Review 764; Kretzmer, 1999, pp. 78–79.

Isn't the refusal to legislate just as much an exercise of democratic will?[40] Indeed, there are examples of statutory bills being overruled by subsequent legislation.[41]

One suspects that the critics' concern is not that democratic decision making will be nullified, but rather that rights concerns will have too much salience or unrepresentative courts too much influence in subsequent debates. The question comes down, then, not to entrenchment, but to whether the adjudication of rights brings anything of value to these issues. Those who voice this objection tend to believe that it simply obfuscates.

In my view, the essential issue is the extent to which rights adjudication has a distinctive and important role to play in the protection of important interests. If that role is significant, and if it differs substantially from the role that legislatures can play, that would go a very long way towards meeting the objections. Because of the difference between statutory and entrenched bills, the objections to statutory bills are tightly constrained. They rely on the adoption of a hard view on the limitation of the judicial role, but without being able to invoke the strongly democratic imperative that underlies many criticisms of entrenched bills. They depend upon a fierce commitment to certainty in the law, but one which may well overstate the level of certainty within legal regimes generally and in any case depends upon the benefits of certainty outweighing benefits derived from adjudication under statutory bills. Or they come down to a strong objection to rights as a useful category of analysis – an objection so strongly held that the critics are unappeased by legislatures' ability, under statutory bills, to engage in greater balancing of interests.

In the rest of this chapter, I concentrate on the positive justification for rights adjudication. That justification will differ substantially from those commonly used to support judicial review on the basis of entrenched bills. The latter are dominated by the constitutional context. They are designed to justify, above all, *final* determination by courts. They therefore advance a simplistic description of judicial and legislative roles, painting the former as an arena of principle and the latter as an arena of interest,

---

40 Goldsworthy (2003, p. 263) makes this argument in the context of provisions like section 33 of the *Canadian Charter of Rights and Freedoms*, which permit the legislature to derogate from provisions of an entrenched bill of rights. The argument is less compelling in that context, for the entrenchment of rights, even if subject to derogation, does structure the debate in a manner that introduces regrettable distortions. The legislature's decision tends to be characterized as an overruling of rights, rather than the adoption of a competing interpretation. Moreover the rights themselves carry the high symbolic charge and high degree of abstraction typical of constitutional provisions. Statutory bills achieve a more appropriate balance. See: Webber, 2003.

41 For example, Quebec's National Assembly passed legislation expressly derogating from the *Charter of Human Rights and Freedoms* in order to overturn the decision in *Ford* v *Quebec* [1988] 2 SCR 712: *An Act to amend the Charter of the French Language*, SQ 1988, c. 54.

log-rolling and power politics in order to argue for the overwhelming superiority of judicial determination.[42] They tend to argue in general and abstract terms.

My argument will have a different character. It assumes the primacy of democratic engagement in the resolution of normative disagreement. But it takes seriously the constitutional lawyer's traditional concern with blending institutional forms to achieve optimal outcomes. Constitutional virtue resides in the arrangement of a variety of institutional structures in a way that takes advantage of the distinctive strengths and minimizes the potential weaknesses of each. Judicial review on the basis of statutory bills can play an important role in such a balance, ensuring that the specific character of each case is considered, clarifying the competing normative demands at issue, and prompting deliberation and democratic decision making on those issues. That role fully justifies the adoption of a statutory bill, so that public norms are made responsive to the complexity of the individual case. Such responsiveness increases the likelihood that justice will be done in the particular case and opens the norms to refinement as a result of insights drawn from their application.

Of course, many of these benefits are attained under entrenched bills. The difference lies in the fact that under statutory bills, the most representative institution – the legislature – retains responsibility for the general norms applicable to society. The legislature can learn from rights adjudication. It may be compelled to confront circumstances that it had previously overlooked or would prefer to overlook. But in the last analysis, it sets the rules.

The Argument for Statutory Bills

Why, if one favours the ultimate normative responsibility of legislatures, would one want to preserve judicial review of legislation?

We can work towards the answer by asking why we preserve an autonomous sphere of decision making for courts at all. Why do our institutions presume that judicial decision making should occur in a manner insulated from legislative control? Why do we value judicial independence, even in political systems that are committed to parliamentary sovereignty?

The answer is not just one of administrative convenience. We don't preserve courts simply because legislatures lack the time to deal with the detailed application of the norms they adopt. If this were so, we would have no objection to legislatures assuming the adjudicative function themselves, replacing the courts whenever they wanted. Nor would we see any objection to bills of attainder, where a statute is used to single out a particular individual for condemnation and punishment. Those actions are matters of concern precisely because we see courts and legislatures as being specially adapted to their distinctive roles. We object to legislative interference with judicial decision making because it disrupts the integrity of the adjudicative process,

---

42 Waldron (1999, esp. pp. 28ff) has been particularly forceful in arguing against this tendency.

replacing a process that is well adapted to judging individual cases with one that is suited to a very different kind of inquiry.

Suppose we imagine a system in which judicial decision making is routinely subjected to direct legislative over-ruling in specific cases. What would be the problem? It would not simply be that the legislature would be overburdened, unable to spend the time on its decisions that courts ideally can. That would indeed be a problem, but it is a problem that flows from the nature of the institution itself: its size; its broad agenda; its focus on articulating a general policy rather than attending to the minutiae of particular cases. The procedures of legislatures are not adapted to the dissection of a particular set of events but rather to the exploration of broad social concerns in a manner that marshals an extensive spectrum of opinion. They are focused on the determination of social facts, not the parochial detail of adjudicative facts. Moreover, legislatures are not subject to the rationalistic controls on evidence and argument, designed to screen out prejudgment and prejudice, that are observed by courts. Legislatures do have their own rationalistic procedures – structured processes for formulating propositions, justifying those propositions, considering alternative formulations, criticising, amending, adopting – all in a manner that draws on the assembled wisdom of the chamber. But these procedures are designed to refine and adopt general propositions, not to secure dependable outcomes in specific cases. Judicial procedures, on the other hand, are entirely focused on the analysis of a specific set of events.

That is the key characteristic of judicial decision making: the focus on the specific case; the attempt to ensure that the application of general norms is attentive to the detail of particular circumstances; the attempt to ensure that in the practical imposition of social norms, individual people and individual circumstances are given their due.

That consideration of the particular case does not simply happen at large, the courts at liberty to impose whatever solution they see fit. They are always mediating between the general norms articulated by the legislature (or derived from the common law) and the detail of the particular case. When the law is clear, the courts' obligation is primarily to find the facts in the case and apply the law accordingly. Even in this situation, the structured focus on the individual circumstances remains highly significant. It forces attention to those particular facts, discouraging one from being so preoccupied with a general principle – or with fear – that one runs roughshod over the individual case. And running roughshod is, of course, a very real possibility, as the cases of wrongful conviction demonstrate.

Moreover, in a decision on common law or where the application of an enactment to the specific facts is open to a range of plausible interpretations – which is very frequently the situation, especially in the contested matters that come before the courts – the consequences of attending to the particular case will not be confined to a simple finding of facts. Immersion in the facts of the case may reveal normative considerations that had not been clearly perceived before. The court's attention to those circumstances may produce a more fine-grained normative understanding, which in turn shapes the interpretation of the common law or statutory rule.[43]

These benefits would not be attained if specific cases were regularly determined in legislative chambers. There, the institutional structures, procedures and numbers of decision makers are all premised on formulating a general rule, on attending to the long view. There would be a very real risk of the particular case being given less than its due, and of the interests of the individuals being sacrificed to that long view.

This is the crucial justification for judicial independence. It is a dimension of judicial decision making that is often obscured in discussions of the merits of judicial review, which tend to focus purely and simply on the elaboration of the general norms, especially on judges' role in determining the normative content of broadly phrased rights. There is good reason why debates over entrenched bills focus on the judges' articulation of the abstract normative content of rights. The extent of normative elaboration that occurs under constitutionally entrenched bills of rights is a critical and problematic dimension of constitutional review, especially because those often-contestable judgments are not subject to legislative revision. But when discussing rights protection more generally, it is wise to remember that judges do not merely expand upon general principles. They have a distinctive role in applying standards to particular cases, in identifying novel normative concerns that emerge from those cases, and in considering the consequences those concerns should have for the application – and therefore the development – of the law. If judges' ability to determine the general normative order of society is constrained (by, for example, enacting the rights guarantees in statutory form, so that the legislature can always revise those guarantees), judges' distinctive engagement with the individual case may become a much more significant dimension of our assessment.

There is a close affinity between this concern with the individual case and individual rights protection. This is true in the most obvious sense: a strong focus on particular cases prevents individual injustices. But the affinity goes further.

Let's resist, for the moment, the temptation to look immediately at express rights protections and examine first the interpretive conventions commonly used by courts to protect rights concerns, starting with the simplest and most generic of these – the principle that in the absence of clear language, courts will not interpret legislation so as to abrogate acquired rights.[44] This too is closely related to courts' distinctive focus on the individual case. Legislators typically have the general run of a rule's application – or, what amounts to the same thing, the central and most obvious cases

---

43 James Boyd White makes this argument with effect noting, 'when the bright light of attention is focused on what we have not seen, or not seen clearly, it almost always reveals a complexity and richness of significance that we had missed, thus putting in question, among other things, our own prior habits of mind and imagination': at pp. 50–51. His emphasis is, above all, on the effect of the encounter on our imagination. My emphasis is on the normative insight that intensive grappling with a specific context can reveal.

44 See, for example: *Colonial Sugar Refining Co* v *Melbourne Harbour Trust Commissioners* [1927] AC 343, 359 (PC) (whether property had impliedly been expropriated by a consolidation of statutes).

of a rule's potential application – in mind when they adopt an enactment. They may have no knowledge of or they may simply overlook specific interests that the law might impair. But courts do encounter these interests in the application of the law to the particular case. The interpretive convention preserves these interests from being swept aside without adequate consideration. That focus on acquired rights has been extended to protect non-pecuniary interests, including many of the interests often protected under bills of rights: rights of property, including the entitlement to compensation when property is expropriated; freedom from warrantless searches; freedom of speech.[45]

In the application of those interpretive conventions to this broader range of concerns, there will be cases in which the impact of the law is a matter of pure inadvertence. A good example appears in the Supreme Court of Canada's decision in *MacKeigan* v *Hickman*.[46] In that case, a Royal Commission had been established to inquire into the wrongful conviction and process of exoneration of a Miq'maq man, Donald Marshall Jr. The Commission sought to compel the attendance of the judges who had sat on the hearing that resulted in his release, to explain the basis for comments they had made which blamed Marshall for his own conviction, and to explain the choice of the panel for that hearing (one of the judges had been Attorney General, and therefore chief prosecutor, at the time of Marshall's conviction). The question before the Supreme Court was whether the judges could be compelled to answer questions about these matters. The relevant provision of the Nova Scotia *Public Inquiries Act* stated that the commissioners 'shall have the power of summoning … any persons as witnesses and of requiring them to give evidence on oath … and to produce such documents and things as the commissioner or commissioners deem requisite to the full investigation of the matters.'[47] The judges who had sat on the panel clearly fell within the category of 'any persons'. Nevertheless, the Supreme Court concluded that 'vague and general statutory language should not be read as displacing fundamental rights'. It held that nothing in the statute 'suggests that the legislators intended to clothe the Commission with power to abrogate the

---

45 See, for example: *A-G* v *DeKeyser's Royal Hotel* [1920] AC 508 (HL) (an intention to compensate will be presumed in an expropriation statute silent as to compensation); *Morris* v *Beardmore* [1981] AC 446 (HL) (legislation requiring the giving of a breath sample not impliedly authorizing police to forcibly enter the individual's home in order to request the sample); *Re Bolton; Ex parte Beane* (1987) 162 CLR 514 (the liberty of the individual protected by declining to find, in a power to detain a deserter from another country's armed forces and to hand him over to that country's officials, an implied power for the foreign authorities to exercise jurisdiction over the individual); *R* v *Home Secretary, Ex parte Simms* [2000] 2 AC 115 (HL) (restrictions on prisoners' interviews with journalists interpreted narrowly so as to permit a prisoner to enjoy a measure of freedom of expression, especially for the purpose of proving his innocence).

46 [1989] 2 SCR 796.

47 RSNS 1967, c. 250, s. 3.

fundamental principle that judges cannot be compelled to testify as to how and why they arrived at their decisions'.[48]

In these circumstances, the Court's interpretation is an accurate assessment of the legislature's intention. Doubtless no one intended to limit judicial independence when adopting section 3 of the *Public Inquiries Act*. No one turned their mind to the possibility, and if they had they would have foreclosed it – if they had thought it worthwhile to weigh down the statute with verbiage meant to protect against such an unusual case. There is very good reason, then, grounded in the best assessment of the legislature's intention, to read the language down. Note that the importance of the interest in question is crucial to the outcome. It is precisely because judicial independence is so important that we presume that the legislature would not have meant to restrict it by such general and anodyne language.

MacKeigan v *Hickman* was a clear case. But often there will be more doubt whether an infringement was intended. The statute's language will be sufficient to authorize an infringement (were it not for the importance of the interest in issue) and in addition, the possible infringement will be much more closely connected to the legislative purpose. A striking example is *Re Bolton; Ex parte Beane*[49] where the statute in question authorized Australian authorities to detain a deserter from another country's armed forces and to deliver him into the custody of the 'service authority of the country to which he belongs', but did not expressly authorize that service authority to exercise power over that individual once handed over, at least in the specific circumstances of this case (there was express authority in a different part of the Act dealing with deserters from forces visiting Australia). In *Re Bolton*, a US citizen who had become a permanent resident of Australia was detained. He had deserted from US forces in Vietnam in 1970, had made his own way to Australia, and had been arrested in 1986 (upon a request made by US authorities in 1982). The High Court concluded that, in light of the importance of the liberty of the individual, the statutory language was not sufficient to permit the US authorities to exercise jurisdiction over the detainee in Australia. He was therefore freed under writ of habeas corpus, and a writ of prohibition was issued forbidding his delivery to the US forces.

Again, had it not been for the importance of the interest in question, the court would almost certainly have found the statute conferred power on the US authorities. Should it have done so in this case? There is good reason for courts to be reluctant to find that an infringement was intended, even when it was (as in this case) much more likely than not. Statutory intent is often less than perfectly clear, not only because of the usual problems of constructing a collective intention (which are significant), but precisely because the legislature's concern is with the long view. Legislators don't foresee all the cases and when they do, they don't perceive them in their full normative complexity or full practical import. Unless the legislative intention is

---

48 *MacKeigan* v *Hickman* [1989] 2 SCR 796, 831 (McLachlin J).

49 (1987) 162 CLR 514 ('*Re Bolton*').

abundantly clear, there is good reason for the courts to interpret legislation so as not to infringe rights, at least when those rights are sufficiently important.

I do not accept, then, the view expressed by some commentators that when interpreting a statute in the light of the requirement that one adopt an interpretation that, so far as possible, respects rights (the interpretive obligation common in statutory bills), the statute's meaning must first be determined in the absence of the rights concerns, and only if more than one meaning exists should rights enter into consideration.[50] This argument understates the extent to which legislative intention is constructed. It takes the elaborate battery of mechanisms used by lawyers to fashion a legislative intention and naturalizes them, treating them as though they produced the actual intent. But the situation is rarely so simple. When interpretation is pursued conscientiously, the interpreter does, in an important sense, strive for a meaning that reflects the aggregated intentions of the legislators, by giving pride of place to the sentence meaning, informed by the interpreter's best estimate of the legislators' subjective intentions.[51] That interpretive ethic is crucial if law is to remain responsive to democratic decision making. But the resulting intention is nevertheless an aggregate, determined by means that necessarily involve judgment. Moreover, in constructing that intention, the interpreter makes manifestly unrealistic assumptions, and does so for reasons that have nothing to do with the attempt to reproduce the legislators' actual intent. The interpreter assumes that in framing the enactment the legislators had in view the whole of the law – or, when the interpreter is considering one section of a statute, that the legislator had in mind the entirety of that statute – assumptions that are prompted more by a desire to achieve consistency in the law than by an attempt to mirror the legislators' subjective intentions. For even if a statute contained clear internal tensions, tensions that the interpreter knew full well were a result of inattention, bargaining, studied ambiguity or an imperfectly executed amendment, he or she would still interpret it in a manner that, to the extent possible, established a coherent meaning. Statutory interpretation is shaped by aims deemed inherent in a legal order, such as presuming – and to some extent assisting – the efficacy of legislation, and fashioning a system of law that makes consistent and non-contradictory demands on its subjects. The interpretive approaches imposed by statutory bills run along similar lines. They ask the interpreter to recognize that some legal interests are substantially more important than others and to take that into account in interpretation. This makes eminent sense, especially when the legislature has itself imposed the obligation, when the ultimate interpretation simply resolves the doubt that is always inherent in the process of interpretation, and when the legislature remains able to infringe the interests as long as it does so with clarity.

---

50 See, for example: Hodge, 2000; Campbell, 2001, pp. 84ff; Evans, 2004; or in less theoretically informed terms Marshall, 2003.

51 This adopts terms with which Hodge (2000) analyses statutory interpretation, drawing upon the work of Jim Evans.

Laws LJ expressed this approach well when he summarized the interpretive obligations imposed by 'constitutional statutes' (including the UK's accession to the European Union and the *Human Rights Act 1998* (UK)) as follows:

> For the repeal of a constitutional Act or the abrogation of a fundamental right to be effected by statute, the court would apply this test: is it shown that the legislature's *actual* – not imputed, constructive or presumed – intention was to effect the repeal or abrogation? I think the test could only be met by express words in the later statute, or by words so specific that the inference of an actual determination to effect the result contended for was irresistible.[52]

This method tends to track what would be the best reconstruction of the legislature's intention in situations like *MacKeigan* v *Hickman*, where the statute is pitched at a very broad level of generality and where it is highly unlikely that the legislature ever intended to authorize a rights violation. In a case like *Re Bolton*, it may well depart from what the legislators would say had been their intention if they were polled on the issue. But the fact is that they have not been polled, and rather than undermine important interests without clear legislative sanction, surely it is better that the interests be preserved, subject to further legislative action if necessary.

Indeed, there is a very good reason to suggest that statutory bills affirm legislative responsibility rather than impair it. The bills themselves are adopted by legislative act. In so doing, the legislature extends the scope for judicial review, but it also subjects that review to a measure of control, defining – and, if necessary, revising at a later stage – the considerations upon which review should proceed. The legislature places its imprimatur on the courts' special attention to rights concerns. It may be best to see statutory bills as seeking to conciliate two kinds of legislative intention – one that concentrates on the specific policy of an act, and the other (a kind of meta-intention) that is focused on establishing overarching considerations that should condition all legislation. Andrew Butler captures this idea when he says that the UK *Human Rights Act 1998* (UK)

> adds a new super-norm dimension to the task of divining parliamentary intention in respect of a particular enactment or provision thereof. No longer will it be sufficient to consider the statute/provision on its own terms, but rather it will be necessary to view it through HRA-tinted glasses, because only in that way will Parliament's true super-intent (Convention compliance where possible) be achieved.[53]

---

52 *Thoburn* v *Sunderland City Council* [2003] QB 151, 186–87 (emphasis in the original). Something like this approach was also adopted in *Westminster Bank* v *Beverley BC* [1971] AC 508, 529 (Lord Reid) (HL), regarding statutory interpretation to preserve acquired rights: the intention to override the rights must be express or 'appear by irresistible inference from the statute read as a whole. But … if there is reasonable doubt, the subject should be given the benefit of the doubt.' For a very fine discussion, see Gearty, 2002, pp. 255ff.

53 Butler, 2000, p. 256. See also *R* v *Secretary of State for Transport; Ex parte Factortame Ltd [No 2]* [1991] 1 AC 603, 659 (HL), regarding Parliament's recognition of the paramountcy

When adopting an Act, legislators may be so preoccupied with the specific policy aim that they neglect the meta-intention. They may be poorly placed structurally to consider the latter both because of the difficulty one has anticipating all the circumstances to which a statute will apply (circumstances that may be necessary to generate the rights concerns) and because their attention is focused on the objective that prompted the legislation, not on the whole gamut of possible conditioning factors. In any real-life setting, legislative consideration is less than comprehensive. Legislators' intentions are particularly acute on some matters, less so on others; focused now on one particular concern, focused later on another. When very important interests are at stake, it may make sense to realize the practical imperfection in legislative consideration and provide mechanisms for protecting the meta-intention.

Even when, at the end of the day, the legislature either disagrees with the court's interpretation or simply wants to set aside rights because of some supervening objective, statutory bills arguably foster rather than constrain democratic accountability. Following an adverse decision, the matter can be brought to the legislature for further debate and decision, now with the rights concerns highlighted. Alternatively, the legislature can simply be clearer on its intention in the first place. In either case the implications of the measure are likely to be more apparent, the debate more acute, and the decision therefore more reflective of democratic consideration. The standard justification of the manner and form requirements in Canadian statutory bills is that by requiring that derogations from rights be express, they play an important signalling function. Before rights can be infringed, all legislators must be put on notice, so that any decision to infringe can be consciously made.

It is true that this accountability may be hard won. The legislation as first enacted may be interpreted narrowly or struck down. As a consequence, it may fail to achieve its objective. Considerable time may elapse before the matter can be brought back to the legislature, given the timing of legislative sessions and charged legislative agendas. But deliberation and debate themselves are time-consuming, yet they are maintained. If the interests protected by statutory bills are sufficiently important, and if adjudication plays a distinctive role in protecting those interests, it is worth accepting delay in those few cases in which the legislature would wish to overturn a judgment.

By specifically authorizing courts to interpret legislation in a manner that respects rights concerns, declare legislation incompatible with the rights protections, or (under the Canadian provisions) declare legislation inoperative that fails to respect rights, statutory bills allow one to take advantage of the distinctive normative insight that comes from courts' engagement with particular cases. Normative understanding is not advanced by articulating fixed positions *a priori*, which then stand in mute contrast to one another. It progresses by uncovering new concerns, grappling with those concerns, and attempting to revise one's position in consequence. Attending to individual cases is an important driver in the development of normative understanding.

---

of European law and the need, in the application of later legislation, to give predominance to that parliamentary 'meta-intent'.

Statutory bills allow one to harness that insight, enabling the focused reflection of courts on the detail of particular circumstances to react back upon our normative presumptions. Courts encounter the unexpected case. They gauge the impact of the statute in that case. And they can suggest how fundamental interests that arise in those cases should be protected in relation to the statutory objective.

This, it seems to me, is a substantial answer to the concern with the open-ended quality of decision making under bills of rights, which was the principal objection to statutory bills identified above. One should not exaggerate the extent of openness. Yes, rights provisions tend to be phrased in general terms – and indeed I favour more specifically targeted rights protections than are found in many bills of rights. But in statutory bills, even that degree of openness is bounded by the fact that most rights adjudication occurs in the context of the interpretation of statutory provisions, where the process remains closely tied to the sphere of operation of that statute. Although the rights are commonly expressed in broad language, their breadth differs from other legal principles only in degree. They lie towards one end of a spectrum of greater or lesser specificity of legal expression, but where other commonly accepted legal principles also occupy the less specific end of the spectrum (for example, the 'best interests of the child'; or the foreseeability test for the existence of a duty in tort). Moreover, under statutory bills, the courts' interpretations always remain subject to the override or, more importantly, redefinition by the legislature. When one considers all this, and when one then considers the particular quality of normative insight obtained from grappling with statutes' application to the overlooked or underappreciated case, the remaining objection to rights review seems fastidious. If one does accept that the interests protected by statutory bills are worthy of special consideration, the balance of benefit favours statutory bills.

Conclusion

The debate over bills of rights often falls into simplifications in which rights are starkly pitted against majorities. Abstract and highly symbolic arguments dominate the field. And too often the participants are either wide-eyed believers in a conception of rights so pristine that disagreement and institutional concerns have no place, or fierce prophets of the impending death of democracy. These positions have some verisimilitude when entrenched bills are in issue (although they still drastically oversimplify). Entrenched bills do create a blunt division in institutional roles, they are often justified in highly symbolic terms, and their advocates rely on exaggerated claims. But there is no reason to reproduce such inflated rhetoric in the context of statutory bills, which have a very different structural context and a substantially different operation. The simplicities blind us to more subtle approaches to institutional structure. One of the important features of constitutionalism on the British model has been its careful attention to – its fine-grained attempt to blend – the strengths of different institutional forms, all within a structure that came to recognize the ultimate sovereignty of parliament. Statutory bills of rights lie very much within that tradition, and careful analysis of institutional architecture should not be displaced by the blunter categories of entrenched bills.

When I first came to Australia 30 years ago, I worked for a mining company in central New South Wales. My partner as an assistant prospecting hand was an Irishman named Seamus Ryan, who had been with the company for many years. We worked in conjunction with a group of drillers from Western Australia. Their comments on Aborigines, often expressed through jokes, were terrible – so terrible that I would have difficulty repeating them today. They used to tease Seamus mercilessly for having once picked up an Aboriginal woman who was hitchhiking. On one occasion I complained to Seamus about these comments. I remember him replying: 'You know, those drillers grew up in the country. Many of their boyhood friends were aborigines.' That didn't make the jokes any less disturbing. But it was an important lesson in how bigotry often works at a level of generality and is much harder to maintain in the face of the very people one is slandering.

It is that insight that underlies the operation of statutory bills of rights. They offer no guarantees of virtue. As in the case of bigotry, people can be resistant to the lessons of the particular case. They can close their ears to them. They can maintain their previous position and pursue it with single-minded vigour. But statutory bills provide one means of fostering the process of attention and revision. They do so by combining adjudication's intense focus on the particular case with, at the end of the day, legislative determination of the general normative order of society.

Authors note: This chapter has benefited from the research assistance of Emma Ferguson, Christina Godlewska, Keltie Mann, Crystal Reeves and Chad Vandermolen, and from comments of Richard Bellamy, Jim Evans, Keith Ewing, Eric Ghosh, Christina Godlewska, Hester Lessard, Brent Olthuis, and seminar participants at the Melbourne Workshop on 'Protecting Human Rights in Australia: Past, Present and Future', the University of South Wales, and University College, London.

References

Allan, J. (2000), 'Turning Clark Kent into Superman: The New Zealand Bill of Rights Act 1990', *Otago Law Review*, **9**: 613.

—— (2001)a, 'Take Heed Australia – A Statutory Bill of Rights And Its Inflationary Effect', *Deakin Law Review*, **6**: 322;

—— (2001)b, 'The Effect of a Statutory Bill of Rights where Parliament is Sovereign: The Lesson from New Zealand', in Campbell, T., Ewing, K.D. and Tomkins, A. (eds), *Sceptical Essays on Human Rights* (Oxford: Oxford University Press), p. 375.

—— (2002a), 'Oh That I Were Made Judge in the Land', *Federal Law Review*, **30**: 561.

—— (2002b), *Sympathy and Antipathy: Essays Legal and Philosophical* (Aldershot: Ashgate).

—— (2003), 'A Defence of the Status Quo' in Campbell, T., Goldsworthy, J. and Stone A. (eds), *Protecting Human Rights: Instruments and Institutions*, Oxford: Oxford University Press, p. 175.

Allan, J. and Cullen, R. (1997), 'A Bill of Rights Odyssey for Australia: The Sirens are Calling', *University of Queensland Law Journal*, **19**: 171.

ACT, ACT Bill of Rights Consultative Committee (2003), *Towards an ACT Human Rights Act: Report of the ACT Bill of Rights Consultative Committee* (Canberra: Australian Government Publishing Services).

Brennan, F. (1998a), *Legislating Liberty: A Bill of Rights for Australia?* (St Lucia: University of Queensland Press).

—— (1998b), *The Wik Debate: Its Impact on Aborigines, Pastoralists and Miners* (Sydney: University of New South Wales Press).

Butler, A. (2000), 'Interface Between the Human Rights Act 1998 and Other Enactments: Pointers from New Zealand', *European Human Rights Law Review*: 249.

—— (2001), 'Implied Repeal, Parliamentary Sovereignty and Human Rights in New Zealand', *Public Law*: 586.

Butler, P. (2004), 'Human Rights and Parliamentary Sovereignty in New Zealand', *Victoria University of Wellington Law Review*, **35**: 341.

Campbell, T. (1996), *The Legal Theory of Ethical Positivism* (Aldershot: Dartmouth).

—— (2001), 'Incorporation through Interpretation', in Campbell, T., Ewing, K.D. and Tomkins, A. (eds), *Sceptical Essays on Human Rights* (Oxford: Oxford University Press), p. 79.

Clapham, A. (1999), 'The European Convention on Human Rights in the British Courts: Problems Associated with the Incorporation of International Human Rights', in Alston, P. (ed.), *Promoting Human Rights through Bills of Rights: Comparative Perspectives* (Oxford: Oxford University Press), p. 95.

Davis, M. (2002), 'New South Wales Bill of Rights Inquiry', *Public Law Review*, **13**: 11.

Davis, M. and Williams, G. (2002), 'A Statutory Bill of Rights for Australia? Lessons from the United Kingdom', *University of Queensland Law Journal*, **22**: 1.

Debeljak, J. (2003), 'The Human Rights Act 1998 (UK): the Preservation of Parliamentary Supremacy in the Context of Rights Protection', *Australian Journal of Human Rights*, **9**: 183.

Egerton, G. (2004), 'Writing the Canadian Bill of Rights: Religion, Politics, and the Challenge of Pluralism 1957–1960', *Canadian Journal of Law and Society,* **19**: 1.

Evans, C. (2004), 'Responsibility for Rights: the ACT *Human Rights Act*', *Federal Law Review*, **32**: 291.

Evans, J. (2004), 'Reading Down Statutes', in Rick Bigwood (ed.), *The Statute: Making and Meaning* (Wellington: Lexis-Nexis), p. 123.

Fitzgerald, P. (1992), 'Section 7 of the New Zealand Bill of Rights Act 1990: A Very Practical Power or a Well-Intentioned Nonsense', *Victoria University of Wellington Law Review*, **22**: 135.

Gearty, C.A. (2002), 'Reconciling Parliamentary Democracy and Human Rights', *Law Quarterly Review*, **118**: 248.

Ghai, Y. (1997), 'Sentinels of Liberty or Sheep in Woolf's Clothing? Judicial Politics and the Hong Kong Bill of Rights', *Modern Law Review*, **60**: 459.

Goldsworthy, J. (2003), 'Judicial Review, Legislative Override, and Democracy', in Campbell, T., Goldsworthy, J. and Stone A. (eds), *Protecting Human Rights: Instruments and Institutions* (Oxford: Oxford University Press), p. 263.

Hiebert, J. (2002), *Charter Conflicts: What is Parliament's Role?* (Montreal: McGill-Queen's University Press).

Hodge, M. (2000), 'Statutory Interpretation and Section 6 of the New Zealand Bill of Rights Act: A Blank Cheque or a Return to the Prevailing Doctrine', *Auckland University Law Review*, **9**: 1.

Hogg, P.W. (1992ff), *Constitutional Law of Canada*, various edns (Toronto: Carswell).

Hovius, B. (1982), 'The Legacy of the Supreme Court of Canada's Approach to the Canadian Bill of Rights: Prospects for the Charter', *McGill Law Journal*, **28**: 31.

Huscroft, G. (2002), 'Rights, Bills of Rights, and the Role of Courts and Legislatures', in Huscroft, G. and Rishworth, P. (eds), *Litigating Rights: Perspectives from Domestic and International Law* (Oxford: Hart Publishing), p. 3.

Irvine, Lord (2003), 'The Impact of the Human Rights Act: Parliament, the Courts and the Executive', *Public Law*: 308.

Joseph, P.A. (1999), 'The New Zealand Bill of Rights Experience', in Philip Alston (ed.), *Promoting Human Rights through Bills of Rights: Comparative Perspectives* (Oxford: Oxford University Press), p. 283.

Klug, F. and O'Brien, C. (2002), 'The First Two Years of the Human Rights Act', *Public Law*: 649.

Kretzmer, D. (1999), 'Basic Laws as a Surrogate Bill of Rights: The Case of Israel', in Philip Alston (ed.), *Promoting Human Rights through Bills of Rights: Comparative Perspectives* (Oxford: Oxford University Press), p. 75.

Marshall, G. (2003), 'The Lynchpin of Parliamentary Intention: Lost, Stolen, or Strained?' *Public Law*: 236.

McDonald, L. (2004), 'New Directions in the Australian Bill of Rights Debate', *Public Law*: 22.

McLean, J., Rishworth, P. and Taggart, M. (1992), 'The Impact of the New Zealand Bill of Rights on Administrative Law', in *The New Zealand Bill of Rights Act 1990* (Auckland: Legal Research Foundation), p. 62.

Optican, S. (1999), 'Search and Seizure in the Court of Appeal – An Essay on the Uses and Misuses of Section 21 of the Bill of Rights', *New Zealand Universities Law Review*, **18**: 411.

Palmer, G. (1992), *New Zealand's Constitution in Crisis: Reforming our Political System* (Dunedin: McIndoe).

Petter, A. (2003), 'Twenty Years of *Charter* Justification: From Liberal Legalism to Dubious Dialogue', *University of New Brunswick Law Journal* (**52**: 187).

Rishworth, P. (1995), 'The Birth and Rebirth of the Bill of Rights', in Grant Huscroft and Paul Rishworth (eds), *Rights and Freedoms: The New Zealand Bill of Rights Act 1990 and the Human Rights Act 1993* (Wellington: Brooker's), p. 1.

Schwartz, H. (1998), 'The Short Happy Life and Tragic Death of the New Zealand Bill of Rights Act', *New Zealand Law Review*: 259.

Starmer, K. (2003), 'Two Years of the Human Rights Act', *European Human Rights Law Review*: 14.

Taggart, M. (1998), 'Tugging on Superman's Cape: Lessons from Experience with the New Zealand Bill of Rights Act 1990', *Public Law*: 266.

Tarnopolsky, W.S. (1975), *The Canadian Bill of Rights*, 2nd edn (Toronto: McClelland and Stewart).

Tomkins, A. (2001), 'Introduction: On Being Sceptical about Human Rights', in Campbell, T., Ewing, K.D. and Tomkins, A. (eds), *Sceptical Essays on Human Rights* (Oxford: Oxford University Press), p. 1.

Waldron, J. (1999), *Law and Disagreement* (New York: Oxford University Press).

Webber, J. (1993), 'Tales of the Unexpected: Intended and Unintended Consequences of the Canadian Charter of Rights and Freedoms', *Canterbury Law Review*, **5**: 207.

—— (2000), 'Constitutional Reticence', *Australian Journal of Legal Philosophy*, **25**: 125.

—— (2003), 'Institutional Dialogue between Courts and Legislatures in the Definition of Fundamental Rights: Lessons from Canada (and Elsewhere)', *Australian Journal of Human Rights*, **9**: 135.

—— (2006), 'Democratic Decision-Making as the First Principle of Contemporary Constitutionalism,' in Bauman, R.W. and Kahana, T. (eds), *The Least Examined Branch: The Role of Legislatures in the Constitutional State* (New York: Cambridge University Press, forthcoming).

White, J.B. (2002), 'Human Dignity and the Claim of Meaning: Athenian Tragic Drama and Supreme Court Opinions', *Journal of Supreme Court History*, **27**: 45.

Williams, G. (2000), *A Bill of Rights for Australia* (Sydney: University of New South Wales Press).

Winterton, G. (1980), 'Can the Commonwealth Parliament Enact "Manner and Form" Legislation?', *Federal Law Review*, **11**: 167.

Chapter 12

Australia's First Bill of Rights: The Australian Capital Territory's *Human Rights Act*

Hilary Charlesworth[1]

Australia's first bill of rights, the Australian Capital Territory's (ACT) *Human Rights Act 2004* (ACT) ('*Human Rights Act*'), came into force on 1 July 2004. Many of the debates about the value of the formal legal protection of human rights engaged in the contributions to this book were reflected in the development of the ACT law. This chapter describes the background to the ACT *Human Rights Act*, the first year of its operation and considers its value as a model for improving the protection of human rights in Australia.

Background to the ACT *Human Rights Act*

In 2001, Jon Stanhope, Leader of the Opposition Labor Party in the ACT, made an election promise that, if his party were elected, he would appoint a committee to consult with the community on whether the ACT should adopt a bill of rights. This was not the first time that this issue had been raised. At the time of the Territory's move to self-government, there was public discussion about introducing a bill of rights as part of the self-government package. Jack Waterford, a prominent Canberra journalist, indeed drafted a bill of rights,[2] but in the end the *ACT Self-Government Act 1988* (Cth) did not include any reference to rights. In 1993, the ACT Attorney-General, Terry Connolly, published an issues paper on an ACT bill of rights (ACT, Attorney-General's Department, 1993) and received a number of submissions in relation to the proposal. A public seminar was held the following year (ACT, Attorney-General's Department, 1994) and early in 1995 the Attorney-General

---

1   Thanks to Gabrielle McKinnon, Director, ACT *Human Rights Act* Project, Regulatory Institutions Network, Research School of Social Sciences, The Australian National University, for her valuable comments and Richard Refshauge SC, ACT Director of Public Prosecutions for providing very helpful information on the operation of the ACT *Human Rights Act 2004* (ACT).

2   The bill prepared by Waterford is contained in Grundy et al, 1996, appendix 9.

circulated an exposure draft of an ACT bill of rights. The Connolly Bill lapsed after the Labor Party lost government at the March 1995 election.

The issue of an ACT bill of rights made little apparent impact on the election campaign in 2001, but a Stanhope government was elected in October of that year. Jon Stanhope took on the portfolios of both Chief Minister and Attorney-General and, in the latter capacity, appointed a four person ACT Bill of Rights Consultative Committee in April 2002. The Committee's terms of reference were broad and non-prescriptive. They charged the Committee to consult on: whether it was 'appropriate and desirable' to enact an ACT bill of rights, what form such a bill might take, what effect the bill might have on executive and judicial powers and what rights should be included in the bill (ACT, ACT Bill of Rights Consultative Committee, 2003, [1.3]). The consultation process took nine months and involved the publication of an issues paper and a pamphlet, 145 submissions, many meetings, both open to the public and with specific community groups, public lectures, seminars and conferences and a 'deliberative poll' (ACT, ACT Bill of Rights Consultative Committee, 2003, [1.6–1.18]). These various forms of consultation all produced a similar result, indicating that there was majority support (approximately two-thirds of those participating) for an ACT bill of rights in principle, although this figure was not broken down according to particular models.

The Consultative Committee presented its report to the Chief Minister in May 2003. It recommended that the ACT adopt a bill of rights, in the form of a *Human Rights Act*, a draft of which was appended to the report. This proposed legislation was unentrenched and set out to create a 'dialogue' about human rights between the branches of government in the ACT as well as the community.[3] The image of a dialogue was drawn from both Canadian and United Kingdom (UK) commentary that emphasized the interaction of interpretation of rights by the judiciary and political and legislative action (Klug, 2000). The dialogue model of human rights protection is in contrast to a model based on judicial review, such as the United States Bill of Rights, which gives the judiciary the final say on the interpretation of rights.

The Human Rights Act proposed by the Consultative Committee covered most of the rights contained in the *International Covenant on Civil and Political Rights*[4] and the *International Covenant on Economic, Social and Cultural Rights*.[5] These international treaties were used as the basis for the catalogue of protected rights largely because there were concerns that if a more tailored and modern set of rights were devised, the Commonwealth government might use its constitutional power to override territories' legislation.[6] The draft legislation included in the report attempted

---

3   See the Preamble to the Human Rights Bill 2003 in ACT, ACT Bill of Rights Consultative Committee 2003, appendix 4.

4   Opened for signature 19 December 1966, 999 UNTS 171 (entered into force 23 March 1976) (*ICCPR*).

5   Opened for signature 16 December 1966, 993 UNTS 3 (entered into force 3 January 1976) (*ICESCR*).

6   *Australian Constitution*s.122.

to break down the traditional distinction drawn between civil and political rights on the one hand and economic, social and cultural rights on the other by defining rights as including elements from both Covenants. For example, clause 2 of the schedule to the draft legislation linked the right to life and the right to an adequate standard of living.[7]

The legislation proposed by the Committee was quickly repudiated by the Opposition. Indeed Shadow Attorney-General Bill Stefaniak had been opposed to any model of a bill of rights from the outset of the consultative process. His major arguments were that existing laws and the common law provided adequate protection for human rights and that a bill of rights would simply produce a 'litigation culture' (Stefaniak, 2002). But there was also considerable opposition to the Committee's proposals within the ACT Cabinet and at the most senior levels of the bureaucracy. Some government departments obtained legal advice that predicted dire budgetary and policy consequences for the ACT if any form of rights protection were enacted. Within the ACT Labor Party, there were general concerns that the Chief Minister's enthusiasm for a bill of rights was electoral folly and specific anxieties about various provisions of the legislation. One contentious issue was whether protection of the right to life, as set out in article 6 of the *ICCPR*, would affect the ACT's relatively liberal abortion laws. Although article 6 has generally been understood not to affect access to abortion, the language of the international formulation of the right was finally amended to make this explicit.[8]

The debate on the draft legislation in the Legislative Assembly was conducted in strong terms. Shadow Attorney-General Stefaniak called it 'the most important and potentially most dangerous legislation we have ever seen in this Territory'.[9] Among other objections, he was critical of the failure to refer to the right to own property, the right to safety and security and the rights of victims of crime (Campbell, 2004, p. 2). He also was concerned that it transferred power from elected politicians to unaccountable judges. Other members of the Opposition described it as a 'can of worms'[10] and predicted that it would allow the circumvention of the parliamentary process by political and legal lobby groups.[11]

Passage of the *Human Rights Act* in the ACT Legislative Assembly prompted the Shadow Attorney-General to introduce a Charter of Responsibilities Bill 2004 in order to temper the 'excesses' and selfishness he associated with the *Human Rights Act*.[12] The structure of the Charter was modelled on the *Human Rights Act*; for example it contained an interpretation clause providing that '[i]n working out the meaning

---

7   *ICCPR* art. 6(1); *ICESCR* art. 11 (1) and (2).

8   See *Human Rights Act 2004* (ACT) s. 9 (2).

9   ACT, *Parliamentary Debates*, Legislative Assembly for the ACT, 25 November 2003, 4577.

10   ACT, *Parliamentary Debates*, Legislative Assembly for the ACT, 2 March 2004, 511 (Jacqui Burke MLA).

11   Ibid. 456 (Steve Pratt MLA).

12   ACT, *Parliamentary Debates*, Legislative Assembly for the ACT, 18 August 2004, 3883. For an analysis of the draft Charter see Kostakidis-Lianos and Williams, 2005.

of a Territory law, an interpretation that is consistent with civil responsibilities is to be preferred to any other interpretation.'[13] In the case of conflicting interpretations under the *Human Rights Act*, the Charter-mandated interpretation was to have priority.[14] The responsibilities covered by the Charter included the responsibility to be honest, the responsibility not to misuse 'economic and political power ... as instruments of domination',[15] the responsibility to confess any breach of the law and to accept appropriate punishment,[16] and a judicial responsibility to take 'community expectations into account when sentencing offenders in criminal matters and in giving judgments in civil claims affecting the community generally.'[17] The Charter was not supported by the government or cross-benchers and was defeated in the Legislative Assembly.

At the time of the passage of the *Human Rights Act* through the Legislative Assembly in March 2004, the prospect of Commonwealth intervention to override the legislation was raised.[18] The Prime Minister had expressed concern in a letter to the ACT Chief Minister that the *Human Rights Act* was a dangerous precedent and that it unnecessarily replicated existing human rights mechanisms (Morris, 2004, p. 3). He later described the Act as 'ridiculous' in a radio interview, (see, AAP, 2004) leading to keen speculation within the ACT that the Commonwealth might intervene to invalidate it. In the event, however, no formal steps were taken to interfere with the legislation.

The *Human Rights Act 2004*

The final form of the *Human Rights Act* followed the Consultative Committee's proposals to a large degree. It is a statutory instrument with no entrenchment provision, as would have been possible under the *ACT Self-Government Act 1988* (Cth). The legislation differs in two significant respects from that proposed by the Consultative Committee: it covers a catalogue of rights derived from the *ICCPR*[19] and omits economic, social and cultural rights; and the methods of implementation it provides do not include a direct right of action against public authorities or an explicit remedy for breach of rights. A proposal by the Consultative Committee that delegated legislation that was incompatible with human rights become invalid

---

13 Charter of Responsibilities Bill 2004 cl 8 ('Charter').

14 Ibid. cl. 8(3).

15 Ibid. cl. 18(1).

16 Ibid. cl. 17.

17 Ibid. cl. 10(5).

18 This would have been possible through Commonwealth legislation under the Territories power set out in s. 122 of the *Australian Constitution*. This section had been the basis of Commonwealth legislation overriding a Northern Territory law allowing euthanasia in 1997.

19 For a discussion of the relationship between the *ICCPR* and the rights included in the ACT *Human Rights Act 2004* (ACT) see Charlesworth, 2004.

also was not implemented. Other forms of implementation recommended by the Committee survived and include:

- an obligation to interpret legislation to be consistent as far as possible with human rights (s. 30);
- Supreme Court jurisdiction to issue a declaration of incompatibility in cases where legislation cannot be interpreted to be consistent with human rights (s. 32); the declaration does not affect the validity of the legislation in question, (s. 39) but the Attorney-General is required to report on governmental responses to the declaration to the Legislative Assembly (s. 33);
- a duty on the Attorney-General to present a written statement on the compatibility of each bill presented to the Legislative Assembly (s. 37);
- pre-enactment scrutiny of all legislation for consistency with human rights by the relevant Standing Committee of the Legislative Assembly (s. 38), which presents a report to government, which then must respond to the report;
- the creation of the Office of Human Rights Commissioner to review laws to ensure compliance with the *Human Rights Act* and to advise the Attorney-General on the operation of the Act (s. 41);
- a duty for government departments to report on their implementation of the *Human Rights Act* in their annual reports (schedule 2).

The *Human Rights Act* also adopted the Consultative Committee's proposal to include provision for a full review of the workings of the legislation after five years of operation.[20] The Stanhope government was dependent on the support of at least two of the three cross-benchers to assure the passage of the *Human Rights Act* and a further one-year review was inserted into the legislation at the insistence of Kerrie Tucker, a member of the Greens Party.[21] The review, to be concluded by 1 July 2006, must include the issue of whether rights contained in the *ICESCR* should be introduced into the *Human Rights Act* as well as 'whether environment-related human rights would be better protected if there were statutory oversight of their operation by someone with expertise in environment protection'.[22]

At the heart of the *Human Rights Act* is an obligation to interpret all ACT legislation to be compatible with specified human rights. The wording proposed by the Consultative Committee was:

> A court or tribunal must interpret a law of the Territory to be compatible with human rights and must ensure that the law is given effect to in a way that is compatible with human rights, as far as it is possible to do so.[23]

---

20 *Human Rights Act 2004* (ACT) s. 44.

21 Ibid. s. 43(1).

22 Ibid. s. 43(2)(b).

23 Human Rights Bill 2003 (ACT) cl. 3, appendix 4 to ACT, ACT Bill of Rights Consultative Committee, 2003.

This interpretative obligation was to apply to both legislation and the common law. The final wording of the obligation is contained in s. 30 (1) of the ACT *Human Rights Act*. It provides:

> In working out the meaning of a Territory law [an Act or statutory instrument], an interpretation that is consistent with human rights is as far as possible to be preferred.

This obligation does not apply explicitly to the common law. Section 30(2) goes on to specify that this interpretative preference is subject to s. 139 of the *Legislation Act 2001* (ACT) (*'Legislation Act'*), which contains a statement of the 'purposive' rule of statutory interpretation in the following terms:

> (1)   In working out the meaning of an Act, the interpretation that would best achieve the purpose of the Act is to be preferred to any other interpretation.

Section 30(3) of the ACT *Human Rights Act* follows s. 138 of the *Legislation Act* to define the term 'working out the meaning of a Territory law' as:

(a) resolving an ambiguous or obscure provision of the law; or
(b) confirming or displacing the apparent meaning of the law; or
(c) finding the meaning of the law when its apparent meaning leads to a result that is manifestly absurd or is unreasonable; or
(d) finding the meaning of the law in any other case.

At first sight, then, s. 30 appears to make a human rights interpretation of legislation available only when it is clear that the Legislative Assembly did not intend otherwise. In this sense it could be read as a codification of the 'principle of legality' by which parliament is assumed not to intend to impinge on basic rights, unless it uses clear words to do so.[24] This may suggest that s. 30 is weaker than both its New Zealand and UK counterparts in promoting a human rights dialogue. The New Zealand courts have read s. 6 of the *Bill of Rights Act 1990* (NZ) as allowing interpretations that conflict with the intention of Parliament,[25] and the House of Lords has described s. 3 of the *Human Rights Act 1998* (UK) as imposing 'a stronger and more radical obligation than to adopt a purposive interpretation in the light of the [European Convention on Human Rights]'.[26] The Explanatory Statement tabled when the ACT *Human Rights Act* was introduced into the Legislative Assembly, however, gives a stronger account of s. 30.[27] It states that s. 30 is 'a new rule of statutory construction' which requires that 'when working out the meaning of a Territory statute or statutory instrument an interpretation that is consistent with human rights must be applied in

---

24 *Al Kateb* v *Godwin* (2004) 208 ALR 124, [19] (Gleeson CJ).

25 *R* v *Poumako* [2000] 2 NZLR 695.

26 *Ghaidan* [2004] 3 WLR 113, [44] (Lord Steyn). The New Zealand and UK approaches are discussed in detail in Charlesworth, 2005.

27 Explanatory Statement, Human Rights Bill 2003 (ACT), available at <http://www. legislation.act.gov.au/es/db_8294/current/rtf/db_8294.rtf>

preference to any other interpretation'.[28] The Explanatory Statement notes the impact of the purposive rule of construction as set out in the *Legislation Act* but explains this partially in reference to the interpretation of the *Human Rights Act* itself:

> Subclause 139(1) [of the *Legislation Act*] requires that Territory laws must be interpreted in a way that best achieves the purpose of the Act. Consequently, the interpretation most beneficial to human rights will best achieve the purpose of the Bill.

> Where there is a choice between two interpretations and both interpretations best achieve the purpose of the statute or statutory instrument, the interpretation that is consistent with human rights must prevail.[29]

However, the Statement goes on to note that '[Section] 30(2) clarifies that if an interpretation that is consistent with human rights would have the affect of defeating the obvious purpose of the statute or statutory instrument the interpretation that is consistent with human rights will not prevail.'[30] It adds:

> The effect of [s.] 30 is that the courts, tribunals, decision makers and others authorised to act by a Territory statute or statutory instrument must take account of human rights when interpreting the law. A statutory discretion must be exercised consistently with human rights unless legislation intends to authorise administrative action regardless of the human right.[31]

It is not yet clear how ACT courts and tribunals will deal with the co-existence in the *Human Rights Act* of a direction to find human-rights-consistent interpretations of ACT legislation and a direction to prefer a purposive approach. The broad meaning given to the term 'working out the meaning' of legislation, which includes displacing the apparent meaning, suggests potential conflict. It is possible that the ACT Supreme Court will use declarations of incompatibility more readily than advised by the House of Lords in the context of the UK legislation as a method of resolving inconsistencies between human rights and legislative intention. Such a course may be encouraged by the fact that the Attorney-General's statements on the human rights compatibility of government bills required by s. 37 have so far been extremely brief and formulaic, giving little insight into the government's assessment of the human rights implications of draft legislation.[32] Sometimes, the government's views on human rights compatibility are set out at more length in the Explanatory Statement which accompanies the introduction of the legislation. The operation of s. 28 of the ACT *Human Rights Act*, which provides that '[h]uman rights may be subject only to reasonable limits set by Territory laws that can be demonstrably

---

28 Ibid. p. 5.

29 Ibid.

30 Ibid.

31 Ibid.

32 Compare the relatively lengthy advices on the human rights consistency of draft legislation prepared in New Zealand, available at <www.justice.govt.nz/bill-of-rights>.

justified in a free and democratic society', will also be significant as a technique for resolving tensions between human rights protection and legislative intent.

The *Human Rights Act* in Operation

Over the first year of its operation, the *Human Rights Act* has not had the dramatic effect on law or politics in the ACT hoped for by its supporters or feared by its critics. Indeed the low public visibility and apparent lack of impact of the legislation has led some of the critics of its introduction to declare it mere symbolism (for example Creyke, 2006) or even a hoax (for example Spry, 2004). The story is, however, more complex.

Within the courts, s. 30 of the *Human Rights Act* has been used gingerly by both the judiciary and legal advocates. As at 1 September 2005, the *Human Rights Act* has been referred to in 13 judgments of the Supreme Court of the ACT, one judgment of the Court of Appeal and one decision of the ACT Administrative Appeals Tribunal.[33] The Act is also cited regularly in bail applications in the Supreme Court. Prosecutors have reported that judges will often refer to the *Human Rights Act* in criminal cases and enquire whether there is a human rights issue involved (Refshauge, 2005).

The first discussion of the interpretative clause in s. 30 was in *R v YL*.[34] Justice Crispin of the ACT Supreme Court used s. 30's direction of a human rights-consistent interpretation to support a reading of legislative provisions he had arrived at through traditional analysis. He invoked s. 11(2) of the *Human Rights Act* (the right of children to protection) to remove any doubt about the use of judicial discretion under s. 20 of the *Supreme Court Act 1933* (ACT) not to coerce a child witness to give evidence against his stepmother. Justice Crispin also read the statutory powers of the Director of Public Prosecutions in light of the rights to a fair[35] and timely[36] trial. In another case before the ACT Administrative Appeals Tribunal, *Re Merritt and the Commissioner for Housing*, s. 30 was briefly and rather desultorily considered in the interpretation of regulations dealing with access to emergency housing.[37] At issue was whether the human rights of children and families to protection (s. 11) should be taken into account in determinations about housing allocation. The Tribunal dismissed the human rights argument put forward by a public housing tenant on the basis that the regulations were clearly worded and had been previously applied in a consistent way. The decision in that case suggests a misunderstanding of the nature of the *Human Rights Act*, with the Tribunal implying that there was a need for

---

33 For an overview see McKinnon, 2005.

34 (2004) 187 FLR 84.

35 *Human Rights Act 2004* (ACT) s. 21.

36 Ibid. s.22.

37 *Re Merritt and Commissioner for Housing* [2004] ACTAAT 37. Robin Creyke (2005) also discusses this case.

ambiguity in the statutory wording before the s. 30 interpretative duty of the *Human Rights Act* came into operation.[38]

Although s. 31 of the *Human Rights Act* specifically allows 'international law, and the judgments of foreign and international courts and tribunals, relevant to a human right' to be used in interpretation, ACT courts have been slow to refer to this type of jurisprudence in cases where the *Human Rights Act* has been invoked. An exception to this wariness is the Supreme Court decision in *R v Upton*.[39] The case concerned an application for a stay of criminal proceedings because of considerable delay in the prosecution. In considering whether the delay could affect the defendant's right to a timely trial set out in s. 22 of the *Human Rights Act*, Connolly J examined UK and New Zealand cases on the right to be tried without delay and relied on the principles they had expounded to grant the application.[40]

The first declaration of incompatibility under the *Human Rights Act* was sought in the case of *I v S*,[41] argued in the Supreme Court before Higgins CJ in August 2005. The case concerned s. 51A of the *Domestic Violence and Protection Orders Act 2001* (ACT) and involved a protection order made against a child. The effect of this provision was to require a respondent to an interim protection order who was absent at the time the order was made to make a written objection within seven days to prevent the order becoming final. The legislation did not provide for the setting aside of the final order even where there was a reasonable explanation for the failure to lodge a written objection. A respondent was required to apply for leave to apply to amend the order, but this could only be granted if the court was satisfied that there may have been a substantial change in the circumstances surrounding the making of the original order. The argument made by the ACT Legal Aid Office on behalf of a respondent to a protection order was that s. 51A breached the right to a fair hearing (set out in s. 21 of the *Human Rights Act*) and that it was not capable of being interpreted to be consistent with human rights. Section 51A had been inserted in 2005, after the entry into force of the *Human Rights Act*, and had gone through the internal governmental human rights scrutiny process. The Explanatory Statement to the draft amending legislation briefly asserted that it did not 'unduly interfere [...] with the civil liberties of the individual' and was thus covered by the '"reasonable limits" exemption under section 28' of the *Human Rights Act* and this assertion was not challenged by the Legislative Assembly's scrutiny of bills committee. The ACT Human Rights Commissioner filed a brief in the Supreme Court supporting the challenge to the legislation and argued that s. 51A breached the rights to equality before the law (s. 8), the right to a fair hearing (s. 21), the right of the child to protection (s. 11) and possibly criminal law procedures (s. 22). Human rights jurisprudence supports the view that s. 51A is inconsistent with human rights

---

38 For a discussion of the case see Evans, 2005.

39 [2005] ACTSC 52 (Unreported Judgment, Connolly J, 1 July 2005).

40 Justice Connolly is a former ACT Attorney-General and had introduced a draft bill of rights into the Legislative Assembly in 1995.

41 (2005) ACTSCA 33.

covered in the ACT *Human Rights Act*[42] and the Supreme Court's judgment in *I* v *S* will provide an interesting signal of how ACT courts will deal with such situations.

The use of the *Human Rights Act* in ACT courts and tribunals has overall been cautious, perhaps a result of the judiciary's and the profession's unfamiliarity with international human rights law and standards. Education programs in the ACT have been minimal compared, for example, to those preceding the introduction of the UK *Human Rights Act 1998* (UK). The private ACT legal profession has also generally tended to dismiss the value of a bill of rights that contains no explicit right of action. Gerard McCoy has speculated that this might be the result of either 'forensic somnolence or intellectual recumbency' (McCoy, 2005), but it is more likely a product of the small size of the Canberra legal community. Transcripts of the argument of cases where the *Human Rights Act* has been raised reveal some confusion about the scope of the legislation. Judgments do not tend to provide much clarity on the way that particular human rights were interpreted or how they affected decisions. This caution is hardly surprising in the context of such unfamiliar legislation and it mirrors the early New Zealand experience with its *Bill of Rights Act 1990* (NZ) where it took almost five years for that legislation to be invoked regularly. The earlier take-up of the UK's *Human Rights Act 1998* (UK) may be explicable by the experience of UK lawyers with human rights litigation under the European Convention of Human Rights and the fact that the UK law provides an explicit right of action against public authorities.

The *Human Rights Act* has affected the operation of the ACT Legislative Assembly's Standing Committee on Legal Affairs which acts as a scrutiny of Bills committee. Section 38 of the *Human Rights Act* provides that the Committee must report to the Assembly about human rights issues raised by bills. The Committee has produced sometimes lengthy reports outlining the human rights implications of draft legislation (Bayne, 2005a). A recurring issue has been the compatibility of proposals for offences of strict or absolute liability with rights such as the presumption of innocence (s. 22(1)) and to liberty (s. 18) (Bayne, 2005b). The Committee has, however, accepted the government's view that strict liability offences can be justified where, for example, a defendant can reasonably be expected to know the requirements of the law (Bayne, 2005b). Some members of the Committee have complained that the Committee does not always have adequate information to take a position of human rights concerns raised by particular bills (Kelly, 2005). Although it has its own (part-time) legal adviser, Peter Bayne, the Committee does not have access to the advice provided by the Department of Justice to the Attorney-General. The government has amended some legislative proposals in light of the Committee's reports, but on other occasions it has not responded to the human rights issues raised. One potentially important issue that is not covered by the scheme created by the *Human Rights Act* is the scrutiny of the human rights implications of amendments made on the floor of the Legislative Assembly.

---

42 For example on the issue of a fair hearing, see *Escalona* v *Spain* [2000] ECHR 202.

Although little public information is available, the greatest impact of the *Human Rights Act* seems to have been on the generation of government and legislative policy. A small Human Rights Unit has been established in the Department of Justice and Community Safety to monitor and support the implementation of the *Human Rights Act* within government. The Unit has published a plain English guide to the legislation guidelines on the development of legislation and policy in light of the *Human Rights Act* (see ACT, Department of Justice and Community Safety, 2004). One issue has been the resources available to this important element of the human rights dialogue. The Unit comprises three lawyers, but is responsible for advising Cabinet and all other government departments about the effect of the legislation. It also prepares the compatibility statements required by s. 37 of the *Human Rights Act*. The brevity of the compatibility statements referred to above is one sign of the resource pressures on the Unit.

Issues that have been considered from a human rights perspective within the ACT executive over the first year of the *Human Rights Act* include sentencing laws, the exclusion from public employment of a person with a criminal record, setting up of roadblocks, the prevention of prisoners from voting, blanket policies of strip-searching of prisoners, the use of children for tobacco test purchases, and the wearing of headscarves in ACT schools (Kelly, 2005; Refshauge, 2005). There have been cases where the Human Rights Unit has counselled government departments that a particular legislative proposal is not consistent with human rights and that, if left unamended, the Attorney-General will be advised not to issue a compatibility statement. As yet, the *Human Rights Act* appears to have reached only a limited echelon of the public service. Its requirements have not yet percolated through the whole of the ACT government and service deliverers and administrative decision-makers are only beginning to be aware of the legislation (Kelly, 2005). Perhaps the most striking use of the legislation is the reference to it in the design brief for a new ACT prison.[43]

An important element of the *Human Rights Act* is s. 28, quoted above, which allows limits to be placed on rights. As yet there has been little guidance from the ACT courts on how this will operate (Refshauge, 2005). Explanatory Statements attached to draft legislation have tended to refer to s. 28 as 'a "reasonable limits" exemption'. This may overly simplify the nature of s. 28 by suggesting that it is a safety net for policies that are considered reasonable by the government, rather than a provision requiring detailed legal justification of any limits to rights. The Legislative Assembly's Standing Committee on Legal Affairs also regards s. 28 as requiring the legislature to make a policy decision in particular cases and has generally been cautious in offering advice on how the elements identified in s. 28 might be balanced (McKinnon, 2005). This approach differs from that taken in other jurisdictions, such as the UK, where comparable provisions have been interpreted as requiring a complex assessment of the importance of the right affected, the nature of the interference with it, the strength of the justification for interference, and the

---

43 See, homepage of the ACT Prison Project at <http://www.cs.act.gov.au/amc/home>.

number and vulnerability of the people likely to be affected (Feldman, 2002). In other words, s. 28 of the *Human Rights Act* relies on the concept of proportionality, rather than the less structured idea of unreasonableness to restrict limitations on rights (McCoy, 2005).

The ACT Human Rights Commissioner, Dr Helen Watchirs, has played a significant role in implementing the *Human Rights Act*. Under s. 41 of the legislation, the Commissioner is required to report to the Attorney-General on reviews of ACT laws, to provide community education and to advise the Attorney-General on anything relevant to the operation of the *Human Rights Act*. Thus far, Dr Watchirs' office has initiated education campaigns in schools and convened community forums about the legislation and made submissions to government on the human rights implications of proposed legislation. The Commissioner's advice that a proposed law permitting the use of electro-convulsive therapy in emergency situations breached human rights led to some amendments of the legislation, although the advice has not been made public. She has also conducted a major review of a youth detention facility in the ACT, Quamby, identifying many areas where practices were inconsistent with human rights, such as strip searches, seclusion, surveillance and lockdown periods (ACT, Human Rights Office). The Quamby report has already persuaded the government to change some of the more draconian juvenile justice policies, although it is not yet clear how many of the Commissioner's recommendations will be implemented.

Conclusion

Australia's 'exceptionalism' with respect to the protection of human rights has been somewhat reduced by the introduction of the ACT *Human Rights Act*. It differs from earlier models of bills of rights discussed in Australia through its dependence on legislative interpretation as the vehicle for human rights protection. The adoption of a human-rights-consistent approach to statutory interpretation has been popular in modern bills of rights because it appears to avoid the charge of democracy-erosion that dogs bills of rights that allow the judiciary to strike down legislation found to breach rights standards (for example Klug, 2000, p. 166) The assumption has been that the new rule of statutory interpretation is less of an interference with the processes of a majoritarian democracy than entrenched protection of human rights: judicial interpretation of laws seems a less interventionist activity than that of invalidation. Indeed, a feature of the marketing of the ACT *Human Rights Act*, as in the case of the *Human Rights Act 1998* (UK), has been that it allows a 'human rights dialogue' between the various branches of government. The preservation of parliamentary supremacy in similar human rights legislation has led however to criticism that the mechanism of human rights interpretation is inadequate to protect human rights. For example, the United Nations Human Rights Committee has questioned the efficacy of the New Zealand and UK human rights laws, recommending that both countries revise them to allow courts to strike down legislation inconsistent with the rights set out in the *ICCPR*.[44] Some Australian supporters of bills of rights were also concerned about what they perceived as a weak ACT model (for example Debeljak, 2004). On the other hand, despite the modesty of the ACT *Human Rights Act*, critics of bills of rights have continued to object to its interference with the democratic process.[45] These critics rarely make clear how human-rights-consistent statutory interpretation differs from judicial interpretation in other contexts and the 'democratic' objection appears more an automatic response to the idea of a bill of rights than one based on the actual terms of the ACT law.

One area where the *Human Rights Act* may assume some importance in the future is in administrative law cases. It could be argued that the legislative articulation of a set of human rights gives rise to a legitimate expectation that those human rights will be considered in the exercise of any statutory discretion or power. Failure to take human rights into account could thus constitute a breach of procedural fairness (Connolly, 2005; McCoy, 2005).

Any assessment of the human rights dialogue approach offered by the ACT *Human Rights Act* must take into account not only the limited resources available to be invested in it but also the small size of the ACT's governmental institutions. Writing before the legislation came into effect, Leighton McDonald (2004, p. 30) noted that

> the quality of the 'dialogue' between these institutions is likely to depend upon the breadth and depth of the surrounding legal/human rights culture, including, for example, the capacities of interest groups, the level of academic interest in any local experiment, and the orientations and expertise of the local legal profession.

As yet, on these indicators, there is only a thin ACT human rights culture, but the *Human Rights Act* is slowly deepening it. Greater transparency about the human rights conversations occurring *within* government, for example by releasing the advice to government by the Human Rights Commissioner and some form of the advice of the government's Human Rights Unit on particular legislative and policy proposals, would further enhance this fledgling culture.[46]

One important effect of the ACT experiment has been to encourage other Australian jurisdictions to consider the introduction of bills of rights. There have

---

44 *Concluding Observations of the Human Rights Committee, New Zealand*, UN Doc A/50/40 (1995) [176] (New Zealand), *Concluding Observations of the Human Rights Committee, United Kingdom of Great Britain and Northern Ireland*, UN Doc (1995) [408–435] (United Kingdom). For further discussion see Leane, 2004.

45 For example Waterford, 2005; see also Albrechtsen, 2005 (on the UK *Human Rights Act 1998* (UK)).

46 The Acting Chief Executive of the Department of Justice and Community Safety, Elizabeth Kelly (2005), has argued that release of the advice of the Human Rights Unit would detract from the creation of a human rights dialogue within government by making agencies reluctant to seek legal opinions on human rights matters.

been some signs of interest in governmental circles in South Australia, Tasmania and Western Australia. Given the strength of the 'States' rights' objections to an Australian bill of rights over the last century (Charlesworth, 2002, pp. 35–6), there is some irony in the fact that the Australian States and Territories now are leading the Commonwealth in this area. In April 2005 the Victorian government established an expert committee to develop proposals for a statutory bill of rights, chaired by Professor George Williams. The 'statement of intent' adopted by the Victorian government to guide the work of the committee closely tracked the features of the ACT *Human Rights Act*. Indeed, the current ACT model may act in this sense to freeze Australian political imaginations and constrain the development of broader models of bills of rights. The ACT *Human Rights Act* itself is unlikely to remain static, however, with the ACT government now preparing the first major review of the legislation. The Chief Minister has indicated interest in amending the legislation to include at least some economic, social and cultural rights and the ACT *Human Rights Act* may thus continue to unsettle Australian legal traditions.

References

Albrechtsen, J. (2005), 'Bill of rights full of risks', *The Australian*, 10 August 2005, p. 12.

Australian Associated Press (AAP) (2004), 'Howard Attacks ACT Gay Adoption Law', *The Sydney Morning Herald*, 8 March 2004.

Australian Capital Territory (ACT), Attorney-General's Department (1993), *Issues Paper on an ACT Bill of Rights* (Canberra: Attorney-General's Department).

ACT, Attorney-General's Department (1994), *A Bill of Rights for the ACT: Record of Proceedings 7 May 1994* (Canberra: Attorney-General's Department).

ACT, ACT Bill of Rights Consultative Committee (2003), *Towards an ACT Human Rights Act* (Canberra: Publishing Services).

ACT, Department of Justice and Community Safety (2004), *Human Rights Act 2004: A Plain English Guide* (Canberra: Bill of Rights Unit), available at <http://www.jcs.act.gov.au/humanrightsact/Publications/ PlainEnglishGuide.doc>.

ACT, ACT Human Rights Office (2005), Human Rights Audit of Quamby Youth Detention Centre (Canberra: Human Rights Office), available at <http://www.hro.act.gov.au/gems/ Quamby%20Audit-final%2030%20June%202005.pdf>.

Bayne, P. (2005a), 'The *Human Rights Act* 2004 (ACT): Developments in 2004', *Canberra Law Review*, **8:** 135.

—— (2005b), 'Pre-enactment dialogue about proposed laws under the influence of the *Human Rights Act 2004* (ACT)', paper presented at a conference on 'Assessing the First Year of the ACT Human Rights Act', 29 June 2005, available at <http://cigj.anu.edu.au/events/ACTBill05.php>.

Campbell, R (2004), 'Libs to seek change to Bill of Rights', *Canberra Times,* 1 March 2004, p. 2

Charlesworth, H. (2002), *Writing in Rights* (Sydney: University of New South Wales Press).

—— (2004), 'Lost in Translation? What Rights are Covered in the ACT *Human Rights Act*?', paper delivered at a conference on Australia's First Bill of Rights, Canberra, 1 July 2004, available at <http://www.gtcentre.unsw.edu.au/Paper-Charlesworth.doc>.

—— (2005), 'Human Rights and Statutory Interpretation', in Corcoran S. and Bottomley S. eds, *Interpreting Statutes* (Sydney: Federation Press).

Connolly, T. (2005), 'Practising Criminal Law under the *Human Rights Act* – No Rogue's Charter', paper delivered at the Conference of Australian Prosecutors, Canberra, 14 July 2005.

Creyke, R. (2006), 'The Performance of Administrative Law in Protecting Rights', in Campbell, T., Goldsworthy, J. and Stone, A., *Protecting Rights Without a Bill of Rights: Institutional Performance and Reform in Australia* (Aldershot: Ashgate), ch. 4.

Debeljak, J. (2004), 'The *Human Rights Act* 2004 (ACT): A Significant, Yet Incomplete, Step Toward the Domestic Protection and Promotion of Human Rights', *Public Law Review*, **15**: 169.

Evans, C. (2005), 'Human Rights Act and Administrative Law Talk', paper presented at a conference on 'Assessing the First Year of the ACT Human Rights Act', 29 June 2005, available at http://cigj.anu.edu.au/events/ ACTBill05.php

Feldman, D. (2002), 'Parliamentary Scrutiny of Legislation and Human Rights', *Public Law*: 323.

Grundy, P., Oakes, B., Reeder, L., and Wettenhall, R. (eds) (1996), *Reluctant Democrats: The Transition to Self-Government in the ACT* (Fyshwick, ACT: The Federal Capital Press of Australia).

Kelly, E. (2005), 'Government in the ACT: A Human Rights Dialogue', paper presented at a conference on 'Assessing the First Year of the ACT Human Rights Act', 29 June 2005, available at <http://cigj.anu.edu.au/events/ ACTBill05.php>.

Klug, F. (2000), *Values for a Godless Age: The Story of the United Kingdom's New Bill of Rights* (London: Penguin Books).

Kostakidis-Lianos, L. and Williams, G. (2005), 'Bill of Responsibilities: Is One Needed to Counter the "Excesses" of the ACT *Human Rights Act 2004*?', *Alternative Law Journal*, **30** (2): 58.

Leane, G. (2004), 'Enacting Bills of Rights: Canada and the Curious Case of New Zealand's "Thin" Democracy', *Human Rights Quarterly*, **26**: 152.

McCoy, G. (2005), 'Sibylline Observations: The Human Rights Act 2004 (ACT)', paper presented at a conference on 'Assessing the First Year of the ACT Human Rights Act', 29 June 2005, available at <http://cigj.anu.edu.au/events/ACTBill05.php>.

McDonald, L. (2004), 'New directions in the Australian bill of rights debate', *Public Law*: 22.

McKinnon, G. (2005), 'The ACT Human Rights Act 2004 – The First Year', paper presented at a conference on 'Assessing the First Year of the ACT Human Rights Act', 29 June 2005, available at <http://cigj.anu.edu.au/events/ACTBill05.php>.

Morris, S. (2004), 'Howard Axe Hangs over ACT's Landmark Bill of Rights', *The Australian*, 3 March 2004, p. 3.

Refshauge, R. (2005), 'The *Human Rights Act 2004* and the Criminal Law', paper presented at a conference on 'Assessing the First Year of the ACT Human Rights Act', June 29 2005, available at <http://cigj.anu.edu.au/events/ACTBill05.php>.

Stefaniak, B. (2002), 'Our laws are enough', *Canberra Times*, 25 April 2002.

Spry, M. (2004), 'ACT's Human Rights Bill Cannot Achieve Its Purpose', *Canberra Times*, 3 February 2004.

Waterford, J. (2005), 'Bills that let judges make laws', *Canberra Times*, 11 June 2005.

Chapter 13

An Australian Rights Council

George Winterton[1]

A Bill of Rights?

Australians have long debated the adoption of a bill of rights, both at Commonwealth and State level. As the report of the New South Wales Legislative Council's Standing Committee on Law and Justice demonstrated, there is broad agreement that greater attention ought to be given to the compatibility of Australian (Commonwealth, State and Territory) law with fundamental principles of human and civil rights and freedoms recognized by the common law and international human rights instruments (treaties and declarations) (NSW Legislative Council Standing Committee on Law and Justice, 2001, especially ch. 5; ACT Bill of Rights Consultative Committee, 2003, ch. 2). The common law is subject to legislation; so while its principles can be employed by judges to protect rights and endeavour to interpret legislation compatibly with the common law (including international human rights principles incorporated therein)[2] (see also Doyle and Wells, 1999, pp. 17–61, 63–65, 70–74; Joseph, 2002, pp. 477–78), the common law offers no protection against unambiguous legislation which trenches upon fundamental rights.[3] Hence, it would be valuable to have some standard – some principles enjoying broad support (if not a consensus) – against which to evaluate legislation, or at least proposed legislation, and to educate the community as to appropriate standards of law and government.

The difficulty is that there is a wide disparity of views as to how such a desirable objective can be achieved; indeed, whether it can be without introducing a detriment which, for many, outweighs the benefits, namely an imperial, or at least 'politicized', judiciary. A constitutional bill of rights introduced into the *Commonwealth Constitution* through s. 128 would obviously offer the greatest protection of rights and freedoms but, unless it resulted merely in a judicial declaration of 'incompatibility',[4] the difficulty of amending such a bill of rights once introduced could eventually lead to inflexibility in public policy, possible obsolescence of rights, judicial imperialism,

---

1   Professor of Constitutional Law, University of Sydney. This paper is based upon 'An Australian Rights Council' (2001), *University of New South Wales Law Journal* **24**: 792.

2   See, e.g., *Coco* v *The Queen* (1994) 179 CLR 427; *Mabo* v *Queensland (No. 2)* (1992) 175 CLR 1, 42 (Brennan J, Mason CJ and McHugh J concurring).

3   See, e.g., *Al-Kateb* v *Godwin* (2004) 219 CLR 562.

4   Cf. *Human Rights Act 1998* (UK) s. 4; *Human Rights Act 2004* (ACT) s. 32.

and 'politicization' of the judicial appointment process even if it included provisions such as the Canadian 'override clause'.[5] Moreover, the prospects of securing referendum approval for the introduction of such a bill of rights are minimal in view of the inevitable controversy it would generate, regarding both what was included and what omitted.[6] One has only to contemplate the debates over rights to abortion, same-sex marriage and adoption, in-vitro fertilization (IVF) treatment, euthanasia, and to strike, or not join a union, as well as the acceptability of capital punishment, mandatory sentences and preventive detention, to see what an impossible 'can of worms' would be opened by such a proposal. Moreover, these are only current issues. The future is bound to raise controversies presently unforeseeable.

A statutory bill of rights at State or Territory level offers greater flexibility since it could be amended more easily, unless, of course, a State or Australian Capital Territory bill of rights was entrenched by a 'manner and form' provision.[7] A non-entrenched statutory bill of rights could be employed by the courts to interpret legislation.[8] It might also constrain the executive government and other public authorities,[9] and even private bodies (such as corporations) and individuals, perhaps even providing for damages for breach of a protected right.[10] But it could be avoided by inconsistent legislation, although it could possibly be protected by an interpretation provision which sought to ensure that inconsistent legislation must expressly declare that it is to operate notwithstanding the bill of rights (see Winterton, 1980, pp. 182–89, 190–91; but see footnote 7).

The Commonwealth could enact a statutory bill of rights to govern the conduct of Commonwealth and Territory executives and the interpretation of Commonwealth and Territory legislation, and it could possibly be 'entrenched' to the extent of requiring inconsistent legislation to provide expressly that it is to operate notwithstanding the bill of rights.[11] Such a statutory bill of rights could be enacted pursuant to

---

5   *Canadian Charter of Rights and Freedoms*, Part I of the *Constitution Act 1982*, s. 33.

6   Cf. the 30 per cent to 68 per cent referendum defeat of the rights proposal in 1988.

7   For the ACT, see *Australian Capital Territory (Self-Government) Act 1988* (Cth) s. 26. Since State legislation contravening a State bill of rights would probably not fall within the *Australia Act 1986* (Cth and UK) s. 6, it is doubtful since *Attorney-General (WA)* v *Marquet* (2003) 217 CLR 545, [80] (but see also [68]) per Gleeson CJ, Gummow, Hayne and Heydon JJ, [215]–[216] per Kirby J whether a State bill of rights could be validly entrenched. See Twomey, 2004a, pp. 184–86; Twomey, 2004b, pp. 293–98.

8   See, e.g., *Human Rights Act 1998* (UK) s. 3; *New Zealand Bill of Rights Act 1990* (NZ) s. 6; *Human Rights Act 2004* (ACT) s. 30.

9   See, e.g., *Human Rights Act 1998* (UK) s. 6; *New Zealand Bill of Rights Act 1990* (NZ) s. 3. The ACT *Human Rights Act 2004* does not include such a provision, contrary to the ACT Bill of Rights Consultative Committee's recommendation (2003, para [4.53]; Draft Human Rights Bill cl. 6 (Appendix 4, p. 5)). The *Human Rights Act 2004* (ACT) applies only to Acts, regulations and bills.

10 See *Simpson* v *Attorney-General* [1994] 3 NZLR 667 (CA) (*Baigent's Case*).

11 See Winterton, 1980, pp. 182–89, 190–91, discussing (inter alia) *R* v *Drybones* [1970] SCR 282. But cf. *Thoburn* v *Sunderland City Council* [2003] QB 151 (QBD), 184 [59] per

ss. 51(xxxix) and 122 of the *Constitution*. However, if a Commonwealth bill of rights were to apply to the States and/or private corporations and individuals, it would need to rest on other powers, especially the 'external affairs' power (s. 51(xxix)), which would require that the provisions of the bill of rights complied with the provisions of an international treaty ratified by Australia. This would exclude a bill of rights modelled on the *Canadian Charter of Rights and Freedoms 1982* or the *European Convention for the Protection of Human Rights and Fundamental Freedoms*,[12] which are generally considered preferable to the *International Covenant on Civil and Political Rights* (ICCPR),[13] which the Commonwealth could implement under its 'external affairs' power. A Commonwealth bill of rights which applied to State legislation[14] would render inconsistent State legislation inoperative pursuant to s. 109 of the Constitution. So far as the States were concerned, it would therefore operate similarly to a constitutionally entrenched bill of rights.

Non-judicial Enforcement

The constitutional and statutory bills of rights considered above would probably be interpreted and enforced by the courts, although the bill of rights could limit the degree to which the courts were involved subject, of course, to constitutional limitations, such as the requirement that the judicial power of the Commonwealth be vested only in courts envisaged by Chapter III of the *Commonwealth Constitution*. However, judicial enforcement is the principal hurdle to adopting a bill of rights, assuming, of course, that agreement on its content could be achieved. As Sir Gerard Brennan has noted, a bill of rights 'purports to convert political into legal debate, and to judicialize questions of politics and morality' (Brennan, 1999, p. 458). Consequently, in interpreting its provisions, courts must 'make political, social and ethical decisions affecting the whole community' (Brennan, 1999, p. 461).

The theoretical and practical appropriateness of leaving such issues to the judiciary is, of course, one of the most debated subjects of constitutional jurisprudence. For present purposes, it suffices to note that many believe that the

---

Laws LJ holding that the United Kingdom Parliament could not validly stipulate against implied amendment or repeal of legislation, although the courts, through the common law, can effectively achieve that result by recognizing 'constitutional statutes' which cannot be impliedly amended or repealed; any amendment or repeal of such statutes must essentially be by express words: at 186–87 [63], 189 [69]. Crane J concurred.

12 Opened for signature 4 November 1950, 213 UNTS 221 (entered into force 3 September 1953).

13 Opened for signature 16 December 1966, 999 UNTS 171 (entered into force 23 March 1976).

14 For example, the draft statutory Bill of Rights circulated by the Hawke Government (Attorney-General Senator Gareth Evans) in 1984, as contrasted with the Australian Bill of Rights Bill 1985 (Cth) (introduced by Attorney-General Lionel Bowen), which would have applied only to Commonwealth legislation. See NSW Legislative Council Standing Committee on Law and Justice, 2001, paras [3.10]–[3.11].

judiciary is an unsuitable repository for such ethical and political questions. Among the main disadvantages in leaving enforcement of a bill of rights to the courts, three of significance for the present writer may be noted. First, and most important, is that application of a bill of rights frequently requires balancing of competing rights and freedoms: the mother's freedom to abort her foetus versus any right to life of the foetus and the father's right to parenthood; the defendant's right to a fair trial versus the media's freedom of expression; the right to free exercise of religion versus the right to equality or freedom from discrimination; freedom from establishment of religion versus freedom of expression, and so on. The balancing of these rights and freedoms can rarely adequately be achieved merely by neutral principled reasoning, which is what an ideal judiciary offers. It requires the input of community values, policy and public opinion; in other words, social, economic, political (in the broad, governmental sense) and ethical considerations, which should be tailored to each application, and may vary over time. It may, for example, be preferable to resolve issues such as the appropriateness of reverse discrimination differently – even inconsistently – for different groups, different situations and different times. The political process subject, ultimately, to the ballot box is a more appropriate mechanism for resolving such dilemmas than the blunt neutrality and consistency of (ideal) courts, essentially because it is more 'democratic' in the sense that ultimate decision-making responsibility rests with the people (the ultimate constitutional sovereigns) and/or their elected representatives. (Leaving these issues to non-ideal courts which implement their own views on such 'legal' issues is, of course, even less justifiable.) Secondly, judicial enforcement of a bill of rights inevitably leads to avoidance of responsibility and 'buck-passing' by the political branches. This is undesirable on many grounds including, in addition to that noted above, that judicial enforcement is costly; may be long delayed, with much damage caused before redress is achieved; is retrospective, thereby creating uncertainty and upsetting existing rights and expectations (Goldsworthy, 2001, pp. 74–75, 78); and many issues are non-justiciable or simply cannot come before the courts. Hence, it is important that the political branches not shirk their responsibility to assess the compatibility of their actions with fundamental human rights norms. Thirdly, it is certainly arguable that 'an increased politicization of the Judiciary, and particularly the judicial appointment process, is an inevitable consequence of the introduction of a bill of rights' (NSW Legislative Council Standing Committee on Law and Justice, 2001, p. xiii). These concerns are reduced if the weaker United Kingdom or New Zealand versions of a bill of rights (which do not authorize the invalidation of legislation), as contrasted with the Canadian or United States models, are adopted, but they are not completely avoided (Allan, 2002, p. 174 (n. 37); Campbell, 2001). A New Zealand critic of its bill of rights jurisprudence has concluded that '[t]here are few differences between what judges *could accomplish* (in the way of "giving life" to "fundamental rights") when operating a New Zealand-type Bill of Rights Act and what they *do accomplish* when operating constitutionalized and entrenched models [emphasis in original]' (Allan, 2001, p. 390).

It has, accordingly, been suggested that 'Parliament [should] become a more effective guardian of human rights rather than handing over this role' to the courts (NSW Legislative Council Standing Committee on Law and Justice, 2001, p. xiv). The New South Wales Legislative Council's Standing Committee on Law and Justice proposed a parliamentary joint House committee, modelled on the Senate's Scrutiny of Bills Committee, to examine draft legislation prior to enactment for compliance with human rights standards, such as the *International Covenant on Civil and Political Rights* (NSW Legislative Council Standing Committee on Law and Justice, 2001, ch. 8). However, while obviously preferable to the complete absence of pre-enactment review, such committees suffer from considerable constraints: time pressure; lack of expertise, only partly ameliorated by the employment of external experts; the difficulty of building up a coherent body of jurisprudence over time; and the ultimate subjection of its work to the vicissitudes of politics. The Senate's Standing Committee on the Scrutiny of Bills, for example, 'expresses no concluded view on whether any provisions offend against its principles or should be amended'.[15] Any proposed amendment of a bill pursuant to the Committee's report must be moved by a Senator, and adverse comments in Committee reports have been ignored for political reasons. Such committees exist in the Senate and in Victoria, Queensland, New South Wales (since 2002) and the Australian Capital Territory. A recent exemplar is the United Kingdom's Joint Committee on Human Rights, established in January 2001 (see Lester, 2002; Feldman, 2002; Feldman, 2004), which one member described as a 'parliamentary watchdog and bloodhound' (Lester, 2002, p. 433; see likewise Lester, 2002, p. 451 ('public watchdog')).

However, parliamentary review of proposed legislation is not an effective substitute for judicial enforcement. This is illustrated by the saga of clause 10 of the Asylum and Immigration (Treatment of Claimants, etc.) Bill 2003/4 (UK), in which an 'ouster' or 'privative' clause would have denied judicial review or appeal to the courts from decisions of a new Asylum and Immigration Tribunal (see Oliver, 2004). As Dawn Oliver relates, the House of Commons passed the Bill notwithstanding strong criticism of the clause by, *inter alia*, the Joint Committee on Human Rights and the House of Commons Constitutional Affairs Committee (pp. 49, 51 respectively). The Government ultimately withdrew the clause 'because of the lack of a government majority in the [House of Lords], concern about the severe implications for vulnerable people ... and the strong line taken by the lawyers in the House [of Commons?]' (p. 52). She concludes that parliamentary scrutiny of bills provides a 'rather fragile protection against the passage of unconstitutional laws. ... It is obvious that purely intra-governmental or intra-parliamentary scrutiny cannot secure due protection of constitutional principles and values' (pp. 52, 54). Consequently, parliamentary scrutiny of proposed legislation will not halt the continuing pressure to follow Canada, New Zealand and now the United Kingdom

---

15 Evans, 2004, p. 358. Similarly, the United Kingdom's Joint Committee on Human Rights: Feldman, 2002, p. 332.

by introducing a bill of rights enforced by the courts.[16] If Australian Parliaments are unwilling to reduce their adherence to parliamentary supremacy, they may in time find themselves overwhelmed by public pressure for a judicially enforceable bill of rights. Whether or not attributable to public pressure, the Australian Capital Territory has proceeded down this path, Victoria plans to do so in 2006 and even New South Wales is beginning to stir in this direction.[17]

An Australian Rights Council

Sir Gerard Brennan has remarked that '[i]f the exercise of political power is to be subjected to a Bill of Rights, there is no institution to which the administration of those provisions can be entrusted save the Courts' (Brennan, 1999, p. 455). But is that necessarily so?

A parliamentary committee does not adequately balance parliamentary supremacy with judicial enforcement of rights; the balance falls too heavily on Parliament's side. However, an alternative compromise is possible. It would combine the following elements: pre-enactment review by an independent, but non-judicial, expert body able to build up a substantial body of human rights jurisprudence, whose reports could not be ignored, either as a matter of law (in the States) or because of the body's prestige (in the Commonwealth). Such a body, here called a 'Rights Council' and modelled loosely on the French *Conseil Constitutionnel*,[18] would protect rights and freedoms through pre-enactment, abstract, quasi-judicial review. Because the constitutional position differs between the Commonwealth and the States, the proposed operation of the Rights Council in the States will be described first.

The Rights Council would ideally comprise five members who should be former judges of an Australian superior court or acknowledged experts in constitutional or human rights law. Serving members of Parliament, public servants and judges would be ineligible. To ensure their acceptability to both sides of politics, Rights Council members should be elected by a two-thirds majority of each House of Parliament or, perhaps, a two-thirds majority at a joint sitting of both Houses in bicameral legislatures. (Germany provides a precedent, since judges of its Federal Constitutional Court are

---

16 See *Canadian Bill of Rights 1960* (Can); *Canadian Charter of Rights and Freedoms*, Part I of the *Constitution Act 1982*; *New Zealand Bill of Rights Act 1990* (NZ); *Human Rights Act 1998* (UK).

17 See *Human Rights Act 2004* (ACT). For comments on the Act, see Debeljak, 2004; Williams, July 2004; Williams, March 2004; Campbell, 2004. For a more sceptical comment, see Winterton, 2004.

18 The *Conseil Constitutionnel* comprises nine members: three appointed by the President of the Republic, three by the President of the National Assembly, and three by the President of the Senate. The President of the *Conseil* is appointed by the President of the Republic. Former Presidents of the Republic are also *ex officio* life members of the *Conseil*. Other members serve for a non-renewable nine-year term. See *Constitution of France* art. 56. Members of the *Conseil* are ineligible to serve as Ministers or members of Parliament: art. 57.

elected by two-thirds parliamentary majorities.)[19] The members of the Rights Council should elect their chair from among its members. A new Rights Council should be elected for each Parliament, unless a national Rights Council is established. Rather than each of the nine Australian jurisdictions having its own Rights Council with possibly divergent interpretations but no superior authority (like the High Court of Australia in judicial matters) able to impose uniformity and consistency, it would be highly desirable for the Commonwealth and the States and Territories to pool their legal resources and jointly establish one national Australian Rights Council comprising five members, two elected by the Commonwealth Parliament (by a two-thirds majority at a joint sitting of both Houses) and three chosen by the State and Territory Parliaments. Since both sides of politics will usually enjoy majorities in various Houses of those Parliaments, election by simple majorities should suffice to necessitate bipartisanship, especially as securing two-thirds majorities in eight Parliaments with thirteen legislative Houses may prove unwieldy. It is envisaged that the six States and two self-governing Territories would agree upon three suitable members. A national Rights Council would, of course, require a specified term of office, say five years, with a member's term perhaps renewable only once. Compulsory retirement at the age of 75 would be appropriate.

The Rights Council would examine the compatibility of proposed legislation with the relevant bill of rights. However, the establishment of a Rights Council is not conditional on the enactment of a bill of rights, since the Council could be empowered to examine proposed legislation by reference to international human rights instruments, whether or not legislatively incorporated into Australian domestic law. The Council would report on the compatibility of the proposed legislation after a quasi-judicial hearing in which arguments for and against were addressed to the Council, preferably by legal counsel (although others should also be entitled to address the Council), and the Council should also be empowered to suggest possible amendments to ensure compatibility with the bill of rights (or international instruments). Ideally, the Rights Council would examine bills just prior to enactment, when parliamentary consideration had concluded. Hence, the appropriate point would be after the bill's Third Reading in the second House (in bicameral Parliaments). The Council should, likewise, examine any bills amended pursuant to an earlier Rights Council report. The operation of a Rights Council is, of course, entirely compatible with a complementary parliamentary committee, such as the Senate's Scrutiny of Bills Committee or the New South Wales Legislation Review Committee. Indeed, it would be desirable for bills reaching the Rights Council to have received the fullest

---

19 The Federal Constitutional Court (FCC) comprises two 'Senates', each of eight judges. Half the members of each Senate are elected by each legislative House. The Lower House (*Bundestag*) elects FCC judges by a two-thirds majority of its 12 member Judicial Selection Committee, which is elected by proportional representation; the Upper House (*Bundesrat*) elects FCC judges by a two-thirds majority vote: *Federal Constitutional Court Act 1951* (Germany) arts 2, 5–7 (as amended): available at <http://www.iuscomp.org/gla/>.

possible consideration both as to policy and compliance with human rights and freedoms.[20]

The role of the Rights Council would be strongly influenced by the provision made for referring proposed legislation for evaluation. The effectiveness of the *Conseil Constitutionnel*, for example, was greatly augmented when sixty members of either legislative House (the National Assembly and the Senate) were empowered to refer legislation to it (prior to promulgation) in 1974. This power had previously lain only in the President of the Republic, the Prime Minister and the Presidents of the two Houses.[21] (The French National Assembly presently comprises 577 members and the French Senate 331 members.) It seems desirable to allow very liberal standing to refer bills to the Rights Council. Hence, the power could be given to every member of the relevant Parliament. If this be considered too liberal, following the French example the power could be given to the Prime Minister, Premier or Chief Minister, the Speaker of the Lower House, the President of the Senate or Legislative Council and, say, five members of a legislative House. This would ensure that the Opposition or a substantial third party would be able to refer bills, especially if the reference were supported by some Independent members of Parliament. Non-members of Parliament who would be directly affected by the proposed legislation and would have standing to challenge it in court (after enactment) were the bill of rights (or the international instruments) judicially enforceable ought, in principle, to be empowered to refer a proposed law to the Rights Council. However, if this be considered inappropriate because it would tend to make the Rights Council too analogous to a court (and thus effectively move it from the legislative to the judicial branch of government, at least in the States), interested non-members of Parliament should, at least, be empowered to intervene in hearings of the Council, subject to obtaining the Council's leave. Provision might also be made for those analogous to *amici curiae* (including non-governmental organizations such as Amnesty International, the International Commission of Jurists or the Australian Press Council) to assist the Rights Council, subject to obtaining its leave to do so.

The Council's pre-enactment (or 'preventive')[22] review would suffer from a disadvantage shared by advisory opinions: the abstract nature in which the legal issues are presented, lacking the advantages of the concrete factual setting and focused adversarial commitment provided by an actual application of legislation. But there are commensurate advantages, including avoidance of the disruption caused by retrospective invalidation of legislation[23] which may have operated for many years, and avoidance of social, economic and political factors which can

---

20 For Canadian and United States support for parliamentary examination of bills' compatibility with constitutional rights requirements, see Hiebert, 2003; Tushnet, 2003, pp. 214–19, 223ff.

21 *Constitution of France* art 61.

22 See Brewer-Carias, 1989, p. 251, discussing the *Conseil Constitutionnel*.

23 Cf. *Ha v New South Wales* (1997) 189 CLR 465, 503–04, 515 regarding prospective overruling.

influence courts when examining the application of legislation in a concrete setting, as is demonstrated by United States Bill of Rights jurisprudence (but cf. Waldron, 2002, pp. 100–01). Moreover, a quasi-judicial body such as the Rights Council could be informed by a wider range of information sources than a court.

Decisions of the *Conseil Constitutionnel* are binding; legislation declared unconstitutional cannot be promulgated.[24] The States would have the power to confer similar power on the Rights Council, but that would effectively bring many of the disadvantages of a judicially enforceable bill of rights, except that the State's actual judiciary would not be involved. The Rights Council would, in effect, operate analogously to a European constitutional court, except that its review function would be abstract (that is, it would not determine actual 'cases or controversies' or 'matters')[25] and would be confined to review pre-enactment. However, the French position should not be followed in this respect. If decisions of the Rights Council were binding, the balance would fall too heavily against parliamentary supremacy. Instead, adapting the *United States Constitution*'s provision regarding congressional overriding of the presidential veto of a bill, Parliament should be empowered to override adverse reports of the Rights Council and enact provisions declared incompatible with the bill of rights (or international human rights instruments) provided a two-thirds majority in each House agrees.[26] This would leave the ultimate decision to Parliament, but the requirement of a supermajority would help to protect minorities and avoid partisan measures. One hopes, with Alexander Hamilton, that 'it will not often happen, that improper views will govern so large a proportion as two-thirds of both branches of the Legislature at the same time' (Cooke, 1961, p. 498 (no. 73)).

---

24 *Constitution of France* art. 62.

25 Employing, respectively, United States and Australian terminology in art. III and ch. III of their respective Constitutions.

26 Cf. *United States Constitution* art. I § 7(3) (overriding presidential veto). The 'override' provision of the *Canadian Charter of Rights and Freedoms* (s. 33) is, of course, also somewhat analogous, though it does not apply to all *Charter* rights, does not require a parliamentary supermajority and, of course, would not avoid many of the vicissitudes of judicial enforcement, including the 'judicialization' of social and political issues and the 'politicization' of the judiciary unless a 'notwithstanding' clause were inserted in virtually every bill. Unlike s. 33, Parliament could not pre-empt an adverse decision; it could only respond to a prior decision by the Rights Council. In fact, s. 33 has rarely been invoked. The requirement of a supermajority in the Rights Council proposal and the Rights Council's likely weaker legitimacy and prestige than that of the courts should make the Rights Council proposal's override mechanism more politically acceptable than that in s. 33 of the *Charter*, though the latter was tarnished by Quebec's employment of it to protect francophone supremacy. For analysis of s. 33, see Kahana, 2002; Leeson, 2000. Australian discussion includes Goldsworthy, 2003, especially pp. 274–78 ('The Desuetude of Section 33'); Williams, 2003, pp. 257–58. George Williams advocated inclusion of such a clause in an Australian bill of rights (at 257). See also Victoria Human Rights Consultation Committee, 2005, [4.4.2] (chaired by George Williams). Charter of Human Rights and Responsibilities Bill 2006 (Vic) clause 31.

The Commonwealth Parliament should also implement the Rights Council proposal, preferably as a component of a national Australian Rights Council. The Commonwealth Parliament could provide for pre-enactment review of bills pursuant to ss. 50(ii) and 51(xxxix) of the *Constitution*, provided that the Rights Council's role preceded passage by the relevant House. But the Commonwealth Parliament (unlike State Parliaments) could not (without a constitutional amendment pursuant to s. 128) require bills which had been passed by both Houses (or by a joint sitting under s. 57 of the *Constitution*) to be approved by the Rights Council prior to enactment, since that would contravene s. 1 of the *Constitution* which vests the legislative power of the Commonwealth in a Parliament comprising the Queen, the Senate and the House of Representatives. Unlike the States, the Commonwealth could not make submission of bills for the Royal Assent conditional upon the prior approval of the Rights Council (see Winterton, 1980, p. 192). Moreover, again unlike the States, the Commonwealth Parliament, or either of its Houses, could not require a bill (for example, one which the Rights Council had held to be incompatible with the bill of rights or human rights standards) to be passed by a supermajority because ss. 23 and 40 of the *Constitution* provide that 'questions arising' in the Senate and House of Representatives, respectively, 'shall be determined by a majority of votes', 'majority' here meaning a simple majority (see Winterton, 1980, p. 191). Hence, without a constitutional amendment, a Rights Council could be given no greater than a merely advisory role in regard to Commonwealth bills.[27] However, such a function would nevertheless be a valuable one; a negative report by an Australian Rights Council comprising several retired High Court justices, for example, would be politically difficult to ignore. Its reports would clearly have greater weight than those of a committee of parliamentarians, even if assisted by external expert advice.

Conclusion

The Rights Council proposal is worthy of implementation, at least initially in one Australian jurisdiction, even if only on a trial basis subject to a 'sunset clause'. It need not await the enactment of even a merely statutory bill of rights, since the Rights Council could be empowered to determine the compatibility of proposed legislation with international human rights treaties or other instruments. The Rights Council could operate in conjunction with a committee of parliamentarians. Indeed,

---

27 A remote precedent of sorts already exists in the power of the Human Rights and Equal Opportunity Commission to examine proposed enactments, when requested to do so by the Minister, to ascertain whether they 'would be inconsistent with or contrary to any human right', and to report thereon to the Minister: *Human Rights and Equal Opportunity Commission Act 1986* (Cth) s. 11(1)(e). See, generally, Kinley, 1999, p. 253, referring also to the *Human Rights Act 1993* (NZ) s. 5(h)(iii). A closer analogue is Major John Cartwright's 1823 proposal for a 'Council of Elders' to 'advise Parliament as to the constitutionality of proposed legislation, with no power either to reject or invalidate it': see Goldsworthy, 1999, p. 219. Cartwright's proposal is outlined in Weston, 1965, pp. 225–26.

it is desirable that it should, but experience suggests that the latter alone is an insufficient protector of rights and freedoms. The establishment of a Rights Council would constitute a minimal first step towards extra-parliamentary[28] protection of the broad range of rights and freedoms usually protected by bills of rights. Indeed, if implemented in the States as suggested here (that is, with its decisions capable of barring the progress of proposed legislation, subject to being overridden by a parliamentary supermajority), the Rights Council would be more effective in protecting rights and freedoms than a judicial declaration of 'incompatibility' which Parliament and the Government can ignore with legal (albeit not political) impunity.[29] In short, the Rights Council offers the advantage of utilizing a bill of rights (or international human rights instruments) as a criterion for evaluating (proposed) legislation without succumbing to the disadvantages inherent in judicial enforcement. It offers many of the benefits of judicial enforcement – including independent expert evaluation of legislation in light of prescribed human rights standards and the building up of a coherent body of indigenous jurisprudence to guide legislatures and other governmental bodies – without the detriments resulting from judicial enforcement, including its retrospectivity, the additional cost and increase in litigation (see Brennan, 1999, pp. 459–60), the likely 'politicization' of the judiciary and the judicial appointment process and, above all, the removal from the people and their elected representatives, who are ultimately accountable to their electors, of ultimate control (subject, theoretically, to a constitutional amendment) over vital issues of social, political and ethical policy (see for example Allan, 2003, pp. 189–90). Moreover, Parliament's power to override the Rights Council's determinations, even in the stronger form recommended for the States, leaves the ultimate decision regarding the enactment of legislation in the 'democratic' hands of Parliament.

In addition to protecting rights and freedoms, the Rights Council could fulfil a valuable function as auditor of the legislature's compliance with human rights precepts. Instead of relying on a few notorious breaches of human rights (see for example NSW Legislative Council Standing Committee on Law and Justice, 2001, para. [5.17]) and impressionistic assessment of the common law's effectiveness as a protector of rights and freedoms (cf. paras [5.23]–[5.31]), the legislature's record of compliance with the carefully reasoned reports of the Rights Council would provide concrete evidence on which to base an informed assessment as to the necessity of enacting a judicially enforceable bill of rights.

---

28 However, from the separation-of-powers perspective, the Rights Council would be an organ located within the legislative branch of government.

29 The Rights Council proposal is, of course, not inherently inconsistent with a judicially enforceable bill of rights, but the combination of both methods of enforcing a bill of rights would be costly, unwieldy, and could create difficulty if the Rights Council's jurisprudence diverged from that of the courts. Realistically, the Rights Council proposal would commend itself principally to those opposed to judicial enforcement. Likewise, it would seem inappropriate for the Rights Council to rule on proposed legislation's compliance with constitutional limitations.

References

Allan, J. (2001), 'The Effect of a Statutory Bill of Rights where Parliament is Sovereign: The Lesson from New Zealand', in Campbell, T., Ewing, K.D. and Tomkins, A. (eds), *Sceptical Essays on Human Rights* (Oxford: Oxford University Press), p. 375.

—— (2002), *Sympathy and Antipathy: Essays Legal and Philosophical* (Aldershot: Ashgate).

—— (2003), 'A Defence of the Status Quo', in Campbell, T., Goldsworthy, J. and Stone, A. (eds), *Protecting Human Rights: Instruments and Institutions* (Oxford: Oxford University Press), p. 175.

Australian Capital Territory Bill of Rights Consultative Committee (May 2003), *Towards an ACT Human Rights Act* (Canberra).

Brennan, Sir G. (1999), 'The Impact of a Bill of Rights on the Role of the Judiciary: An Australian Perspective', in Alston, P. (ed.), *Promoting Human Rights through Bills of Rights: Comparative Perspectives* (Oxford: Oxford University Press), p. 454.

Brewer-Carias, A.R. (1989), *Judicial Review in Comparative Law* (Cambridge: Cambridge University Press).

Campbell, R., 'Top Judge Applauds ACT Bill of Rights', *Canberra Times*, 4 March 2004, p. 2.

Campbell, T. (2001), 'Incorporation through Interpretation', in Campbell, T., Ewing, K.D. and Tomkins, A. (eds), *Sceptical Essays on Human Rights* (Oxford: Oxford University Press), p. 79.

Cooke, J.E. (ed.) (1961), *The Federalist* (Middletown, Conn.: Wesleyan University Press).

Debeljak, J. (2004), 'The Human Rights Act 2004 (ACT): A Significant, Yet Incomplete, Step Toward the Domestic Protection and Promotion of Human Rights', *Public Law Review*, **15**: 169.

Doyle, J. and Wells, B. (1999), 'How Far Can the Common Law Go Towards Protecting Human Rights?', in Alston, P. (ed.), *Promoting Human Rights through Bills of Rights: Comparative Perspectives* (Oxford: Oxford University Press), p. 17.

Evans, H. (ed.) (2004), *Odgers' Australian Senate Practice*, 11th edn (Canberra: Australian Government Publishing Service for Department of the Senate).

Feldman, D. (2002), 'Parliamentary Scrutiny of Legislation and Human Rights', *Public Law*: 323.

—— (2004), 'The Impact of Human Rights on the UK Legislative Process', *Statute Law Review*, **25**: 91.

Goldsworthy, J. (1999), *The Sovereignty of Parliament: History and Philosophy* (Oxford: Clarendon Press).

—— (2001), 'Legislative Sovereignty and the Rule of Law', in Campbell, T., Ewing, K.D. and Tomkins, A. (eds), *Sceptical Essays on Human Rights* (Oxford: Oxford University Press), p. 61.

—— (2003), 'Judicial Review, Legislative Override, and Democracy', in Campbell, T., Goldsworthy, J. and Stone, A. (eds), *Protecting Human Rights: Instruments and Institutions* (Oxford: Oxford University Press), p. 263.

Hiebert, J.L. (2003), 'Parliament and Rights', in Campbell, T., Goldsworthy, J. and Stone, A. (eds), *Protecting Human Rights: Instruments and Institutions* (Oxford: Oxford University Press), pp. 231–46.

Joseph, P. (2002), 'The Demise of Ultra-Vires: A Reply to Christopher Forsyth and Linda Whittle', *Canterbury Law Review*, **8**: 463–79.

Kahana, T. (2002), 'Understanding the Notwithstanding Mechanism', *University of Toronto Law Journal*, **52**: 221.

Kinley, D. (1999), 'Human Rights Scrutiny in Parliament: Westminster Set to Leap Ahead', *Public Law Review*, **10**: 252.

Leeson, H. (2000), 'Section 33, The Notwithstanding Clause: A Paper Tiger?', *Choices*, **6** (4): 3.

Lester, A. (2002), 'Parliamentary Scrutiny of Legislation under the Human Rights Act 1998', *European Human Rights Law Review*: 432.

New South Wales Legislative Council Standing Committee on Law and Justice (October 2001), *Report No. 17: A NSW Bill of Rights* (Sydney).

Oliver, D. (2004), 'Constitutional Scrutiny of Executive Bills', *Macquarie Law Journal*, **4**: 33.

Tushnet, M. (2003), 'Non-judicial Review', in Campbell, T., Goldsworthy, J. and Stone, A. (eds), *Protecting Human Rights: Instruments and Institutions* (Oxford: Oxford University Press), pp. 213–29.

Twomey, A. (2004a), 'Manner and Form Limitations on the Power to Amend State Constitutions', *Public Law Review*, **15**: 182.

—— (2004b), *The Constitution of New South Wales* (Sydney: Federation Press).

Victoria Human Rights Committee (2005), *Report: Rights, Responsibilities and Respect*, (Melbourne).

Waldron, J. (2002), 'Eisgruber's House of Lords', *University of San Francisco Law Review*, **37**: 89.

Weston, C.C. (1965), *English Constitutional Theory and the House of Lords 1556–1832* (London: Routledge & Kegan Paul).

Williams, G. (2003), 'Constructing a Community-Based Bill of Rights', in Campbell, T., Goldsworthy, J. and Stone, A. (eds), *Protecting Human Rights: Instruments and Institutions* (Oxford: Oxford University Press), p. 247.

—— 'Finally, Australia's First Bill of Rights', *Australian Financial Review*, 12 March 2004, Weekend Review p. 4.

—— 'ACT Bill of Rights a Good Starting Point', *Australian Financial Review*, 2 July 2004, p 63.

Winterton, G. (1980), 'Can the Commonwealth Parliament Enact "Manner and Form" Legislation?', *Federal Law Review*, **11**: 167.

—— 'Rights Code Test', *Lawyers Weekly*, 30 July 2004, p. 11.

Chapter 14

Human Rights Strategies: An Australian Alternative

Tom Campbell[1]

The remarkable rise of human rights discourse and human rights institutions over the last fifty years (Bobbio, 1996; Loughlin, 2000, pp. 197–214) is under threat through a number of recent trends. One such threat derives from the selective intervention by militarily powerful nations in the affairs of sovereign states on the grounds (or pretext) that these rogue states are particularly heinous human rights violators (Moore, 1998; Ignatieff, 2001). Another threat is the increasing identification of the human rights that really matter with the economic policies and rhetoric of global economic powers to the neglect of alternative systems of social values (Held, 1989). A third threat to the standing of human rights, and the one with which this book is principally concerned, is the utilization of human rights discourse to promote the power of courts to override legislation on the basis of their interpretation of constitutionalized human rights: a form of juristocratic power that undermines that tradition of discursive electoral democracy which seeks to operationalize a commitment to the political and moral equality of all citizens within a polity (Tushnet, 1999). These three trends combine to damage the reputation of institutionalized 'human rights', particularly in the eyes of those people who combine a genuine concern for the wellbeing of the impoverished and oppressed peoples of the world with a belief in democratic mechanisms that manifest equal respect for all human beings.

Rights and Bills of Rights

The extent to which supporting human rights has come to be identified with championing court-centred bills of rights is reflected in the incomprehension that often greets the contention that there are human rights reasons for opposing bills of rights (Waldron, 1993). It is now a common assumption that a bill of rights, interpreted and applied by courts, is in itself an embodiment of human rights, so that, absent such a system of governance, a polity is, for that reason alone, defective in human rights terms. Thus a principal argument put forward by influential commentators

1 Professorial Fellow, Centre for Applied Philosophy and Public Ethics, Charles Sturt University, and Visiting Professor, School of Law, King's College London. Warm thanks are due to Dr Craig Taylor for his helpful comments on a draft of this chapter.

on the Australian human rights scene is that Australia is a human rights backwater because it does not have a bill of rights (Charlesworth, 2002, p. 14; Williams, 2004, pp. 17, 92).

Similar assumptions underlie the standard response to critics of US-style bills of rights to the effect that such critics are naïve about democracy (both in theory and practice) and about law and legal theory (which have moved far beyond the fairytale of legal formalism to a general acceptance of the inevitability of judicial law-making). Those who oppose judicial review through bills of rights are held to have a crude 'majoritarian' conception of democracy that ignores the problem of minorities (by which is meant oppressed not powerful minorities) (Dworkin, 1990), and to be simply uninformed about the fact that judges actually make law as a matter of daily practice (Charlesworth, 2002, pp. 71-74). Such dismissive reactions to human rights critiques of court-centred bills of rights underestimate both the deliberative developments in democratic theory that address the task of extending political participation in other ways (Barber, 1984; Fishkin, 1991; Habermas, 1996; Held, 1996; Bohman and Rehg, 1997; Uhr, 1998; Koh and Slye, 1999; Dryzek, 2000), and the painstaking work done to expound and defend systems of political theory and jurisprudence that can sustain in practice the distinction between law-making and law-application on which democracy and the rule of law depend (Schauer, 1991; Goldsworthy, 1997).

These tactics are, however, often rhetorically successful because they resonate with their audiences' (sometimes justified) contempt for politicians, and the (often-justified) admiration which many educated people, especially lawyers and law students, feel for high-profile activist judges who champion undoubtedly progressive causes. Given these predispositions, it is sailing against the wind in human rights waters to argue against the view that human rights are better served when judges rather than elected representatives determine what our basic rights and duties amount to in practice.

A further difficulty in persuading people that there must be better ways of promoting human rights than the transfer of substantial political power to judiciaries is that opposition to court-centred bills of rights is assumed to stem from the conservative assumption that human rights are currently adequately protected in Australia. The thesis that, in human rights terms, things are far from perfect but that the situation will be made worse overall by such constitutional changes is simply not heard. Many opponents to court-centred bills of rights are indeed complacent about Australia's currently disappointing human rights politics, but the human rights case against such bills of rights does not depend on this complacency.

In this context it is important that two lines of argument be developed. The first, which is stated rather than argued in this chapter, is the warning that human rights are diminished when we seek to cure democratic deficiencies by anti-democratic devices. This is a warning that could be accompanied by a reminder of the historically weak performance of courts in the protection of rights, and the achievements of democratic systems in implementing political rights, such as the universal right to vote, basic rights of association in the employment sphere, anti-discrimination legislation, and the fundamental social and economic rights provided for by the now at risk welfare states, all of which can be illustrated by identifying the human rights provisions that exist in contemporary Australian law (Kinley, 1998).

The second line of argument, which is the main focus of this chapter, is the articulation of alternative political and constitutional strategies for improving the human rights performance of democratic systems without resort to an enlargement of the law-making power of courts. This requires a constructive, imaginative and radical response which acknowledges the fact that electoral democracy, while itself an institutionalization of human rights, has its own human rights weaknesses, particularly where political debate and decision making either fail to reflect the views of the electorate, or the democratic process is captured by illegitimate self-preferences of statistical majorities or, more frequently, powerful minorities.

In developing this second theme, this chapter outlines why democracies require to be engaged with human rights, identifying the chief human rights problems of modern democracies and the deficiencies of currently fashionable human rights regimes, before going on to suggest ways these may be addressed by cultural and constitutional changes that build on the strengths of the Australian political tradition. One of these strengths is the relatively non-partisan role of parliamentary committees in a bicameral federal system, particularly the Senate Standing Committee for the Scrutiny of Bills, which examines draft legislation to see whether or not it conflicts with individual rights (Horrigan, 2003, pp. 247–51). The powers, membership and functions of this widely admired Committee could be developed to provide a strong parliamentary platform for the furtherance of human rights. A second strength is the comparatively good Australian record of human rights legislation, such as the *Racial Discrimination Act 1975* (Cth), the *Sex Discrimination Act 1984* (Cth) and the *Disability Discrimination Act 1992* (Cth). This is an important type of legislation that could be given heightened legal status above that of ordinary legislation by the assumption that human rights legislation takes priority over ordinary legislation in any apparent conflict between the two types of law. A third strength of the Australian polity is the historically significant popular support for human rights at home and abroad and for fair play generally. While some governments are (much) more aware than others of human rights, Australians generally are highly supportive of what they stand for, domestically and internationally. This ingrained rights awareness provides a basis for developing an Australian human rights regime that enjoys the sort of wide popular support that cannot easily be ignored by governments.

Drawing on and developing these existing human rights strengths, I propose that Australia adopt a 'democratic bill of rights'. This declaration would affirm the basic interests that set down social, political and economic goals, against which the performance of governments and other organizations could be assessed. The mere existence of such a bill would have educational and cultural advantages, but its political effectiveness would depend on the institutional mechanisms that are needed to enlist the support of the human rights strengths of the Australian polity. In order to keep human rights on the political agenda and generate the political will to implement a bill of rights, ways would have to be found to make it more difficult for governments to sideline the human rights issues of the day. The mechanisms for implementing such a bill would have to embed in the political system ways of encouraging collective responsibility for articulating and achieving human rights objectives.

From the range of Australian institutions that currently concern themselves with human rights (see Kinley and Martin, 2004), I focus here on the idea of developing the role and powers of the Parliament in promoting human rights protection. In particular, it is suggested that a Joint Parliamentary Committee on Human Rights could be created not only to scrutinize draft legislation, but also to hold inquiries, and bring forward proposed reforms that contribute to a comprehensive set of human rights legislation with an enhanced legal status that would be respected and enforced by Australian courts. The proposal for a constitutionally entrenched democratic bill of rights supported by radically reformed Parliamentary procedures is presented as an exemplar of the sort of political arrangements that could serve as an effective alternative to court-centred bills of rights. This line of thought takes up and develops proposals made by David Kinley for pre-legislative scrutiny of legislation, in his proposal, directed towards achieving legislative compliance with the *International Covenant on Civil and Political Rights*[2] (Kinley, 1999; also Hiebert, 1998). I suggest a more radical form of this suggestion which writes an Australian Bill of Rights into the terms of reference of a Human Rights Committee (similarly in Brennan, 1998). The Committee could be composed of members of both Houses of Parliament, drawn from all parties with a minimal representation in either House. This builds on and goes beyond developments in New South Wales where, following a report of the NSW Parliament Standing Committee on Law and Justice (2001), a Legislation Review Committee was established to scrutinize legislation in part from a human rights perspective. Enhancing the protection of human rights through such changes in the political system and curtailing the tendency of courts to take on a de facto legislative role in creating human rights law opens the prospect of a distinctive path towards a more effective human rights regime that respects the human right to political equality.

Institutional Alternatives

To design and evaluate the institutional alternatives for implementing human rights, we have to be aware of the political function of human rights discourse and the historical weaknesses of standard types of human rights regime. This section outlines the critical assumptions I am making in this regard that prompt the proposal to promote a democratic bill of rights.

---

2   Opened for signature 16 December 1966, 999 UNTS 171 (entered into force 23 March 1976).

The Need for Human Rights in a Democracy

The idea of human rights is to identify those aspects of the life of all human beings whose protection and furtherance ought to be guaranteed in all political systems. They are affirmations of what is valuable about all human beings and the institutional requirements for the realization of these values that both legitimize and limit the powers of governments, businesses and other social institutions. Human rights establish standards against which to measure social, economic and political arrangements. They enable us to locate and correct individual and systemic injustice, oppression, inequality and suffering and establish priority goals that ought to be attained in any tolerably humane and enlightened society.

While human rights have direct application as to how individuals ought to treat each other, they are particularly directed at the conduct of governments and other powerful organizations. Political power is necessary to secure the wellbeing of human beings because they are social beings who need to live together in an organized and relatively peaceful manner. The paradox of politics is that the powers that governments must have to promote wellbeing can and are used by those who hold political power to benefit themselves at the expense of those they are meant to protect and support.

The rationale for democratic government is to enable the detection and correction of such abuses and provide motivation for those who hold or seek power to govern in the general interest. This is achieved by a symbiotic mixture of free elections for government office; freedom of speech, information and association; and the development of a culture in which individuals have an informed concern for all members of society and not just for themselves and their families.

In such societies there are considerable conflicts based on clashes of individual interests, and also significant disagreement about what is in the general interest, both in terms of conflicting values (what constitutes wellbeing, autonomy, justice and equality, and how such values as are agreed can best be implemented), and who should have the right to make decisions about these contentious matters. The basic democratic method is that issues be widely debated and then settled through the election of representatives whose duty is to form a government to implement the policies that they believe promote their preferred instantiations of the values and methods endorsed by the electorate.

This process enables decisions to be made in ways that formally recognize that each person's view has equal political weight. It also enables individuals to protect their self-interest against the misuse of government power. This is a somewhat crude but relatively effective method of ensuring that government does not neglect the perceived interests of a majority of the population. While some theories of democracy take the matter no further, in that elections are seen purely as ways to protect the self-interest of the voters, most theories ascribe to the voter the capacity and the will to be influenced also by their judgment as to what is fair and just for the population as a whole, so that the electoral decision reflects a variable mix of calculated self-interest and impartial moral judgment.

The reality of particular democracies is, of course, often quite different. Often democracies fail to curtail the influence of powerful economic and military minorities, sometimes through corruption and often through the manipulation of public opinion. Majority decision making is often ill-informed, narrowly self-interested and short-sighted. Sometimes the majority decisions reached are clearly unfair to minorities whose interests are unjustly sacrificed to those of the majority. Historical examples are not hard to come by. On the Australian political scene we might cite as current examples the continuing relative deprivations of indigenous people and the lack of substantial recognition of their interests as the original inhabitants, oppressive laws against voluntary euthanasia, inadequate services for disabled people (particularly those suffering from mental illness), failure to protect children at risk, harsh treatment of asylum seekers, acquiescence in child poverty and gross economic inequality, readiness to introduce potentially oppressive anti-terrorist legislation, the use of mandatory sentencing for juvenile offenders (in Western Australia and the Northern Territory), and the Commonwealth Government's repeated and forceful rejection of quite reasonable criticism of these policies by the UN Committee on Human Rights.

As democratic theory itself posits, governments have an inevitable tendency to promote sectional interests and neglect the wellbeing of their citizens. This is a major reason for instituting democratic institutions. But democracies themselves remain prone to these same tendencies. They can readily be manipulated by powerful groups, and do not work when a society is divided into major groupings with perceived conflicting interests. No democratic institutions can guarantee that they will work as their justifying rationales dictate that they should. Democratic governments have a built-in bias towards the abuse of the power that they are designed to control. This means that there is a perpetual imperative to reassert human rights values and to work out how they may be better protected. The articulation and promotion of human rights is an important part of the endeavour to make democracies more democratic and protect both majorities and minorities against ever-present internal and external threats to their wellbeing.

Bills of rights, as affirmations of the core values and institutions of a democracy, can be seen as part of a set of measures designed to protect democracy against its undemocratic tendencies. They do this first by making public declaration of the justifying ideology of the society in question, and by implication of all justified systems of government. In so doing they provide a set of criteria by which voters can evaluate the performances of governments, and so register their consent, dissent, and, in extreme cases, their legitimate rebellion. More positively, bills of rights set goals for governments of a sort that can be used to justify the use of force in the enforcement of their laws and decisions.

To fulfil these functions bills of rights must be regarded primarily as moral declarations – statements of those aspects of human existence to which we ascribe the highest intrinsic value or deem to be essential for the realization of these values (Dworkin, 1996). The intrinsic values include life itself, and the elements of a worthwhile existence: liberty, happiness and security, and those features of social life that are instrumentally essential to their realization: law, democratic government, health care, family life, personal property and economic opportunity. The rights that bills of rights seek to promote – human rights – are essentially moral rights, rights that stand in judgment above all actual laws, customs and social practices. As such, human rights provide a major part of the moral basis both for the justification of the constitution and practice of government and for placing limitations on the power of governments and other potential sources of harm. Human rights discourse articulates the moral groundings of the duties of political and social obligation including the duty to rebel against political, social and economic tyranny and oppression (Nagel, 2002).

The fundamentally moral status of human rights tends to be obscured in those aspects of the contemporary human rights movement that look upon human rights as a type of legal right which is to be found in certain instruments of international law, such as the *International Covenant on Civil and Political Rights* (1966), and in the constitutions of those states that have identifiable bills of rights that are interpreted and enforced by courts. Thus it is common for a country's human rights record to be assessed by: whether or not it is a signatory to certain international conventions; whether it has been criticized by various UN committees; and whether it has a constitution with a court-centred bill of rights, that is, a statement of rights that is interpreted and applied by courts with the power of judicial review of legislation, enabling the courts to invalidate otherwise binding legislation in so far as, in the opinion of the courts, it violates human rights. While these facts provide important evidence about the actual circumstances of the inhabitants of the countries concerned, they do not in themselves constitute the enjoyment of human rights.

For instance, as has been pointed out, it is commonly argued that Australia is backward or reluctant about human rights simply because it has not implemented all its international human rights treaty obligations or does not have such a bill of rights. This mistakes an assessment of means for an assessment of ends. Signing up to international 'human rights' treaties and adopting a court-centred bill of rights are possible ways of promoting human rights, but they should not be identified with having and enjoying the rights themselves. There are other ways of protecting and furthering the interests at stake. Indeed, it is evident that sometimes international conventions and bills of rights can serve to diminish human rights, legitimating violations of human rights, including the rights and freedoms of democratic governance. It is therefore a conceptual and practical mistake to accept the often-assumed identity of human rights and either the international law of human rights or the constitutional rights within particular states.

Despite the fundamentally moral nature of human rights, bills of rights or other institutional devices that give expression to human rights are necessary for the realization of the fundamental moral commitments embedded in human rights discourse. Indeed, the very terminology of 'bills' and 'rights' has an irreducibly institutional flavour and the moral significance of human rights discourse includes a commitment to provide effective mechanisms for the protection and furtherance of the basic values that feature in declarations of human rights, and these must evidently include legal mechanisms. The language of rights is a language of entitlements, and this is a notion that makes little sense where there is no way of securing that to which one is entitled when it is under threat (O'Neill, 1996, pp. 131–214). Affirmations of rights give rise to the legitimate expectation that there are or should be effective ways of ensuring that certain human interests are adequately protected. In fact, it may be argued that, where there is in general no way of securing a claimed 'right', then there is no such right in that society, even though there ought to be.

This inherent demand for effective protection implicit in the concept of rights gives some credence to the claim that without a judicially enforced bill of rights, human rights are not protected. While equating human rights protection with having a court-enforced bill of rights is a mistake, the concept of rights does contain an implicit assumption that the interests identified by such rights are deserving of effective and priority implementation. To have a human right gives rise, amongst other things, to a legitimate claim for relevant protections, either through legislation, judicial intervention, improved economic policies or simply better management. This is why rejection of direct application of bills of rights by courts requires supplementation by proposals for alternative mechanisms for securing rights' objectives.

Judicial Review and Human Rights

Given the above scenario, it is not, perhaps, surprising that those who see the democratic importance of human rights favour having a bill of rights that courts can use to limit the power of elected government to counterbalance the tendency of democracies to lose their way. This appears an obvious solution to the ongoing problem of abuse of government power, which democracy ameliorates but does not exclude. They note the special interests of elected politicians who neglect human rights in order to retain or gain power, the capacity of homogeneous majorities to dominate the rest of society, and the vulnerability of disadvantaged groups under any political system. It is argued that a balancing political force with a special brief is needed to guard against these standing dangers. The relative detachment of courts from everyday political disputes and the competition for political power make them an obvious choice for the role of an impartial umpire to oversee the democratic political process to keep it democratic both in process and in outcome (Freeman, 1990).

The diagnosis of the democratic weaknesses of actual democracies is not in doubt. Indeed such defects are what give rise to the need for human rights to be declared and enforced. But there are grave objections to the proposed cure for the ailments in question. Most of these derive from the evident fact that general statements of abstract human rights, while they may have the ring of moral self-evidence, are compatible with a wide array of different particular social policies which radically conflict with each other. Given disagreements as to the implications of such values as 'freedom of speech' and how these values are best promoted, judicial review of legislation on human rights grounds means that controversial political issues are thereby determined by a small group of legal professionals who are not politically accountable to the people, whose human right it is to collectively make their own decisions (Campbell, 1999).

These objections relate both to the effectiveness of outcomes and to the process or methods of entrenched judicially enforced bills of rights. Most of these objections involve emphasizing one core feature of all bills of rights: they are very simple and highly general statements of rights, cast in abstract terms. Such statements can have great value in providing a communal sense of direction and promoting social cohesion, but they engender enormous disagreement when it comes down to saying what they are to mean in practice and making concrete decisions that impact on social outcomes (Waldron, 1994).

The 'interpretation' which courts must undertake, when exercising this power of judicial review on the basis of bills of rights that contain simple statements of rights, accompanied in modern bills by a list of considerations that may override these rights, is quite unlike the interpretation required to apply ordinary laws. To decide what does and what does not unduly interfere with the privacy of the citizen, for instance, is a complex and controversial political matter that cannot be achieved without drawing on debatable political values and beliefs. Bills of rights are in general so vague that they do not have meaning at the level of specificity required to determine whether any actual type of conduct or rule is or is not a violation of human rights. The abstraction of general statements of human rights is such that in the application of a bill of rights to an actual case in a court of law it is necessary in effect to legislate what the rights in question are to mean in concrete terms, or to draw on the previous decisions of courts that have, individually or collectively, legislated in this way. A court-centred bill of rights leaves it to judiciaries to translate such general principles as 'the right to life' into the sort of specific decisions that outlaw capital punishment, or restrict access to abortion services, that allow or permit voluntary euthanasia, or sanction or prohibit rationing of health care, or permit the production of human embryos for stem-cell research. We may agree on general human rights principles, such as the dignity of human existence, the basic equality of all human beings and the wickedness of inflicting unnecessary human suffering, but we disagree as to what these fundamental principles require in practice. Even when we do agree on more specific points, such as the right to vote, the right to express our opinions and our right to equality of opportunity, there is enormous and reasonable disagreement about the content and limitations to be placed on such rights (Waldron, 1999, Part III).

Common law jurisdictions have a long history of courts developing the law, albeit in modern times within limits set by pre-existing legislation. There is frequently no harm and often much good in courts developing and updating the law on the basis of the real-life cases that come before them. Courts have the advantage of seeing how general laws impact on a sample of individual cases. Yet, crucially for democracy, parliaments have been able to assert their authority by countermanding such judicial developments with new legislation. Legislatures and the governments that dominate them have a broader vision than that provided by a perhaps untypical sample of individual cases, more resources to work through the implications of legislation and usually some sort of mandate for the policies that lie behind it.

Entrenched and court-enforced bills of rights are defended principally on the ground that they are necessary to protect vulnerable minorities against persistent majorities. Certainly, no one can deny that individuals and groups are capable of acting with extreme selfishness. Indeed the main argument in favour of majority rule is that rich and powerful minorities will otherwise use the instruments of government to feather their own nests. But the cure – giving power to judges to override majorities – contradicts the justification for that cure – respecting the equality and dignity of the individual human being (Waldron, 1993). If we are not all equal when it comes to having an opinion on justice, rights and the common good, then what is left of the ideal of human equality on which human rights are founded? The cure removes such contentious matters of moral opinion from the democratic process, so that citizens are excluded from having any power to determine the specific rights that are to apply in their society. This is in clear contravention of the idea that the moral views of every human being are to be given equal respect. It is a violation of our autonomy, our dignity and our self-esteem. Inevitably majorities can get it wrong, as can judges and politicians, bureaucrats and minorities. But a democratic system, with its emphasis on representation, freedom of speech and assembly, transparency, accountability and the rule of law, is designed to minimize and correct the mistakes that we make in governing ourselves. Moreover, in the light of legitimate disagreement as to what the 'right' answer is with respect to the specific content of human rights, there are strong intrinsic grounds for using a decision-making mechanism that gives equal weight to the opinions of everyone.

In practice, few human rights goals can be achieved by law-making alone, and many human rights objectives do not require passing and implementing laws. Yet, a crucial aspect of the debate about bills of rights, including what form, content and mode of implementation they should have, is whether legal implementation of such rights should be by way of democratically endorsed legislation alone or also by way of judicial law-making whereby general statements of human rights are rendered specific by the decisions of (unelected) judges rather than of (elected) legislatures. The choice between these approaches can be viewed as simply a matter of deciding which mechanism, or combination of mechanisms, best protects human rights. That is a complicated and difficult question of fact, the answer to which depends to a considerable extent on the nature and circumstances of the societies in question and how their institutions operate. Legal mechanisms and democratic processes can have unpredictable results and are both quite capable of legitimating as 'human rights' practices that are in fact gross violations of human rights.

However, the alternative means on offer (human rights legislation or judicial review) are not themselves on equal terms with respect to human rights. Democratic ways of deciding what the law is to be are an invariable constituent of any contemporary list of human rights. Autonomy, self-determination, the right to debate and vote on the laws that bind us, these are paradigm human rights. This means that, in choosing between achieving human rights objectives through human rights legislation or through human rights based judicial review, we are not choosing between mechanisms that are in themselves neutral with respect to human rights, but between one mechanism which is itself an expression of at least some human rights and another mechanism which is not. For these reasons it is argued that judiciaries should feature in democratic human rights regimes as independent adjudicators of those facts that are relevant to the application of existing human rights laws to particular circumstances, but not as makers of those laws. This is not, of course, the end of the matter. Human rights have to do with more than democratic rights. It may be that we have to sacrifice some human rights in order to protect others. Autonomy may have to give way to life, to security, to wellbeing, or vice versa. Nevertheless, other things being equal, it is clearly preferable, from the human rights point of view, to adopt a democratic means of governance.

It is often argued that these 'counter-majoritarian' objections to judicial review are exaggerated because in practice courts do not stray far from majority opinion. This is indeed generally how things work out over significant periods of time, with courts sometimes being ahead and sometimes behind prevailing public opinion. Judges are appointed by the executives whose actions they are meant to control. Security of tenure protects their independence from immediate political pressure but does not often alter the political views they had on appointment (Edwards, 2002; Atrill, 2003). If this is the case then a bill of rights is likely to be of little help in countering the views of majorities who are neglectful of the wellbeing of vulnerable minorities (Ewing, 2004). Further, courts are likely to block reforms as societies change, thereby entrenching conservative opinion.

Moreover, court-centred bills of rights can be used to undermine the capacity of majorities to defend their legitimate interests against powerful minorities. Bills of rights of a sort capable of being implemented by courts inevitably emphasize liberty over wellbeing, thus giving the opportunity for those with appropriate resources to counter reforms that promote the general wellbeing by reducing property rights, including the right to use money to manipulate political opinion and serve the interests of business over consumers. Court-centred bills of rights have frequently been used to stall progressive policies aimed at general wellbeing and have rarely been of much assistance with respect to the wellbeing of the majority of citizens.

Such conclusions may appear depressing to advocates of human rights. It seems that no one can be trusted to do the right thing in politics or in law. It would, however, be naïve to think otherwise. The eternal problem of political philosophy and political science is how citizens can guard the guardians. In every political system someone or some body must have the final say. If we seek to supervise that body then the supervising institution has the decisive voice. If we respond by dividing power between different centres, then this amounts to a negation of political power, which favours the status quo. To admit that democratic procedures do not always get it right does not mean that there must be a better way of processing disagreement than by debate and majority decision making. In the case of democracy we can always know that at least something is right, namely the maximization of individual autonomy with respect to collective decision making and showing respect for the views of everyone equally, but we cannot ensure, or even know, whether the decisions taken are the outcome of honest moral opinions or foolishness or selfishness, or some mixture of these and more. In a democracy we can always argue, persuade and hope to change the decisions with which we disagree.

There are other, more subsidiary, arguments against a court-centred bill of rights: they create uncertainty, increase litigation, and raise expectations that are bound to be disappointed. Where such bills are activated, this leads to the politicization of the judiciary and a consequent loss of respect for courts in general. Further, the broad approach to legal 'interpretation' called for in the human rights context becomes generalized throughout the legal system, thus weakening democratic control and the rule of law (Campbell, Ewing and Tomkins, 2001). These arguments, which cannot be developed here, have sufficient force to encourage the search for compromise solutions to the problem of protecting human rights without undermining democracy. These compromises seek to combine the virtues of human rights based judicial review with the basic right of a people to self-determination.

Compromise Solutions

It is generally agreed that purely declaratory bills of rights, while having some educational value, cannot address the crucial problem of limiting the powers of governments. On the other hand, full judicial review is widely regarded as democratically problematic. Hence the search for some compromise that allows for partial or correctable forms of judicial review of legislation (ACT Bill of Rights Consultative Committee, 2003).

There are many strategies on offer. Some of these are briefly analysed here to distinguish them from the proposed democratic bill of rights, which, if it is viewed as a compromise, is at the democratic end of the spectrum. This critical overview of compromise solutions suggests that, as far as the compromise is achieved, this is because courts take care not to come into conflict with legislatures, thus undermining the alleged point of having a bill of rights, namely to constrain governments. However, the compromises do not in fact sufficiently constrain courts, because of the many interpretive devices open to courts and the political difficulty of challenging judicial activism, so that courts are able to go beyond the limits set for them by the compromise solutions. From time to time they do so, with unpredictable consequences.

One compromise solution to the tension between judicial review and democracy is to opt for a statutory rather than a constitutional bill of rights. A statutory bill of rights is not entrenched, and is therefore subject to alteration or repeal by normal democratic process, thereby in theory giving the elected legislature the last word. A statutory bill could authorize judicial review and the override of other legislation, but in practice such bills tend only to license courts to interpret legislation so as to render it compatible with the enacted bill of rights. New Zealand (*Bill of Rights Act 1990*) and the UK (*Human Rights Act 1998*) are key examples of this type of statutory bill, recently joined by the Australian Capital Territory (*Human Rights Act 2004* (ACT)).

Such arrangements appear to have the evident advantage that, if legislatures do not like what the judges do with their interpretive powers, they can change the bill to bring the courts into line. However, in practice this is not easy to do since such 'intervention' is taken to undermine the publicly perceived purpose of having a bill of rights, namely to circumscribe legislatures. Hence countering court decisions that favour particular individuals and groups by legislation is something that is rarely feasible (Huscroft, 2004).

This may not seem to matter if a court's use of a bill of rights is confined to an interpretive role of resolving ambiguities in favour of a reading that they regard as most compatible with the rights enumerated in the bill. However, judges who see themselves as guardians of human rights have a number of strategies which go under the name of 'interpretation' which enable them to make what they will, not only of bills of rights but also of the legislation that may be said to conflict with such bills. Taking the moral high ground, they argue that an instrument designed to protect human rights should not be construed narrowly and legalistically, in effect licensing themselves to modify the relevant legal texts to achieve what they consider to be just. Even where the text and legislative history of a bill are absolutely clear, they can get around this by reading in exceptions.

New Zealand provides the best examples of what has been done by judiciaries in the name of human rights contrary to the express intentions of a statutory 'interpretive' bill of rights (Allan, 2001; Rishworth, 2004). There, the courts have become skilled at finding unclarities and ambiguities on which to hang the opportunity to override what would otherwise be plain enough texts. The mere fact that a provision seems to conflict with a court's current understanding of some element in a bill of rights is itself sufficient to trigger 'interpretation', a process that can in effect extend to deleting or adding certain words in order to make the legislation accord with their reading of the bill. This is justified by saying that it is to be assumed that parliaments do not intend to legislate contrary to a bill of rights, therefore the laws they enact can be modified in whatever way is necessary to ensure that they do not violate the bill or charter (as interpreted by the courts). This is sometimes justified in terms of what is grandly referred to as a 'principle of legality' whereby ordinary legislation is in effect displaced if it is judged to be in conflict with 'fundamental rights' (Griffith, 2000). Similar points can be made in relation to empowering or requiring courts to pay attention to international law when interpreting legislation.

In practice the outcome of such compromise solutions is an unpredictable mix of decisions in which courts either subordinate their views on the human rights in question to the more democratically legitimate authority, or overstep their interpretive powers to intervene in ways to which it is difficult for legislatures to respond. In other words they are either ineffective or, in terms of the purpose of the compromise strategies, overly ambitious.

A somewhat different compromise solution is used in Canada where an entrenched *Charter of Rights and Freedoms*[3] is used for the purpose of judicial review. The

---

3 *Canadian Charter of Rights and Freedoms*, Part I of the *Constitution Act 1982.*

Charter's s. 33 is a 'notwithstanding' clause whereby a Parliament can override a protected right by indicating that a statutory provision is to apply notwithstanding the provisions of the *Charter*. There had been hopes of thereby retaining a serious political input into the determination of specific *Charter* rights (Russell, 1991, pp. 293-309; Bushell and Hogg, 1997). Yet, clearly if the notwithstanding override were routinely used, the *Charter* would be ineffective. Moreover, this device has the unfortunate effect of presenting genuine disagreements about what constitutes the right in question as a situation in which the courts stand for rights and the parliament stands against rights, when what is in fact going on is a disagreement about what these rights are. In Canada, for one reason or another, the notwithstanding provision is rarely used. This means that there is in reality little dialogue between courts and Parliament, and little sense that Parliament is a source of legitimate interpretations of the *Charter* (Huscroft and Brodie, 2004).

Less problematic, in theory, is the device utilized in the UK *Human Rights Act 1998* whereby courts can issue 'statements of incompatibility' which do not invalidate legislation that they deem incompatible with the European Convention on Human Rights, but enable Parliament to adopt a fast-track procedure for amending such legislation, should it choose to do so. In practice, courts prefer to use their power to interpret the legislation so as to make it compatible, thus evading the less effective device of declaring an incompatibility. Parliament can reject such rewritings in subsequent legislation but this in turn can be evaded through creative interpretation. Moreover, in this process, it is the legal not the political definition of the human rights at issue that is the focus of debate. The UK *Human Rights Act* makes the assumption that it is a Parliament's duty to legislate in accordance with prior legal definitions of human rights rather than in accordance with its own concretizations of the abstract rights contained in the European Convention.

It would appear that all of these devices, in so far as they are designed to limit the powers of courts, come up against the capacity of courts to circumvent legislative provisions that seek to protect democratic rights. However, in practice, this happens only sporadically. In so far as the compromise arrangements are intended to make governments more human rights conscious, they disappoint, in that courts rarely take an unpopular line. In either case they tend to weaken political responsibility for the pursuit of rights by distancing it from the democratic process without providing much that is tangible in return.

A Democratic Bill of Rights

If the compromise solutions tried so far are either disappointingly ineffective or seriously undemocratic, we may wish to turn to the idea of a democratic bill of rights combined with appropriate political institutions to work out democratically the meaning and application of rights listed in such a bill. The aim would be to retain responsibility for the detailed formulation of human rights with elected governments, but bring pressure on these governments to resist their inherent tendency to negate the very norms that justify democracy as a system of government.

A democratic bill of rights is not simply a bill of democratic rights. Rather, it is a democratically adopted, articulated and applied bill of rights covering all areas of human wellbeing. A bill of rights is democratic if, in the first place, it is directly endorsed by the electorate, and in the second place, if it is institutionalized through constitutional provisions that relate primarily to improving the democratic political process. The thesis is that it is desirable to adopt democratic bills of rights as a basis for the stimulation and assessment of legislative and policy proposals that promote human rights. The objective is to replace the idea of an entrenched judicially enforced bill of rights with an entrenched democratic bill of rights.

The challenge here is to work out how to give a democratic bill of rights sufficient leverage to counter those aspects of democratic polities that are potentially antithetical to human rights without unduly compromising the democratic principle of the sovereignty of the people. A democratic bill of rights is a bill that is institutionalized so as to channel the legislative and governmental activities of the state, with the courts being involved only in the enforcement of such human rights legislation as is enacted by the Parliament and of any constitutional provisions relating to the political implementation of the bill of rights. The objective of a democratic bill of rights is to bring pressure on the system to make it more responsive to human rights considerations.

The key institutions involved, comprising a democratic bill of rights, a Human Rights Committee, and human rights legislation, require the support of other instruments and institutions which also draw on the entrenched democratic bill, such as the office of the Ombudsman, and an independent Human Rights Commission whose role would be to investigate complaints, conduct inquiries and promote human rights educationally. This in turn requires the support of an active civil society invigorated by a variety of non-governmental organizations with a focus on specific human rights issues.

Ideally, a democratic bill of rights would be entrenched through constitutional amendment, which would give the citizens ownership of the bill, greatly enhancing its legitimacy and hence its political status and operative force. Alternatively, the bill could be enacted by Parliament after endorsement in a nationwide referendum. This is much easier than constitutional amendment but sufficiently potent constitutionally to make it politically very difficult for Parliament to amend it without holding further referenda. A democratic bill of rights is not directly enforceable by courts, except with respect to certain constitutive and procedural requirements relating to the function of the Human Rights Committee and, perhaps also, the Human Rights Commission and the enhanced legal standing of human rights legislation.

Entrenchment itself has considerable significance when considering the symbolic and educational functions of a bill of rights. At its best, such a bill could be a unifying ideology on the basis of which is developed a culture of rights that impacts on both national politics and international relations. However, there is no doubt that human rights are taken more seriously when they are accompanied by judicial review of legislation. It is important, therefore, to underpin a democratic bill of rights with some constitutional basis that will lead seasoned political players as well as morally concerned citizens to take it seriously.

One way of achieving this objective in Australia is to adopt a Human Rights Amendment to the *Constitution* that establishes a joint standing committee of both Houses of Parliament – a Joint Standing Committee on Human Rights – with certain constitutionally guaranteed powers. Building on the model of existing parliamentary committees, in particular the Senate Standing Committee for the Scrutiny of Bills, the Human Rights Committee would have the right and the duty to examine all proposed legislation and to require new legislation to be brought forward on the basis of their understanding of what is required to implement the bill of rights. The prime focus of the committee would be on achieving a comprehensive set of human rights legislation, that is, legislation directed at the implementation of specific human rights objectives, such as non-discrimination and freedom of expression (Campbell, 2005).

Scrutiny mechanisms already exist in the Australian Parliament and in four States and one Territory. For instance, the Senate Scrutiny of Bills Committee has the task of analysing proposed legislation to see whether it 'trespasses unduly on personal rights and freedoms' (Senate Standing Committee for the Scrutiny of Bills, 2003, p. 1) and, if it appears to do so, bringing this to the attention of the Senate. This committee operates in a relatively non-partisan way and can be quite forceful in its dealings with ministers and in its reports to the Senate concerning proposed legislation that might affect individual rights. Similar arrangements are in place in Queensland, Victoria, New South Wales and the Australian Capital Territory.

A Human Rights Committee could have much wider powers and responsibilities than existing scrutiny committees. What I have in mind are specific enforceable procedural requirements that keep the human rights agenda firmly on the table. How this can be done is a constitutionally tricky issue, which cannot be adequately addressed here, since parliamentary procedures are not traditionally justiciable. The procedures I have in mind include more than the publication of the Committee's reports and recommendations. It includes the power of the Committee to delay the legislative process to give it time to consider bills that it considers to have potential human rights implications. It includes the power of the Committee to require that legislation be brought forward within a particular time frame to deal with what it perceives to be human rights deficits, and to hold public enquiries on these matters.

While a Human Rights Committee could not block legislation for long and would be unable to require that legislation be passed, it would have the power to obtain responses to points it raises with the government department that is sponsoring the legislation, cross-examine the government minister concerned and be able to make available to the Parliament as a whole any material on which the bill's sponsors rely, call witnesses, receive submissions and obtain expert advice. Its powers of delay could ensure that time is given for internal and external debate to take place. The idea is to give such a committee a position that is similar to but politically stronger than that enjoyed by powerful Congressional Committees in the USA.

All this could involve both a shift of power from government to Parliament and an opportunity to provide the basis for much wider public debate than current Parliamentary procedure facilitates, dominated, as it is, by the government of the day. The purpose and powers of the Human Rights Committee can be seen as part of a wider development to give more effective and less adversarial tasks to members of the parliament who are not government ministers, thus making the Parliamentary system more thoughtful and forward looking (Marsh and Yencken, 2004).

An obvious parallel here is the Joint Committee on Human Rights introduced into the UK Parliament following on the *Human Rights Act 1998*, itself modelled to some extent on the Australian Senate Standing Committee for the Scrutiny of Bills.

The UK Human Rights Committee has already made some impact on the extent and quality of debates in the British Parliament, although little by way of significant change in the substance of legislation has resulted (Feldman, 2002, Irvine, 2003). It could be expected that the more extensive powers of the proposed Australian Committee on Human Rights, together with the existing constitutional powers of the Senate, a much more powerful body than the House of Lords in the UK, would give it considerably more influence.

In addition to the somewhat negative role of scrutinizing proposed legislation, the Committee would have the power and resources to draw on the bill of rights to investigate possible human rights failures both in domestic situations and in foreign policy. Moreover a process could be designed to give members of the legislature the right to bring what they view as human rights deficits to the notice of the Human Rights Committee in which a minority vote would be sufficient to generate a constitutional requirement for legislative time being given over to addressing the issue. In this way all ambitious politicians would have an incentive to become human rights advocates.

Currently such committees as exist tend to scrutinize legislation in the light of what are perceived to be fundamental common law rights, international treaty obligations and the human rights jurisprudence deriving from court-centred bills of rights around the globe. This is a large rag-bag of data, much of it deriving from earlier times and other places from which much of value can be gleaned in a haphazard way. Having a popularly endorsed bill of rights to act as a framework for its deliberations, the Committee will be freed from the legal contexts from which the decisions of constitutional courts in different jurisdictions have emerged, and will have legitimate recourse to a much wider, more ethical, corpus of literature that approaches the articulation of human rights as a moral rather than a legal matter, albeit one that has legal consequences through the enactment of human rights legislation.

The sources that the Human Rights Committee would be entitled and expected to take into account in its deliberations on the bill of rights would include domestic and international human rights documents and jurisprudence, as well as philosophical, political, economic and social writing on human rights. In addition, the Committee would be bound to receive petitions and hold hearings, and have powers to require the cooperation of government departments and ministers and to compel witnesses and evidence in dealing with the full range of its business. The objective would not be to anticipate possible legal decisions, but to determine important moral questions about the nature and content of rights.

Inevitably, the Human Rights Committee would be significantly affected by the demands of party politics, although this could be considerably muted by arrangements to ensure some continuity of membership, drawn from both Houses, and, perhaps, by giving disproportionately high representation by minor parties or other ways of bolstering the non-partisan traditions of key standing committees. Moreover, the work of the Human Rights Committee would be supplemented by an independent Human Rights Commission, along the lines of a broader and better resourced version of the existing Australian Human Rights and Equal Opportunity Commission, whose independence from government would be guaranteed by constitutional amendment or backed by a referendum held prior to the adoption of the democratic bill of rights. The Commission would have extensive powers of investigation and mediation, and a particular role in the scrutiny of legislation and procedures that have a bearing on the rights and duties of Members of Parliament as well as broad educational goals.

The crucial difference between a democratic bill of rights and the various compromise solutions outlined above is that no power would be given to courts to interpret legislation in the light of the bill of rights, international law or foreign precedents, other than those that have been adopted into positive law via statute. Rather, the duty of courts with respect to human rights would be to apply such human rights provisions as have been enacted by Parliament in the process of implementing the bill of rights or implementing international human rights treaties. Courts would be required to give such human rights legislation priority over subsequent ordinary legislation unless this is clearly negated by the explicit words of the enactment. Human rights legislation would thus have the status of 'constitutional statutes',[4] or 'super statutes' (Eskridge and Ferejohn, 2001), that are not liable to implied repeal by later statutes.

The objective of such constitutional and other related changes would be to provide both a symbolic and practical focus for the human rights aspirations of the Australian people, and to create powerful institutional mechanisms for ensuring that human rights issues are more adequately addressed and resolved, without undermining key democratic human rights. One advantage of this approach is that it would enable the adoption of a bill of rights that is not only straightforward and non-legalistic in content but which incorporates a broad range of economic, social and cultural rights as well as the more traditional civil and political rights that are central in court-centred bills of rights. This offers the prospect of a more politically balanced bill of rights than is likely to emerge in the context of judicial review, which inevitably favours civil and political rights over social and economic ones.

A second advantage is the type of consideration that would feature in the difficult choices that arise when rights clash or require more detailed specification, or have to be balanced against public goods such as economic progress and national security.

---

4   *Thoburn* v *Sunderland City Council* [2002] 3 WLR 247.

These choices can be couched and debated in the moral and political terms that are appropriate to these matters, rather than in technical legal terms that inevitably distort the moral issues at stake and are accessible only to legal elites (Mandel, 1989). Further, the human rights advantage of a democratic bill of rights is its superior democratic legitimacy and its potential for garnering broad consensual support for human rights objectives.

The progressive potential of such a broadly conceived bill of rights is considerable. Courts are aware of their lack of democratic legitimacy in striking down legislation and their lack of competence in developing laws with social and economic ends. As a result they rarely stray beyond what they see as their business with respect to human rights, concentrating on those matters with which they are familiar, such as criminal law and process. A democratic bill of rights need not be restricted in content or application by such fears of illegitimacy and incompetence and is in a position to encourage more dramatic moral leadership than courts can supply.

Another major advantage of a democratic bill of rights is that it would focus not just on the dangers of government overactivity (in which bills of rights originally featured), but would also address the other sources of human rights violations. In particular it can address the dangers of corporate power: the power without responsibility enjoyed by those who control our major corporations and operate under the continual temptation to use productive enterprises as if they were their personal possessions. Similarly, human rights at work and in business could thus become a major ingredient of a democratic bill of rights. The human rights of workers, consumers, suppliers, customers and investors could feature centrally in such a bill.

Conclusion

Australia needs some fresh human rights initiatives. Whether or not we think it desirable, it is highly unlikely that the *Constitution* will be amended to include a bill of rights for the purpose of judicial review of legislation. The Australian Capital Territory has recently enacted an interpretive bill of rights along the lines of the UK *Human Rights Act 1998*. It may be that other Australian Territories or States may adopt similar compromise versions of bills of rights that will (perhaps unintentionally) transfer significant legislative power to courts or else have little in the way of significant outcomes. Either way, this is likely to engender either disillusionment about human rights if it leads to more legal activity with little tangible result, or more hostility to human rights if these new powers are exercised to further the preferred values of activist judges. It is hard to imagine, for instance, the Australian public accepting their abortion laws being determined by judicial opinions as to the 'right to life'.

In these circumstances it is appropriate to build on the strong Australian record with respect to human rights legislation and the Australian experience of using Parliamentary committees to raise and press human rights issues in the political arena. These traditions give a basis for the adoption of a non-justiciable but fully entrenched bill of rights that would serve to unite the aspirations of those who are committed to human rights goals, and which fits with the democratic sensibilities of the Australian people.

A democratic bill of rights is an Australian alternative to court-centred bills of rights with greater potential to realize tangible and lasting human rights outcomes. Given popular endorsement and a consensual commitment of executive government and elected representatives, sometimes referred to as a 'culture of rights', such a constitutional arrangement would also go some way towards satisfying the aspirations of all those who appreciate the role of human rights in a democracy. Its impact could be important, particularly with respect to community education in human rights and the formal recognition of the moral duty of majorities not simply to protect their own interests but to have regard to the equal rights of all citizens. Such attitudes cannot be legislated into existence but, given suitable institutions, they could readily emerge within a developed democracy such as Australia, and, in so far as this is achieved, this must provide the strongest possible basis for the protection and furtherance of human rights.

Were a democratic bill of rights to materialize, 'Australian exceptionalism' over human rights could be transformed from a negative and critical label for human rights backwardness, to a positive feature, identifying a distinctive alternative to current domestic human rights regimes, one which gives responsibility for human rights articulation and oversight to those who have the human right to make such decisions.

References

ACT Bill of Rights Consultative Committee (2003), *Towards an ACT Human Rights Act* (Canberra: ACT Government).

Allan, J. (2001), 'The Effect of a Statutory Bill of Rights where Parliament is Sovereign: The Lessons from New Zealand', in Campbell, T., Ewing, K.D. and Tomkins, A. (eds), *Sceptical Essays on Human Rights*, Oxford: Oxford University Press.

Atrill, S. (2003), 'Keeping the Executive in the Picture: A Reply to Professor Leigh', *Public Law*: 415.

Barber, B. (1984), *Strong Democracy: Participatory Politics for a New Age* (Berkeley: University of California Press).

Bobbio, N. (1996), *The Age of Rights*, trans. A. Cameron (Cambridge: Polity Press).

Bohman, J. and Rehg, W. (eds) (1997), *Deliberative Democracy: Essays on Reason and Politics* (Cambridge, Mass.: MIT Press).

Brennan, F. (1998), *Legislating Liberty: A Bill of Rights for Australia?* (Brisbane: University of Queensland Press).

Bushell, A.A. and Hogg, P.W. (1997), 'The Charter Dialogue Between Courts and Legislatures', *Osgoode Hall Law Journal*, **35** (1): 75–124.

Campbell, T. (1999), 'Human Rights: A Culture of Controversy', *Journal of Law and Society*, **26**: 6–26.

—— (2005), 'Legislating Human Rights', in Wintgens, L. (ed.), *The Theory and Practice of Legislation: Essays in Legisprudence* (Aldershot: Ashgate).

Campbell, T., Ewing, K.D. and Tomkins, A. (eds) (2001), *Sceptical Essays on Human Rights* (Oxford: Oxford University Press).

Charlesworth, H. (2002), *Writing in Rights: Australia and the Protection of Human Rights* (Sydney: University of New South Wales Press).

Dworkin, R.M. (1990), *A Bill of Rights for Britain* (London: Chatto & Windus).

—— (1996), *Freedom's Law: The Moral Reading of the American Constitution* (Cambridge, Mass.: Harvard University Press).

Dryzek, J. (2000), *Deliberative Democracy and Beyond: Liberals, Critics, Contestations* (Oxford: Oxford University Press).

Edwards, R.A. (2002), 'Judicial Deference under the Human Rights Act', *Modern Law Review*, **65**: 859–82.

Ewing, K.D. (2004), 'The Futility of the Human Rights Act 1998', *Public Law*: 829–52.

Eskridge, W.N. and Ferejohn, J. (2001), 'Super-Statutes', *Duke Law Journal*, **50**: 1215–76.

Feldman, D. (2002), 'Parliamentary Scrutiny of Legislation and Human Rights', *Public Law*: 323–48.

Fishkin, J.S. (1991), *Democracy and Deliberation: New Directions for Democratic Reform* (New Haven: Yale University Press).

Freeman, S. (1990), 'Constitutional Democracy and the Legitimacy of Judicial Review, *Law and Philosophy*, **9**: 327–70.

Goldsworthy, J. (1997), 'Originalism in Constitutional Interpretation', *Federal Law Review*, **25**: 1–50.

Griffith, J.A.G. (2000), 'The Brave New World of Sir John Laws', *Modern Law Review*, **63**: 159–76.

Habermas, J. (1996), *Between Facts and Norms: Contributions to a Discourse Theory of Law and Democracy*, trans. W. Rehg (Cambridge: Polity Press).

Held, D. (1989), *Political Theory and the Modern State: Essays on State, Power and Democracy* (Cambridge: Polity Press).

—— (1996), *Models of Democracy*, 2nd edn (Stanford, Calif.: Stanford University Press).

Hiebert, J L. (1998), 'A Hybrid-Approach to Protect Rights? An Argument in Favour of Supplementing Canadian Judicial Review with Australia's Model of Parliamentary Scrutiny', *Federal Law Review*, **26** (1): 115–38.

Horrigan, B. (2003), *Adventures in Law and Justice: Exploring Big Legal Questions in Everyday Life* (Sydney: University of New South Wales Press).

Huscroft, G. (2004), 'Thank God We're Here: Judicial Exclusivity in Charter Interpretation and Its Consequences, *Supreme Court Law Review*, **25**: 241.

Huscroft, G. and Brodie, I. (eds) (2004), *Constitutionalism in the Charter Era* (Toronto: LexisNexis Butterworths).

Ignatieff, M. (2001), *Human Rights as Politics and Idolatry*, ed. Gutmann, A. (Princeton: Princeton University Press).

Irvine, Lord (2003), 'The Impact of the Human Rights Act: Parliament, the Courts and the Executive', *Public Law*: 308–25.

Kinley, D. (ed.) (1998), *Human Rights in Australian Law: Principles, Practice and Potential* (Sydney: Federation Press).

Kinley, D. (1999), 'Parliamentary Scrutiny of Human Rights: A Duty Neglected?', in Alston, P. (ed.), *Promoting Human Rights through Bills of Rights: Comparative Perspectives* (Oxford: Oxford University Press), ch. 5.

Kinley, D. and Martin, P. (2004), 'The Institutional Mediation of Human Rights in Australia', in Boreham, P., Stokes, G. and Hall, R. (eds), *The Politics of Australian Society: Political Issues for the New Century*, 2nd edn (Sydney: Pearson Education).

Koh, H.H. and Slye, R.C. (eds) (1999), *Deliberative Democracy and Human Rights* (New Haven: Yale University Press).

Loughlin, M. (2000), *Sword and Scales: An Examination of the Relationship between Law and Politics* (Oxford: Hart Publishing).

Mandel, M. (1989), *The Charter of Rights and the Legalization of Politics in Canada* (Toronto: Wall & Thompson).

Marsh, I. and Yencken, D. (2004), *Into the Future: The Neglect of the Long Term in Australian Politics* (Melbourne: Black Inc.).

Moore, J. (ed.) (1998), *Hard Choices: Moral Dilemmas in Humanitarian Intervention* (Lanham, MD: Rowan & Littlefield Publishers).

Nagel, T. (2002), *Concealment and Exposure* (Oxford: Oxford University Press).

O'Neill, O. (1996), *Towards Justice and Virtue: A Constructive Account of Practical Reasoning* (Cambridge: Cambridge University Press).

Rishworth, P. (2004), 'Common Law Rights and Navigation Lights: Judicial Review and the New Zealand Bill of Rights', *Public Law Review*, **15**: 103.

Russell, P.H. (1991), 'Standing Up for Notwithstanding', *Alberta Law Review*, **29**: 293–309.

Senate Standing Committee for the Scrutiny of Bills (2003), *Second Report* (Canberra: Commonwealth of Australia).

Schauer, F. (1991), *Playing by the Rules: A Philosophical Examination of Rule-based Decision-making in Law and in Life* (Oxford: Clarendon Press; New York: Oxford University Press).

Standing Committee on Law and Justice (2001), *A New South Wales Bill of Rights* (Sydney: NSW Government).

Tushnet, M. (1999), *Taking the Constitution Away from the Courts* (Princeton: Princeton University Press).

Uhr, J. (1998), *Deliberative Democracy in Australia: The Changing Place of Parliament* (Melbourne: Cambridge University Press).

Waldron, J. (1993), 'A Rights-Based Critique of Constitutional Rights', *Oxford Journal of Legal Studies*, **13**: 18–51.

—— (1994), 'Freeman's Defense of Judicial Review', *Law and Philosophy*, **13**: 27–41.

—— (1999), *Law and Disagreement* (Oxford: Clarendon Press; New York: Oxford University Press).

Williams, G. (2004), The Case for an Australian Bill of Rights: Freedom in the War on Terror (Sydney: University of New South Wales Press).

Index

www.ingramcontent.com/pod-product-compliance
Ingram Content Group UK Ltd.
Pitfield, Milton Keynes, MK11 3LW, UK
UKHW020401010325
455677UK00021B/571